Frontiers of Citizenship

Frontiers of Citizenship is an engagingly written, innovative history of Brazil's black and indigenous people that redefines our understanding of slavery, citizenship, and the origins of Brazil's "racial democracy." Through groundbreaking archival research that brings the stories of slaves, Indians, and settlers to life, Yuko Miki challenges the widespread idea that Brazilian Indians "disappeared" during the colonial era, paving the way for the birth of Latin America's largest black nation. Focusing on the postcolonial settlement of the Atlantic frontier and Rio de Janeiro, Miki argues that the exclusion and inequality of indigenous and African-descended people became embedded in the very construction of Brazil's remarkably inclusive nationhood. She demonstrates that to understand the full scope of central themes in Latin American history – race and national identity, unequal citizenship, popular politics, and slavery and abolition – one must engage the histories of both the African diaspora and the indigenous Americas.

Yuko Miki is Assistant Professor of History and affiliated faculty of Latin American and Latino Studies at Fordham University. Her work has been awarded the Best Article Prize from the Latin American Studies Association (LASA) Brazil Section and the Coordinating Council for Women in History. She lives in New York City.

D1073793

Afro-Latin America

Series Editors

George Reid Andrews, *University of Pittsburgh*
Alejandro de la Fuente, *Harvard University*

This series reflects the coming of age of the new, multidisciplinary field of Afro-Latin American Studies, which centers on the histories, cultures, and experiences of people of African descent in Latin America. The series aims to showcase scholarship produced by different disciplines, including history, political science, sociology, ethnomusicology, anthropology, religious studies, art, law, and cultural studies. It covers the full temporal span of the African Diaspora in Latin America, from the early colonial period to the present and includes continental Latin America, the Caribbean, and other key areas in the region where Africans and their descendants have made a significant impact.

A full list of titles published in the series can be found at:
www.cambridge.org/afro-latin-america

Frontiers of Citizenship

A Black and Indigenous History of Postcolonial Brazil

YUKO MIKI

Fordham University, New York

CAMBRIDGE
UNIVERSITY PRESS

CAMBRIDGE
UNIVERSITY PRESS

University Printing House, Cambridge CB2 8BS, United Kingdom

One Liberty Plaza, 20th Floor, New York, NY 10006, USA

477 Williamstown Road, Port Melbourne, VIC 3207, Australia

314-321, 3rd Floor, Plot 3, Splendor Forum, Jasola District Centre, New Delhi - 110025, India

79 Anson Road, #06-04/06, Singapore 079906

Cambridge University Press is part of the University of Cambridge.

It furthers the University's mission by disseminating knowledge in the pursuit of education, learning and research at the highest international levels of excellence.

www.cambridge.org
Information on this title: www.cambridge.org/9781108405409
DOI: 10.1017/9781108277778

First published 2018
First paperback edition 2019

A catalogue record for this publication is available from the British Library

ISBN 978-1-108-41750-1 Hardback
ISBN 978-1-108-40540-9 Paperback

Cambridge University Press has no responsibility for the persistence or accuracy of URLs for external or third-party internet websites referred to in this publication, and does not guarantee that any content on such websites is, or will remain, accurate or appropriate.

For my mother, Masako Miki

Contents

Figures and Table

Table

Acknowledgments

When a Tokyo native spends years writing a book on the history of black and indigenous Brazilians, a common question is, why? To that I can only respond that it is the result of many encounters with extraordinary people I have come to know over the years, and I apologize for any names I may have missed.

I was fortunate to attend an undergraduate institution with an exceptional faculty that encouraged students to test their boundaries and pursue their interests. I am deeply indebted to Anthony Molho and Meera Viswanathan at Brown, two scholars who took the extra time to mentor and inspire me with their love of learning. At New York University (NYU), my advisor Michael Gomez's deep intellectual engagement with the African diaspora is matched by his dedication to his students, and my appreciation only grows as the years pass. Barbara Weinstein has shown me the magical combination of sheer brilliance, boundless generosity, and irrepressible humor; how fortunate I am to have been at NYU when the city welcomed her home. Sinclair Thomson has been a serene ray of light who cleared many an intellectual storm. It is thanks to him that I took the leap into indigenous history. Ada Ferrer has been a model of acuity, rigor, and imagination. Her classes kindled passions and heated debates, a wonderful experience that inspires my own teaching.

Danny Dawson is the origin story of many people, and I am no exception. He taught me about *quilombos* and the incredibly rich cultures of people of African descent in the Americas; he has opened paths that have led to incredible discoveries. I am delighted and honored to be among his many "children." I also express my deep gratitude to Mestre João Grande, who introduced me to the richness of Brazilian history and has taught me that knowledge assumes many forms. Billy Acree, Marcela Echeverri, and Laurie Lambert deserve special thanks for being amazing friends and colleagues who kept me on track and ensured that this book would see the light of day.

The cohort of fellow graduate students at NYU infused my time there with amazing intellectual energy, and many continue to enrich my life. Thanks to Jennifer Adair, Lina Britto, Michelle Chase, Joaquín Chávez, Greg Childs, Anne Eller, Tanya Huelett, Ebony Jones, Natasha Lightfoot, Tyesha Maddox, Aldo Marchesi, Toja Okoh, Alison Okuda, Michelle Pinto, Gabriel Rocha, Hillina Seife, Ernesto Seman, Carmen Soliz, Cristina Soriano, Federico Sor, Jonathan Square, Franny Sullivan, and Matt Vitz, among others. My gratitude also goes to Tamara Walker, Sarah Sarzynski, and Zeb Tortorici, who with others in our writing group read and commented on early chapter drafts.

This book would not have been possible without the expertise and dedication of the staff in archives and repositories in Brazil, many of whom accommodated my tight research schedule and allowed me to access rare holdings. In Rio de Janeiro they include the National Archive, the National Library, the Brazilian Historical and Geographic Institute, the Museum of the Indian, and José Bessa (for the Capuchin archive); in Espírito Santo, the Public State Archive in Vitória and the First Notarial Office in São Mateus; and in Bahia, the Public State Archive in Salvador and the Diocese of the Co-Cathedral of Santo Antônio in Caravelas. In Lisbon and New York, I thank the Arquivo Histórico Ultramarino and the New York Public Library. In addition, I thank the various institutions whose support enabled my research and writing, including the Office of the Dean at Fordham University, the Center for the Humanities and the Office of the Dean of Washington University in St. Louis, the Warren Dean Memorial Fund, the Tinker Foundation, and the Office of the Dean and the Henry M. MacCracken Fellowship at NYU.

At Washington University in St. Louis I found a wonderful group of colleagues, including Sonia Lee, Paul Ramírez, Iver Bernstein, Shefali Chandra, Maggie Garb, Bret Gustafson, Carolina Hausmann-Stabile, Shino Hayashi, Peter Kastor, Sowande' Mustakeem, Kaori Nakata, Derek Pardue, Tim Parsons, Mark Pegg, Azusa Tanaka, Selma Vital, Lori Watt, and the incomparable Jean Allman. At Fordham University, Kirsten Swinth, Sal Acosta, Wes Alcenat, Doron Ben-Atar, Ed Bristow, Saul Cornell, Aimee Cox, Arnaldo Cruz-Malave, Chris Dietrich, Claire Gherini, Barry Goldberg, Richard Gyug, David Hamlin, Samantha Iyer, Maryanne Kowaleski, Hector Lindo-Fuentes, Chris Maginn, Eric Marmé, Durba

Mitra, Fawzia Mustafa, David Myers, Silvana Patriarca, Nick Paul, Beth Penry, Carina Ray, Thierry Rigogne, Clara Rodríguez, Grace Shen, Asif Siddiqi, Daniel Soyer, Steven Stoll, Magda Teter, Ebru Turan, Susan Wabuda, and Rosemay Wakeman have provided a supportive, collegial community, one that keeps running thanks to Sandra Arnold, Natasha Obeng, Audra Furey-Croke, and Isaac Tercero. I also thank my many students at the two institutions who have challenged me to consider the wider scope of my work, and my predecessor, Christopher Schmidt-Nowara (in memoriam), who kindly helped my research when I was still a grad student.

João Reis, Hal Langfur, and Steven Stoll generously and thoroughly read and commented on an earlier version of this book, pushing me to make bolder claims and surprising discoveries in familiar sources. Stuart Schwartz's seminar was a thrilling introduction to colonial Brazil; his path-breaking work has inspired this book in many ways. In the United States, at various points I also received invaluable commentary and support from George Reid Andrews, Ana Lúcia Araújo, Ikuko Asaka, Manuel Barcia, Herman Bennett, Judy Bieber, Jonathan Bogarín, Kim Butler, Celso Castilho, Amy Chazkel, Oscar de la Torre, Tracy Devine-Guzmán, Roquinaldo Ferreira, Brody Fischer, Jan French, Jim Greene, Marc Hertzman, Martine Jean, Mary Karasch, Gabi Kuenzli, Eric D. Langer, Kittiya Lee, MaryAnn Mahony, Florencia Mallon, Kirsten Schultz, Daryle Williams, James Woodard, and Eric Zolov. Kamau Brathwaite, Robert Farris Thompson, and Robin D.G. Kelley also provided early inspiration.

Arguably the best perk of working in Brazil is the incredibly welcoming community one can find there, which makes all the difference. Flávio Gomes and João Reis have mentored this project from its earliest stages. I also thank Maciel de Aguiar, José Bessa, Adriana Campos, Olivia Gomes da Cunha, Walter Fraga, Henrique Espada Lima, Izabel Missagia de Mattos, John Monteiro (in memoriam), Marco Morel, Eliézer Nardoto, Álvaro Nascimento, Maria Hilda Paraíso, Sandro Silva, Carlos Eugênio Líbano Soares, and Regina Xavier. Urano Cerqueira de Andrade is the best researcher, period. In Rio, Espírito Santo, and Bahia, I am grateful for the kindness of Carlo Alexandre, Fabricio Archila, Dalivia Bento Bulhões, and Flávio Tongo and their families, Father Eurico, Jaco Galdino, Aki Katai, Carlos Benedito de Souza, Mestres Paulinha, Janja, and Poloca, Mestre Zé Carlos, Izabel Zyro, and Hugo Bellucco, and fellow US-based historians Patricia Acerbi, Teresa Cribelli, and Okezi Otovo. Special thanks go to Zeca Ligiéro, Giovanna Xavier, Mauricio

Barros de Castro, Ruth Torralba, Martin Ossowicki, and Alessandra Tosta and their families for their brilliance and friendship. This book is also in loving memory of Frede Abreu, a man of incomparable charm and kindness who helped researchers and travelers from around the world from his office in the Instituto Mauá. I hope this book will find a place in his library.

At Cambridge, I thank my editor, Debbie Gershenowitz, who championed this book from early on; the Afro-Latin America Series editors, George Reid Andrews and Alejandro de la Fuente, who embraced a book that is also about the indigenous Americas; Kris Deutsch, Robert Judkins, Salam Mazumder, and Terry Kornak; and the two anonymous reviewers whose close reading and thoughtful comments have allowed me to envision the larger reach of this work. Caroline Traugott has taught me to be a better writer; Bill Nelson is a great cartographer; and Erik Carter, a wonderful jacket designer.

An earlier version of Chapter 1 was published in *Slavery & Abolition* 35:1 (2014), and a part of Chapter 5 appeared in the *Americas* 68:4 (2012).

As the years pass I am increasingly aware of how migration has defined my own life. In no small way my ties to home owe to my decades-long friendship with Erika Hirokawa, Anna-Marie Farrier, Chikako Kobayashi, Kaoru Nishikawa, Yuki Moriuchi, and Aika Yamazaki. I also thank Dagan Bayliss, Jeremy Harley, Tatsuya Imai, Danny Massey, Yuko Kitajima Miller, Nyneve Minnear, Chijioke Okeke, Gordon Walker, and Chris Yoon for their many years of friendship and inspiration. Ben Moser introduced me to Brazil and the beauty of the Portuguese language while we were at Brown. I wish I saw everyone more often.

My extended family in Japan, especially my grandparents, Ikuko and Teiichi Yamada, and the late Kikuye Miki, has wondered what exactly I have been doing in the United States since I left for college at eighteen. I am deeply grateful to all of them for offering me countless opportunities in life. I express the deepest gratitude and love for my mother, Masako Miki, who "let her dear child travel," as the Japanese saying goes, and has unconditionally supported my decidedly nonmedical pursuits (I am a doctor, at least). To her I dedicate this book. In the United States I thank Marilyn Ontell, Elan Bogarín, Troy Herion, and the Abanor and Woolley families for welcoming me into their fold. Jonathan Bogarín has been a patient, loving companion through many moments since our meeting in front of a Brooklyn brownstone. He has remained my greatest friend, advocate, support, and voice of common sense through extended research trips to Brazil, a long-distance marriage, and now, as the father of our child. Ayumi came into our lives three years ago, her name embodying the oceans spanned by our family histories. In not a few moments, I have doubted the compatibility of parenting and completing this book. I can now say that this book exists in spite of – and because of – her. Thank you, Jonathan and Ayumi, for all these gifts, and for the journeys that await us.

Note on the Text and Currency

I have decided to preserve the nineteenth-century orthography for people's names, as modernizing them seemed to create an awkward facsimile of the women and men whose life stories appear in the sources. The one exception is Teófilo Ottoni, a widely known public figure, whose name I modernized. I have modernized place names, since many of them continue to exist in the present. All translations are mine unless otherwise noted. The Brazilian currency was based on the *milréis* during the empire (1822–89). One milréis was written as 1$000, and one thousand milréis equaled one *conto* (1:000$000).

Abbreviations

ABN	Anais da Biblioteca Nacional
ACRJ	Arquivo dos Capuchinhos, Rio de Janeiro
AHU	Arquivo Histórico Ultramarino, Lisbon
AN	Arquivo Nacional, Rio de Janeiro
APEB	Arquivo Público do Estado da Bahia, Salvador
APEES	Arquivo Público do Estado do Espírito Santo, Vitória
BA	Bahia
BN	Biblioteca Nacional, Rio de Janeiro
CA	Corte de Apelação
CPSM	Cartório Primeiro de São Mateus, Espírito Santo
CRL	Center for Research Libraries
ES	Espírito Santo
Fl.	Folha
HAHR	*Hispanic American Historical Review*
IHGB	Instituto Histórico e Geográfico Brasileiro
JLAS	*Journal of Latin American Studies*
Mc	Maço
MG	Minas Gerais
MS	Manuscript
RAPM	*Revista do Arquivo Público Mineiro*
RIHGB	*Revista do Instituto Histórico e Geográfico Brasileiro*
Ser.	Série
STR	Slave Transaction Records

Introduction

A Frontier on the Atlantic

Atop the highland plateaus of the Brazilian interior began the eastward journey of many rivers and streams. Coursing through the forest down rugged mountain slopes, they flowed beneath a lush, dense canopy of purple jacaranda, *sapucaia*, and *inga* trees. The fragrance of passionflowers filled the air, their long garlands grazing the waters running below. Begonias accented the forest verdure with their red, white, and blue blossoms. Among the trees echoed the songs of *arará* parrots, their iridescent plumage capturing the light filtering through the foliage. The hum of insects reverberated through the air. The rivers and streams snaked north and south as they continued their descent, sometimes flowing over a waterfall. The mountains ceded to gentler slopes, sand gradually replaced earth, and coconut trees soared above the banks. Finally, when an archipelago of mangroves began to dot the rivers' increasingly brackish waters, their journey was at an end. Seagulls circled above as whales surfaced to breach before swimming away toward the nearby Abrolhos islands. It was the Atlantic Ocean.

By the beginning of the nineteenth century, the sumptuously verdant forest through which these rivers coursed had long since vanished on much of Brazil's Atlantic seaboard. Surviving indigenous groups had retreated inland as settlements spread along the coast, among them the bustling port cities of Salvador in the northeast and Rio de Janeiro further south, where various African languages were as commonly heard as Portuguese. Sugarcane fields dotted the coastal wetlands, its cultivators voraciously consuming the forest to feed the flames of sugar production. The scars left by human endeavor were also visible further inland. In

the highlands of Minas Gerais, two centuries of gold and diamond mining that had fed the opulence of the Portuguese empire, slash-and-burn
agriculture, and cattle ranching had wreaked havoc on the forest, leaving
grassy patches and bare, stripped earth in their wake. It was thus startling
to encounter, heading east from these lands toward the coast, a narrow
strip of seemingly undisturbed forest still remaining. Here was a frontier
on the Atlantic.[1]

"One can travel for days without discovering a single sign of life,"
observed a European traveler in the region on the eve of Brazil's independence (1822).[2] His solitude amidst the dense forest canopy was no
illusion. For over a century preceding his journey, the Portuguese Crown,
jealously safeguarding against the smuggling of gold and diamonds from
the interior to the coast, had prohibited the settlement of the Atlantic
littoral in southern Bahia and Espírito Santo captaincies. This prohibition had coalesced with the tenacious resistance of the region's indigenous
populations to preserve the territory against all but the most adventurous,
the desperately poor, or a fugitive slave (Figure 0.1).

As the mines ran dry, however, the allure of the remaining forest and
its bounty became irresistible, attracting a growing stream of settlers by
the dawn of the nineteenth century. Thus, as the traveler continued his
journey up the coast, he felt his solitude dissipate. He soon encountered
a hamlet of Indians, and further along, the sight of manioc fields framed
a small town of handsome, tile-roofed buildings and a port from where
goods were shipped to towns and cities along the coast. African slaves
tilled the fields as their Portuguese or mestizo master watched impassively
from the house. A team of men hacked through the dense forest to clear
a path from the mountainous interior to the coast.[3] In the decades following the traveler's journey, this migration of settlers and their slaves
into indigenous territory would permanently transform the Atlantic frontier, the remaining forest and its inhabitants removed to make way for
roads and railroads, coffee and manioc. Encouraging these initiatives was
the Portuguese Crown, which had relocated across the ocean to Rio de
Janeiro in 1808 to flee Napoleon's Iberian invasion and gradually relin-
quished its prohibition on the region's settlement. From the comfort of
its "tropical Versailles," the monarchy welcomed settlers as a way to

[1] Warren Dean, *With Broadax and Firebrand: The Destruction of the Brazilian Atlantic
    Coastal Forest* (Berkeley: University of California Press, 1995), 80, 97–102, 115.
[2] Maximilian Wied-Neuwied, *Viagem ao Brasil nos anos de 1815 a 1817* (São Paulo:
    Companhia Editora Nacional, 1958), 184–85.
[3] Ibid., 174–75.

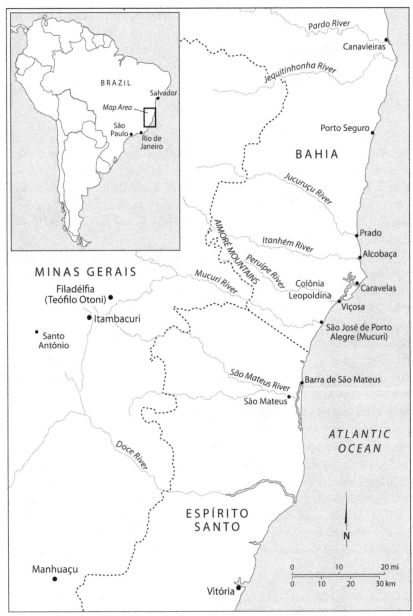

FIGURE 0.1 Brazil and the Atlantic Frontier. Adapted from Izabel Missagia de Mattos, *Civilização e Revolta: os Botocudos e a catequese na província* de Minas (São Paulo: EDUSC ANPOCS, 2004), courtesy of the author. Map by Bill Nelson Cartography.

introduce progress to a distant region they considered "infested" by wild
Indians and vagabonds.[4]

Progress remained an ambiguous aspiration on national independence
in 1822 and the beginning of the Imperial period (1822–89). Under the
rule of Pedro I, who stayed in the former colony after his father, João VI,
and the rest of the royals returned to Portugal, Brazil became the lone
monarchy in a sea of Spanish American republics. The elite entrusted
with chartering the course of the new nation looked with consternation
upon the large African-descended, indigenous, and mixed population,
whom they considered an impediment to national progress. Even so,
they ensured slavery's preservation, the bedrock of their own wealth and
power. The trans-Atlantic slave trade would continue until 1850, and
Brazil would garner the ignominy of becoming the last nation in the
Americas to abolish slavery, in 1888.

Yet if such a reliance on slavery cast Brazil's propensity for progress
into doubt, its leaders also delineated a remarkably inclusive vision of
citizenship that suggested a sanguine national future. In the new Constitution of 1824, Brazilian citizenship was extended to all those born
free on Brazilian soil regardless of race or color. This included Brazilian-
born slaves, once freed. Brazil's inclusiveness stood in sharp contrast to
the United States, where race was employed to deny citizenship to Indians, slaves, and freeborn blacks until the Fourteenth Amendment (1868)
defined citizenship inclusively and unconditionally by birth or naturaliza-
tion – and that too came with many restrictions.[5] Brazil's racially inclusive
nationhood was reaffirmed in 1845 when the reigning Emperor Pedro II
gave his official approval to an essay written for the Brazilian Historical
and Geographic Institute celebrating the nation's origins in its unique
heritage born from the mixture of the "three races" – Indian, African,
and Portuguese.[6]

This discourse of race mixture and harmony has become a powerful if contested marker of Brazilian national identity ever since. Mobi-
lized by Afro-Brazilian activists to argue for greater inclusion in the

---

[4] Kirsten Schultz, *Tropical Versailles: Empire, Monarchy, and the Portuguese Royal Court
in Rio de Janeiro, 1808–1821* (London: Routledge, 2001).

[5] James Holston, *Insurgent Citizenship: Disjunctions of Democracy and Modernity in
Brazil* (Princeton, NJ: Princeton University Press, 2008), 52–63. In spite of the Fourteenth Amendment, Indians were not granted full citizenship until 1924, and Jim Crow
legislation continued to deny full citizenship to African Americans.

[6] Karl Friedrich von Martius, "Como se deve escrever a História do Brasil," *Revista de
Historia de América* 42 (1956). The essay was originally published in 1845.

later nineteenth and early twentieth centuries, the idea gained international acclaim in the 1930s in its incarnation as a "racial democracy" – anthropologist Gilberto Freyre's contention that Brazil was free of racial prejudice because of its long history of race mixture. Promoted during the nationalist fervor of the first Getúlio Vargas presidency (1930–45), this racial nationalism also served as a strong rebuke of the Jim Crow violence of the United States. Similar mixed-race national identities also emerged in other Latin American nations including Cuba, Mexico, and Colombia.[7]

Racialized national identities can make sense only when grounded in the historical specificities of each place. It would thus seem that the Atlantic frontier, where enterprising Portuguese descendants tilled the earth among native daughters and enslaved future citizens – in the very moment when Pedro II was praising the union of the "three races" – would offer the ideal conditions wherein Brazil's racially inclusive nationhood could be forged. This book tells a different story. From the eve of independence in 1822 until the years following the end of monarchical rule in 1889, the Atlantic frontier became a theater of staggering anti-indigenous violence and the entrenchment of African-based slavery. Through an examination of frontier settlement in post-independence Brazil, it argues that the exclusion and inequality of indigenous and African-descended people became embedded in the very construction of an inclusive nationhood and citizenship. Far from being an irrelevant national periphery, the frontier was the very space in which the boundaries and limitations of Brazilian citizenship were defined. At the heart of these conflicts were enslaved people of African descent, whose labor enabled the opening of the Atlantic forest, and autonomous Indians – indigenous peoples who had not become incorporated into Portuguese settler society – whose lands became the staging ground of settler colonialism. These were women and men whose civic, cultural, and racial heterogeneity did not dovetail with emerging national ideas about a

---

[7] Paulina L. Alberto, *Terms of Inclusion: Black Intellectuals in Twentieth-Century Brazil* (Chapel Hill: University of North Carolina Press, 2011); Thomas E. Skidmore, *Black Into White: Race and Nationality in Brazilian Thought* (Durham, NC: Duke University Press, 1993); Peter Wade, *Blackness and Race Mixture: The Dynamics of Racial Identity in Colombia* (Baltimore: Johns Hopkins University Press, 1993); Ada Ferrer, *Insurgent Cuba: Race, Nation, and Revolution, 1868–1898* (Chapel Hill: University of North Carolina Press, 1999); Marixa Lasso, *Myths of Harmony: Race and Republicanism during the Age of Revolution, Colombia 1795–1831* (Pittsburgh: University of Pittsburgh Press, 2007); Darío Euraque, *Conversaciones históricas con el mestizaje y su identidad nacional en Honduras* (San Pedro Sula, Honduras: Centro Editorial, 2004).

homogeneous Brazilian people (*povo brasileiro*); examining their lives on the Atlantic frontier allows us to see the fissures in Brazil's inclusionary nationhood.[8]

Focusing our attention on the frontier opens new avenues for understanding nation-building in postcolonial Brazil and other Latin American nations. At the most fundamental level, this book understands frontiers as spaces with a contested relationship to the nation-state. At the time of independence, Brazil was a vast territory consisting of disparate former captaincies and multiple frontiers, both external and internal, in a territory larger than the continental United States. With the exception of the interior mines, settlement was concentrated on the littoral. Much of the territory from the Amazon to the disputed borders with Spanish America in the far West and South was part of the new nation but in name only, under the control of indigenous populations, local and regional power networks, and competing claims of possession. As a monarchy, Brazil may have been spared the political destabilization that rocked the Spanish American republics after independence. Still, the nation-state enjoyed an uncertain presence on the frontiers, similarly to northern Mexico, the Eastern Andes, the Argentina Pampas, or Patagonia. The Atlantic frontier was no exception.[9]

Yet if frontiers were important features of Brazil's physical territory, the frontier as a concept did not enjoy the prominence it did in US historiography. As several scholars have noted, this was due at least in part to Brazilian historians' resistance to Frederick Jackson Turner's nationalistic, and much criticized, argument that the westward frontier and the availability of free land engendered the uniquely democratic spirit of the United States. Such an idea appeared absurd to Latin American nations wherein frontier expansion consolidated the power of large

---

[8] An earlier work on the creation of inequality on the frontier is Alida C. Metcalf, *Family and Frontier in Colonial Brazil: Santana de Parnaíba, 1580–1822* (Austin: University of Texas Press, 2005).

[9] For example, Ricardo Donato Salvatore, *Wandering Paysanos: State Order and Subaltern Experience in Buenos Aires during the Rosas Era* (Durham, NC: Duke University Press, 2003); Walter Mario Delrio, *Memorias de expropiación: sometimiento e incorporación indígena en la Patagonia, 1872–1943* (Bernal, Buenos Aires: Universidad Nacional de Quilmes, 2005); Erick D. Langer, *Expecting Pears from an Elm Tree: Franciscan Missions on the Chiriguano Frontier in the Heart of South America, 1830–1949* (Durham, NC: Duke University Press, 2009); Tamar Herzog, *Frontiers of Possession: Spain and Portugal in Europe and the Americas* (Cambridge, MA: Harvard University Press, 2015); Evelyn Hu-DeHart, *Yaqui Resistance and Survival: The Struggle for Land and Autonomy, 1821–1910* (Madison: University of Wisconsin Press, 2016).

landowners and encouraged exploitation.[10] If anything, Brazilianists preferred the *sertão* (pl. *sertões*) – the backlands, the wilderness, the uncivilized interior – whose colonial exploration and settlement became the subject of major national historiographies.[11] However, recent scholarship has breathed new life into studies of the frontier in the Americas. These works see both internal and external frontiers as spaces of contact, permeability, and negotiation. As one historian has described it, the frontier "encompasses the notion of the fringes of empires, wilderness, disputed territories between different groups of colonists and rival populations, and an open area for seeking resources and trade opportunities."[12]

This fluidity, which allows us to account for the role of indigenous and African-descended people in shaping frontier dynamics, is essential to understanding the postcolonial frontier. Explored throughout this book are the multitude of interactions among Indians, people of African descent, settlers, and state agents on the Atlantic frontier. We will also

[10] Frederick Jackson Turner, *The Frontier in American History* (New York: Henry Holt and Co., 1921); Warren Dean, "The Frontier in Brazil," in *Frontier in Comparative Perspectives: The United States and Brazil* (Washington, DC: Latin American Program, Wilson Center, 1990), 15–27; *Contested Ground: Comparative Frontiers on the Northern and Southern Edges of the Spanish Empire*, ed. Donna Guy and Thomas Sheridan (Tucson: University of Arizona Press, 1998), 7–10; Ligia Osorio Silva, "Fronteira e identidade nacional," in *Anais do V Congresso Brasileiro de História Econômica*, 2003; Hal Langfur, "Frontier/Fronteira: A Transnational Reframing of Brazil's Inland Colonization," *History Compass* 12, no. 11 (November 1, 2014): 845–46.

[11] Among the classic works are Euclides da Cunha, *Rebellion in the Backlands (Os Sertões)* (Chicago: University of Chicago Press, 1944); João Capistrano de Abreu, *Chapters of Brazil's Colonial History, 1500–1800*, trans. Arthur Brakel (New York: Oxford University Press, 1998); Sérgio Buarque de Holanda, *Caminhos e fronteiras* (São Paulo: Companhia das Letras, 1995). For how the sertão and its explorers, the *bandeirantes*, have informed modern paulista history and identity, see Barbara Weinstein, *The Color of Modernity: São Paulo and the Making of Race and Nation in Brazil* (Durham, NC: Duke University Press, 2015).

[12] Quote from Fabricio Prado, "The Fringes of Empires: Recent Scholarship on Colonial Frontiers and Borderlands in Latin America," *History Compass* 10, no. 4 (April 1, 2012): 319; José de Souza Martins, *Fronteira: a degradação do outro nos confins do humano* (São Paulo: Editora Hucitec, 1997); Cynthia Radding, *Landscapes of Power and Identity: Comparative Histories in the Sonoran Desert and the Forests of Amazonia from Colony to Republic* (Durham, NC: Duke University Press, 2005); Juliana Barr, *Peace Came in the Form of a Woman: Indians and Spaniards in the Texas Borderlands* (Chapel Hill: University of North Carolina Press, 2007); Hal Langfur, *The Forbidden Lands: Colonial Identity, Frontier Violence, and the Persistence of Brazil's Eastern Indians, 1750–1830* (Stanford, CA: Stanford University Press, 2006); "Frontier/Fronteira"; Richard W. Slatta, "Comparing and Exploring Frontier Myth and Reality in Latin America," *History Compass* 10, no. 5 (May 1, 2012): 375–85; Herzog, *Frontiers of Possession*.

trace how these interactions shaped, and were shaped by, state policy and
elite discourse at the local, national, and transnational levels. To do so
reveals the complex ways in which the nation was formed simultaneously
on the frontier and at the center. This approach allows us to depart from
defining the frontier as the disorganized "margin" into which the state
gradually extended its control. Rather, the frontier was the very space in
which the relationship between race, nation, and citizenship were daily
tested and defined; therefore the frontier itself was central to Brazil's
postcolonial history.

Such processes come into especially sharp focus on the Atlantic frontier, the once forbidden lands of the Portuguese Crown where the
provinces of Minas Gerais, Bahia, and Espírito Santo converged.[13] As
destructive methods exhausted the mines in the Minas Gerais interior,
the region, its long coastline skirting one of the last remaining stretches
of original Atlantic forest in southern Bahia and Espírito Santo, became
the object of aggressive colonization in the nineteenth century. Elites and
colonists imagined these lands as virginal and empty, but local native
populations, called the Botocudo Indians (discussed later), had long been
its inhabitants, engaged in their own alliances and interethnic warfare
over territorial control and political power. The contact and negotiation
that had previously shaped limited Indian–settler relations increasingly
ceded to conflict as interest in their land and labor intensified in the
late colonial period, spurring the Portuguese monarch to declare a just
war against them in 1808 that would continue after independence. The
Botocudo captured the grotesque fascination of Brazilians and foreigners
as epitomes of the irredeemable savage who, even though native to the
soil, existed outside of civilization. As such, the history of the Botocudo,
who became the objects of both ruthless violence and acculturative policies, is particularly illustrative of the ambiguities and limited possibilities
of indigenous citizenship (Figure 0.2).

Equally important, it was African slavery that drove the settler colonization of indigenous lands. By mid-century, slave labor would propel the region – centered on the northern Espirito Santo town of São
Mateus and the southern Bahian immigrant plantation colony of Colônia
Leopoldina – into a major manioc flour and coffee producer for the
domestic (and occasionally international) market. A powerful proslavery oligarchy emerged that would fight abolition tooth and nail until
the eleventh hour. Tracing slavery's expansion and consolidation on the
Atlantic frontier after independence shows how inseparable it was from

---

[13] Langfur, *The Forbidden Lands.*

FIGURE 0.2 *A Family of Botocudos on a Journey. Source:* Maximilian Wied, *Travels in Brazil* (London: Henry Colburn & Co., 1820). Courtesy of the John Carter Brown Library at Brown University.

the violent colonization of indigenous territory. It also demonstrates how the frontier, in its incorporation into the nation, became the space wherein noncitizens were reproduced.

The impossibility of understanding frontier history without accounting for African and indigenous experiences leads us to the crux of this book. Why has Brazilian postcolonial history been so focused on people of African descent and comparably so little on the indigenous? Of course, demography can partly explain the imbalance: on the eve of independence, Brazil had a total population of about 4.4 million, of which 2.5 million were free and enslaved people of African descent, compared to the approximately 800,000 so-called "wild" or autonomous Indians. This was a precipitous decline from the estimated 5 million who inhabited it in the beginning of the sixteenth century.[14] Yet there are deeper

[14] In 1817/1818 the population estimates were for free people of color – 585,000; slaves – 1.93 million; whites – 1.043 million. According to Perdigão Malheiro's statistics cited by Conrad, there were 259,400 "free" Indians, but the information does not specify whether or not they were settled on Indian villages, so I have opted to cite Oliveira's figure instead. For statistics on African slaves and the slave population, see Robert Edgar Conrad, *The Destruction of Brazilian Slavery, 1850–1888* (Berkeley: University of California Press, 1972), 283; Dale Torston Graden, *From Slavery to Freedom in*

epistemological reasons that need to be addressed. Scholarly and public perception alike widely accept Brazil as Latin America's – or indeed, the Americas' – black nation par excellence, particularly given the legacy of 5 million Africans (ten times greater than in North America) who arrived on its shores during the three centuries of the trans-Atlantic slave trade. To let this figure speak for itself, however, occludes our own hand in mapping Latin America with racialized historical narratives. Many of us follow well-trodden paths, organizing our knowledge about Latin America into black and indigenous, slavery and Indian republics, Brazil and the Caribbean versus Central America and the Andes. Even as a growing body of historical scholarship has shed light on the shared experiences of the black and indigenous people throughout the Americas, these remain largely colonial in focus. In the case of Brazil, scholarship on the postcolonial period has been overwhelmingly about African-descended people and their Atlantic world connections forged by slavery, collectively reinforcing the nation's identification with blackness.[15]

Recognizing how such racialized narratives continue to shape our historical inquiries leads to more pernicious aspects of their very genesis. The familiar story that native populations simply "disappeared" as they were decimated by settlers and disease in the colonial period and replaced by African slaves has become the commonplace explanation for their marginal place in postcolonial Brazilian and Caribbean history. Through a close attention to postcolonial indigenous history, policy, and anti-indigenous violence, this book documents the deliberate production of indigenous "extinction" in the mid-nineteenth century by a diverse array of interests from settlers to Indian administrators and a domestic and

---

Brazil: Bahia, 1835–1900 (Albuquerque: University of New Mexico Press, 2006), 17–21. For the indigenous population, see Mércio Pereira Gomes, *The Indians and Brazil* (Gainesville: University Press of Florida, 2000), 249; João Pacheco de Oliveira, "'Wild Indians,' Tutelary Roles, and Moving Frontier in Amazonia: Images of Indians in the Birth of Brazil," in *Manifest Destinies and Indigenous Peoples*, ed. David Maybury-Lewis, Theodore Macdonald, and Biorn Maybury-Lewis (Cambridge, MA: Harvard University Press, 2009), 98.

[15] Peter Wade, *Race and Ethnicity in Latin America* (London and New York: Pluto Press, 2010), Chapter 2; George Reid Andrews, *Afro-Latin America, 1800–2000* (Oxford: Oxford University Press, 2004); Barbara Weinstein, "Erecting and Erasing Boundaries: Can We Combine The 'Indo' And The 'Afro' In Latin American Studies?," *Estudios Interdisciplinarios de América Latina y el Caribe* 19, no. 1 (2007). Among the recent works in the history of black and indigenous people are the various studies in Matthew Restall, ed., *Beyond Black and Red: African-Native Relations in Colonial Latin America* (University of New Mexico Press, 2005); Matthew Restall, *Black Middle: Africans, Mayas, and Spaniards in Colonial Yucatan* (Stanford, CA: Stanford University Press, 2013); Rachel Sarah O'Toole, *Bound Lives: Africans, Indians and the Making of Race in Colonial Peru* (Pittsburgh: University of Pittsburgh Press, 2012).

international scientific community. Indian extinction's invention was integral to the very forging of a racially inclusive national identity, negating the possibility of indigenous citizenship even as Indians were celebrated symbolically as progenitors of the nation. Too often our understandings of Brazilian postcolonial history have taken this elision for granted; nor have we sufficiently questioned what purpose such elisions have served. Continuing to exclude the indigenous as historical subjects uncritically reproduces the nineteenth-century idea of their incompatibility with the nation. Attention to the frontier therefore allows us to critically reevaluate this powerful racial paradigm that has shaped our understandings of Latin American history.[16]

That said, the objective of this book is not to "reinsert" Indians back into postcolonial Brazilian history. Rather, it focuses on the connections of black and indigenous histories and argues that each is necessary to understand the other, particularly so if we are interrogating the relationship between race, nation, and citizenship. A rich scholarship on the African diaspora has enlightened us about the myriad ways in which race and slavery shaped black people's access to citizenship during and after slavery, paralleling how racial discourses played a powerful role in indigenous people's political projects and citizenship rights in the Andes and Central America.[17] Yet a fuller understanding of the fundamental issues

[16] This issue has been specifically addressed by Vânia Moreira, who argues that the idea of *mestiçagem* as Brazil's national identity has been primarily responsible for the erasure of Indians as historical subjects, from von Martius's essay to Caio Prado Jr.'s *Formação do Brasil Contemporâneo* (1942). Vânia Moreira, "História, etnia e nação: o índio e a formação nacional sob a ótica de Caio Prado Júnior," *Memoria americana*, no. 16–1 (June 2008): 63–84.

[17] This is a large list that includes George Reid Andrews, *Blacks & Whites in São Paulo, Brazil, 1888–1988* (Madison: University of Wisconsin Press, 1991); Hebe Maria Mattos de Castro, *Das cores do silêncio: os significados da liberdade no sudeste escravista, Brasil século XIX* (Rio de Janeiro: Arquivo Nacional, 1995); Florencia E. Mallon, *Peasant and Nation: The Making of Postcolonial Mexico and Peru* (Berkeley: University of California Press, 1995); Charles Walker, *Smoldering Ashes: Cuzco and the Creation of Republican Peru, 1780–1840* (Durham, NC: Duke University Press, 1999); Mimi Sheller, *Democracy after Slavery: Black Publics and Peasant Radicalism in Haiti and Jamaica* (Gainesville: University Press of Florida, 2000); Laurent Dubois, *A Colony of Citizens: Revolution & Slave Emancipation in the French Caribbean, 1787–1804* (Chapel Hill: University of North Carolina Press; Omohundro Institute, 2004); James E. Sanders, *Contentious Republicans: Popular Politics, Race, and Class in Nineteenth-Century Colombia* (Durham, NC: Duke University Press, 2004); Olivia Maria Gomes da Cunha and Flávio dos Santos Gomes, *Quase-cidadão: histórias e antropologias da pós-emancipação no Brasil* (Rio de Janeiro: Editora da Fundação Getúlio Vargas, 2007); Rebecca J. Scott, *Degrees of Freedom: Louisiana and Cuba after Slavery* (Cambridge, MA: Belknap Press of Harvard University Press, 2008); Peter F. Guardino, *Peasants, Politics, and the Formation of Mexico's National State: Guerrero, 1800–1857* (Stanford, CA: Stanford University Press, 1996); Brooke Larson, *Trials of Nation Making:*

that postcolonial Latin American nations confronted – such as slavery and abolition, the unequal access to citizenship, and constructions of racialized difference and national identity – can be realized only by accounting for the histories of both black and indigenous people. Such an approach is especially needed for Brazil, where the intellectual history of *mestiçagem* (race mixture) of black, Indian, and white has been only tenuously connected to the social histories of the nineteenth century, which have focused on slavery, Africans and Afro-Brazilians, and black–white relations. Eliding Indians cannot sufficiently account for the constructions of racialized hierarchies and unequal access to citizenship that were foundational to the very construction of Brazil's inclusive nationhood. To study the interconnectedness of indigenous and black histories in the context of nation-building both complicates and enriches the translocal frameworks of the African diaspora and the Atlantic world that have had a ground-breaking impact on the study of Brazilian slavery and post-emancipation. At the same time, this book places the history of Brazilian Indians in fuller dialogue with the literature on Indians and the Liberal Age in Spanish America.

This book presents the history of race, nation, and citizenship in Brazil through the interconnected histories of black and indigenous people. The study assumes six analytical lenses: slavery and citizenship; popular politics; race and nation; law and violence; geography; and labor and abolition. Race and citizenship are organizing concepts in every chapter, while some themes, such as geography and law, weave throughout the book but take center stage in specific chapters. It is my hope that the methodological and conceptual tools presented in each chapter, and the book as a whole, will be useful to scholars of Brazil and the Americas in general. A chapter outline is provided at the end of this introduction.

A reader expecting a plethora of stories of black–Indian solidarity may be disappointed. Presuming interracial unity and similarity of experience would risk producing a homogenizing subaltern narrative that obscures enlightening tensions and differences. What this book does is show the contingent and often surprising ways in which black and indigenous histories overlapped and shaped each other. These complexities would remain hidden if we focused only on Brazil's African descendants. Black and indigenous people's exclusion and inequality were embedded in the very

---

Liberalism, Race, and Ethnicity in the Andes, 1810–1910 (Cambridge and New York: Cambridge University Press, 2008); Natasha Lightfoot, *Troubling Freedom: Antigua and the Aftermath of British Emancipation* (Durham, NC: Duke University Press, 2015).

construction of an inclusive nationhood and citizenship. Studying the two groups together reveals the uneven ways in which their citizenship was articulated, understood, and contested. For example, while many scholars have discussed the 1824 Constitution's exclusion of enslaved people from citizenship, few have recognized how autonomous Indians were also excluded according to the same rationale of their "living outside of society." Nor have scholars of slavery documented the resurgence of indigenous slavery that coincided with the expansion of African slavery in the nineteenth century. Yet if this suggested their analogous status, by the 1880s, diverging legal regimes for slaves and Indians, as evidenced by two cases of extravagant violence in the Atlantic frontier, signaled the expanding citizenship opportunities of enslaved people that paralleled the total legal exclusion of Indians. Alternately, the book also draws attention to the strikingly similar, racialized discourse of vagrancy and need for labor discipline used by missionaries, state officials, and abolitionists toward freedpeople and Indians during the implementation of gradual abolitionist laws in the 1870s and 1880s. While such discourses, employed in the name of citizenship preparation, helped confine both groups to servile labor and thus to a second-class status, freedpeople and autonomous Indians expressed radically different criticisms of such agendas.

Two important revelations emerge from a close attention to black and indigenous people's interactions with settlers and state agents, law and discourse. First, we are able to see their shifting positions in relation to each other and to the racialized hierarchies embedded in constructions of citizenship and nation. Second, the variegated ways in which black and indigenous people interpreted, took advantage of, and rejected their terms of exclusion and unequal citizenship reminds us that while many imagined and claimed citizenship on their own terms, it was not always or necessarily their desired objective. If such a contention seems to contradict the rich scholarship on black and indigenous intellectual and political histories of citizenship in the Atlantic world, this book proposes otherwise. For just as studies of popular royalism have enlightened us to the complex political worlds of nonelite actors, the lives of black and indigenous people on the Atlantic frontier remind us that citizenship was but one among many political possibilities. It is our work to recognize these many visions, rather than folding them into a unified, linear narrative that concludes with the achievement of citizenship.[18]

---

[18] James H. Sweet, *Domingos Álvares, African Healing, and the Intellectual History of the Atlantic World* (Chapel Hill: University of North Carolina Press, 2011); Marcela

The rest of this introduction will offer the reader a little more insight into the place that would become the Atlantic frontier.

The Atlantic Frontier: The Place and the People

For a place of great fame in Brazilian history, the Atlantic frontier is remarkably little-studied. The "Discovery Coast," as its northern end is known today, was the first landing place of the Portuguese explorer Pedro Álvares Cabral in 1500, in the present-day southern Bahia state. Cabral and his crew had been headed for India until winds and currents sharply pulled them off course. Sighting a tall mountain, they dropped anchor and soon encountered several men of a "dark brown, rather reddish color" carrying bows and arrows who appeared to welcome the accidental arrivals. In the company of native peoples, the party erected a cross and delivered their first mass.[19] Administration of the new but still disputed land began in 1533 with the initiation of the captaincy system under King João III, who divided the Brazilian coastline into fifteen parcels that he ceded to twelve Portuguese noblemen (*fidalgos*) to hold as lord proprietors. The fidalgos were granted certain rights and privileges of dominion in return for obligations to colonize, populate, and develop the economy of their captaincy. Pero de Campos Tourinho received the captaincy where Cabral anchored, which was named Porto Seguro or safe port. To its south, separated by an unconfirmed border, was the captaincy of Espírito Santo, ceded to Vasco Fernandes Coutinho. Porto Seguro and Espírito Santo remained sparsely settled for much of the colonial period even as sugar mills were quickly erected all along the Atlantic littoral, worked by mainly by indigenous slaves.[20]

Several key factors contributed to such sparse settlement. In the early decades after Cabral's arrival, the Portuguese Crown showed only luke-warm interest in its American possession while its attention remained captivated by the lucrative trade with India. Meanwhile, the establishment of sugarcane plantations on the Brazilian coast in the 1530s and

---

Echeverri, *Indian and Slave Royalists in the Age of Revolution: Reform, Revolution, and Royalism in the Northern Andes, 1780–1825* (New York: Cambridge University Press, 2016).

[19] Letter of Pero Vaz de Caminha to the King of Portugal, May 1, 1500, in Stuart B. Schwartz, *Early Brazil: A Documentary Collection to 1700* (New York: Cambridge University Press, 2010), 1–9.

[20] Stuart B. Schwartz, *Sugar Plantations in the Formation of Brazilian Society: Bahia, 1550–1835* (Cambridge and New York: Cambridge University Press, 1985), 17.

1540s, encouraged by the Crown, enjoyed mixed success. The majority were concentrated in the northeast beyond Porto Seguro, in large part due to more amicable relations with local Indian populations.[21] Porto Seguro, by contrast, was inhabited by extremely hostile indigenous populations whom the Portuguese called the Aimoré. "The captaincies of Porto Seguro and Ilhéus (to its north) are destroyed and nearly depopulated due to fear of these barbarians," the chronicler and planter Gabriel Soares de Souza remarked in 1587. "The mills produce no sugar as the Indians killed all their slaves and people... So great is the [settlers'] fear that simply hearing 'Aimorés' makes them abandon their properties." Later chroniclers similarly described Porto Seguro's depopulation.[22] As such, even as the city of Salvador in Bahia began to flourish, having been established the royal capital in 1549, the Atlantic frontier continued to languish, with only a few Jesuit *aldeias* (Indian villages) and sugar plantations standing. The Jesuits were more successful further south in Espírito Santo with their missions in Reis Magos (today Nova Almeida) and Santa Cruz. According to one historian, the Atlantic frontier remained, with the exception of Amazônia, one of the most sparsely settled areas in all of Brazil.[23]

Another unique circumstance ensuring the region's sparse settlement began in the 1690s with the discovery of gold in the landlocked captaincy of Minas Gerais ("general mines"), just to the interior of Porto Seguro and Espírito Santo. The gold cycle launched one of the most opulent and brutal periods in Brazil's colonial era. Africans who survived the horrors of the Middle Passage were transported to the mines where a ruthless labor regime exploited, at its apogee, more than 100,000 slaves.[24] Yet if the gold rush unleashed the floodgates of speculation and environmental destruction on Minas Gerais and its indigenous population, the Atlantic littoral was spared. This was because the Crown, jealously guarding its mining monopoly, placed tight controls on the transport of gold and

---

[21] Ibid., 17–19.
[22] Gabriel Soares de Sousa, *Tratado Descritivo do Brasil em 1587*, ed. Francisco Adolpho de Varnhagen (Recife: Fundação Joaquim Nabuco Massangana, 2000), 42–43; Engel Sluiter, "Report on the State of Brazil, 1612," *HAHR* 29, no. 4 (November 1, 1949): 527–28; Fernão Cardim, *Tratados da terra e gente do Brasil*, ed. Ana Maria de Azevedo (Lisboa: Comissão Nacional para as Comemorações dos Descobrimentos Portugueses, 1997), 197–98.
[23] Vânia Moreira, "Índios no Brasil: marginalização social e exclusão historiográfica," *Diálogos Latinoamericanos* 3 (2001): 93–94; Haruf Salmen Espindola, *Sertão do Rio Doce*, Coleção História (Governador Valadares, MG: Editora Univale, 2005), 74.
[24] Mariza de Carvalho Soares, "Descobrindo a Guiné No Brasil Colonial," *RIHGB* 161, no. 407 (2000): 82.

precious minerals, allowing only three overland routes through the rocky, dangerous terrains to distant ports.[25] The Crown expressly closed off the most direct route to the Atlantic through Porto Seguro and Espírito Santo beginning in 1701 in order to maintain its right to the royal fifth on all gold production and to discourage tax-evading smugglers and foreign rivals.[26] Due to such policy, the Atlantic littoral was effectively sealed off from explorers and settlers in spite of – or due to – its natural bounty and the many rivers and streams linking the interior to the coast. Over time the region came to be known as the Forbidden Lands, which was spared the ravages of the gold mines, sugar plantations, and tobacco farms. Indians and a smattering of others, including fugitive slaves and the free poor, here found refuge from colonial expansion.[27]

However, arguably much more effective than Crown policy in discouraging settlement on the Atlantic frontier was the native population, whose ongoing resistance to colonialism sparked fantasies of wandering, man-eating savages. The indigenous groups in the area included the Puri, Makoni, Malali, Maxacali, Panhame, Kumanaxó, Monoxó, Kutaxó, Kopoxó, Pataxó, and Kamakã. Most prominent, however, were those whom the Portuguese collectively called the Botocudo, a name that likely derived from the *botoque*, or barrel lid, that was thought to resemble the wooden disks that some Indians inserted in their ear lobes and lower lips.[28] None of these natives referred to themselves by this name. The Botocudo were therefore an indigenous people that came into existence through coerced tribalization, or ethnogenesis, resulting from the destabilizing effects of colonialism. "Indians" too were a European creation, of course, for indigenous peoples of the Americas did not perceive any unity among themselves. According to Hal Langfur, the Botocudo "coalesced as an identifiable people largely as a product of their contact with, struggle against, and representation by encroaching settlers."[29]

---

[25] Langfur, *The Forbidden Lands*, 32.   [26] Ibid., 34–35.

[27] Maria Hilda Baqueiro Paraiso, "O tempo da dor e do trabalho: a Conquista dos Territórios Indígenas nos Sertões do Leste" (doctoral dissertation, Universidade de São Paulo, 1998); Langfur, *The Forbidden Lands*; Espindola, *Sertão do Rio Doce*.

[28] Langfur, *Forbidden Lands*, 24. For colonial views, see John M. Monteiro, "The Heathen Castes of Sixteenth-Century Portuguese America: Unity, Diversity, and the Invention of the Brazilian Indians," *HAHR* 80, no. 4 (2000): 697–719.

[29] James Lockhart and Stuart B. Schwartz, *Early Latin America: A History of Colonial Spanish America and Brazil* (Cambridge and New York: Cambridge University Press, 1983), 31; Langfur, *The Forbidden Lands*, 30; Hal Langfur, "Introduction: Recovering Brazil's Indigenous Pasts," in *Native Brazil: Beyond the Convert and the Cannibal, 1500–1900* (Albuquerque: University of New Mexico Press, 2014), 14. On ethnogenesis

Their defining characteristic was their resistance to Portuguese expansion, rather than any cultural, material, or linguistic criteria.[30] Mostly Macro-Gê speakers who lived as seminomadic hunters and foragers, they tended to move about in small bands and depended on the land for their material and spiritual well-being. They derived from a variety of indigenous groups inhabiting the Atlantic seaboard. The small number of survivors today identify themselves as Krenak. Further complicating ethnic identification, some labels were taken from leaders or descriptively given by other groups, such as Maxacali ("reunion of tribes"), Naknenuk ("not of the land"), or Giporok ("bad").[31] Sometimes these groups were identified as Botocudo "subgroups," and at other times as their enemies. In the interest of narrative clarity, however, this book utilizes the terms Indian and Botocudo unless there is a specific other ethnicity or subgroup provided, following the practice of other scholars. It is important to remember that in most instances, only by this name do they become visible in the historical record. Furthermore, while offensive war was officially only against the Botocudo, its repercussions extended to all those who lived in the region, producing new interethnic hostilities and alliances.

The Portuguese disdain for the Botocudo was part and parcel of their invented indigenous genealogies. In the early colonial period, settlers and explorers, with their limited knowledge, had grouped local indigenous populations into two broad types to whom they ascribed essentialized, contrasting qualities. On one hand were the Portuguese-friendly Tupi (Tupinambá). In the nineteenth century, during the height of Romantic Indianism, Emperor Pedro II and his court celebrated the Tupi as the origin of the Brazilian people and symbols of the nation. On the other hand were the hostile Tapuia, whom the Portuguese considered to be the ancestors of the Aimoré, the Indians who had fiercely fended off the earliest settlers.[32] The Aimoré, whom the Portuguese accused of

---

in the larger Atlantic world, see James Sidbury and Jorge Cañizares-Esguerra, "Mapping Ethnogenesis in the Early Modern Atlantic," *The William and Mary Quarterly* 68, no. 2 (April 1, 2011): 181–208.

[30] Maria Hilda Paraiso as cited in Judy Bieber, "Catechism and Capitalism: Imperial Indigenous Policy on a Brazilian Frontier, 1808–1845," in *Native Brazil: Beyond the Convert and the Cannibal, 1500–1900*, ed. Hal Langfur (Albuquerque: University of New Mexico Press, 2014), 168.

[31] Bieber, "Catechism and Capitalism," 168; Marco Morel, "Cinco imagens e múltiplos olhares: 'descobertas' sobre os índios do Brasil e a fotografia do século XIX," *História, Ciências, Saúde* 8 (2001): 1042, n. 4.

[32] Monteiro, "Heathen Castes."

cannibalism, were in turn believed to be the Botocudos' predecessors.[33] These colonial epistemologies based on simple binaries – good and bad, friendly and hostile, Christianized and heathen, tame and wild, civilized and savage – continued to inform indigenous policies and justify anti-indigenous violence for the entire nineteenth century.[34]

By the early eighteenth century the Portuguese had elevated the Botocudo into the sui generis embodiment of savagery. Fear of Botocudo aggression and cannibalism became a powerful deterrent to settlement of the Atlantic frontier, which remained remarkably free from the tentacles of colonization until the middle of the century (Figure 0.3). By then, however, it had become evident that aggressive and wasteful technologies had depleted the mines and wreaked havoc on the land. Those whose hardscrabble life had always been subject to the vagaries of the mining economy now found themselves compelled to search for alternative sources of livelihood. Soon, fantasies of untapped gold and diamond reserves and the allure of precious timber and land in the Atlantic frontier began overtaking their fear of the native inhabitants. The Botocudo evolved in the settler imagination from a danger to be avoided at all costs into an infestation obstructing access to virginal terrain. If indigenous hostility had long been the invisible barrier protecting the Atlantic frontier, with the depletion of the mines it would evolve into its opposite – the pretext for violent conquest.

Beginning inland in eastern Minas Gerais in the 1760s, the unraveling of the Forbidden Lands gradually moved east into the Atlantic frontier, producing escalating conflicts between settlers and Indian groups. Prince Regent João VI's 1808 declaration of a just war against the Botocudo of Minas Gerais, Porto Seguro, and Espírito Santo was therefore but an official recognition of the settler initiative that had been decades in the making.[35] Far from being a culmination, however, the Botocudo Wars,

---

[33] Ibid., 703; Langfur, *The Forbidden Lands*, 24. Barickman has questioned scholars' association of the Aimoré with the Botocudo. While I agree that we cannot draw a clear ethnographic connection, what matters is that they were *perceived* by colonists and later Brazilians to be related because of their hostility. See B. J. Barickman, "'Tame Indians,' 'Wild Heathens,' and Settlers in Southern Bahia in the Late Eighteenth and Early Nineteenth Centuries," *The Americas* 51, no. 3 (January 1, 1995): 336 n. 29. Teófilo Ottoni however surmised that the Botocudo were too stupid to be the descendants of the valiant Aimoré. Teófilo Benedito Ottoni, *Notícia sobre os selvagens do Mucuri* (Belo Horizonte: Editora UFMG, 2002).

[34] Early chroniclers did not just perceive two indigenous groups. In fact, they recorded a whole variety of groups, but in terms of how colonial settler–Indian relations and indigenous policy took shape, the Tupi–Tapuia binary remains most relevant.

[35] Langfur, *The Forbidden Lands*.

FIGURE O.3 Botocudo Indians in the colonial imagination. Although highly dubious, their association with cannibalism stirred fears among white and black people alike and became the pretext for anti-indigenous violence. This image is noteworthy for the presence of black people among both the victims and their attackers. *Source:* Alberto Lamego, *A terra Goicatá á luz de documentos inéditos* (Paris: L'Édition d'Art, 1913). Courtesy of Marco Morel.

which would be in effect until 1831, would only help facilitate an unrelenting wave of anti-indigenous violence in the ensuing decades. Entering the postcolonial period as hated "wild" Indians and targets of just war, the Botocudo were effectively excluded from Brazilian citizenship and would be repeatedly exposed to the brutal consequences of their ambiguous place in the new nation.

The Crown was initially displeased by the bursts of local settler initiative, unwilling to relinquish its tight control over the mines and the land and river pathways linking them to the Atlantic. Economic realities and the inability to stem the settler tide soon changed its outlook. The Crown also recognized the Atlantic frontier as a space in which to realize a new vision for its empire in the tropics. This realization led to its inaugurating a new policy of economic and racial development that would fundamentally transform the region and impact later iterations of indigenous and black citizenship. The seeds of these changes had been planted decades before the Crown's arrival in Brazil in 1808. Just as Brazil's mining yields began drying up in the mid-eighteenth century, across the Atlantic ocean,

Sebastian José de Carvalho e Melo, the future Marquis of Pombal (ruled 1750–77), was ushering Portugal into the era of Enlightened despotic rule. With a keen eye toward tightening metropolitan control over the colonies and increasing administrative efficiency in a manner echoing the Bourbon Reforms in Spanish America, Pombal appointed new *ouvidores* (royal judges) to the captaincy of Porto Seguro in the 1760s.[36] This appointment, which entrusted the ouvidores with overseeing the captaincy's economic development and settlement, marked a clear departure from the Forbidden Lands policy.[37] The ouvidores were also responsible for the secular administration of Indians after Pombal expelled the Jesuits in 1759 (the Order was expelled from Spanish America in 1767), based on a new body of legislation known as the Directorate of Indians. The Directorate's main objective was to transform Indians into royal vassals through acculturation into Portuguese society.[38]

Meanwhile, eight new townships (*vilas*) were established on the littoral between 1759 and 1800, some of which were former Jesuit aldeias: Belmonte, Vila Verde, Transcoso, Prado, Alcobaça, Vila Viçosa, São José de Porto Alegre, and soon, São Mateus. All were adjacent to, or at the mouth of, numerous interconnected rivers linking Minas Gerais to the Atlantic coast, whose potential as new commercial shipping and transportation routes excited countless speculators and adventurers. Population in Portuguese-controlled areas doubled between 1780 and 1820 to more than 16,000, reversing the abandonment that had long characterized the region.[39] Administrative borders were also redrawn. In 1763 Pombal authorized ouvidor Couceiro de Abreu to extend Porto Seguro's jurisdiction over its southern neighbor, the *comarca* (juridical district) of São Mateus in Espírito Santo captaincy, that also included the coastal settlement of Barra de São Mateus to which it was connected by the eponymous river. The comarca of São Mateus extended as far south as the Doce River, one of the principal waterways connecting Minas Gerais to the Atlantic (Figure 0.4). This measure extended Porto Seguro's

---

[36] "Aviso do secretário do Estado dos Negócios do Reino, Conde de Oeiras, Sebastião José de Carvalho e Melo, aos governadores do Estado do Brasil, referente à criação da Ouvidoria do Porto Seguro, nomeando para ela, o bacharel Thomé Couceiro de Abreu," April 28, 1763, AHU-ACL_CU_005 Cx. 150 Doc. 11523, AHU; "Decreto do Rei D. José ao Conselho Ultramarino nomeando o corregedor da comarca de tomar o bacharel Thomé Couceiro de Abreu para ouvidor da nova Ouvidoria da capitania de Porto Seguro," April 2, 1763, AHU-ACL_CU_005 Cx. 150 Doc. 11510, AHU.

[37] Langfur argues that the very reason for the renewed colonization of these lands was spurred by sharply declining outputs that were already prevalent by the mid-eighteenth century, much prior to the official Crown declaration of the Botocudo Wars in 1808.

[38] Barickman, "Tame Indians," 337.   [39] Ibid., 331.

FIGURE 0.4 Early-nineteenth-century travelers eagerly explored the Atlantic frontier, serving as both witnesses and proponents of its settlement. The Doce, which coursed through Botocudo territory, was one of the region's principal rivers. *Source: Excursion up a Branch of the Rio Doce*, from Maximilian Wied, *Travels in Brazil* (London: Henry Colburn & Co., 1820). Courtesy of the John Carter Brown Library at Brown University.

territory to incorporate a large swath of the Atlantic frontier. The annexation stimulated São Mateus' economic development, transforming it into an important producer of manioc flour that was shipped through Barra and exported to the rest of Porto Seguro, Salvador, and eventually as far as Rio.[40] Henceforth São Mateus identified administratively, politically, and economically with Porto Seguro and later Bahia. São Mateus was finally reverted to Espírito Santo during independence, when the new province of Bahia absorbed the rest of Porto Seguro and Ilhéus captaincies into its borders.[41]

[40] Marquis de Pombal to Ouvidor Thomé Couceiro de Abreu, April 30, 1763, Arquivo de Marinha Ultramar, Registro de Ordens Régias Livro 4 (1758–1765) fls. 198 and following, reprinted in Eliezer Nardoto and Herinéa Lima, *História de São Mateus* (São Mateus, ES: Editorial Atlântica, 2001), 33–35 n.7; Gabriel Augusto de Mello Bittencourt, *Café e modernização: O Espírito Santo no século 19* (Rio de Janeiro: Ed. Cátedra, 1987), 22, 58–60. For farinha production and African-based slavery in Porto Seguro, see Barickman, "Tame Indians," 332.

[41] The exact administrative relationship of Porto Seguro to Bahia during the late colonial period remains unclear. A separate captaincy along with Ilhéus since the early colonial

After independence, the region forming the Atlantic frontier became two new comarcas: Caravelas in southern Bahia, including the towns of Caravelas, Viçosa, São José de Porto Alegre, Alcobaça, and Prado; the other was São Mateus, comprising São Mateus and Barra de São Mateus, across the new provincial border in Espírito Santo.[42] The residents developed regional networks transcending administrative borders that often included those from northern Minas. The region would maintain a conflictive relationship with the provincial and national governments, at times eagerly agreeing with their policies of development and Indian administration, and at other times tenaciously resisting its visions of national integration and progress, including abolition.

These towns of the Atlantic frontier were tucked in among territories inhabited by various indigenous groups. Many of the settlers were the poor from Minas Gerais in search of new opportunities in lands cleared for settlement by anti-Indian military operations. On the northern end were the majority indigenous town of Prado (pop. 1,036) and the small but prosperous manioc-producing town of Alcobaça at the mouths, respectively, of the Jucuruçu and Itanhém Rivers. Among Alcobaça's nearly 900 residents were Portuguese, Azoreans, black slaves, and Chinese coolies who had been sent from the tea plantations in Rio de Janeiro. Alcobaça and Prado both traded their food and tools with the Pataxó Indians, who maintained a wariness toward the settlers. The Pataxó had allied with the Maxacalí Indians against Botocudo incursions. Near Alcobaça were some small properties worked by slaves, including a manioc farm run by an Englishman.[43]

Just south of Alcobaça was Caravelas, the largest town in the region and the seat of the comarca. Lined with several streets and well-kept homes with colorful ceramic tiles, it had a total population of 3,552, 40 percent of which (1,434) were black and *pardo* slaves. Ships arrived

period, Porto Seguro was at some point between the late eighteenth and early nineteenth century integrated into the Captaincy-General of Bahia as a comarca, but different sources provide different titles. For example, a 1759 survey of the captaincy of Bahia refers to Porto Seguro as both a captaincy and a comarca. By independence, however, it was definitively part of the new province of Bahia. Barickman, "Tame Indians," 334.

[42] *Almanak Administrativo, Mercantil e Industrial da Bahia*, 1855, 124; *Almanak (ES)*, 1885, 158. The region of São Mateus addressed in this book thus comprises the territory from the border with Bahia down to the Doce river. São Mateus was elevated from town to city status in 1848.

[43] Wied-Neuwied, *Viagem ao Brasil*, 174–196–217; Barickman, "Tame Indians." The population for Alcobaça is from Maximilian. Barickman gives Alcobaça's population at 1,841 for 1818.

to its ample harbor from Pernambuco, Bahia, Rio de Janeiro, and Espírito Santo to trade in its cotton, manioc flour, and whale oil. Further down the coast past a thicket of mangroves and sandy banks was Vila Viçosa, another manioc-producing town whose local municipal chamber repeatedly clashed with the European coffee planters of nearby Colônia Leopoldina, located on the Peruípe River connecting the two locales, over land titles. Marking the southernmost border of Bahia province after independence was the Mucuri River and São José de Porto Alegre, the poor, mostly indigenous hamlet where the Mucuri met the Atlantic. It was here that the aforementioned European traveler had encountered a captain leading a multiracial team of workers clearing a road from the interior. At the southern end of the Atlantic frontier was the newest and already prosperous town of São Mateus, located up the river from the town of Barra de São Mateus. Of its 3,120 residents in 1820, 42 percent (1,336) were black and pardo slaves. São Mateus' growing economy of timber and manioc exports (60,000 *alquieres* – a unit of 36.3 kg – annually circa 1815–17) pitted the residents against the various indigenous groups living along the river, with such tensions spilling over into interethnic hostilities. On its north bank were the Kumanaxó, Pataxó, and Maxacalí, who had joined forces against the Botocudo on the southern bank. Further up the São Mateus River, the military outpost of Galvêas was founded to prevent hostile Indians from reaching the town. One could occasionally hear the drumming of African slaves drifting over from properties tucked away among forests of jacaranda and cashew.[44]

Compared to the Indians, the African-descended population in these early years was much more obscure. Around independence, African slavery was still small compared to major cities and plantation zones, but was already approaching half of the population in larger towns such as São Mateus and Caravelas. They appear fleetingly in sources, for example in the ouvidores' prohibition of black–indigenous marriages and godparentage (an important indicator of interracial affective relationships), or baptismal and marriage registries from Alcobaça in the 1780s that include black and *pardo* (mixed-race) slaves who accompanied their masters from Ilhéus. Also present were freedpeople and the free poor from Minas Gerais who had arrived to seek new opportunities. However, the sources are frustratingly opaque regarding free people of color, a situation that sharply contrasts with the high visibility of slavery and the enslaved

---

[44] Wied-Neuwied, *Viagem ao Brasil*, 170–72.

after independence. For this reason this book focuses mostly on enslaved people of African descent and the Botocudo.[45] Yet even for the enslaved, only scattered documentation exists that sheds light on their points of sale and presumed origins, particularly for the late eighteenth and first half of the nineteenth century. The limited evidence indicates that the majority of the region's African-descended, enslaved population arrived after independence with the expansion of slavery into the Atlantic frontier. Most were employed in small-scale manioc flour production, but others worked on the few coffee plantations there. With the perennial labor shortage in the Atlantic frontier, so important did African slavery become that large slaveholders in São Mateus and Colônia Leopoldina accrued outsize economic and political influence, going to extreme lengths to keep their human property. Attention to the enslaved thus reveals not only how essential their labor was to frontier development, but also the tremendous obstacles that lay in their pathway to emancipation. Through their lives on the Atlantic frontier we can see the ways in which enslaved people resisted, challenged, and negotiated the boundaries and meanings of slavery, freedom, and citizenship.[46]

This book travels between the Atlantic frontier and Rio de Janeiro, following the movement of Indians and slaves, settlers and missionaries, laws and knowledge, national policy and local practice. On the ground, provincial borders between Bahia, Espírito Santo, and Minas Gerais meant little to those who regularly traversed them. The many meanings that the various actors in this book gave to the territory – as a space of liberation from bondage, of power and sustenance, of economic opportunity, or of darkness to be brought into the light of civilization – provide an important lens onto the conflicts over race, nation, and citizenship in nineteenth-century Brazil.

---

[45] "Instrucções para o governo dos indios da Capitania de Porto Seguro, que os meus Directores hão de praticar em tudo aquillo que se não encontrar com o Directorio dos Indios do Gram Pará" (July 27, 1777, appendix to n. 9492), 372–76, in *ABN* 32 (1910); Baptismal and Marriage records from the parish of Santo Antônio de Caravelas, transcribed and annotated by Father Olavo Timmers in the 1960s, Co-Catedral do Santo Antônio de Caravelas.

[46] For the sake of narrative clarity, this book utilizes the terms "slave," "enslaved," and "slavery" to refer enslaved people of African descent. The exception is Chapter 1, where both indigenous and African slavery are addressed. In addition, the expression "African slavery" is used to signify the enslavement of Africans and their Brazilian-born descendants.

Chapter Overview and a Note on the Sources

Chapter 1 addresses the relationship between black and indigenous slavery and citizenship. It begins with a discussion of the 1824 Constitution, whose remarkably inclusive definition of citizenship was premised on the implicit exclusion of black slaves and Indians. Such exclusions were reproduced on the Atlantic frontier, which relegalized Indian slavery during the Botocudo Wars at the same time as the expansion of African slavery into the region. The reader is introduced to Colônia Leopoldina, a European immigrant colony founded in southern Bahia on the eve of independence whose transformation into a slave plantation exposed the failures of the Crown and state to "civilize" the frontier through white, free labor. Chapter 2 focuses on popular politics. It examines the many ways in which black and indigenous people experienced and interpreted frontier nation-building from roughly the 1820s to the 1850s, including violent confrontation with masters and settlers, strategic negotiations, and sometimes, citizenship claims. Rather than framing all examples under the rubric of a universal aspiration for citizenship, this chapter argues that it was but one among a variety of possibilities. The chapter demonstrates how state expansion was shaped by the very people whom it sought to exclude. Race and national identity are the central themes of Chapter 3. This chapter argues that the officialization of *mestiçagem* (race mixture) as a uniquely inclusive Brazilian national identity in the mid-nineteenth century – a purported "solution" to the twin problems of a large African and persistent "wild" Indian population – was inseparable from the active promotion of indigenous extinction. Acculturative indigenous policies intended to "civilize" Indians for national inclusion worked in tandem with settler violence, Romantic artistic movements, and the emerging science of race to elevate indigenous extinction into a fact. The chapter also demonstrates how racial ideas about Indians shaped corresponding ideas about Afro-Brazilians in surprising ways.

The nexus of law, violence, and citizenship in the final years of slavery and imperial rule is the subject of Chapter 4. By comparing two cases of extravagant violence from the early 1880s, this chapter demonstrates the diverging relationship of enslaved and indigenous people to the nation's body of laws. The first example is a white family that castrated and clandestinely murdered one of its slaves who impregnated his mistress, and the second, the settler massacre of an entire indigenous village. In spite of the violent outcomes for both, the chapter argues that the cases reveal the growing legal inclusion of enslaved people that paralleled the effective legal exclusion of Indians. This chapter also examines specific practices of violence through the lens of gender, power, and legitimacy in the 1880s. Chapter 5 illuminates the uses and meanings of geography by a group of female and male *quilombolas* (maroons) of São Mateus in 1880–81, and an antislavery insurrection rumor in which some of them were implicated in 1884. Through the concept of "insurgent geographies," it shows how enslaved people used their own territorial claims to assert a specific vision of citizenship and antislavery politics in the absence of legal avenues for freedom. The chapter also traces the adventures of the legendary quilombola Benedito, whose life has been richly recounted in local oral histories but with little archival research until now. Labor and abolition are addressed in Chapter 6. The impending abolition of slavery (1888) reinvigorated an interest in indigenous labor as local slaveholders resisted abolitionism with increasing violence and demagoguery. This chapter argues that missionaries, state officials, and abolitionists shared remarkably similar ideas about the need to discipline black and indigenous people through labor regimes with the goal of preparing them for a servile citizenship. Such a vision, furthermore, was intimately tied to the contest for territorial control. The chapter concludes with a discussion of black and indigenous people's radically different criticisms of their limited citizenship at the end of the nineteenth century.

Archives are both bountiful and exasperating to the historian seeking to write about black and indigenous people in postcolonial Brazil. From the outset one must contend with the separation of black and indigenous lives that is already produced in the archive, which creates the illusion of a nation where only one side – usually of African descent – existed. Sources are qualitatively and quantitatively uneven to the extreme, and rarely does a single type of source address both populations. By piecing them together like a puzzle, a more complex history begins to come into focus. A project such as this also requires a critical reading of the multiple voices intoning indigenous people's extinction by the last three decades of the nineteenth century. Romantic artistic celebrations of colonial Indians and anthropological studies of Botocudo skulls, both of which promoted views that justified Indian extinction at the time, and since have informed scholars of racial thought, must be read against reports of rampant anti-indigenous violence on the ground. Nor are we privy to a well-balanced chorus of black and indigenous voices. The richness of slave testimonies in court records, for example, has no counterpart among the indigenous. A wide variety of sources, from police, administrative, and court records to laws, inventories, censuses, memoirs, missionary correspondence, public works and engineering proposals, travel narratives, scientific texts, ethnographies, and newspapers, among others, have been used to fill in this gap. Yet as historians, we are naturally at home among the irregular and kaleidoscopic bounty of the historical record, for it is here that enlightening and surprising stories emerge.

I

Outside of Society

Slavery and Citizenship

The Swiss and German colonists who arrived in southern Bahia on the eve of Brazil's independence found themselves in the middle of a vast warzone. The Portuguese Crown had given them a land grant (*sesmaria*) in 1818 in what was then Porto Seguro, a captaincy of small towns and hamlets on the Atlantic frontier, worlds apart from the bustling coastal cities of Salvador, Recife, and Rio de Janeiro. The region was the field of a "just war" against the Botocudo Indians. This war, declared by the Prince Regent João VI in 1808 but long in the making, authorized the Indians' enslavement, violent subjugation, and land seizure. Once feared and avoided by the Portuguese as savages and cannibals, the Botocudo were now seen as an infestation to be removed from an otherwise pristine, virginal terrain ripe for the taking.

Brazilian nationhood would thus inaugurate amidst the conquest of the Atlantic frontier. Spanning a vast area from the interior mountains to the ocean, these formerly "forbidden lands" may not have been the El Dorado some had dreamt of. Still, they seduced newcomers with the promise of untapped diamond mines, navigable rivers, high-quality timber, and plenty of cultivable land tantalizingly close to the ocean. European immigrants embodied the Crown's hopes of civilizing this indigenous territory with the introduction of white, free labor. The settlement, which the immigrants named Colônia Leopoldina, would play an important role in colonizing the Atlantic frontier over the course of the nineteenth century. Doubtless the settlers did not foresee the remarkable cycle of violence they would help unleash in the nation after independence, engulfing immigrants and Brazilians, Indians and blacks in countless territorial conflicts for decades to come.

By the mid-nineteenth century these European colonists would be among the most powerful coffee producers in the region. Yet their wealth was not the result of innovative agricultural technology or Indian subjugation alone. Driving their ascent was a growing labor force of enslaved Africans and their descendants who toiled daily in the oppressive heat of the southern Bahian sun to tend to the colony's vast coffee and manioc fields. The colonists' success was enabled by the expansion of African slavery into frontier lands, where it forcefully converged with Indian enslavement, last abolished in the late eighteenth century but relegalized during the Botocudo Wars. The enslavement of black and indigenous people became foundational to the incorporation of the Atlantic frontier into the nation from which, as slaves and "savages," they themselves were excluded.

Paralleling the violence of the frontier were the debates on Brazilian citizenship taking place in the parliament of the newly independent Brazil. The 1824 Constitution presented a remarkably inclusive, liberal idea of citizenship that extended it to Brazilian-born freedpeople. Yet its ambiguities and exclusions reflected the political elite's unwillingness to recognize Africans, Indians, and slaves as members of the new nation. To examine the constitutional debates and the territorial incorporation of the Atlantic frontier together is to see not two disconnected spheres but rather two simultaneous and confluent processes of nation-building. From its inception, the new Brazilian nation engendered exclusions in both spheres by forging a legal and physical geography of slavery and quasi-citizenship of its black and indigenous people.

"Merely Brazilian": Early Debates and Silences on Citizenship, 1823–1824

Pedro I declared Brazilian independence in September 1822 and was proclaimed emperor in October.[1] A year later, the General Constituent and Legislative Assembly met to define the new constitution's parameters of Brazilian citizenship. Deciding who would be included within – and excluded from – the nation was no simple feat in a vast territory where political unity was far from achieved.[2] Proslavery interests

---

[1] Roderick J. Barman, *Brazil: The Forging of a Nation, 1798–1852* (Stanford, CA: Stanford University Press, 1988), 99.

[2] According to Holston, about one-third of the population in 1819 (excluding autonomous Indians) was enslaved. James Holston, *Insurgent Citizenship: Disjunctions of Democracy and Modernity in Brazil* (Princeton, NJ: Princeton University Press, 2008), 67.

also successfully maintained the trans-Atlantic trade, defeating its critics
and ensuring that liberalism in post-independence Brazil would coex-
ist with slavery. In the heated discussions, Indians and slaves became
key groups through which the terms of inclusion and exclusion were
defined.

The debate was unleashed by Senator Nicolau Vergueiro of São Paulo,
who proposed to amend Article 5 of the Constitutional Project for the
Empire of Brazil. Vergueiro suggested amending the language "[o]f the
members of the society of the Empire of Brazil" by replacing "members of
society" with "citizen." He believed the change was necessary given the
presence of "slaves and Indians who are Brazilian but not part of society"
to whom the Constitution would not apply.[3] His view was seconded
by Manoel França of Rio de Janeiro, who contended that birthplace
made one Brazilian but did not automatically confer citizenship. In his
view, "enslaved *crioulos* [Brazilian-born slaves] are born in Brazilian
territory but are not Brazilian citizens. We must make this distinction:
a Brazilian is he who is born in Brazil; a Brazilian citizen is he who
has civil rights." His argument extended to the indigenous people, who
were also required to meet civilizational criteria. "Indians who live in the
forests are Brazilians, but nevertheless are not Brazilian citizens as long
as they do not embrace our civilization," he argued, adding that "wild"
Indians "in their savage state . . . cannot be considered part of the 'great
Brazilian family.'"[4] Both referred only to autonomous Indians. Following
their arguments, Francisco Carneiro of Bahia explicitly excluded slaves
and Indians from citizenship. "Our intention is to determine who are
Brazilian citizens," he began, "for once we know who they are, the others
can be called simply Brazilian, for being born in the country, as slaves,
crioulos or Indians, etc." In no uncertain terms Carneiro affirmed that
the "Constitution does not deal with [them], because they do not enter
in the social pact." Slaves and Indians were "*merely Brazilian* but do not
belong to so-called civil society and do not have any rights beyond mere
protection."[5] These representatives agreed that citizenship could not be
conferred by birthplace alone – the principle of *ius soli*. Brazilian-born
slaves and Indians were excluded from its purview, the former because
of their enslaved status and the latter for lacking civilization. França

---

[3] *Annaes do Parlamento brazileiro, Assembléa constituinte, 1823*, Vol. 5 (H. J. Pinto,
1880), 211, 232.
[4] Ibid., 211.   [5] Ibid., 228–29. Italics added.

described these variations as a problem of the "heterogeneity of our population."[6]

If the exclusion of slaves and autonomous Indians was asserted, the possibilities for a future inclusion were left open. Brazilian-born slaves were best placed in this regard. The representatives supported citizenship for manumitted Brazilian slaves with little controversy. Scholars have noted that this support was based not on the principle of universal citizenship but rather on a liberal defense of slavery. Proslavery representatives calculated that providing *libertos* (freedpeople) with the possibility of individual liberty and citizenship would ultimately help maintain the existing social order of slave society.[7] The same possibilities were closed down for African libertos, whom many openly disdained. Almeida e Albuquerque of Pernambuco, for example, questioned, "How is it possible that a man without a homeland, virtue, nor customs, seized by a hateful commerce from his land and brought to Brazil, could just by virtue of his master's will suddenly acquire such rights in our lands?" He considered Africans among those who should not be given the right to citizenship since they lacked a "certain aptitude for the good of society and do not have moral qualities." He found it unacceptable that manumission would automatically grant citizenship to Africans when Europeans were required to naturalize.[8] A striking defense of African libertos' citizenship came from Silva Lisboa of Bahia, who squarely blamed Europeans, and in particular the Portuguese, for the slave trade. He criticized the "hateful caste distinctions that exist based on differences in color" and urged the Assembly not to promote "new inequalities" that would result from granting citizenship only to Brazilian libertos.[9] Silva Lisboa clashed with and was ultimately defeated by Maciel da Costa of São Paulo, who blamed Africans' "barbaric compatriots" for selling them into slavery. He viewed their enslavement as a contract that Brazilians had already fulfilled, and that citizenship was not owed them. A recent governor of French Guiana under Brazilian rule, da Costa had seen up close the tumultuous events

---

[6] Ibid., 211.

[7] Andréa Slemian, "Seriam todos cidadãos? Os impasses na construção da cidadania nos primórdios do constitucionalismo no Brasil (1823–1824)," in *Independência: história e historiografia*, ed. István Jancsó (São Paulo: Editora Hucitec, 2005), 846; Rafael de Bivar Marquese and Márcia Regina Berbel, "A ausência da raça: escravidão, cidadania e ideologia pró-escravista nas Cortes de Lisboa e na Assembléia Constituinte do Rio," in *Território, conflito e identidade*, ed. Cláudia Maria das Graças Chaves and Marco Antonio Silveira (Belo Horizonte: Argumentum, 2007), 63–88.

[8] *Annaes do parlamento*, 1823, 234, 259.   [9] Ibid., 262.

of the French colonies rippling out from St. Domingue. He argued that
public security was more important than "philanthropy" and suggested
that limiting citizenship to Brazilian libertos would help maintain social
order by driving a wedge between them and Africans.[10]

Compared to the libertos, much greater ambiguity shrouded the citizenship possibilities of Indians. First, advocates of Indian exclusion were
addressing only the autonomous Indians, many of whom were being
enslaved through just war precisely during these debates. The eligibility of
aldeia Indians – those who had become Portuguese vassals and resided in
state-sponsored villages, subject to separate laws from the autonomous –
was left undefined.[11] Teixeira Vasconcellos of Minas Gerais pointed out
this omission in França's earlier argument, noting that he seemingly
excluded all Indians from citizenship although "they are born free and
live in Brazil." Speaking of aldeia Indians, he contended that if they are
"part of the social pact, there is no reason to exclude them." Similarly,
José de Alencar of Ceará argued that "an Indian who 'enters our society,'
savage as he is, is a citizen." Yet tellingly, neither of these comments
were followed up, perhaps based on an implicit assumption that aldeia
Indians required no special discussion.[12] Second, unlike those for manumission for Brazilian libertos, there were no clear criteria according to
which autonomous Indians would be eligible for citizenship. França himself suggested that "we will give them the rights of a citizen once they
embrace our customs and civilization." Francisco Montesuma of Bahia
agreed that Indians could enter the "family that constitutes the Empire"
as soon as they wished and suggested that the Constitution "establish a
chapter that discusses the methods of inviting them into the cradle [of
our society]."[13] However, the Assembly's deliberations on these matters

---

[10] Ibid., 264; João Severiano Maciel da Costa, *Memória sobre a necessidade de abolir a introdução dos escravos africanos no Brasil: sobre o modo e condições com que esta abolição se deve fazer; e sobre os meios de remediar a falta de braços que ela pode ocasionar* (Coimbra: Imprensa da Universidade, 1821), 23–24; Slemian, "Seriam todos cidadãos?," 844; Marquese and Berbel, "A ausência da raça."

[11] Beatriz Perrone-Moisés, "Índios livres e índios escravos: os princípios da legislação indigenista do período colonial (séculos XVI a XVIII)," in *História dos índios no Brasil*, ed. Manuela Carneiro da Cunha (São Paulo: Editora Schwarcz, 1992), 117–22.

[12] Fernanda Sposito, *Nem cidadãos, nem brasileiros: Indígenas na formação do Estado nacional brasileiro e conflitos na província de São Paulo (1822–1845)* (São Paulo: Alameda, 2012), 36–37. Under Pombal, aldeia Indians lost their special protected status and became equal to other vassals after the Directorate of Indians was abolished in 1798. An exception was the recently settled, who were given orphan status.

[13] *Annaes do parlamento*, 1823, 236.

were abruptly terminated in November 1823 when it was dissolved by Pedro I, who replaced it with a new commission that included six of the former representatives, headed by Maciel da Costa. It was they who put the final stamp on the Constitution promulgated in March 1824.

In a striking departure from the specificity in the discussions held in the Constituent Assembly, the 1824 Brazilian Constitution was both explicit and remarkably vague about who qualified as a citizen. According to Article 6, "Brazilian citizens are those born in Brazil, either freeborn or freed, even if the father is a foreigner, once he is no longer in service of his nation." Also included were the foreign-born children of a Brazilian father, and the illegitimate children of a Brazilian mother who came to establish residence in the Empire. Finally, Portuguese residing in Brazil who had pledged allegiance to independence, as well as naturalized foreigners of any faith, also qualified.[14] Latin America's largest slave society thus granted citizenship to all free and formerly enslaved persons born in Brazil.[15]

As notable as its inclusiveness, however, were the Constitution's silences. There was no mention of gender qualifications. Nor were there any racial criteria by which citizenship was made available to a Brazilian-born freedperson. Such deracialized citizenship contrasted with the race-based exclusion of native-born black and indigenous people in the United States.[16] African libertos, however, were completely excluded from the Constitution. Although they could potentially naturalize like European immigrants, they were considered stateless persons encouraged to self-deport rather than lay claim to Brazilian citizenship.[17]

[14] Full text of the 1824 Constitution: http://pdba.georgetown.edu/Constitutions/Brazil/brazil1824.html#mozTocId158438.

[15] Brazilian citizenship could be comparable to that of Colombia, which initially granted it to all slaves and Indians. However, by 1843, Colombian citizenship was restricted by property, income, and by 1850, literacy, as in many other Spanish-American republics. In Brazil these restrictions would be placed in 1881. Brooke Larson, *Trials of Nation Making: Liberalism, Race, and Ethnicity in the Andes, 1810–1910* (Cambridge and New York: Cambridge University Press, 2008), 81–82; James E. Sanders, *Contentious Republicans: Popular Politics, Race, and Class in Nineteenth-Century Colombia* (Durham, NC: Duke University Press, 2004), 20; Sidney Chalhoub, "The Precariousness of Freedom in a Slave Society (Brazil in the Nineteenth Century)," *International Review of Social History* 56, no. 3 (2011): 415.

[16] Holston, *Insurgent Citizenship*, 60, 87; Hebe Maria Mattos de Castro, *Das cores do silêncio: os significados da liberdade no sudeste escravista, Brasil século XIX* (Rio de Janeiro: Arquivo Nacional, 1995).

[17] Manuela Carneiro da Cunha, *Negros, estrangeiros: os escravos libertos e sua volta à África* (São Paulo: Ed. Brasiliense, 1985), 74–81; Barbara Weinstein, "Slavery, Citizenship, and National Identity in Brazil and the U.S. South," in *Nationalism in the New*

The Constitution also maintained a total silence on Indians. Article 6's principle of *ius soli* (birthplace) implied that all Indians were citizens, but the preceding Assembly debates clearly demonstrated the representatives' consensus over the exclusion of autonomous Indians.[18] As for Montesuma's earlier suggestion that it include a chapter on methods to invite these Indians into society, the matter was discussed but ultimately voided in the final version of the Constitution, and a follow-up attempt to devise a national policy of catechism and civilization in 1826 would also fail.[19] In fact, only in 1845, when the Brazilian state had achieved greater centralization under Pedro II, would there be a national body of legislation for Indian incorporation. The Constitution therefore at best implied, but never affirmed, their inclusion. Its silence on Indian citizenship could partly be explained by the inability of representatives deliberating the matter in Rio de Janeiro to confront the diversity of indigenous groups and local laws across Brazil of which they had little experience or knowledge. But more fundamentally, a central problem in defining Indian citizenship was its impossibility – since according to the political elite's ideas about race and culture, to enter the social pact, Indians needed to be civilized, and in doing so, they were no longer Indian.[20]

Their resulting omission of Indians was criticized in the frontlines. Guido Marlière, the French-born Director-General of Indians of Minas Gerais who lived among the Botocudo, decried in 1825 that the "Constitution qualifies freed slaves as citizens. But the Indians, *Senhores*

World, ed. Don Harrison Doyle and Marco Antonio Villela Pamplona (Athens: University of Georgia Press, 2006), 260. Pressures to self-deport would mount especially after the 1835 Malê revolt. Led by mostly Muslim West African slaves and freedpeople, the Malê Revolt that took place in January in Salvador, Bahia terrified Brazilian slaveholding society and led to stringent measures against Africans in Brazil, including deportation.

[18] During the colonial period, Indians were royal vassals, while African-descended slaves were technically not. Russell-Wood and Schultz have shown, however, that the latter were sometimes able to request and receive royal protection. After the Court's arrival in Rio de Janeiro, slaves claimed vassal status in order to receive royal intervention against their masters' abuses. A. J. R. Russell-Wood, "Acts of Grace: Portuguese Monarchs and Their Subjects of African Descent in Eighteenth-Century Brazil," *JLAS* 32, no. 2 (May 2000): 307–32; Kirsten Schultz, *Tropical Versailles: Empire, Monarchy, and the Portuguese Royal Court in Rio de Janeiro, 1808–1821* (London: Routledge, 2001), Chapter 5.

[19] Fernanda Sposito, "Liberdade para os índios no Império do Brasil: A revogação da guerra justa em 1831," *Almanack* 1 (2011): 61–62. The documents from this haphazard national survey (from Espírito Santo, Goiás, Paraíba, Ceará, Minas Gerais, São Paulo, Pernambuco, and Piauí) are available in Naud, "Documentos sôbre o índio brasileiro, 2a parte" and analyzed in John M. Monteiro, "Tupis, Tapuias e Historiadores: Estudos de História Indígena e do Indigenismo" (São Paulo: Tese de Livre Docência, UNICAMP, 2001), Chapter 7.

[20] Sposito, *Nem cidadãos*, 33, 93–94.

Proprietários, born in this immense land that we inhabit, have not received this title! That is our equality!" Confusion over their status was evident in Marlière's referring to them later as "Indian Citizens" – an oxymoron in the minds of many legislators.[21]

Finally, the Constitution was also distinguished by what James Holston has called its "inclusively inegalitarian" nature. It extended citizenship to many but was simultaneously predicated on the unequal distribution of rights. Nowhere was this more evident than in the absence of the word "equality." Brazil's idea of citizenship differed fundamentally in this regard from North American and French models based on the "all-or-nothing" distribution of rights.[22] Rights were separated into civil and political rights, the latter reserved only for a few and distributed unevenly among three levels of citizens: passive citizens, active voting citizens, and active electors, the last of whom had to be born free.[23] The vast majority were passive citizens who could not vote. Brazilian *libertos* made some important gains, including the right to own property without restriction, maintain a family, inherit and bequeath, be a legal guardian, and represent themselves at court and before the state. However, they could vote only in primary elections and were ineligible to work as public servants.[24] The political exclusion of women was not mentioned at all, because it was so evident to legislators as to not warrant special mention.[25] Even

---

[21] Letter by Guido Marlière to the President of Minas Gerais, July 25, 1825, in Naud, "Documentos sôbre o índio brasileiro, 2a parte," 317. Jurist Perdigão Malheiro noted that José Bonifácio's dual proposal in 1823 to gradually abolish slavery and institute a national plan for Indian civilization was annulled by the dissolution of the Constituent Assembly in November 1823, resulting in a constitution that avoided both issues. Agostinho Marques Perdigão Malheiro, *A escravidão no Brasil, ensaio histórico-jurídico-social*, Vol. 2 (Rio de Janeiro: Typographia Nacional, 1866), 134–35. The Constitution's inclusive yet ambiguous language has contributed to disagreements over Indian citizenship. On one side is James Holston, who has argued that the principle of ius soli extended citizenship to all Indians (although some were orphans), while Fernanda Sposito has explicitly stated that Indians, along with women and slaves, were excluded.

[22] Holston, *Insurgent Citizenship*.

[23] Hebe Maria Mattos de Castro, *Escravidão e cidadania no Brasil monárquico* (Rio de Janeiro: Jorge Zahar, 2000), 20–21; Chalhoub, "Precariousness of Freedom," 413–16.

[24] Holston, *Insurgent Citizenship*, 79, 90. Men had to meet the 100 *mil-réis* minimum income requirement to vote in primary elections. Most domestic servants, all underage citizens, and all women were also passive citizens. As José Murilo de Carvalho has noted, even this right to vote was not, in practice, understood as political participation in the nation, but was strictly bound to local struggles and boss politics. José Murilo de Carvalho, *Cidadania no Brasil: o longo caminho* (Rio de Janeiro: Civilização Brasileira, 2001), 35.

[25] Women were also permanently disqualified from active citizenship. Brazil was hardly unique in its silence on women's political qualification; Holston found the US and French Constitutions also silent on women. Holston, *Insurgent Citizenship*, 87, 90.

the representatives at the Constituent Assembly who disagreed over various matters had no qualms about the inequality of citizenship itself. As Andrea Slemian has observed, the constitution was a "model of liberal citizenship that adopted, without trauma, the idea of society as naturally unequal."[26]

Inequality and exclusions, both explicit and implicit, were thus central to the definition of citizenship in the Brazilian constitution. Citizenship was constructed around not only active and passive, free and slave, but also civilized and uncivilized. All slaves and autonomous Indians were excluded from the constitution's purview because they existed "outside of the social pact." Yet although Brazilian slaves had a pathway to eventual citizenship, such possibilities did not challenge the existence of slavery itself. This maintenance of slavery ensured its expansion in postcolonial Brazil.

For Indians, the constitution's apparently inclusive language based on birthplace and free status was deliberately silent on their eligibility. No representative affirmed the citizenship of aldeia Indians, while a cohesive set of legislations to realize autonomous Indians' eventual inclusion was abandoned.[27] The Botocudo Wars and other offensive wars created the opening for many Indians to enter the nation as slaves, a condition that would haunt them long after the wars and Indian slavery were officially ended. This ambiguous citizenship status placed Brazilian Indians in a vulnerable, legal gray area that would effectively erode their rights and protections over the course of the nineteenth century. Like libertos given only partial or conditional manumission and threatened by a precarious hold on citizenship, Indians became quasi-citizens from the moment of the nation's birth, at best eligible for an uncertain future citizenship.[28] If state policies deliberated in Rio seemed irrelevant in a politically fragmented new nation, they would converge with war and slavery on the Atlantic frontier.

---

[26] Slemian, "Seriam todos cidadãos?," 840.

[27] Such silence echoes many state officials' reluctance to acknowledge Indians' right to liberty after its declaration between 1755 and 1758. Hal Langfur and Maria Leônia Chaves de Resende, "Indian Autonomy and Slavery in Colonial Minas Gerais," in *Native Brazil: Beyond the Convert and the Cannibal, 1500–1900*, ed. Hal Langfur (Albuquerque: University of New Mexico Press, 2014), 151–59.

[28] Rebecca Scott documents the similarly precarious claim on freedom that the freedwoman Adélaïde Métayer/Durand had to fight for in her journey from St. Domingue to Cuba, then Louisiana. Rebecca J. Scott, "Paper Thin: Freedom and Re-Enslavement in the Diaspora of the Haitian Revolution," *Law and History Review* no. 4 (2011): 1061–88.

Civilizing with Slavery: The Curious Life of Colônia Leopoldina

Colônia Leopoldina's creation in southern Bahia on the eve of independence was enabled by the Crown's fusion of settler occupation with indigenous conquest. In his authorization of the Botocudo Wars in Bahia, Espírito Santo, and Minas Gerais, João VI had clearly stated his territorial objectives.[29] They included the navigation of the Doce River (the principal river linking Minas Gerais to the Atlantic through Espírito Santo captaincy) and special concessions to "those who want to settle those precious, auriferous terrains that are today abandoned due to the fear caused by the Botocudo Indians." He provided generous incentives to prospective settlers, including sesmarias, debt forgiveness, and freedom from paying the royal tax for ten years. The Crown also created eight infantry divisions to protect the settlers, the Doce River Divisions, reaching from Minas to the borders of Espírito Santo and Bahia.[30] In 1811, three years after declaring the Botocudo Wars, João VI approved assistance for 3,000 colonists who had "entered in the lands free from the invasion of barbarian Indians" in the Porto Seguro captaincy. These lands which, in the language of just war, were "rescued" from the "anthropophagous Botocudo Indians" were distributed as land grants among the new arrivals. By this year, 381 sesmarias were granted in a single military district.[31]

Following these grants, in 1818, the Crown began sponsoring immigrant agricultural colonies in the region in accordance with João VI's 1808 decree authorizing land grants to foreigners. With assistance from the governor of Bahia, in June of 1819 the German naturalist Georg Wilhelm Freyreiss and five fellow immigrants from Switzerland and Hamburg received their grant. A few years later they were joined by other Swiss and Germans including Jan Martins (João Martinho) Flach and Georg Anton von (Jorge Antônio) Schaeffer. They named their colony after Maria Leopoldina of Austria, who would shortly become the empress on João VI's return to Portugal and the accession to the throne of his son, Pedro I, who decided to remain in Brazil with his new consort

---

[29] These cartas regias date from May 13, November 5, and December 12, 1808. Maria Hilda Baqueiro Paraiso, "Os Botocudos e sua trajetória histórica," in *História dos índios no Brasil*, ed. Manuela Carneiro da Cunha (São Paulo: Editora Schwarcz, 1992), 416.

[30] Carta Regia, Manuela Carneiro da Cunha (ed.), *Legislação indigenista no século XIX: uma compilação, 1808–1889* (São Paulo: Comissão Pró-Indio de São Paulo, 1992), 57–60; Judy Bieber, "Catechism and Capitalism: Imperial Indigenous Policy on a Brazilian Frontier, 1808–1845," in *Native Brazil: Beyond the Convert and the Cannibal, 1500–1900*, ed. Hal Langfur (Albuquerque: University of New Mexico Press, 2014), 173–74. According to Bieber, the eighth division was established later in 1820.

[31] Cunha, *Legislação indigenista*, 73–76; Bieber, "Catechism and Capitalism," 173.

after independence.[32] Schaeffer was a colonization agent with close ties to Pedro I and José Bonifácio, Brazil's "father of independence," who encouraged Schaeffer to invite Germans to settle near Colônia Leopoldina.[33] Between 1818 and 1829, other immigrant colonies would be established throughout Brazil, including three more in southern Bahia; Nova Friburgo in the province of Rio de Janeiro; São Leopoldo and São Pedro de Alcântara in the nation's extreme south (today Rio Grande do Sul and Santa Catarina); and Santo Amaro, Itapecerica, and Rio Negro in the province of São Paulo.[34]

Colônia Leopoldina was located on nearly 11,000 hectares of heavily forested land inhabited by Pataxó, Maxacali, and Puri Indians on the banks of the Peruípe River, 20 miles northwest of Vila Viçosa. A natural canal linked the Peruípe to the Caravelas River and the Atlantic Ocean through a labyrinth of mangroves. Large ships arriving from Salvador and Rio de Janeiro were able to navigate this route up to the Port of São José near the colony. With the expansion of its agricultural production, the colony's relative proximity to the ocean proved invaluable for its ability sell its products to Salvador, Rio, and Europe. At its apogee, the colony would extend nearly 53 square kilometers on both sides of the Peruípe River.[35] In exchange for the Crown's sponsorship that included land, livestock, and tools, the colonists were required to observe stringent residency and production regulations. Among these, the most difficult to meet were those regarding labor. In an 1820 decree the Crown required the grantees to work half the land with the labor of their own families, and to distribute the other half among other immigrants whom they were responsible for securing. This effectively prohibited the use of slave labor. In this way the Crown asserted its intent to settle these newly acquired lands with white, free labor.[36]

---

[32] Residents of Colônia Leopoldina to Auguste Tavel, Consul of Commerce of the Swiss Confederation, July 12, 1832, IA6–154, AN; Auguste Tavel to Francisco Carneiro de Campos, Minister and Secretary of Foreign Relations, July 17, 1832, IA6–154, AN.

[33] Alane Fraga do Carmo, "Colonização e escravidão na Bahia: a Colônia Leopoldina (1850–1888)" (M. A. thesis, Universidade Federal da Bahia, 2010), 27.

[34] Ibid., 14; Sílvia Cristina Lambert Siriani, "Os descaminhos da Imigração alemã para São Paulo no século XIX – aspectos políticos," *Almanack* 2 (2005): 92; M. Thereza Schorer Petrone, *O imigrante e a pequena propriedade, 1824–1930* (São Paulo: Brasiliense, 1982), 7–37. Rio and São Paulo were also the names of the respective provinces after independence. Schaeffer original received a sesmaria for his own colony, Frankental (1822), which was later absorbed into Colônia Leopoldina. The area of Rio Negro later became part of the state of Paraná.

[35] Carlos H. Oberacker Jr., "A Colonia Leopoldina-Frankental na Bahia meridional," *RIHGB* 142, no. 354 (1987): 125–26.

[36] Ibid., 128–33.

The spectacular failure of this racialized free labor project in the ensuing decades reveals its incompatibility with the incorporation of Brazil's frontiers, where slavery proved vital to their settlement and economic development. And if Colônia Leopoldina's transformation into a thriving slave plantation community suggested the disconnect between the central government and the frontier, and the inability of the former to extend its authority over the latter, the separation of the two was much less crystalline in practice. Even as it criticized the colony, the state took no concrete action to foster free labor in the frontiers as it ceded to profitability and proslavery interests. Colônia Leopoldina's trajectory embodied a territorial incorporation process that expanded the geography of noncitizens in the incipient nation.

Two traveling Italian missionaries had introduced coffee into southern Bahia in the late eighteenth century. By the time the Swiss and German immigrants arrived, small-scale coffee cultivation was already underway. It was only under Colônia Leopoldina, however, that it would flourish, leading to the establishment of Bahia's only coffee plantation economy, with some of the *fazendas* (plantations) approaching the size of the great estates of southeastern Brazil. Its coffee would command popularity in Rio and even Europe.[37] Only in the second half of the nineteenth century did São Mateus also begin cultivating coffee, spurred by the coffee frontier expanding from the Paraíba Valley farther south.

The first slaves were introduced to Colônia Leopoldina by 1824 in spite of the Crown's stipulations for free labor. While the exact reasons for this turn to slave labor are unclear, the absence of further immigrant arrivals was an important factor. The correlation of these two issues is evident in a letter addressed to Pedro I by the Swiss immigrant and Rio de Janeiro transplant João Flach, who requested royal assistance to bring more immigrants to the colony and also mentioned introducing fifteen slaves and an overseer.[38] According to B. J. Barickman's calculations,

---

[37] B. J. Barickman, *A Bahian Counterpoint: Sugar, Tobacco, Cassava, and Slavery in the Recôncavo, 1780–1860* (Stanford, CA: Stanford University Press, 1998), 27–28. Barickman notes that coffee production expanded in Bahia as a whole in the first half of the nineteenth century, but that in the 1850s, the province supplied only 2 percent of Brazil's coffee exports.

[38] Jan Martins Flach to His Imperial Majesty, October 5, 1824, C-815,15, BN/MS. Oberacker's theory that the "xenophobia" of the immigrants' Brazilian neighbors, who derided their toiling with their own hands, forced them to use slave labor seems questionable given how comfortably they adopted the culture and economy of slavery. Nor is it likely that the death of the colony's co-founder, Freyreiss, cemented its proslavery course, since Freyreiss lauded the benefits of slavery and supported only a gradual abolition, believing libertos to be incapable of freedom. Oberacker,

in 1820 the region as a whole had 3,529 African-descended slaves.[39] This racial landscape would change dramatically as Colônia Leopoldina overwhelmed the surrounding properties in both production and the slave population, and as São Mateus also accelerated its manioc production through slave labor.[40]

Slave prices were low in the early years, their purchases facilitated by immigrant-owned and Brazilian firms that extended credit to the colonists. Some of the wealthier Leopoldina colonists would later set up their own lending businesses.[41] The uptick in the slave population soon aggravated conflicts with their immigrant masters. Many of the enslaved ran away to the sparsely settled indigenous hinterlands to establish *quilombos* (maroon settlements).[42] The colony experienced its first major uprising in 1832 when Schaeffer's slaves shot another planter, dragged Schaeffer's wife back to his plantation, and beat her mercilessly. The original colonists were wary of Schaeffer for leaving "his blacks in an entire insubordination, an ominous example for the blacks on other plantations." They complained to the Swiss consul that Schaeffer's slaves, "armed with rifles, went to the Leopoldina plantations to incite the blacks there to join them and kill the whites." Having experienced racial conflict firsthand, they were eager to discipline their slaves and discourage them from raising a "fearless hand on whites without receiving the punishment they deserve."[43] By the 1840s, the colonists collectively owned more than a thousand slaves. Still, some of them may have admitted that such an economy was not what the Brazilian government had envisioned when it had granted them land. The real problem was not that slaves were fleeing and revolting, but that they were in the region at all.

"Apontamentos," 132; Georg W. Freyreiss, "Viagem ao interior do Brasil nos annos de 1814–1815," *Revista do Instituto Historico e Geographico de São Paulo* XI (1906): 226–27.

[39] B. J. Barickman, "'Tame Indians,' 'Wild Heathens,' and Settlers in Southern Bahia in the Late Eighteenth and Early Nineteenth Centuries," *The Americas* 51, no. 3 (January 1, 1995): 332–33. Barickman gives the total number at 4,835 for the larger region that extended further north to the town of Porto Seguro.

[40] São Mateus is discussed in more depth in Chapter 2.

[41] Johann Jakob von Tschudi, *Reisen durch Südamerika* (Leipzig: F. A. Brockhaus, 1866), 366; Carmo, "Colonização e escravidão," 32–33.

[42] For the region's quilombolas in the early nineteenth century, see Chapter 2.

[43] Residents of Colônia Leopoldina to Tavel, Consul of Commerce of the Swiss Confederation, July 12, 1832; Tavel to Campos, Minister and Secretary of Foreign Relations, July 17, 1832. In 1835 Schaeffer was also attacked by a *mameluco* (Indian-white) person in his own home.

The Crown's prohibition of slavery on these land grant colonies was founded on a specific vision of race and civilization that it aspired to realize in frontier territories. The Portuguese royals who relocated their seat of empire to Rio de Janeiro in 1808 were disconcerted by the bustling black slave society that welcomed them. While recognizing Brazil's utter dependence on the forced labor of black women and men, the royal court and the Brazilian imperial government that followed considered the sizeable African-descended population a fundamental problem. The court envisioned the empire as a homogeneous political body, and white European immigrants played a key role in its desire to facilitate the exclusion of "barbarous" African "foreigners" from participation in civil society.[44] Such racialized fears of Africans became especially pronounced in the aftermath of the Haitian Revolution. In 1821 the aforementioned Maciel da Costa warned that with a racial inundation of Africans, "Brazil will be mistaken for Africa" and raised alarm about a "Kingdom of Congo" growing in its midst. Costa was confident that "it would not be difficult to increase our white population with European émigrés" and specifically promoted agricultural colonies as the best way to acquire hard-working laborers who could set an example in a society too dependent on slaves.[45]

These anti-African sentiments became pronounced in the wake of the 1835 Malê Revolt in Salvador, led by Muslim West African slaves, that shook all of Brazil to its core with the fear of an African takeover.[46] That year the Bahian politician and planter Miguel Pin e Almeida, who sought to establish an immigration company, urged his compatriots to extirpate the "African cancer" and promote immigrant free labor. He explicitly linked free labor with civilization and nation-building, arguing that it was the "most solid basis for the prosperity of a new state," the only way for converting "wilderness into cities, and forests into tilled fields."[47] At the same time, a general population shortage prompted the Minister of Empire to encourage European immigration and Indian civilization.[48]

---

44 Schultz, *Tropical Versailles*, 207–9. Europeans were foreigners who could become Brazilians, while Africans faced tremendous hurdles.

45 Costa, *Memoria*, 34–35, 60, 73.

46 João José Reis, *Rebelião escrava no Brasil: a história do levante dos malês em 1835* (São Paulo: Companhia das Letras, 2003).

47 Miguel Calmon du Pin e Almeida, *Memoria sobre o estabelecimento d'uma companhia de colonisação nesta provincia* (Salvador: Typographia do Diario de G. J. Bezerra e cia, 1835), 9–10.

48 José Ignacio Borges, "Relatório da repartição dos negócios do Império apresentado à Assembléa Geral legislativa, 1835" (Rio de Janeiro: Typographia Nacional, 1836), 21, CRL.

Scholars have noted the rise of immigration debates during the later nineteenth century, when the economic and political elite of Rio de Janeiro
and São Paulo, realizing the inevitability of abolition, advocated for European immigrants as a replacement for slave labor. However, the Crown's
early prohibition of slave labor from immigrant colonies and its favoring
German and Swiss immigrants indicate that by the early nineteenth century it already saw white immigration as an antidote to Africanness and
slavery.[49]

At the same time, the predominance of African slaves and the lack of
free labor were not the only problems immigration was meant to assuage.
Most of the early immigrant colonies were founded in the hinterland,
where they were intended to fulfill multiple purposes.[50] First, as Colônia
Leopoldina's location and period of founding attested, immigrants were
above all the agents of settlement and colonization of frontier territories undergoing violent state incorporation. This included both internal
and inter-imperial frontiers such as those in the extreme south.[51] Second,
the immigrants served as a buffer against enemies of the state – whether
hostile Indians or foreign powers, especially Spanish forces in Rio de la
Plata – and offered manpower in the service of war. Thus São Pedro, Rio
Negro, and Nova Friburgo were, like Colônia Leopoldina, in indigenous
territory. The aforementioned Schaeffer was an immigrant recruiter who
brought in Germans to serve as colonists and mercenaries, 3,000 of whom
served in the Cisplatine War (1825–28) against the United Provinces of
Rio de la Plata.[52] Third, immigrants promised to improve these frontier
regions, which the elite considered backward, with a welcome dose of economic development and European civilization. A local judge expressed his
admiration for the colony's cleared fields and orderly rows of coffee trees
as embodiments of European-style progress and exclaimed, "If only all of

---

[49] For debates on slave versus freed and immigrant labor, see, for example, Celia Maria
Marinho de Azevedo, *Onda negra, medo branco: o negro no imaginário das elites –
século XIX* (Rio de Janeiro: Paz e Terra, 1987); George Reid Andrews, *Blacks & Whites
in São Paulo, Brazil, 1888–1988* (Madison: University of Wisconsin Press, 1991); Verena
Stolcke, *Coffee Planters, Workers, and Wives: Class Conflict and Gender Relations on
São Paulo Plantations, 1850–1980* (New York: St. Martin's Press, 1988). The literature
on immigration also focuses predominantly on the central and southern regions of
the nation. A good discussion of early immigration efforts under João VI is Siriani,
"Descaminhos da Imigração alemã."
[50] Schultz, *Tropical Versailles*, 210.
[51] Siriani, "Descaminhos da Imigração alemã," 93; Petrone, *O imigrante e a pequena
propriedade*, 25–37.
[52] Siriani, "Descaminhos da Imigração alemã," 95. The Cisplatine War, fought between
Brazil and the future Argentina over control of the border territory, would result in the
founding of the Oriental Republic of Uruguay.

FIGURE 1.1 Enslaved Africans and their descendants cleared the Atlantic forest for settlements and roads connecting the interior to the coast. *Source: Defrichement d'une forêt*, from Johann Moritz Rugendas, *Voyage pittoresque dans le Brésil* (Paris: Engelmann & Cie., 1835).

Brazil had roads like these!"[53] Finally, João VI had envisioned making the immigrants into small proprietors who would form an intermediary class between large landowners and slaves and complement the large estates by producing for the domestic market.[54] After independence, official support for Colônia Leopoldina continued under Pedro I, who ordered the local government to assist the immigrants in encouraging the "great advantages that it could bring to the State" (Figure 1.1).[55]

Enthusiasm for immigration and economic development of Bahia's southernmost region grew as the system of slave-based production itself was increasingly cast into doubt. The 1840s were beset by economic crisis as Bahia's commerce was shaken by the ravages of the federalist Sabinada

[53] João Antonio de Sampaio Vianna to Manoel Ferreira Lagos, August 31, 1841; and "Breve notícia da primeira planta de café que houve na comarca de Caravelas, ao sul da província da Bahia," June 20, 1842, BN/MS.

[54] Petrone, *O imigrante e a pequena propriedade*, 17.

[55] 'Aviso do Principe Regente para que se preste todo o auxílio aos colonos estabelecidos em Leopoldina, comarca de Porto Seguro' (Rio de Janeiro, August 22, 1821), Lata 8, Pasta 31, IHGB.

revolt (1837–38).[56] The province had lost its former trading partners during the revolt to more stable rivals. The loss also extended overseas, where Bahia found its access to West and West Central African markets cut off by the increased presence of the British in Atlantic waters as they hunted down illegal slavers, many of them headed for Brazil. Aggravating the crisis was the impending abolition of the trans-Atlantic slave trade by the Brazilian government, a measure largely ignored when the original law was passed in 1831, but now an increasingly plausible reality as British ships patrolled the Atlantic waters with greater frequency. Indeed, the Eusébio de Queirós Law of 1850 – which shifted prosecution of slave-trading from local courts to special imperial tribunals – would finally end the trade, signaling the beginning of the end of slavery in Brazil, and a crisis in all economic practices based on it.[57]

By the mid-nineteenth century, the confluence of international political pressure, antislavery initiatives, and federalist strife in Salvador instigated an economic crisis in Bahia that threatened the future of African-based slavery. The dour economic climate and labor crisis made European immigrants seem increasingly desirable at the same time that Bahian state officials, eager for a solution, looked with heightened interest toward the colonization of the southern part of the province. Bahian president Joaquim Vasconcellos waxed enthusiastic about the prospects and believed that southern Bahia could settle more than 600,000 colonists.[58] His sentiments were echoed in 1857 by another Bahian president who grandly proclaimed that "casting our eyes upon the southern districts shows us that lying there, underdeveloped, are vast and rich lands between the ocean and the sertão, awash by [many] rivers . . . What vast grounds for a great colonization!"[59]

At first glance, then, Colônia Leopoldina was exactly what the province needed: Europeans contributing to the settlement and economic development of the nation's hinterlands. But instead of enthusiasm there was growing skepticism and criticism. The problem was that Colônia Leopoldina was not, strictly speaking, a European immigrant colony. Its coffee production was doing well, President Vasconcellos admitted in 1842, but much more would be accomplished, he insisted, if all

---

[56] Hendrik Kraay, *Race, State, and Armed Forces in Independence-Era Brazil: Bahia, 1790s-1840s* (Stanford, CA: Stanford University Press, 2004).

[57] Joaquim José de Vasconcellos, President of Bahia, "Falla (BA)," 1842, 10, CRL.

[58] Ibid., 9.

[59] J. L. V. Cansansão de Sinimbú, President of Bahia, "Falla (BA)," 1857, 83, CRL.

TABLE 1.1 *Colônia Leopoldina: White and Slave Population, 1824–1857*

Year	No. of Properties	Whites/Free	Black Slaves
1824	20		15 min. (Flach)
1832	18	86	489
1840	55		1,036
1848	37	130	1,267
1851	43	65 "pessoas de familia"	1,243
1852		54 Europeans, 400 Brazilians	1,600
1857		200 whites	2,000 (approx.)

Note: Numbers for Indians, settled and autonomous, were not available, although the nearby town of Prado had a 43% Indian population in the 1840s, and more individuals of indigenous ancestry were likely included among pardos (10%) and mamelucos (2%). Maria Rosário de Carvalho. "Índios do sul e extremo sul baianos: Reprodução demográfica e relações interétnicas." In *A presença indígena no Nordeste: processos de territorialização, modos de reconhecimento e regimes de memória*, edited by Ana Stela de Negreiros Oliveira and João Pacheco de Oliveira. Rio de Janeiro: Contra Capa, 2011, 374.
Sources: BN/MS – C-815, 15; AN–IA6–154; APEB – Agricultura/4603–3 and Justiça/2329; CRL–Falla (BA), 1848, 44; Tölsner, *Die Colonie Leopoldina in Brasilien*, 3; Pederneiras, "Comissão de Exploração do Mucury," s/n; Costa, *Comarca de Caravellas*, 19.

agriculture were done by free workers.[60] Five years later, diminishing the allure of the province's only prosperous colony was another president's observation that "it is a shame that all this [coffee and manioc flour] is not produced solely by free workers."[61] An engineer assessing the lack of economic development in southern Bahia soon after the cessation of the trans-Atlantic slave trade also warned that although the colony was the region's only economic engine, its slave-based economy had only further stymied the necessary transition to free labor.[62]

In short, the enlightened European colony had degenerated into a slave plantation. In 1832 Colônia Leopoldina counted 18 plantations run by 86 whites and 489 slaves. By 1858, 39 years after its founding, it was home to 40 plantations, 200 free European- and Brazilian-born residents, and close to 2,000 slaves (Table 1.1). A German physician named Karl Tölsner, who resided in the colony during the 1850s,

[60] Vasconcellos, President of Bahia, "Falla (BA)," 9.
[61] Antonio Ignacio de Azevedo, President of Bahia, "Falla (BA)," 1847, 20, CRL.
[62] Innocencio Velloso Pederneiras, *Commissão de exploração do Mucury e Gequitinhonha. Interesses materiaes das comarcas do sul da Bahia. Comarcas de Caravellas e Porto Seguro. Relatório do capitão do imperial corpo d'engenheiros, I.V. Pederneiras, chefe da mesma commisão* (Bahia: Typographia de João Alves Portella, 1851), 10.

attributed the growth of the slave population to their good treatment, a claim disputed by its Brazilian neighbors.[63] About half of the colony's slaves were African born in the first half of the nineteenth century, and were gradually superseded by Brazilian-born slaves in the second half, as the planters focused on the slaves' reproduction to ensure the maintenance of their work force.[64] The colony's growth trajectory exposed how much the poster child of European immigration had veered off course, an embarrassment to the nation-building aspirations of the Brazilian political elite. Far from showcasing the marvels of European free labor, the immigrants comfortably delegated the backbreaking work of coffee production to their slaves. Colônia Leopoldina's economic success became a bitter testament to the fact that the conquest and settlement of the Atlantic frontier was accomplished not by European enlightenment and civilization, but by the enslaved labor of Africans and their descendants that it was meant to eradicate (Figure 1.2).

By the middle of the nineteenth century, public attitudes toward the colony were downright chilly, sharply contrasting with the accolades of times past. Brazilians and foreign observers alike criticized the colony for depending on slave labor instead of encouraging further European immigration. Their negative assessment remained unchanged even when the colony's coffee, known by the name of Café de Caravelas, became renowned throughout Brazil for its superior quality. The harshest critics claimed that Colônia Leopoldina could no longer be considered a colony, as it was now "inhabited by a great majority of foreigners who own coffee plantations, whose cultivation is handled by approximately 2,000 slaves." Subsequent to these dismissals, the darling of colonization

---

[63] Karl August Tölsner, *Die colonie Leopoldina in Brasilien. Schilderung des anbaus und der gewinnung der wichtigsten, dort erzeugten culturproducte, namentlich des kaffees, sowie einiger anderen* (Göttingen: Gebrüder Hofer, 1860), 3.

[64] According to assessments of Colônia Leopoldina's planter inventories conducted by a team of linguists, the proportion of African slaves on the colony remained at around 50 percent of the total adult slave population until the late 1850s. Of the seventeen colonists' inventories they located, only four gave ethnicities, including the following: Angola, Monjolo, Nagô, Jejê, Cabinda, Moçambique, Benguela, Haussa, Benin, Calabar, São Tomé, and Rebola. Between 1847 and 1872, Central Africans of various origins were the most numerous, but the Nagô were the single most represented. Dante Lucchesi, Alan N. Baxter, and Ilza Ribeiro, *O português afro-brasileiro* (Salvador: UFBA, 2009), 89–90; Dante Lucchesi and Alan N. Baxter, "Un paso más hacia la definición del pasado criollo del dialecto afro-brasileño de Helvécia (Bahia)," in Klaus Zimmermann (ed.), *Lenguas criollas de base lexical espanola y portuguesa* (Madrid: Iberoamericana and Frankfurt: Vervuert, 1999), 131–38. On the reproduction and high fertility rates of the colony's slaves, see Carmo, "Colonização e escravidão," 106–7.

FIGURE 1.2 Colônia Leopoldina's coffee, produced by slaves, was shipped from a local port on the Peruípe River to the rest of Brazil and sometimes, Europe. *Source: Convoi de café*, from Jean Baptiste Debret, *Voyage pittoresque et historique au Brésil* (Paris: Firmin Didot frères, 1834). From the New York Public Library.

ventures, though economically vibrant, began to disappear from official government reports in a clear indication of its diminishing worth and promise.

The Swiss and German immigrants may have been content with their accomplishment: vast, orderly coffee fields tended by a few thousand slaves had replaced formerly uncultivated virgin lands "infested" with "savage" Indians. But this was undeniably far from the conception of racial and economic progress the Brazilian government had envisioned – one that, in practice, it had done little to support. In fact, a budgetary law in December 1830 had totally suspended any state financial assistance to the colonies or the introduction of new immigrants, leaving the colonists to their own devices, which the colony's critics failed to mention. Proslavery interests had likely passed the law, suspicious of free labor and of immigrant small landownership creating a class that would encroach upon their power. By taking no concrete action to discourage slave labor or provide material support for an immigrant colony, even Colônia Leopoldina's critics ultimately allowed slavery to grow.[65] Meanwhile, other early colonies around Brazil similarly stagnated, while those

---

[65] Costa, *Comarca de Caravellas*, 19; Alvaro Tiberio de Moncorvo Lima, President of Bahia, "Falla (BA)," 1856, 79, CRL; Municipal Justice of Caravelas to Herculano Ferreira Penna, President of Bahia, February 10, 1860, Colonial/Justiça/Caravelas/Mc 2332, APEB; Tschudi, *Reisen durch Südamerika*, 366; Siriani, "Descaminhos da Imigração alemã," 93. See also Robert Avé-Lallemant, *Viagem pelo norte do Brasil no ano de 1859* (Rio de Janeiro: Instituto Nacional do Livro, Ministério da Educação e Cultura, 1961), 151–52.

that thrived, such as Cantagalo and Macaé in Rio de Janeiro, had also transformed into slave-based coffee plantations.[66]

Despite the colony's detractors, however, its planters remained indifferent to their fall from grace. Slave-based coffee cultivation continued. With the scarcity of free laborers and a dearth of alternatives, black slavery was the planters' lifeline, one they would defend until the very end. They would suppress abolitionism with violence even as the rest of the nation had come to accept it. The colony was the very place where the region's legendary maroon leader, Benedito, would be gunned down on the eve of abolition after years on the run (see Chapter 5).

Examining the trajectory of Colônia Leopoldina allows us to trace the expansion of African-based slavery into the nation's indigenous frontiers, challenging a well-established idea that it extended into empty lands.[67] Its twisted journey, however, was more than just another chapter in the consolidation of nineteenth-century slave-based plantation economies, as we have seen in various regions of Brazil, as well as Cuba, Puerto Rico, and the United States. Rather, its original purpose embodied the aspirations of an emerging nation – to foster racial whitening, civilization, and colonization of the frontiers through a fusion of indigenous conquest, European immigration, and economic development. That it lasted and prospered as a slave plantation zone until the eve of the twentieth century, at the same time that a slave-owning oligarchy was also emerging in nearby São Mateus, vividly exposes how much slavery expansion was fundamental to Brazilian nation-building. It was a process that both relied on and engendered people who, as Africans and slaves, resided in but were excluded from the nation.

---

[66] Petrone, *O imigrante e a pequena propriedade*, 26.

[67] Among the important works examining slavery and indigenous history in nineteenth-century frontier regions are Barickman, "Tame Indians"; Mary Karasch, "Slave Women on the Brazilian Frontier in the Nineteenth Century," in *More than Chattel: Black Women and Slavery in the Americas*, ed. David Barry Gaspar and Darlene Clark Hine (Bloomington: Indiana University Press, 1996), 79–96. Maria Hilda Baqueiro Paraiso, "O tempo da dor e do trabalho: a Conquista dos Territórios Indígenas nos Sertões do Leste" (doctoral dissertation, Universidade de São Paulo, 1998); Izabel Missagia de Mattos, *Civilização e revolta: os Botocudos e a catequese na província de Minas* (São Paulo: EDUSC ANPOCS, 2004); Marcelo Sant'Ana Lemos, "O índio virou pó de café? a resistência dos índios Coroados de Valença frente à expansão cafeeira no Vale do Paraíba (1788–1836)" (M. A. thesis, Universidade do Estado do Rio de Janeiro, 2004); Hal Langfur, *The Forbidden Lands: Colonial Identity, Frontier Violence, and the Persistence of Brazil's Eastern Indians, 1750–1830* (Stanford, CA: Stanford University Press, 2006); Mary Ann Mahony, "Creativity under Constraint: Enslaved Afro-Brazilian Families in Brazil's Cacao Area, 1870–1890," *Journal of Social History* 41, no. 3 (2008): 633–66.

"Perfect Captivity": Indian Slavery in the Nineteenth Century

While Colônia Leopoldina's immigrants pioneered large-scale, African slave-based plantation agriculture on the Atlantic frontier, another form of slavery – of Indians – was already in practice in the region. In the early nineteenth century, the conquest and settlement of these territories instigated the violent merger of African and indigenous slavery. The entanglement of these two histories of bondage compels us to question the commonplace acceptance of indigenous slavery as the "first slavery," a colonial practice superseded by African-based slavery long before the nineteenth century.[68] João VI had justified offensive war in his 1808 declaration as the only viable option to subdue what he reviled as a hostile, "atrocious anthropophagous race." The Botocudos' alleged cannibalism and hostility to Portuguese rule were enumerated as necessitating violent measures, and just wars legalized their enslavement. Captured Indians, along with those "rescued" from hostile Indians, became prisoners of war who were forced to serve their captors for a minimum of ten years, and for as long as their "ferocity" lasted. It was a very convenient setup for settlers needing a labor force.[69]

---

[68] There is remarkably little scholarship dedicated to postcolonial indigenous slavery in Brazil, on its own or in relation to African-based slavery. I am very indebted to conversations with Izabel Mattos, Marco Morel, the late John Monteiro, and José Bessa. A key work is Maria Hilda Baqueiro Paraiso, "As crianças indígenas e a formação de agentes transculturais: o comércio de kurukas na Bahia, Espírito Santo e Minas Gerais," in *Resistência, Memória, Etnografia*, ed. Luiz Savio de Almeida, et al. (Maceió, AL: UFAL, 2007). The most important work on colonial indigenous slavery remains John M. Monteiro, *Negros da terra: índios e bandeirantes nas origens de São Paulo* (São Paulo: Companhia das Letras, 1994). See also Barbara A. Sommer, "Colony of the Sertão: Amazonian Expeditions and the Indian Slave Trade," *The Americas* 61, no. 3 (2005): 401–28; Barbara A. Sommer, "Why Joanna Baptista Sold Herself into Slavery: Indian Women in Portuguese Amazonia, 1755–1798," *Slavery & Abolition* 34, no. 1 (March 1, 2013): 77–97; Mary Karasch, "Catechism and Captivity: Indian Policy in Goiás, 1780–1889," in *Native Brazil: Beyond the Convert and the Cannibal, 1500–1900*, ed. Hal Langfur (Albuquerque: University of New Mexico Press, 2014), 198–224.

[69] Cunha, *Legislação indigenista*, 57–60. In the case of the just wars against the Kaingang of São Paulo, Langfur demonstrates that 1808 was not the pivotal point in indigenous policy in the Minas hinterlands, but rather a culmination of a violent anti-indigenous policy that dated back to the 1760s when settlement of eastern Minas Gerais first began in earnest. João VI had already authorized the Minas government to conduct offensive warfare in 1801, and the Bahia government in 1806. See Langfur, *The Forbidden Lands*. For discussions of just war, see Perrone-Moisés, "Índios livres e índios escravos," 123–27. For offensive wars around Brazil around independence, see Monteiro, "Tupis, Tapuias."

Indian slavery was inseparable from the clamor for territorial control accelerating in the early nineteenth century. Around the same time as the Botocudo Wars, offensive wars were also declared against the Kaingang, Xavante, Karajá, Apinayé, and Canoeiro Indians in Brazil's other frontier regions from São Paulo to Goiás, Ceará, and the Amazon.[70] For instance, just six months after he declared the Botocudo Wars, João VI authorized another offensive war against the *bugre* (a derogatory term denoting savages) Indians in São Paulo.[71] In southern Bahia, Baltazar da Silva Lisboa, the royal judge of Ilhéus who was entrusted with opening roads from the interior, affirmed the necessity of just war given the "projects that cannot be realized while the barbarians remain in their savage state...making necessary the use of troops accustomed to this type of war." Writing less than a decade before the founding of Colônia Leopoldina, he optimistically observed that by subjugating the Botocudo, "the state will have power, wealth, and population, and these very fertile lands will attract many colonists, who will produce mountains of wealth."[72]

The enslavement of "hostile" Indians remained relegalized until a decade after independence, outlasting the transition from colony to nation alongside African-based slavery. It was abolished the very same year, as was the trans-Atlantic slave trade (1831), a fact little noted by scholars of nineteenth-century slavery. Portuguese law had always guaranteed the freedom of aldeia Indians, who were their allies in the colonial project. Yet it had maintained an irregular stance regarding autonomous Indians, alternately abolishing and relegalizing their enslavement. If repeated laws abolishing Indian slavery were a bitter testament to the difficulty of implementing them, the Crown's periodic reauthorization of legal enslavement derived from what it considered the impossibility of freedom for all Indians, given the preponderance of hostile Indians. Indian slavery had most recently been abolished and Indian freedom affirmed between 1755 and 1758 by the royal administrator, the future Marquis of Pombal, who

---

[70] Patrícia Melo Sampaio, "Política indigenista no Brasil imperial," in *O Brasil imperial*, ed. Keila Grinberg and Ricardo Salles, Vol. 1, 1808–1831 (Rio de Janeiro: Civilização Brasileira, 2009), 181; Karasch, "Indian Autonomy," 205–6.

[71] For the decree, see Cunha, *Legislação indigenista*, 62. Indians are nearly invisible in the vast scholarship on coffee regions of the Center-South, but important recent work promises to open up our understanding of Indians in these regions after independence, including Lemos, "O índio virou pó de café?"; Sposito, *Nem cidadãos*.

[72] Baltazar da Silva Lisboa to Conde de Linhares, Minister of Empire and Foreign Affairs, January 31, 1810, Lata 109 Doc. 14, IHGB.

expelled the Jesuits and secularized Indian administration.[73] After it was legalized anew in 1808, the total silence on Indians in the 1824 Constitution meant that the status of autonomous Indians, whom Brazilian representatives considered to live outside of the social pact, remained unaddressed, with many effectively entering the new nation as slaves. The legal ambiguity about their status would help maintain de facto Indian slavery long after its abolition in 1831, just as the trans-Atlantic slave trade to Brazil continued after the 1831 prohibition.[74]

Sources abound with episodes of staggering violence against the Botocudo and other indigenous groups in the Bahia–Espírito Santo borderlands in the first decades of the nineteenth century. Prince Maximilian Wied-Neuwied, who was traveling through Brazil on the eve of independence, captured the severity of the violence when he observed that

there has been no truce for the Botocudos, who were exterminated wherever they were found, without regard for their age or sex. Only from time to time, in certain occasions, are small children spared and cared for. This war of extermination was executed with the utmost perseverance and cruelty, since [the perpetrators] firmly believed that [the Indians] killed and devoured all enemies that fell into their hands.[75]

What Maximilian may not have known was that this "war of extermination" was only in its early stages. Over the course of the nineteenth century, the violence of settler expansion would combine with a complex amalgam of policies, racial theories, and science to devastate the lives of indigenous people of the Atlantic frontier.

Contrary to what this anti-indigenous violence suggests, however, Brazilian indigenous policy in the years following independence was not exterminationist. On the contrary, it was assimilationist. While the new national government would not devise a nation-wide indigenous policy until 1845, it generally advocated *brandura*, or "gentleness," in

---

[73] Perrone-Moisés, "Índios livres e índios escravos"; Mércio Pereira Gomes, *The Indians and Brazil*, 3rd ed. (Gainesville: University Press of Florida, 2000), 60–64; Langfur and Resende, "Indian Autonomy," 152.

[74] The 1831 legislation against the trans-Atlantic trade, passed under British pressure, was largely ineffective. Portugal had agreed to abolish the trade north of the equator in 1815. The trans-Atlantic trade in general was finally abolished in 1850, though contraband trade continued for approximately another decade. For recent scholarship on the 1831 law, see Beatriz Gallotti Mamigonian and Keila Grinberg (eds.), "Dossiê: "Para inglês ver? Revisitando a lei de 1831"," *Estudos Afro-Asiáticos* 1–3 (2007).

[75] Maximilian Wied-Neuwied, *Viagem ao Brasil nos anos de 1815 a 1817* (São Paulo: Companhia Editora Nacional, 1958), 153.

the treatment of Indians even as it conducted offensive war against its
enemies. In his "Notes on the Civilization of the Wild Indians of Brazil"
(1823), Minister of Empire José Bonifácio de Andrada e Silva mapped
out a state policy, drawing largely on the late colonial policies of Pombal and based on peaceful means to civilize Indians through productive
labor regimes. The "Notes" explicitly criticized the offensive wars that
"in a century so enlightened such as ours, in the Court of Brazil," had
allowed for "the Botocudo, the Puri of the North, and the Bugres of
Guarapava [to be] converted once again from prisoners of war into miserable slaves." He insinuated that Indian slavery was as anathema to
Brazil's progress as African slavery, an allegation that put him at odds
with the nation's powerful slaveocracy. José Bonifácio envisioned the
incorporation of all Indians, aldeia-residing and autonomous (along with
mulattoes and blacks), into Brazilian nationhood through civilization and
miscegenation. Doing so would "tie the reciprocal interests of the Indians
with ours, and from them create *one sole body of the nation* – stronger,
educated, and entrepreneurial."[76] His homogenizing vision echoed the
prevalent view, shared by members of the Constituent Assembly, that
Indians did not constitute a society of their own but rather, existed outside
of it. Nor was José Bonifácio interested in preserving indigenous societies
or indigenous citizenship, for the goal of assimilation was for Indians to
cease existing as a distinct group. As Manuela Carneiro da Cunha has
noted, assimilation was not considered destructive to indigenous society, as the latter was seen as nonexistent in the first place.[77] Although
José Bonifacio was driven into exile and his proposal thrown out when
Pedro I dissolved the Constituent Assembly, his "gentle" approach, based
on assimilation, set the tone for subsequent national indigenous policy
(discussed further in Chapter 3).[78]

Far away from the comforts of Rio de Janeiro, the challenges of
implementing a national indigenous policy were immediately evident. An
attempt to do so in 1826 failed. Meanwhile, in 1831, with the end of just

[76] Cunha, *Legislação indigenista*, 347–60. Italics mine.
[77] Manuela Carneiro da Cunha, *Antropologia do Brasil: mito, história, etnicidade* (São Paulo: Editora Brasiliense, 1986), 170.
[78] John Hemming, *Amazon Frontier: The Defeat of the Brazilian Indians* (Cambridge, MA: Harvard University Press, 1987), 173. For example, the Imperial decision of May 23, 1823 and the decrees of January 28, 1824 and that of October 18, 1825 advocate *brandura* and civilization and admonish locals for resorting to retaliatory violence against the Botocudo. Cunha, *Legislação indigenista*, 106, 111–114, 125.

war, Botocudo slavery was abolished one last time.[79] Rather than being freed, however, Indians were juridically transformed into orphans under state guardianship. Their new legal status as the nation's children placed them in a condition similar to that of emancipated Africans and recent libertos. The Justice of Orphans was responsible for overseeing them until they were deemed ready to be emancipated and enter society, meanwhile ensuring that Indians were paid for their labor and protected from reenslavement, and eventually baptized.[80] While such measures could be taken as a concrete step to begin incorporating "wild" Indians into the nation as citizens, settlers residing in the Botocudo warzone who had been benefiting from Indian slavery were threatened by this state intervention. State institutions on their part lacked the enthusiasm and funds to enforce brandura policies, all of which contributed to the collapse of Indian civilizing ventures premised on government–settler cooperation.

A case in point was the swift failure of the government-funded aldeia of Biririca in the São Mateus hinterland. Biririca's objectives were to relocate Indians onto fertile lands along the river to be trained for agricultural work, and to send them to Rio de Janeiro to serve in the navy. The Espírito Santo government, however, increasingly preoccupied with the proliferation of quilombos throughout the province, showed only lukewarm interest in Biririca. The São Mateus Municipal Chamber finally authorized its establishment in 1841 after turning down several requests to fund other aldeias. It expected Biririca to capitalize on the "daily communication that these Indians have had over nine years with the town's inhabitants, selling, buying, and working on the fazendas with compensation."[81] However, an overall lack of government investment,

---

[79] Sposito, "Liberdade para os índios"; Paraiso, "Crianças indígenas," 74. Sposito contends that in 1831, just wars were revoked in Minas Gerais and São Paulo only; Paraíso, on the other hand, contends it was a general revocation. I am adhering to Paraíso's analysis.
[80] Cunha, *Legislação indigenista*, 24–25,137–53. Africans who were illegally enslaved and then apprehended after 1831 were considered *emancipados* and turned over to the Justice of Orphans, like Indians. I disagree with Holston that autonomous Indians were included as orphan-citizens with independence; see Holston, *Insurgent Citizenship*, 67. On the ambiguities and limitations of citizenship (including the creation of active and passive citizens) for *emancipados* and *libertos*, see Cunha, *Negros, estrangeiros*, 68–85; Castro, *Escravidão e cidadania no Brasil monárquico*; Beatriz Gallotti Mamigonian, "O direito de ser Africano livre: os escravos e as interpretações da Lei de 1831," in *Direitos e justiças no Brasil: ensaios de história social*, ed. Silvia Hunold Lara and Joseli Maria Nunes Mendonça (Campinas, SP: Editora UNICAMP, 2006).
[81] Municipal Chamber of São Mateus to José Joaquim Machado de Oliveira, President of Espírito Santo, March 16, 1841, Governadoria Ser. Accioly Liv. 351 Fl. 546, APEES.

aggravated by sabotage and general hostility from area settlers who saw the aldeia interfering in their access to indigenous laborers, led to its collapse by 1848. Biririca was unable to settle a single Indian, and no other aldeia was founded thereafter.[82]

Differing conceptualizations about indigenous labor held by the state and frontier settlers exposed the fragilities of Indian citizenship. The state viewed labor regimes as a means to civilize autonomous Indians by transforming them into a settled, productive peasantry to prepare them for eventual citizenship. On the other hand, many settlers, particularly those without access to black slaves, simply coveted servile workers and had no qualms about enslaving Indians. The Brazilian government allowed Indians to work for individuals under a contract in the Regulation of Missions (1845), its one major national indigenous law of the nineteenth century. But leaving the contracts in the hands of private citizens ensured that much of the labor effectively went unremunerated. Many settlers "paid" Indians with *cachaça*, a sugarcane-derived spirit, which contributed to the spread of alcoholism.[83] In fact, another reason for Biririca's failure owed to the state's attempt to resettle indigenous families there and prevent them from going to individual properties, where they risked reenslavement and abuse.[84]

However, settlers were not the lone enthusiasts of Indian slavery. The state's reticence about Indian citizenship and lack of a cohesive civilization plan translated into an ambiguous indigenous policy that was officially "gentle" yet simultaneously condemned and enabled Indian slavery.[85] During the Botocudo Wars, captured Indians were turned over to individual settlers for a minimum period of ten to fifteen or, if they were children, twenty years. The settlers were responsible for feeding, dressing, educating, and Christianizing their slaves in exchange for their labor

---

[82] Luiz Pedreira Couto Ferraz, "Relatório (ES)," 1847, 32, CRL; Luiz Pedreira Couto Ferraz to Municipal Chamber of São Mateus, April 13, 1848, Governadoria Ser. 751 Liv. 181 Fl. 17–17v, APEES; Luiz Pedreira Couto Ferraz, President of Espírito Santo to Manoel Alves Branco, Minister of Empire, October 11, 1847, IJJ9–362-ES, AN.

[83] For the Regulation see Cunha, *Legislação indigenista*, 191–99, especially item 28. The Regulation is discussed further in Chapter 3. For settlers paying Indians with alcohol, see Vânia Moreira, "Índios no Brasil: marginalização social e exclusão historiográfica," *Diálogos Latinoamericanos* 3 (2001): 103–5.

[84] Manoel Joaquim de Sá e Mattos to Francisco Jorge Monteiro, May 5, 1844, Polícia Ser. 2 Cx. 8 Mç 41 Fl. 302–303, APEES.

[85] Carlos Henrique Gileno, "A legislação indígena: ambigüidades na formação do Estado-nação no Brasil," *Caderno CRH* 20, no. 49 (April 2007): 123–33. Perdigão Malheiro condemned the absurdity of this approach. Malheiro, *Escravidão no Brasil*, 2:136–37.

as a way to prepare them for eventual participation in society as full citizens.[86] Indigenous slavery thus had a perversely pedagogical objective that linked government and individual interests. Unsurprisingly, pedagogy was not foremost on anyone's agenda. The French traveler Auguste de Saint-Hilaire noted that settlers used this promise in order to trick the Botocudo into giving up their children, whom they sold for 15 to 20 mil reis. Government officials also lent each other Indian laborers who had to clear roads through what had been their own lands to facilitate settlers and commerce. The president of Espírito Santo was particularly eager to "borrow" indigenous laborers from Minas Gerais since it was "difficult, if not impossible, to find free day laborers or slaves to work in these far flung locations... For now we can only count on Indians."[87] After the abolition of Indian slavery in 1831, as we have seen, these enslaved Indians were transformed into orphans under the guardianship of a judge. The judge possessed the power to distribute them as free laborers to those in his sphere of influence. Many judges abused this privilege liberally, amassing great personal wealth.[88]

This slippery slope of state-sanctioned Indian civilization and slavery created many opportunities for abuse that lasted long after Indian slavery was officially abolished. Particularly appalling was the enslavement and trafficking of Indians, especially their children, who were known as *kurukas*.[89] Saint-Hilaire aptly decried that "in Brazil was repeating what happens on the Coast of Africa: tempted by the prices that the Portuguese paid for the children, the Botocudo captains fought one another to obtain children to sell." The demand for kurukas profoundly destabilized intra-indigenous relations. For example, two Botocudo groups in northern Minas had been nearly annihilated by wars to obtain kurukas for the Portuguese.[90] Kuruka slavery also touched many other indigenous groups, aldeia-residing and autonomous, with more than a few settlers intentionally mislabeling their victims as Botocudo in order to justify

---

[86] Paraiso, "Crianças indígenas," 58–59. The same model was employed for emancipated Africans.

[87] Auguste de Saint-Hilaire, *Viagem pelas provincias de Rio de Janeiro e Minas Geraes, v. 2* (São Paulo: Companhia Editora Nacional, 1938), 127; Herculano Ferreira Penna, President of Espírito Santo to José Carlos Pereira de Almeida, Minister of Empire, April 25, 1846, IJJ9–362-ES, AN.

[88] Holston, *Insurgent Citizenship*, 74.

[89] *Kuruka* was the indigenous (*borum*) term for child. Although sounding similar to the Quechua term *kuraka*, which signified an Andean lord, they are not related.

[90] Auguste de Saint-Hilaire, *Rio de Janeiro e Minas Gerais*, 127, 183.

their enslavement.[91] Little is known about kuruka slavery in nineteenth-century Brazil, partly due to the sparse attention given to indigenous slavery during the Empire, but also because of its smaller numbers and extralegality. Unlike African slavery, which has produced volumes of registries, bills of sale, and inventories, kuruka slavery suffers from a dearth of documentation. Nonetheless, kurukas appear in the historical record frequently enough to force us to question what this slavery reveals about indigenous people's status in postcolonial Brazil.

Kurukas were employed for a variety of purposes. The majority were captured, traded, and used by unscrupulous settlers as domestic servants and farm laborers and at times to harvest the prized jacaranda wood. Some wealthy individuals considered them a sign of social prestige and gave each other kurukas as favors and gifts. Soldiers in Espírito Santo and Minas Gerais "gifted" seven Botocudo kurukas to Pedro I in the early 1820s to be educated in the schools, which Marco Morel has identified as slavery, since the children were owned by soldiers who had attacked and killed their parents.[92] Children were generally preferred to adults because of their supposedly greater propensity toward assimilation. Even Saint-Hilaire, who vocally denounced kuruka slavery, was determined to obtain his own Botocudo child. His repeated requests were refused by the *cacique* (indigenous leader) Johaima, who poignantly told the Frenchman that the "Portuguese took almost all our children, promising us they would return, but we never saw them again." When Saint-Hilaire insisted, Johaima evoked the Portuguese lexicon of Indian civilization to deflect him, stating that "since we would like to cultivate the earth, we couldn't dispense of our children." He added that the whites had enough women to give them children, and that they "didn't need to come looking for Botocudos."[93] Saint-Hilaire was not the only white person who had difficulty comprehending why Indians did not want to give up their children. A Portuguese director of Indians who marveled at their capacity to mourn the loss of children remarked, "One cannot remove a

[91] Paraiso, "Crianças indígenas," 62–67.

[92] Marco Morel, "Independência, vida e morte: os contatos com os Botocudos durante o primeiro reinado," *Dimensões*, no. 14 (2002): 108–9. The original document clearly states the name of the Botocudo children and the military personnel who 'gave' or 'offered' them to the Emperor. See Guido Marlière, Letter, April 6, 1825, *RAPM* 10 (1910): 593–94.

[93] Saint-Hilaire, *Rio de Janeiro e Minas Gerais*, 145–46. Saint-Hilaire did finally obtain a child from a different Botocudo cacique, first a prepubescent girl whom he then exchanged for a boy whom he called "my Botocudo," but the child later disappeared.

single child from them because as parents, although savages, they adore their children as much as we do."[94]

Especially problematic was the state's involvement in kuruka slavery. Children on aldeias were nurtured to become go-betweens to assist in bringing autonomous Indians into Portuguese villages. In Espírito Santo, indigenous families protested their children's being sent away to serve in remote regions by claiming that they were "national Indians" and thus citizens (a rare, valuable instance) and should be exempt from such treatment. An even more troubling example was the Director of Indians of said province, who regularly coerced aldeia Indians to give up their children, including boys as young as eleven and girls as young as three. He liberally distributed seventy-two kurukas to prestigious persons in 1834, arguing that it was the best means to transform "wild animals" into a "useful population that this province needs." Sexual abuse was likely.[95] Finally, in its worst iteration, settlers massacred entire Indian villages and seized their children in a practice known as *matar uma aldeia*, which Chapter 4 investigates in depth. These repeated examples of Indian slavery on the Atlantic frontier, sometimes illegal and other times disguised as tutelage, all point to the de facto lack of legal protection for Indians and the inability and unwillingness of the state to curtail the practice when it was not itself participating.[96]

That said, some Indians also entrusted the care of their children to missionaries and settlers and were not strictly victims of slave raids or coercion. Paraíso has argued that the Indians did this out of poverty, the desire for objects, and a lack of perspective about the future. The aforementioned Director of Indians especially targeted orphaned children whose relatives were more inclined to give them up in exchange for objects.[97] The US traveler Thomas Ewbank was horrified to encounter Indian mothers from drought-stricken Ceará in Rio de Janeiro selling their sons to the navy in desperation. However, sending their children to outsiders was also an important means for Indians to negotiate their survival amidst growing settler occupation. They "offered their children to

---

94 Bieber, "Catechism and Capitalism," 181.   95 Paraiso, "Crianças indígenas," 62–78.

96 Holloway and Chalhoub have demonstrated the nineteenth-century Brazilian state's unwillingness to meddle directly in private master–slave relations, an attitude which may explain its not prosecuting (despite censuring) Indian slavery. Thomas H. Holloway, *Policing Rio de Janeiro: Repression and Resistance in a 19th-Century City* (Stanford, CA: Stanford University Press, 1993), 115–22; Chalhoub, "Precariousness of Freedom," 408–9.

97 Paraiso, "Crianças indígenas," 64–69.

captivity" under local settlers in order to secure themselves against raids, appease hostilities, and establish strategic alliances and patronage protection. For example, the Botocudo of the Mucuri River Valley "gifted" several kurukas to the *mineiro* (from Minas Gerais) senator Teófilo Ottoni, who was seeking to establish himself in their lands. They told him that the purpose was to ensure that Ottoni "remained tame," another instance in which the Botocudo manipulated the Portuguese lexicon of Indian civilization.[98] In Bahia and Espírito Santo some Indians worked sporadically alongside black slaves but sold their children to local settlers. Among them were the residents of Colônia Leopoldina, where many Botocudo came to seek refuge from other settlers, sometimes requesting baptism as a way to cement their alliance. A few Indians had even become peasants on the colony's lands.[99]

Even so, the precariousness of these alliances was exemplified by an incident at São José de Porto Alegre south of the colony, where kuruka ownership was common. A group of Indians residing in the interior had been selectively sending their youth to the hamlet's missionary and settlers until the latter, coveting the financial rewards promised by their kuruka-seeking neighbors, invaded the Indians' settlements and seized their children, destroying the burgeoning alliance. The next year, a resident of the same hamlet massacred a group of fourteen Botocudo headed by a leader identified as Jiporok, in retaliation for his killing of a local family. Widely reported as the epitome of Botocudo savagery, Jiporok's attack had in fact been motivated by the family's kidnapping of his own children.[100]

---

[98] Thomas Ewbank, *Life in Brazil, Or, A Journal of a Visit to the Land of the Cocoa and the Palm with an Appendix, Containing Illustrations of Ancient South American Arts* (New York: Harper & Brothers, 1856), 323; Teófilo Benedito Ottoni, *Notícia sobre os selvagens do Mucuri* (Belo Horizonte, MG: Editora UFMG, 2002), 46–55. Ottoni later took a kuruka boy to Rio and put him in the navy arsenal to educate him; the boy died.

[99] Ottoni, *Notícia*, 56; Charles Frederick Hartt, *Thayer Expedition: Scientific Results of a Journey in Brazil, by Louis Agassiz and His Travelling Companions: Geology and Physical Geography* (Boston: Fields, Osgood & Co., 1870), 601–2; João Corrado Bachmann-Eiske to Caetano Vicente de Almeida, Jr., January 29, 1848, Colonial/Agricultura/Colonia e Colonos/Colônia Leopoldina/Mc 4603–3, APEB. Márcio Lemos analyzes baptism registries to demonstrate that the Coroado in Valença, RJ also established networks with influential local residents, including many slaveowners, although he does not discuss the giving of *kurukas*. Lemos, "O índio virou pó de café?," 143–45.

[100] Vicar Antonio Miguel de Azevedo to Caetano Vicente de Almeida, Jr., August 8, 1844, Colonial/Justiça/Caravelas/Mc 2330, APEB; Ottoni, *Notícia*, 109; 200–4.

Indians were also trafficked in an interprovincial trade. The concentration of documents denouncing Indian slavery and trafficking in the mid-to late-1840s suggests that they were not immune to the scramble for slave labor sparked by the impending prohibition of the trans-Atlantic slave trade in 1850.[101] Children and adults were enslaved and sold as far as Rio de Janeiro. The Indian slave trade has been nearly invisible in the history of nineteenth-century Brazil, since the number of trafficked Indians was likely minuscule compared to that of black slaves. There are no comprehensive numbers available beyond the estimated 600 to 700 Botocudo dispersed among three towns in northern Minas in the 1820s; 72 sent away by the Espírito Santo Director of Indians in 1834; and the 52 held privately without a contract in Rio de Janeiro in 1845.[102] Thomas Ewbank was startled to learn that "Indians appear to be enslaved as much almost as negroes, and are bought and sold like them" in Rio as late as 1845.[103] The same year, a decree demanded vigilance for children destined for other provinces without evidence of a contract or consent from their parents or guardians. The shipping of an indigenous woman from São Mateus to a resident in Rio de Janeiro also sparked concerns about the trafficking of Indians to private citizens for whom they worked without a contract. The city's Justice of Orphans expressed concern that these Indians, taken advantage of for their "natural simplicity," were held in a "quasi perfect captivity."[104] Two years later, the president of Espírito Santo cautiously praised the economic progress of São Mateus, noting how its planters had "managed to domesticate the Botocudo and employ them in their agriculture in exchange for sustenance and clothing." He nonetheless remained wary of illegal enslavement and advocated establishing government-funded aldeias as a way to keep tabs on Indian laborers and the individuals they served. The plan never materialized.[105]

---

[101] More than a million illegally enslaved Africans entered Brazil between 1825 and 1850.

[102] In 1845, the police of the city of Rio de Janeiro counted fifty-two Indians, male and female, of various ages who were laboring in private residences without a contract, even though they were nominally dependents or "being educated." The police described them as being "almost reduced to the condition of slaves." Joaquim Marcellino de Brito, "Relatório da repartição dos negócios do Império apresentado à Assembléa Geral legislativa, 1845" (Rio de Janeiro: Typographia Nacional, 1846), 25, CRL.

[103] Ewbank, *Life in Brazil*, 323; cited in Manuela Carneiro da Cunha, *História dos índios no Brasil* (São Paulo: Editora Schwarcz, 1992), 146.

[104] Cunha, *Legislação indigenista*, 199–200; *Diario do Rio de Janeiro*, September 29, 1845.

[105] Ferraz, President of Espírito Santo to Branco, Minister of Empire, October 11, 1847.

Kuruka slavery, like that of Africans illegally brought to Brazil after 1831, was an open secret. When the issue surfaced again in 1841, the Espírito Santo president showed no surprise but lamented that the "barbaric and abominable custom of buying wild Indians from the forests" was *still* in effect.[106] The Justice of Law in São Mateus was one of the few who did contest the practice, seeking to prosecute Indian enslavement as a violation of Article 179 of the Criminal Code that criminalized the reduction of free people into slavery. Yet he also claimed that the Indians were coming to settlers' homes of their own free will without coercion, contradicting his acknowledgment that their living conditions were increasingly dire. Beyond the disingenuous insinuation that Indians were willingly enslaving themselves was the harsh reality of disappearing lands and livelihood, rendering them ever more vulnerable to captivity.[107]

Legally speaking, indigenous and African-based forms of slavery were not identical. Among Brazilian-born blacks, slavery was an inheritable biological condition before the Free Womb Law of 1871, while Indians legally became slaves through capture in just war but did not inherit their condition. Black slaves could potentially purchase their freedom or be manumitted, but no such options were available for Indians, who were held in captivity for the royally designated period or until they were "civilized," a completely subjective condition.[108] Yet to examine the process of frontier settlement is to see how these two forms of slavery overlapped temporally, geographically, and experientially. Black and indigenous people shared the devastating experiences of enslavement, sales and trafficking, forced migration, and the rupture of families. Even if Indian slavery

---

[106] José Joaquim Machado de Oliveira, Registro da Correspondência do Governo com a Câmara [Autoridades Civis e Militares da Vila] de S. Mateus, January 31, 1841, Governadoria Ser. 751 Liv. 167 Fl. 21–21v, APEES.

[107] Mattos to Monteiro, May 5, 1844. The Criminal Code was promulgated in 1830, followed by the Criminal Justice Code in 1832 that established the norms of its application. Boris Fausto, *A Concise History of Brazil* (Cambridge: Cambridge University Press, 1998), 87.

[108] In his study of indigenous and African slavery in colonial Curitiba, Stuart Schwartz has argued that slaveholders viewed the two groups differently in religious and ideological terms. Masters served as godparents for Indian slaves whom they considered to be under their tutelage, unlike blacks. While I have not found the baptismal records to corroborate this argument for the Bahia–Espírito Santo borderlands in the nineteenth century, this chapter emphasizes the importance of the actual experience, rather than perceptions, of enslavement. Stuart B. Schwartz, *Slaves, Peasants, and Rebels: Reconsidering Brazilian Slavery* (Chicago: University of Illinois Press, 1996), 143–47.

sometimes assumed the guise of contractual labor or tutelage, the actual experience was often one of "perfect slavery."[109]

As the new nation grappled with the challenges of extending its sovereignty over its vast domain, frontier settlement gave concrete form to the exclusion of black and indigenous people. African-based slavery, not free white labor, drove the process, fusing with and accelerating Indian persecution and enslavement. Frontier settlement and incorporation thus relied on the deliberate creation of people who were "outside of the social pact" and whose existence was yet embedded in the very construction of a liberal Brazilian citizenship.

Black and indigenous people's enslavement also exposed the ambiguity of citizenship and its precondition, freedom. For if both African and Brazilian slaves were legally entitled to a future manumission, that possibility was contingent on the master's will or on the slave's ability to self-purchase. Neither was widely available where labor was scarce. Furthermore, as Sidney Chalhoub has shown, African and native-born slaves and freedpeople in nineteenth-century Brazil were subjected to an abundance of conditional manumissions, revocations of freedom, and restrictions to full citizenship.[110] So while Africans were actively discouraged from becoming citizens, even Brazilian *libertos* discovered that their access to citizenship was ominously elusive, always threatened by the potential to be trapped in a purgatory of "half-freedom," or worse, to fall back from citizen to slave.

The precariousness of freedom also threatened indigenous lives. One who perceived it was Manoel Mascarenhas, the Espírito Santo president, who decried the deleterious effects that child trafficking had on Indian civilization. He presumed the Indians would prefer to live in the hinterland where they maintained their freedom, rather than enter the "cradle of society" where they witnessed their children being reduced to slavery by people who were "free like them."[111] That Indians entered Brazilian society as slaves casts a harsh light on a central question. Were Indians free? And if so, were they citizens? By 1844 when Mascarenhas spoke, there was no legal Indian slavery in Brazil. It continued brazenly in practice, however, sometimes assuming the guise of tutelage or informal labor arrangements. Their "perfect" enslavement exposed just how imperfect

---

[109] Cunha, *História dos índios no Brasil*, 199.
[110] Chalhoub, "Precariousness of Freedom"; Scott, "Paper Thin."
[111] Manoel de Assis Mascarenhas to Police Chief of Espírito Santo, April 2, 1844, Polícia Ser. 2 Cx. 8 Mç 41 Fl. 151, APEES.

were the laws governing Indian citizenship, which remained as ambiguous as it was in the 1824 Constitution. The Swiss naturalist J. J. von Tschudi succinctly captured the problem when criticizing the war of extermination against Indians in the Mucuri Valley, which was continuing "in spite of the beautiful, but unfortunately defective Brazilian Constitution."[112]

To say that in Brazil's early postcolonial decades the state had no bearing on events on the Atlantic frontier is to ignore the ways in which Brazilians, from the national political elite down to the local settler – whether through indifference or direct involvement – allowed slavery, legal and illegal, to propel its settlement and incorporation. Fears of an African Brazil and praise for the civilizing promises of white immigrant labor translated into no material support for Colônia Leopoldina, whose transformation into a slave plantation the state, noting its profits and ceding to proslavery interests, criticized only from afar. Having maintained offensive war against "hostile" Indians, it did little to enforce the abolition of Indian slavery and sometimes participated itself. State and frontier thus converged, ensuring that the inequalities and exclusions of Brazilian citizenship reproduced themselves through the creation of slaves and quasi-citizens who resided within, yet did not have the rights to, Brazil's national territory. How black and indigenous people experienced and interpreted these terms of their inclusion and exclusion and sometimes articulated their own terms, is the subject of the next chapter.

[112] Tschudi, *Reisen durch Südamerika*, 263.

2

Rebels, Kings, Soldiers

Popular Politics

"A people so behind in civilization!" Such were the unflattering words Manoel Pontes, the president of Espírito Santo, used to describe the residents of São Mateus in 1833, just two years after the end of the Botocudo Wars and the first abolition of the trans-Atlantic slave trade. He may have been referring to any number of things ailing the town: a nativist uprising led by a rowdy group of mixed-race residents in the sertão; a vigilante massacre of Botocudo Indians; the Botocudo attacking the properties of São Mateus residents; and the hydra-like tenacity of the region's quilombos that residents feared could culminate in a Haitian Revolution–like race war.[1] It was in such a chaotic atmosphere that the town increasingly prospered from the growth of its manioc flour exports, a prosperity that had not managed to dispel – but rather, encouraged – what Pontes saw as total disorder prevailing in the town and the surrounding region.

Amidst the political turbulence of independence and the abdication of Pedro I in 1831, agitating multiple regions across Brazil, state expansion into the Atlantic frontier was forced to contend with the very people it excluded from the nation. With European immigration swiftly failing, civilization now signified the extension of slave-based agriculture and the domestication of "wild" Indians whose labor and lands would serve settler needs. However, the Brazilian-born and African slaves and Indians possessed radically different ideas about the course of state expansion, challenging the imposition of centralized authority on the frontier and rendering it a highly fraught, often violent process. These challenges

---

[1] Manoel José Pires da Silva Pontes to Aureliano de Sousa e Oliveira Coutinho, Minister and Secretary of Justice, December 22, 1833, IJ1–729-ES Fl. 64, AN.

would assume numerous forms, from direct confrontations with settlers and uprisings to citizenship claims expressed through legal rights and royalist political culture. This chapter examines the various ways in which black and indigenous people interpreted and contested nation-building on the Atlantic frontier through the lens of popular politics.

To speak of nation-building in the frontier during these early post-independence decades may seem premature, even irrelevant, especially when our focus is on the enslaved and indigenous. The people at the center of this chapter bore little resemblance to the elite creole patriots in Benedict Anderson's work on the emergence of nationalism. In a counterpoint to Anderson, José Murilo de Carvalho has contended that at the end of the colonial period, before the arrival of the Portuguese court, there was no *pátria brasileira*, but only an "archipelago of captaincies" without any political or economic unity. Claims of pátria were largely provincial in scope, and the idea remained ambiguous after independence.[2] Indeed, the black and indigenous people who appear in this chapter were not, in most instances, framing their ideas and actions in terms of nation or its complement, citizenship; nor were most Brazilians or Latin Americans at the time. It is still imperative to recognize the very direct ways in which they confronted and grappled with the forces of state expansion and the narrow avenues of inclusion offered by liberal nationhood.

Saint Domingue on the Frontier

The town of São Mateus, which reverted to the original Espírito Santo after independence, was emerging as an important economic hub in the sparsely inhabited province. In the early nineteenth century it was the lone interior town, located upriver from the coastal settlement of Barra de São Mateus (today Conceição da Barra). Its main section, including the cathedral and municipal chamber, were located on the south side of the São Mateus (Cricaré) River atop a bluff nearly 100 feet high that overlooked the port and the river slowly winding through the valley below. The São Mateus had originated as two separate rivers in the Minas interior, merging as it flowed east and entered Espírito Santo territory. Manioc fields encircled the town, and on the river banks outside the

---

[2] Benedict R. O'G. Anderson, *Imagined Communities: Reflections on the Origin and Spread of Nationalism* (London and New York: Verso, 1991), Chapter 4; José Murilo de Carvalho, *Cidadania no Brasil: o longo caminho* (Rio de Janeiro: Civilização Brasileira, 2001), 76–77.

main quarters could be found the simple dwellings and gardens of settled Indians. The Atlantic forest, ever vulnerable to the onslaught of slash-and-burn agriculture, still covered the north bank. Packets and steamers from Rio de Janeiro, Vitória, and Salvador traveled past Barra upriver to the port at the river's edge, where they were met by a bustling square lined with warehouses and offices of merchants and slave-trading firms. Criss-crossing the square's stone-laid pavement were slaves hauling heavy bags of manioc flour.

The slave population swiftly increased from 1,336 in 1820 to a high of 3,029 in 1827, outnumbering the free white population by 3.5 to 1 and the free colored population by 2 to 1. Indians, both aldeia-residing and autonomous, were barely accounted for, beyond the 433 settled Indians in 1820 and 783 in 1827.[3] In 1824, 20 percent (2,654) of the province's entire enslaved population resided in São Mateus. The majority worked in manioc flour cultivation, enabling the town to become, by 1826–27, virtually the province's lone economic engine, with exports tripling from 60,000 alquieres in 1815–17 to nearly 186,000 alquieres in 1826.[4] The slave population would drop after the trans-Atlantic slave trade was definitively abolished in 1850, to 2,213 in 1856. Even so, the town continued to produce 173,610 alquieres in 1852. By the time the slave population recovered to 2,813 in 1872, São Mateus had shifted to the more lucrative cultivation of coffee.[5]

In spite of the town's economic importance, however, many considered it akin to a lawless bandit lair. Agreeing with Pontes's earlier view, the Justice of the Peace complained that "in this town nothing works to instill obedience and respect for authority, since what rules here are knives, pistols, and rifles." He further observed that in the town and its

---

3 For 1820 see B. J. Barickman, "'Tame Indians,' 'Wild Heathens,' and Settlers in Southern Bahia in the Late Eighteenth and Early Nineteenth Centuries," *The Americas* 51, no. 3 (January 1, 1995): 333. For 1827 see Ignacio Accioly de Vasconcellos, *Memoria Statistica da Provincia do Espírito Santo no Anno de 1828* (Vitória: Arquivo Público Estadual, 1978), 39.

4 Maximilian Wied-Neuwied, *Viagem ao Brasil nos anos de 1815 a 1817* (São Paulo: Companhia Editora Nacional, 1958), 170; Vasconcellos, *Memoria statistica*, 50. The 1826 statistic is for the entire province; however, Vasconcellos then notes that all the farinha came from São Mateus. For 1852 see José Bonifacio Nascentes d'Azambuja, "Relatório (ES)," 1852, mapa 4, CRL.

5 Brazil and Directoria Geral de Estatística, *Recenseamento da população do Imperio do Brazil a que se procedeu no dia 1º. de agosto de 1872* ([Rio de Janeiro]: [A Directoria], 1873). For the shift to coffee see Maria do Carmo de Oliveira Russo, "A escravidão em São Mateus, ES: economia e demografia (1848–1888)" (doctoral dissertation, Universidade de São Paulo, 2011).

hinterland, "each person believes himself to be a Magistrate and has no obedience nor respect for authority."[6] The confluence of several disorderly events fed such negative images. In 1843 alone, sailors murdered each other, Indians hired to hunt down a fugitive slave mistakenly killed and decapitated a cattle rancher, slaves shot quilombolas, and a rumor of a slave insurrection circulated. These images remained even when São Mateus would, by 1848, become, "for its geographic position, the most frequented port on the entire littoral between Rio and Bahia." For the then-president, Luiz Ferraz, the problem was the "large number of sailors, many deserters, and other criminals from various provinces, who all go there to seek refuge and cover."

However, by far the greatest problem stymying lawmakers and settlers were the quilombos. Ferraz feared they "could be of fatal consequence to the safety of individuals and property," and his successor added that they were "an evil that without a doubt will compromise the future tranquility of the province, our existence, fortune, and possessions."[7] Quilombos tenaciously reemerged and multiplied on the Atlantic frontier every time an expedition was sent out to destroy them, fed by fugitive slaves from São Mateus and beyond who were attracted by the lax law enforcement. When the largest slave insurrection in Espírito Santo history erupted further south in the town of Queimado in 1849, the townspeople were terrified that some of the participants had come to seek refuge in São Mateus, joining other fugitive slaves from Caravelas, southern Bahia, and preemptively seized all weapons from their slaves.[8]

Since the beginning of the nineteenth century, fortune seekers who had been arriving into the region clamoring for sesmarias and other spoils of the Botocudo Wars had been utterly unprepared for the resistance of their own slaves. By fleeing into the hinterland or engaging in open revolt, the enslaved claimed the Atlantic frontier as a space of freedom from bondage. Their actions often engendered clashes with their masters but also with Indians and state agents.

---

[6] José dos Santos Porto to José Francisco d'Andrade e Almeida Monjardim, Vice President of Espírito Santo, January 3, 1833, IJ1–729-ES, AN.

[7] Luiz Pedreira Couto Ferraz, "Relatório (ES)," 1848, 7–8, CRL; Antonio Joaquim de Siqueira, "Relatório (ES)," 1849, 7, CRL.

[8] Francisco José Alves Pereira to José Ignacio Accioly de Vasconcellos, April 20, 1849, Governadoria Ser. Accioly Liv. 58, APEES; Francisco José Alves Pereira to José Ignacio Accioly de Vasconcellos, May 28, 1849, Governadoria Ser. Accioly Liv. 58 Fl. 192, APEES. For the Queimado insurrection see Affonso Claudio, *Insurreição do Queimado: episódio da história da Província do Espírito Santo* (Vitória, ES: Editora da Fundação Ceciliano Abel de Almeida, 1979).

In November 1822, soon after Brazil proclaimed its independence, São Mateus had its own taste of the African scare. A violent uprising of "free and enslaved Africans . . . against whites and *pardos* (mixed-race people)" sent the townspeople into a panic. The two suspected master-minds were the Africans Claudio Ferreira de Jesus and Luis Benguela, one of whom was reportedly slated to become the rebels' king. de Jesus and Benguela were released for lack of evidence, but subsequent events suggest that it was not a mere conspiracy rumor.[9] In the five years following the revolt, quilombos and slave uprisings continued to proliferate around Caravelas and São Mateus, fueling fears of a Haiti-like race war. By 1827 nearly a hundred slaves had established quilombos in São Mateus's outskirts, attacking women and murdering travelers on public roads. Slaves demanded that their frightened owners treat them "with the humility of servants" before abandoning them to join the quilombolas. São Mateus residents referred to the earlier African uprising led by de Jesus and Benguela when expressing dread that their town would be "reduced to another island of São Domingos (St. Domingue), for they have no other plan, as our experience and certainty have shown in the year 1822."[10] Three months later, in June 1827, the fear of racial violence and the inversion of master–slave relations again shook the residents of São Mateus. Seeing that more than ninety of their slaves "no longer courted the whites as was customary" and seemed poised to seize control of the town, they again expressed fear that they would have to relive the events of 1822, which they recalled as a "slave uprising in this region with the most cruel deaths."[11]

Slave resistance equally abounded in southern Bahia. In 1828 a quilombo was destroyed and burned to the ground in Caravelas. Its members called their settlement an "empire" and had clearly prepared themselves for war against their invaders, arming themselves with firearms, bows, and arrows and fortifying the quilombo with hidden traps and stakes. The anti-quilombo expedition, which included Indians, killed

---

[9] November 16, 1822, Colonial/Insurreições escravas/Mc 322, APEB; João José Reis, *Slave Rebellion in Brazil: The Muslim Uprising of 1835 in Bahia* (Baltimore: Johns Hopkins University Press, 1993), 55–58. Many thanks to João Reis for kindly sharing this source.

[10] Residents of São Mateus to Municipal Chamber of São Mateus, March 10, 1827, Governadoria Ser. Accioly Liv. 351 Fl. 33–34, APEES; Residents of São Mateus to Municipal Chamber of São Mateus, March 23, 1827, Governadoria Ser. Accioly Liv. 351 Fl. 31–32, APEES.

[11] Residents of São Mateus to Municipal Chamber of São Mateus, June 27, 1827, Governadoria Ser. Accioly Liv. 351 Fl. 36, APEES.

three quilombolas and captured several men and women but allowed the injured leader to escape. Yet even with the destruction of this particular quilombo, nearly a hundred quilombolas remained at large in the surrounding forests. The lone bush captain entrusted with leading anti-quilombo expeditions around Caravelas was forced to recognize the futility of his work. Indeed, the Caravelas Justice of the Peace complained that "there will always be fugitive slaves in these forests, because they are dispersed, there are many fields, and the slaves numerous, with more than fifty, eighty, or one hundred captives, with only one bush captain in this district."[12] The 1832 uprising on Schaeffer's plantation in Colônia Leopoldina nearby was a reminder that plantation slaves were equally capable of damage. By 1843, Caravelas's African slave population alone would reach more than 3,000, many of whom continued to establish their own quilombos. The local police complained that "they threaten the safety of all inhabitants, becoming so audacious as to knock down doors, seize goods that farmers transport to their fields, and carry slave women away to their citadel by force, against their will."[13]

The origins of the slaves on the Atlantic frontier in the first half of the nineteenth century are opaque. An 1833 document listing twenty-five female and male fugitive slaves in São Mateus offers fleeting insight: two were Angolan (West Central African), one Nagô (Yoruba), and one *crioulo* (native-born). To this short list we may add the aforementioned Luis Benguela (also West Central African). Similar origins were recorded among the African slaves in Colônia Leopoldina.[14] Although historians have long demonstrated that slave "nations" used in the slave trade are approximations at best, we can conclude that Africans from broadly distinct geographic origins were enslaved alongside native-born slaves on the Atlantic frontier, and that both groups fled and revolted.[15] By

---

[12] Manoel Feliciano Cajazeira to Manoel Ignacio da Cunha, President of Bahia, August 22, 1828, Colonial/Justiça/Caravelas/Mc 2328, APEB; José Eduardo Monteiro to President of Bahia, November 22, 1834, Colonial/Justiça/Caravelas/Mc 2328, APEB.

[13] Antonio Jacinto da Siva Guimarães to Joaquim José Vasconcellos, President of Bahia, February 16, 1843, Colonial/Polícia/Delegados/Mc 3001-1, APEB.

[14] For the Colony's slave origins, see Chapter 1. Residents of São Mateus to Municipal Chamber of São Mateus, February 16, 1833, Governadoria Ser. Accioly Liv. 66 Fl. 26–28, APEES. Even the most detailed demographic study of slavery in São Mateus provides data on slave origins (the vast majority local) only from 1863. Russo, "Escravidão em São Mateus," 126–29.

[15] So far there appears to be no cohesive information on the origins of the region's slaves with the exception of those on Colônia Leopoldina, whether their African origins or their point of purchase in Brazil. Included in the sources I do have is a record of baptisms between 1772 and 1790 in Alcobaça, adjacent to Caravelas, which contains evidence of

mid-century, the next slave generation was Brazilian-born, resulting in important intergenerational ties between Africans and their Brazilian-born kin.

The economic damages that quilombos and slave revolts caused to frontier settlements were formidable. Settlers lost an already limited labor force and suffered destruction of their property and decreased productivity. Slave resistance likely played a significant role in the sharp decline in manioc flour production in Caravelas, Vila Viçosa, Alcobaça, and Prado in the first half of the nineteenth century.[16] Fighting quilombolas and slaves proved to be as costly. Militiamen who participated in anti-quilombo *entradas* (expeditions) returned to their properties in the hinterland to discover, to their chagrin, that slaves had stolen their livestock and destroyed their fields.[17] An 1846 law in Espírito Santo established a military force to combat quilombos and capture fugitive slaves in the province, but the force swiftly disbanded because of high maintenance

"Guiné" slaves. Guiné was often a generic term for West Africa or even African slaves in the sixteenth to seventeenth centuries. In the subsequent two centuries most West Africans were brought from the Bight of Benin, the Bight of Biafra, and Senegambia. Source: "Compendio do Primeiro Libro de Batizados da Freguezia de S. Bernardo da Nova Vila de Alcobaça," Collection of the Co-Cathedral of Santo Antonio in Caravelas, Bahia. On the general debate about assessing slave origins in the Americas and the forging of ethnicities, see, for example, Gwendolyn Midlo Hall, *Slavery and African Ethnicities in the Americas: Restoring the Links* (Chapel Hill: University of North Carolina Press, 2005); Michael A. Gomez, *Exchanging Our Country Marks: The Transformation of African Identities in the Colonial and Antebellum South*, 1st ed. (Chapel Hill: University of North Carolina Press, 1998); John K. Thornton, *Africa and Africans in the Making of the Atlantic World, 1400–1800* (Cambridge and New York: Cambridge University Press, 1998). For Brazil in particular see, for example, the various works by João Reis; Mieko Nishida, *Slavery and Identity: Ethnicity, Gender, and Race in Salvador, Brazil, 1808–1888* (Bloomington: Indiana University Press, 2003); James Lorand Matory, *Black Atlantic Religion: Tradition, Transnationalism, and Matriarchy in the Afro-Brazilian Candomblé* (Princeton, NJ: Princeton University Press, 2005); Juliana Barreto Farias et al., *No labirinto das naçoes: africanos e identidades no Rio de Janeiro, século XIX* (Rio de Janeiro: Arquivo Nacional, 2005); Mariza de Carvalho Soares, *People of Faith: Slavery and African Catholics in Eighteenth-Century Rio de Janeiro* (Durham, NC: Duke University Press, 2011); James H. Sweet, *Domingos Álvares, African Healing, and the Intellectual History of the Atlantic World* (Chapel Hill: University of North Carolina Press, 2011).

[16] B. J. Barickman, *A Bahian Counterpoint: Sugar, Tobacco, Cassava, and Slavery in the Recôncavo, 1780–1860* (Stanford, CA: Stanford University Press, 1998), 87. According to Barickman, at the beginning of the century these districts produced nearly 130,000 alquieres of manioc flour (*farinha*) that it sent to Salvador and other markets, but by the 1840s, the shipments "barely surpassed 76,000 alquieres." He is inconclusive about the reason for this decline, attributing it to the possible introduction of coffee, an export crop, which resulted in the falling production of farinha for the internal market.

[17] Residents of São Mateus to Municipal Chamber of São Mateus, June 27, 1827.

costs. Four years later, the provincial president Filippe Leal expressed his
exasperation that "nothing has been accomplished regarding the quilombos," which he likened to a "terrible cancer to the province's agriculture."
Leal blamed their proliferation on the costly and useless anti-quilombo
units as well as on individuals who protected fugitive slaves in exchange
for their labor.[18]

However, the damage was far beyond economic. Colônia Leopoldina's
failure had affirmed that it was not European free labor but slavery that
would drive the settlement of the frontier. Through flight, revolt, and
the creation of their own "empires" and African kingdoms, the enslaved
crushed settler dreams of prosperity and state ambitions of civilizing the
frontier. Africans figured prominently in these early examples, no doubt
fighting in their own race war against "whites and pardos" who forced
them into servility. The region's reputation as a place of chaos was in
large part attributable to its successful remapping by the slaves as a space
of freedom. Yet in doing so, they also engendered new alliances and
hostilities with various indigenous groups, settlers, and state agents who
made their own territorial claims.

Speaking of Rights

As quilombos proliferated in the borderlands of Bahia and Espírito Santo,
a different kind of struggle against slavery was also fomenting in the 1840s
and 1850s. Complementing the oppositional politics of flight and revolt,
the enslaved claimed a direct relationship with the monarchy and the
state. They spelled out their own terms of national inclusion by voic-
ing their political vision as royal subjects and citizens whose freedom
was guaranteed by these powers. The first documented incident took
place in September 1843, three years after the end of Brazil's tumultuous
regency period (1831–40) when Pedro II, the son of Pedro I, assumed the
throne. A general emancipation rumor circulated through southern Bahia
and northern Espírito Santo, sparked by the royal wedding of Pedro II
to Teresa Cristina in Naples earlier that year. With the new empress's
arrival imminent in late August, São Mateus residents began hearing
that the emperor had freed all the slaves. Slaveowners were alarmed

---

[18] Joaquim Marcellino da Silva Lima, Vice President of Espírito Santo, "Falla (ES)," 1846,
6–8, CRL; Flippe José Pereira Leal, President of Espírito Santo, "Falla (ES)," 1850, 9–11,
CRL. For a general discussion of quilombos and slave revolts in Espírito Santo, see Vilma
Paraíso Ferreira de Almada, *Escravismo e transição: o Espírito Santo (1850–1888)* (Rio
de Janeiro: Graal, 1984), 154–74.

that the emancipation rumor had assumed the guise of a royal act that had emanated personally from the emperor to the enslaved. They feared that their slaves, increasingly audacious and disobedient, were joining hands with quilombolas and other dangerous elements from southern Bahia to launch an insurrection. Law enforcement preemptively seized all weapons in their slaves' possession, along with powder and shot. As terrifying as were actual, armed slaves, however, was the circulation of dangerous rumors that could incite even more. To prevent the emancipation rumor from spreading to Barra, authorities also kept watch over the quilombolas and forty-five sailors who arrived in late September who could potentially carry the dangerous rumor along their maritime routes.[19]

The 1843 insurrection rumor drew on a rich Atlantic world culture of popular royalism reaching from the Kingdom of Kongo to the Tupac Amaru rebellion in Peru.[20] Popular royalism found especially fertile ground in Brazil, a colony and nation under monarchical rule. Once dismissed as evidence of popular political naïveté among people supposedly unable to comprehend the greater promise of republicanism, scholars have now recognized popular royalism as an important political expression in its own right. Many blacks and Indians, slaves and peasants understood royal figures to be a source of justice to whom they pledged their loyalty and expected certain rights and privileges in return. African and European ideas of kingship also overlapped.[21] Kongolese political philosophy, for example, held that a king should rule fairly and unselfishly in the public interest, no matter how great his power. Slaves

---

[19] João Bento de Jesus Silvares to Wenceslau de Oliveira Bello, President of Espírito Santo, August 25, 1843, Polícia Ser. 2 Cx. 7 Mç 38h Fl. 43, APEES; José Alvares da Cunha to Francisco Jorge Monteiro, September 26, 1843, Polícia Ser. 2 Cx. 8 Mç 39 Fl. 150, APEES.

[20] This is a growing list. Aside from those mentioned in this chapter, see, for example, María Elena Díaz, *The Virgin, the King, and the Royal Slaves of El Cobre: Negotiating Freedom in Colonial Cuba, 1670–1780* (Stanford, CA: Stanford University Press, 2000); David A. Sartorius, *Ever Faithful: Race, Loyalty, and the Ends of Empire in Spanish Cuba*, 2013; Sergio Serulnikov, *Subverting Colonial Authority: Challenges to Spanish Rule in Eighteenth-Century Southern Andes* (Durham, NC: Duke University Press, 2003); Marcela Echeverri, *Indian and Slave Royalists in the Age of Revolution: Reform, Revolution, and Royalism in the Northern Andes, 1780–1825* (New York: Cambridge University Press, 2016).

[21] Elizabeth W. Kiddy, "Who Is the King of Congo? A New Look at African and Afro-Brazilian Kings in Brazil," in *Central Africans and Cultural Transformations in the American Diaspora*, ed. Linda M. Heywood (Cambridge and New York: Cambridge University Press, 2001), 156.

in colonial Brazil similarly appealed to Portuguese monarchs whom they considered to be "above the law"; a monarch, with his absolute authority, would intercede on their behalf regarding manumission, abuse, and other conflicts with their masters.[22] After the royal family's arrival in Rio de Janeiro in 1808, the imperial relationship between the monarch and his subjects was redefined, encouraging slaves and Indians in the capital and surrounding captaincy to claim vassal status and make direct appeals to the monarch. Slaves and Indians seeking royal intervention increased, as did the number of freedom suits and manumission requests in Rio de Janeiro sent by slaves directly to the king between 1808 and 1831.[23] The slaves' belief in monarchical protection of them – and even monarchical granting of freedom – was already evident when João VI had stopped in Salvador in 1808 on the royal family's way to Rio de Janeiro. The city's slaves sang that his presence would put an end to the brutal punishment prescribed them by the governor of Bahia. Even more hopeful were those carrying the sedan chair of his son, Pedro I, when the family arrived to the capital: "Our master has arrived, Slavery is over."[24]

Royalism was therefore a political idea that resonated with African as well as Brazilian-born slaves, whose belief in royal protection was strengthened by the monarchy's continued presence in Rio after independence. Such beliefs did not always dovetail with the emperor's and the new state's ambiguous relationship to slaves. Prior to independence, the monarchy could uphold its absolute power by intervening upon a slave owner's authority over his slave. In this sense, a slave was able to enhance monarchical power by receiving protection as its vassal.[25] After independence, however, the emperor and state were more hesitant to intervene. Until 1871, manumission was considered a private matter left entirely to the masters' discretion. Only in 1871 would the Rio Branco law entitle slaves to self-purchase; until then it was, like the slaves' right to

[22] John K. Thornton, "'I Am the Subject of the King of Congo': African Political Ideology and the Haitian Revolution," *Journal of World History* 1993, 191; A. J. R. Russell-Wood, "Acts of Grace: Portuguese Monarchs and Their Subjects of African Descent in Eighteenth-Century Brazil," *JLAS* 32, no. 2 (May 2000): 327–30.

[23] Maria Regina Celestino de Almeida, "Reflexões sobre política indigenista e cultura política indígena no Rio de Janeiro oitocentista," *Revista USP* 79 (2008): 94–105; Keila Grinberg, "Freedom Suits and Civil Law in Brazil and the United States," *Slavery & Abolition* 22, no. 3 (2001): 73.

[24] Kirsten Schultz, *Tropical Versailles: Empire, Monarchy, and the Portuguese Royal Court in Rio de Janeiro, 1808–1821* (London: Routledge, 2001), 166.

[25] Ibid., 173.

amass *pecúlios* (slave savings), a customary right.[26] Some slaves also took the initiative to file freedom suits beginning in the 1850s, claiming illegal captivity on the basis of the 1831 law abolishing the trans-Atlantic slave trade.[27] However, prior to 1871 neither the emperor nor the government could legally manumit slaves, as doing so would infringe upon masters' private property rights. Still, Pedro I had performed the role of a just, magnanimous monarch by "rewarding" with liberty Bahian slaves who had fought for the cause of independence. In such cases the state arranged for the slaves' manumission and compensated their owners for their lost property.[28] Such precedents gave the enslaved compelling reasons to perceive themselves as beneficiaries of a royally decreed emancipation.

That said, the Atlantic frontier was a different space from the densely populated urban centers of Rio de Janeiro and Salvador, at the heart of the court and its rituals of royal pageantry. That the earliest example of an imperially mandated emancipation rumor in the region dates from the early 1840s indicates that if royal presence had been sporadic at best until then (save for a relationship with certain settled Indians, discussed later), its greater political and economic integration and growing information networks were now enabling the enslaved to conceptualize a new relationship to the sovereign as their protector and emancipator. Only six years later, in 1849, would another royally inspired slave insurrection ignite, this time in Queimado, further south in Espírito Santo. The Queimado insurrection was carried out by nearly fifty armed slaves who believed that the "Queen" had interceded, through a local Capuchin priest, to grant them their freedom. While Vilma Almada has posited that the slaves were alluding to England, which was increasing pressure on Brazil to cease the slave trade through the Aberdeen Act in 1845, it is also plausible that they were referring to the Brazilian Empress.[29] These

---

[26] Sidney Chalhoub, *Visões da liberdade: uma história das últimas décadas da escravidão na corte* (São Paulo: Companhia das Letras, 1990), 136; and "The Politics of Silence: Race and Citizenship in Nineteenth-Century Brazil," *Slavery & Abolition* 27, no. 1 (April 2006): 76. The *pecúlio* became a legal right in 1871.

[27] There is a growing scholarship on reinterpretations of the 1831 law, many of which are included in Beatriz Gallotti Mamigonian and Keila Grinberg (eds.), "Dossiê: "Para inglês ver? Revisitando a lei de 1831"," *Estudos Afro-Asiáticos* 1–3 (2007). Uses of this law are further discussed in Chapter 6.

[28] Hendrik Kraay, "Arming Slaves in Brazil from the Seventeenth Century to the Nineteenth Century," in *Arming Slaves: From Classical Times to the Modern Age*, ed. Christopher Leslie Brown and Philip D. Morgan (New Haven, CT: Yale University Press, 2006), 163–65.

[29] Almada, *Escravismo e transição*, 171. Matt Childs has also uncovered evidence of Cuban slaves in the Aponte Rebellion making reference to emancipation decreed by English

rumors circulated well in advance of Pedro II's actual visit to Espírito Santo, which would happen only in 1860 (with São Mateus excluded from his itinerary), suggesting that the monarchy's physical distance did not preclude the enslaved from believing in royal intercession.[30] Meanwhile, the cessation of the trans-Atlantic slave trade in 1850 unleashed a crisis on the Atlantic frontier, aggravating its chronic labor shortage. The Eusébio de Queirós law signaled the definitive end of the brazenly illegal importation of Africans that had been continuing since the initial cessation of the trade in 1831.[31] Brazilians could no longer rely on an endless supply of Africans to replenish their servile labor force. The law was but an important step in the direction of gradual abolition, which would not happen for almost four decades. Many scholars have demonstrated the 1850 law's variable impact on slave labor across Brazil.[32] After the law, between mid-1850 and mid-1881, nearly 222,500 slaves were sold in the internal slave trade from the Northeast sugar regions (especially Pernambuco and Bahia) to the highly capitalized coffee plantation zones of the Center-South (Rio de Janeiro and São Paulo), peaking in the 1870s at nearly 10,000 per year.[33] However, if the availability of slave, free, or freed labor allowed Pernambucan sugar planters to weather the loss of slave labor, the Atlantic frontier had no such backup to draw on.[34] São Mateus's enslaved population would fall

monarchs. Matt D. Childs, *The 1812 Aponte Rebellion in Cuba and the Struggle against Atlantic Slavery* (Chapel Hill: University of North Carolina Press, 2009), 160–61.

[30] Levy Rocha, *Viagem de Pedro II ao Espírito Santo*, 2a. ed. (Rio de Janeiro: Revista Continente Editorial, 1980), 8.

[31] The law for British eyes or "lei pra inglês ver" referred to the first law abolishing the trans-Atlantic slave trade, in 1831. The law garnered this name because it was believed to exist solely in order to appease British abolitionist pressures, and was brazenly ignored. Hence another law was passed in 1850, and this time it took hold, although illegal trading continued for another decade or so.

[32] This is a long list that includes classic works such as Stanley J. Stein, *Vassouras, a Brazilian Coffee County, 1850–1900: The Roles of Planter and Slave in a Plantation Society* (Princeton, NJ: Princeton University Press, 1985); Peter L. Eisenberg, *The Sugar Industry in Pernambuco; Modernization without Change, 1840–1910* (Berkeley: University of California Press, 1974).

[33] For a detailed analysis of the internal slave trade, see Robert W. Slenes, "The Brazilian Internal Slave Trade, 1850–1888: Regional Economics, Slave Experience, and the Politics of a Peculiar Market," in *The Chattel Principle: Internal Slave Trades in the Americas*, ed. Walter Johnson (New Haven, CT: Yale University Press, 2004), 325–70. Richard Graham in the same volume notes how some slaves were sold from Rio Grande do Sul, and that Minas Gerais was also an important destination.

[34] Recent research has shown that most Pernambucan slaves sold in the internal trade came from the interior and not from the coastal sugar plantations, where sugar planters' identities as slaveholders remained strong. Celso Thomas Castilho, *Slave Emancipation*

to 2,213 in 1856. The enslaved population grew in Colônia Leopoldina, southern Bahia (see Table 1.1), but remained concentrated in the colony and did not mitigate the general population shortage.[35] What the region did have, however, were Indians. That this was still a frontier region with a substantial indigenous population remaining, unlike other parts of the littoral that had already ceded to sugar and coffee cultivation and had much longer histories of settlement, helps explain the increase in indigenous enslavement and trafficking on the Atlantic frontier in the years around 1850.[36]

It was in a similar atmosphere of crisis that another rumor about a general slave emancipation emerged in São Mateus in October 1851. This time the slaveholders, who misinterpreted the news of the Eusébio de Queirós Law as a decree of general emancipation, were to blame for originating the rumor. Their anxious conversations were overheard by their slaves, who conferred with a few sailors and concluded that their masters were colluding with local authorities to hide the news about their emancipation. Slaveowners immediately feared a violent uprising and proceeded to destroy local quilombos, disarm slaves, ban public gatherings, and isolate slaves who were suspected of maintaining contact with quilombolas.[37] As with the 1843 rumor, authorities were particularly wary of quilombolas' spreading dangerous information, owing to the

---

and Transformations in Brazilian Political Citizenship (Pittsburgh, PA: University of Pittsburgh Press, 2016), 67–68.

[35] São Mateus' overall African-based slave population remained stable and small throughout the nineteenth century, with 2,654 slaves in 1824, 2,213 in 1856, and 2,500 in 1876, with a high of 2,813 in 1872. Almada, *Escravismo e transição*, 118; Innocencio Velloso Pederneiras, *Commissão de exploração do Mucury e Gequitinhonha. Interesses materiaes das comarcas do sul da Bahia. Comarcas de Caravellas e Porto Seguro. Relatório do capitão do imperial corpo d'engenheiros, I.V. Pederneiras, chefe da mesma commisão* (Bahia: Typographia de João Alves Portella, 1851), 6–11.

[36] The Paraíba Valley, the heart of Rio de Janeiro's coffee region, was Coroado Indian territory, which became eroded by the opening of a principal road between Rio de Janeiro and Minas Gerais in the 1810s, a process that became definitive with the cultivation of coffee in the 1830s. João VI, the prince regent who authorized the Botocudo Wars, also authorized the road. The Coroado were conscripted into the Navy until the 1810s but appear not to have been used as agricultural laborers. Marcelo Sant'Ana Lemos, "O índio virou pó de café? A resistência dos índios Coroados de Valença frente à expansão cafeeira no Vale do Paraíba (1788–1836)" (M. A. thesis, Universidade do Estado do Rio de Janeiro, 2004).

[37] The police lieutenant, Reginaldo Santos, refers to his interrogation of the suspected slave insurgents, but the records are unfortunately unavailable. What we do have are his references to the content, which are included in the sources cited here. Manoel dos Passos Ferreira to Reginaldo Gomes dos Santos, December 15, 1851, IJ1-434-ES, AN; Reginaldo Gomes dos Santos to Antonio Tomás Godoy, January 26, 1852, IJ1-434-ES,

quilombolas' vast social networks and their mobility in criss-crossing the provincial border.

However, investigations revealed no insurrectionary plans. Rather, on hearing the rumor, the enslaved became convinced that the cessation of the trade also promised their freedom. As a policeman reported, "there [were] ideas among the slaves to demand this *right* (which they are convinced had been granted them) that their masters are hiding."[38] The slaves were so confident of their freedom that they saw no need to resort to agitation or violence, and had in fact planned to gather at church on Christmas to hear the priest deliver the wonderful news. By using the language of state-guaranteed rights they made a powerful claim for their inclusion within the Brazilian nation. The enslaved believed that the "central government" had collectively emancipated them, surmising that it was ready to force masters to free them when it discovered the masters' collusion with local authorities to obstruct their emancipation. A local police officer scoffed that the enslaved were "deluded into believing that freedom emanates from the Government, which will force masters to guarantee it." Yet by believing the state to possess the legal and political authority to override private master–slave relations, the enslaved also expected it to protect their collective right to freedom above the masters' individual right to property. If the 1843 rumor framed emancipation as an act of royal beneficence, this time, the enslaved understood it as a legal action taken by the state to ensure their right to freedom.

Slaveholders derided what they called the slaves' "delusions" of freedom, for they had concocted an "imaginary law on their emancipation" and were "persuaded of the existence of this law." However, what the enslaved did was imagine a law about their freedom *into* existence. They were imagining, and thereby forging on their own terms, a nation in 1851 that was ready to include them, even if in reality the state would not recognize their right to self-purchase for two more decades, and general emancipation would not happen for another thirty-seven years.[39] By claiming freedom as a state-guaranteed right and law, they effectively refuted their

---

AN; Reginaldo Gomes dos Santos to José Bonifacio Nascentes d'Azambuja, President of Espírito Santo, December 15, 1851, IJ1–434-ES, AN.

[38] Bernardo José de Castro to Reginaldo Gomes dos Santos, October 13, 1851, IJ1–732-ES, AN.

[39] Ibid.; Santos to Godoy, January 26, 1852. The idea of conceptualizing an "intellectual world of the enslaved" in the realm of Enlightenment thought and law can be found in Laurent Dubois, "An Enslaved Enlightenment: Rethinking the Intellectual History of the French Atlantic," *Social History* 31, no. 1 (February 1, 2006): 1–14.

exclusion from the social pact and declared their right to citizenship – a citizenship that was not manifested as official politics or the vote but was based, as José Murilo de Carvalho has noted, on an emerging notion of citizens' rights and the state's obligations.[40] The enslaved of 1851 differed from their counterparts involved in slave revolts and quilombos discussed earlier that were explicitly adversarial to settler society. Slaves' insistence on the arrival of emancipation and inclusion would become even more pronounced in later decades: in 1866, the Paraguayan War led many slaves to believe it was fought for their freedom; again in 1871, slaves interpreted the Law of the Free Womb as a general emancipation.[41] But whether they chose flight, revolt, or claims of monarchical protection and rights, the enslaved explicitly rejected the servitude that had been foundational to the settlement of the Atlantic frontier.

Masters and Refugees of the Land

On their own, these examples of slaves' freedom claims suggest that Brazilian nationhood, especially under Pedro II, was ever more inclusive. Yet to recognize the impact of slavery expansion into indigenous territory forces us to confront a much more complex history. If São Mateus' prosperity was attributable to its slaves, in 1856 the *Jornal do Commercio* also reminded readers of the "shadow of terror… that it ruthlessly instilled among the miserable savages, terminating them without compassion and with brutality." The town was "living, throbbing evidence of the convenience of the system of terror used against the miserable inhabitants of the forests." The article highlighted Colônia Leopoldina as the lone counterexample – of prosperity achieved through amicable relations with the Indians – by conveniently omitting the fact that it was a slave plantation.[42]

Indigenous groups in the Atlantic frontier, including the Pataxó, Maxacali, Puri, Botocudo, and Kamakã, had been in growing contact with settlers since the late eighteenth century. Violent encounters were undoubtedly frequent but not exclusive; many Indians had found ways to negotiate with the Portuguese through trade, work arrangements, settlement in aldeias, and alliances, even during the height of the Botocudo

---

[40] Carvalho, *Cidadania no Brasil*, 75.   [41] See Chapter 4.

[42] *Companhia do Mucury. História da empresa. Importância dos seus privilégios. Alcance de seus projetos* (Rio de Janeiro: Typographia Imperial e Constitucional de J. Villeneuve e Comp., 1856), 17–18.

Wars. However, by the middle decades of the nineteenth century, opportunities for negotiation became increasingly unviable, frequently ceding
to violent confrontations. Such conflicts were born from the merger of
ideology and geography. The Brazilian state's goal of bringing "wild"
Indians into social pact through "civilization" effectively meant that the
only way in which the seminomadic Botocudo could qualify as citizens
was by transforming into settled farmers and developing the desire for
accumulation of private property. As Judy Bieber has shown, however,
such goals were incompatible with Botocudo cultural preferences and
subsistence practices. Acquiring material goods made little sense to them,
since they carried their possessions on their backs from place to place.
Private land ownership was equally senseless for people who foraged for a
living. But if such differences led to the failure of indigenous policies in the
first post-independence decades, by mid-century, increased settler presence and new legislation diminished the Botocudo's ability to negotiate
and ensure their survival. For many Botocudo, national incorporation did
not augur the promises of citizenship but instead brought greater expo-
sure to settler violence, territorial loss, starvation, and forced migration.
Some chose life on the aldeia, while many others chose confrontation,
with devastating consequences.

From the late colonial period, many indigenous groups in the Atlantic
frontier had chosen selective interaction with settlers. Sometimes they
sought out alliances in order to combat rival native groups.[43] A particularly important practice was trade, which enabled Indians to obtain useful
objects and trinkets from settlers and missionaries, such as axes, machetes,
nails, fishhooks, beads, and clothing, which they exchanged with items
such as beeswax, bows, and arrows, and sometimes their own labor.[44]
Some Indians chose to strategically settle on aldeias, which became a
common source of misunderstanding. For indigenous groups living on
the peripheries of settler expansion, aldeias often served as a temporary
solution to complement their subsistence, so when periods of scarcity

---

[43] Hermenegildo Antonio Barbosa d'Almeida, "Viagem ás vilas de Caravelas, Viçosa, Porto
Alegre, de Mucury, e aos rios Mucury, e Peruípe," *RIHGB* 8, no. 4 (1846): 446–47;
Municipal Chamber of São Mateus to José Joaquim Machado de Oliveira, President of
Espírito Santo, March 16, 1841, Governadoria Ser. Accioly Liv. 351 Fl. 546, APEES;
Izabel Missagia de Mattos, *Civilização e revolta: os Botocudos e a catequese na província
de Minas* (São Paulo: EDUSC ANPOCS, 2004), 167–69.

[44] Judy Bieber, "Catechism and Capitalism: Imperial Indigenous Policy on a Brazilian
Frontier, 1808–1845," in *Native Brazil: Beyond the Convert and the Cannibal, 1500–
1900*, ed. Hal Langfur (Albuquerque: University of New Mexico Press, 2014), 170.

passed, they would retreat into the forest. The Portuguese, by contrast, believed that Indians came to settle on aldeias ready for catechism and were enraged when they left, which tended to happen when aldeias ran out of goods to distribute.[45] A particularly illustrative example of these different perceptions was a group of Maxacali who had arrived in Caravelas to flee Botocudo aggression. Although they were baptized by the local priest, they remained disinterested in adopting agriculture and abandoned the aldeia when the supply of food, iron tools, and clothes ceased. Migrating to Tocoyos in Minas Gerais, they concealed their knowledge of Portuguese in order to pass as autonomous Indians who had come into settler contact for the first time. The Maxacali received a new supply of goods from the local government until their "ruse" was discovered. When confronted by a local military captain about having taken advantage of the colonists to obtain food, the Maxacali leader replied, "My people aren't used to eating only corn and potatoes; they need meat, but in this area the Botocudo destroyed the hunt."[46]

Underlying the Maxacali's creative response to settler expansion was a struggle between settlers, various indigenous groups, state agents, and slaves over the dominion of the frontier geography. Settlers scrambling to claim their piece of land and quilombolas fleeing into the forests were no match for the indigenous population, whose foraging lifestyle depended on the intricate knowledge of its streams, fruit-bearing trees, and hunting grounds. "The greatest caution is needed for all those who enter alone into these immense forests without knowing them a little, or possess an extraordinary ability of the Indians in finding their way," the German traveler Prince Maximilian observed on the eve of independence. "Europeans are still very weak in the immense forests of eastern Brazil . . . Should the savages unite to attack the common enemy, the coast would soon fall again under their power, since those who fled the cities know the Europeans' weaknesses very well."[47]

By mid-century, however, Indians' dominion over the region was significantly eroded. Settler expansion and the intra-Indian conflicts it aggravated forced many Botocudo out of São Mateus and its hinterland north toward Bahia, where new tensions erupted with other Botocudo and indigenous groups already residing there. The archives allow us to trace

---

[45] Ibid., 184.
[46] Auguste de Saint-Hilaire, *Viagem pelas provincias de Rio de Janeiro e Minas Geraes,* Vol. 2 (São Paulo: Companhia Editora Nacional, 1938), 173–77.
[47] Wied-Neuwied, *Viagem ao Brasil,* 313.

this movement. Botocudo-related conflicts begin to dwindle in sources about São Mateus in the 1840s and 1850s, simultaneously increasing in southern Bahian sources. Already in 1844 the Espírito Santo president observed that the Indians of São Mateus "no longer appear in large numbers as they had before, having retreated to Mucuri [in southern Bahia and northern Minas]."[48] A Capuchin missionary similarly noted that the so-called "wild Indians of Mucuri" were the same Indians who used to appear in São Mateus, but had moved north to Caravelas and Porto Seguro in southern Bahia.[49] Increasingly, these "original masters of the land" were becoming its refugees.

The state's plan to transform the Botocudo into property-owning farmers combined with settler encroachment to fundamentally threaten their seminomadic, foraging- and hunting-based subsistence.[50] The Botocudo had vigilantly guarded their territorial claims even prior to the settlers' arrival, and trespassing upon tribal hunting and foraging grounds was a common cause of conflict. Several travelers observed nonlethal battles between rival Botocudo groups when one entered another's hunting grounds (Figure 2.1). Most Gê groups confined their hunting, fishing, and gathering to particular areas in order not to invite conflict over resources with other indigenous groups. Foraging also required seasonal migration to take advantage of seasonal resources such as fruits, vegetables, fish, and game. In the dry season, for example, the Botocudo traveled afar to gather coconuts and the fruits of the sapucaia tree.[51] But higher population densities began to compromise their ability to forage and hunt without straining the environment's ability to provide. In this regard quilombolas could be as threatening as settlers, since their flight into indigenous lands could further strain available resources and invite unwanted expeditionary forces. While Europeans believed "wandering" Indians had no notion of land ownership and infested virgin lands, one missionary recognized the importance of territory to them when complaining that the "savages consider themselves the only owners, and absolute masters, of

---

[48] Ferraz, "Relatório (ES)," 24.
[49] Fr. Caetano de Troina to President of Bahia, September 24, 1846, Colonial/Justiça/Caravelas/Mc 2333, APEB.
[50] Judy Bieber, "Of Cannibals and Frenchmen: The Production of Ethnographic Knowledge in Early Nineteenth-Century Brazil," *Interletras: Revista Transdisciplinar de Letras, Educação e Cultura* 1, no. 5 (December 2006), www.interletras.com.br/ed_anteriores/n5/arquivos/v5/artigointerestudosSneadWertheimEliane.pdf.
[51] Bieber, "Catechism and Capitalism," 178–79; Hal Langfur, *The Forbidden Lands: Colonial Identity, Frontier Violence, and the Persistence of Brazil's Eastern Indians, 1750–1830* (Stanford, CA: Stanford University Press, 2006); Saint-Hilaire, *Rio de Janeiro e Minas Gerais,* 137.

FIGURE 2.1 As hunters and foragers, the Botocudo relied on the land for their survival, and the crossing of territorial boundaries could lead to conflict among rival groups. *Source: Single Combats of the Botocudos*, from Maximilian Wied, *Travels in Brazil* (London: Henry Colburn & Co., 1820). Courtesy of the John Carter Brown Library at Brown University.

the land. They do not let anyone else occupy their lands, and wage war against any who try" including "slaves and white workers in all lands in the comarca of Caravelas."[52]

Conflicts abounded in the area surrounding Prado and São José de Porto Alegre in southern Bahia, to which many Indians had migrated. The Botocudo attacked properties on the towns' outskirts, leading residents to abandon their properties and leave behind destroyed fields, and sometimes human casualties. As Hal Langfur reminds us, violent attacks on colonists drew on a logic internal to an indigenous society, one that can be discerned often only dimly in the sources. At a particular historical moment, indigenous motivations might be influenced by native cosmology and prophesy, epidemic disease, claims of competing headmen and kin-ordered groups, revenge, the search for food, or, to varying degrees, the centuries-long historical experience of violent clashes with Portuguese.[53] It is thus important to consider to the best of our

---

[52] Troina to President of Bahia, September 24, 1846.
[53] Langfur, *The Forbidden Lands*, 229.

ability the multifaceted significance of Botocudo attacks on settler property. Stealing crops and livestock would increase their subsistence base, while destroying fields could mount economic damage, similarly to attacks practiced by quilombolas. However, sometimes the acts were more symbolic. Bieber has suggested the Botocudo practiced a cultural rejection of agriculture.[54] One example suggests the possibility that the Botocudo killed livestock to avenge disease-induced deaths that they attributed to the ill will of settlers who employed Indian laborers.[55] Drawing on research on the Xavante by David Maybury-Lewis, Bieber also posits that field labor was disdained among the Botocudo, for whom agriculture disrupted the gendered division of labor in which men hunted and women foraged, cooked, took care of children, and transported everything on trek.[56]

The Botocudos' attack on a Prado farmer hinted at the narrowing avenues of negotiation. In October 1844 the farmer, Lourenço da Costa, encountered more than seventy Indians on his property. Costa provided them with manioc flour and slaughtered one of his cattle. Like many residents who coveted Indian laborers outside of state regulation, he attempted to settle them onto his property privately with the aid of a resident *lingua* (an Indian or mixed-race interpreter). The Indians left and returned the following day, "more audacious," and demanded food. Matters seemed at peace until a few days later when more than 100 Indians appeared at daybreak in great agitation, which Costa sensed was caused by extreme hunger. Rejecting Costa's attempt to appease them with food, the Indians killed seven of his slaves and injured three others, including his son.[57] Particularly significant was their murder of Costa's slaves, suggesting their awareness of the slaves' economic value to settlers and their vulnerability within the social and racial hierarchies of settler society.[58] In the wake of the incident a local judge wondered what could

---

[54] Bieber, "Catechism and Capitalism," 185.

[55] Botocudo belief in witchcraft appears later in this chapter and again in Chapter 6.

[56] Bieber, "Catechism and Capitalism," 186–87. Brett Rushforth's superb study of indigenous slavery in colonial New France also discusses how captors humiliated their male slaves by forcing them to perform women's work, including agriculture. Brett Rushforth, *Bonds of Alliance: Indigenous and Atlantic Slaveries in New France* (Chapel Hill: University of North Carolina Press; Omohundro Institute, 2012), Chapter 1.

[57] José Lourenço da Costa to Leovigildo d'Amorim Felgueiras, December 29, 1844, Colonial/Justiça/Caravelas/Mc 2330, APEB; Leovigildo d'Amorim Felgueiras to Caetano Vicente de Almeida, Jr., December 30, 1844, Colonial/Justiça/Caravelas/Mc 2330, APEB.

[58] Langfur, *The Forbidden Lands*, 239–42.

be done to "break the fury of these tyrannical people," especially since the soldiers stationed to protect Prado had all deserted out of fear, preferring imprisonment to confronting the Indians.[59]

The state's ideals of Indian civilization limited its capacity to comprehend their plight. Discussing the Costa incident, the President of Bahia did understand that the Indians in Prado, "forced by hunger, [had] come to the settlements with weapons in hand to commit disturbances, devour cattle and plantations" because they had "little space to subsist in an uncultivated forest as wandering hordes." Yet he ultimately criticized them as "children of brute nature who consider themselves masters of all that the land produces." Echoing the common belief that hunting and foraging were evidence of laziness, he suggested that the only feasible solution was for the Indians to learn the "love for work" in order not to prejudice hardworking farmers. He further remained hopeful that the estimated 10,000 Indians living along the Mucuri River could become a settled peasantry following the example set by the Puri and Botocudo further south along the Doce River.[60]

Another important motivation for Indian retaliation against settlers was the illegal kidnapping and enslavement of Indian children (kurukas) by settlers and their Indian allies, as addressed in Chapter 1. A family or small group was profoundly destabilized by the loss of one or two children, particularly since foraging cultures typically space out their children through postpartum sexual taboos and late weaning so that women do not have to carry more than one child at a time when on the move.[61] The Botocudo in the Mucuri Valley were known to harbor fugitives who could provide them with firearms, which served them when they "suspected that someone wanted to steal their children, whom they zealously [protected]."[62] The most notorious case of kuruka slavery in the region, mentioned previously, involved a settler family known as the Violas who resided in the kuruka-trading town of São José de Porto Alegre. In May 1845 a group of Botocudo led by their captain (whom observers mistakenly called Jiporok) assaulted the Viola family on their farm, murdering three and stealing a slave and two children.[63] The incident came to embody what settlers and state officials saw as the Indians' innate

---

[59] Felgueiras to Almeida, Jr., December 30, 1844.
[60] Francisco José Sousa Suares d'Andrea, President of Bahia to Manoel Antonio Galvão, Minister and Secretary of State, March 27, 1845, IJ1–707-BA, AN.
[61] Bieber, "Catechism and Capitalism," 180–81.
[62] Troina to President of Bahia, September 24, 1846.
[63] Jiporok was also sometimes used to designate a Botocudo subgroup.

violence and treachery, having taken place soon after 2,100 of them had
been led to São José by a missionary. The Archbishop of Bahia denounced
them as "hordes" who "lived among beasts in the forests of our vast continent" and were "a true affront to civilization."[64] The attack seemed
to affirm the impossibility of Indian civilization. Only later did Teófilo
Ottoni reveal that, in fact, the group had been under the rule of a lingua
who collected dues from kuruka-owning settlers. The Violas owned two
kurukas but refused to either pay their dues or return them, prompting
the attack through which the captain reclaimed what turned out to be, in
fact, his own children. Although he eventually agreed to be settled under
Ottoni's guidance, a resident in the São Mateus hinterland massacred him
and fourteen of his people before it could occur.[65]

For many state agents and settlers, the invention of indigenous savagery
was essential to justify, and even render necessary, the use of violence.[66]
Any attempt to comprehend indigenous experiences on the nineteenth-
century Atlantic frontier requires us to venture beyond the cacophony of
hateful language that drowns out state and settler violence and negates
the possibility of indigenous negotiation and resistance. Accusations of
cannibalism were the most salient example, of which scholars remain
skeptical given the paucity of hard evidence and the spike in allegations
during times of intensifying settler conflict.[67] In February 1845 an anti-
Indian entrada was organized in Prado to avenge their attack on another
settler. The entrada traveled into the forests and fired into the Indians'
settlement, murdering three adults and capturing four kurukas, two boys
and two girls. "Without the use of violent means, no favorable result will
come about in that town," the expedition leader justified his actions to
the Bahian president, "considering the dissimulation and wickedness of
these barbarians, who never hesitate to offend us." He called the Indian
chief "one of the most barbaric and bloodthirsty of heathens."[68] Steeped

---

[64] Archbishop of Bahia to Francisco José Sousa Suares d'Andrea, President of Bahia, March
26, 1845, IJ1–707-BA, AN.
[65] Ottoni, "Notícia Sobre os Selvagens do Mucuri," 200, 204.
[66] Michael Taussig, "Culture of Terror – Space of Death. Roger Casement's Putumayo
Report and the Explanation of Torture," *Comparative Studies in Society and History*
26, no. 3 (July 1, 1984): 152.
[67] Langfur, *The Forbidden Lands*, 243–46. Mattos, in *Civilização e revolta*, claims that
cannibalism existed in Botocudo cosmology but not in practice. This myth endured until
the Pojixá became extinct in the early twentieth century.
[68] Bernardo José do Rosario to President of Bahia, February 12, 1845, Colo-
nial/Polícia/Delegados/Mc 3001–1, APEB; Pedro Rodrigues Alcantara to Bernardo José
do Rosario, February 15, 1845, Colonial/Polícia/Delegados/Mc 3001–1, APEB.

in a paternalist ethos, settlers invariably viewed any sign of resistance or conflict as incontrovertible evidence of the Indians' perfidiousness and ingratitude. Expecting Indians to be loyal and thankful for their generosity, the apparent lack of such qualities encouraged settlers to retaliate.

Settlers believed they lived in a state of siege, and officials fanned the flames. Echoing the earlier fears of an African race war, the Justice of Alcobaça described Prado as being dangerously close to becoming a "victim of the most terrible carnage."[69] His counterpart in Caravelas requested assistance from the Bahian president, urgently describing the "aggressions that [the residents] fear from the savages around the Mucuri River, who have appeared recently in growing numbers, showing hostility, as can be seen from their painting themselves in many colors, which to them signifies 'war.'"[70] The same criminalizing language was used for the Botocudo as quilombolas such that they "circulate around this comarca, appearing in various points around it, destroying fields, killing whomever they find on the roads." Not coincidentally, both groups epitomized the disorder marring orderly frontier settlement.[71]

Nation-building in the frontier presented the Botocudo with terms of national inclusion that were fundamentally incompatible with their way of life. "Civilizing" the seminomadic Botocudo through settled agriculture and property accumulation was considered the only way to prepare them for citizenship. When such methods failed, settlers and state agents were quick to denounce indigenous "savagery" and resort to violence. Increasing settlement and disappearing land directly diminished possibilities for negotiation and indigenous survival, and for most of the Botocudo, citizenship was meaningless if not destructive. A striking quality of the archival sources on Indians in the 1840s and 1850s is the sheer virulence that far exceeds what is found in contemporary sources decrying slave insurrections and quilombos, even though both were feared and detested. Bloodthirst, carnage, barbarism, anthropophagy: such terms only fed the idea, present since the colonial period, that the Botocudo were more akin to wild beasts than people and needed to be "tamed" through violence. Through their own fictions of indigenous cannibalism and savagery,

[69] Felgueiras to Almeida, Jr., December 30, 1844.
[70] Caetano Vicente de Almeida Almeida, Jr. to President of Bahia, November 9, 1846, Colonial/Justiça/Caravelas/Mc 2330, APEB.
[71] Caetano Vicente de Almeida, Jr. to President of Bahia, May 31, 1844, Colonial/Justiça/Caravelas/Mc 2330, APEB.

settlers engendered a culture of terror that seemed to make necessary their extravagant violence.[72]

Still, the Botocudo did not simply capitulate. Through negotiation and conflict, they thwarted state and settler incursion until it was less feasible. Approaching a view of frontier settlement through their experiences should help lay to rest any notion that Brazilian Indians had simply disappeared by the nineteenth century. Nation-building on the Atlantic frontier was forced to contend with the indigenous population, who challenged and reshaped its course, often with irreparable consequences.

Performing Citizenship: The Botocudo Guido Pokrane

Violent conflict was not the only mode of indigenous encounters with settlers and the state. Even amidst diminishing possibilities for negotiation, some Indians were able to create new opportunities by claiming identities as royal subjects and citizens. No better example exists than Guido Pokrane, who garnered accolades from the Brazilian elite as a model Indian. A Botocudo chief born in Cuieté, Minas Gerais, Pokrane's influence extended among the so-called Botocudo of the South along the Doce River Valley into Espírito Santo. Pokrane represents a controversial "success story" in the annals of state-sponsored Indian civilization. In his relatively short life, he became an agent of state expansion, in the process mastering the role of the ideal royal subject and deftly manipulating the rituals of patronage and civilization to amass considerable power. Pokrane used his position as a successful peasant, go-between, Christian, and soldier to gain social mobility and the rights of citizenship that were denied the majority of Botocudo in a period of rampant anti-indigenous violence.[73] At the same time, his persecution of other Indians and his claiming of rights as a privilege aggravated existing intra-Indian tensions and helped curtail Indian citizenship as a whole.

Pokrane demonstrated his political astuteness as early as 1824, when the French-born Guido Marlière, famed for his "pro-Indian" policies and appointed by the new Brazilian government to settle the Botocudo of the Doce River, appeared on a trinket-loaded canoe.[74] He followed Marlière

---

[72] Taussig, "Culture of Terror – Space of Death." Anti-indigenous violence is discussed in depth in Chapter 5.

[73] For a rich discussion of Pokrane and other cultural mediators or "go-betweens" in Eastern Minas Gerais, see Judy Bieber, "Mediation through Militarization: Indigenous Soldiers and Transcultural Middlemen of the Rio Doce Divisions, Minas Gerais, Brazil, 1808–1850," *The Americas* 71, no. 2 (2014): 227–54.

[74] For background on this fascinating figure, see Bieber, "Cannibals and Frenchmen."

back to his military outpost and became his godson, receiving his new godfather's name at his baptism. Though it was still at the height of the Botocudo Wars, Marlière had advocated brandura, declaring that he would tame Indians with "bullets of maize over those of lead." Marlière arrived in Brazil with the Portuguese court and continued to view Indians as royal vassals after independence whose rights to the land, guaranteed by their "Natural Rights, and many Laws of the Kings of Portugal," were being ignored by unscrupulous settlers.[75] Pokrane symbolically performed his conversion from savagery to civilization by removing his lip disc and encouraged his fellow Botocudo to do the same. Such was his dedication that he risked his own life to facilitate his fellow Indians' conversion, falling victim to an arrow that garnered him the epithet *Pokrane*, or crippled arm.[76] In the meantime he succeeded his father to rule over nearly 300 Botocudo in the Manhuaçu aldeia in Cuieté. Under him the aldeia transformed into a thriving farm, producing enough to feed expeditions and settlers along the Doce River in addition to his own group. He managed the aldeia with an iron fist. As a leader he secured obedience by meting out discipline and punishment to transgressors, including those who refused to work, and garnered official praise for his exemplary leadership.[77]

Frontier zones with a sparse military force relied heavily on armed Indians and blacks, whether slave or free, to combat quilombolas and hostile Indians. Marlière headed six mostly indigenous military divisions stationed along the Doce River, and Pokrane became a soldier in the 4th and later 6th division in Cuieté, swiftly making himself indispensable to the Director of Indians. While many Indians, like slaves and freedpeople, were forced into compulsory military service, especially in the navy, some recognized an opportunity for social advancement both under the colonial militia and the National Guard that replaced it in 1831.[78] As Marlière's lingua, Pokrane was soon entrusted with pacifying various warring groups to the north and south of the province, including the

---

[75] Guido Marliere, "April 6, 1825. S. Tenente General," *RAPM* 10 (1906): 595.

[76] Luiz Pedreira Couto Ferraz, "Apontamentos sobre a vida do Índio Guido Pokrane, e sobre o francez Guido Marlière (September 13, 1855)," *RIHGB* 18, no. 20 (1895): 427–29; "O índio Guido Pocrane," *Diario do Rio de Janeiro*, July 2, 1840.

[77] Filipe Joaquim da Cunha Castro Castro, "Expedição ao Rio Doce, November 9, 1832," *RAPM* 10 (1912): 86–87; Ferraz, "Apontamentos," 430–31; *Diario do Rio de Janeiro*, July 10, 1840.

[78] Vânia Moreira, "A guerra contra os índios botocudos e a formação de quilombos no Espírito Santo," *Afro-Ásia* 41 (2010): 74–75; and "De índio a guarda nacional: cidadania e direitos indígenas no Império (Vila de Itaguaí, 1822–1836)," *Topoi* 11, no. 21 (2010): 127–42; Bieber, "Cannibals and Frenchmen."

Coroado, Puri, and Naknenuk and Krakmun Botocudo, a position he would use to settle personal scores. He harbored a particular animosity for the Puri. Meanwhile, mounting conflicts with colonists, no doubt spurred by differing views on indigenous treatment, led to Marlière's resignation in 1829, followed by his death in 1836. After his departure Pokrane remained in the military and probably joined the National Guard.[79]

With Indian citizenship left ambiguous in the Constitution, some Indians seeking to affirm it recognized military service as key to proving their qualifications and gaining social mobility. Those who served Marlière in the military as go-betweens called themselves "national Indians" to distinguish themselves from autonomous Indians.[80] After 1831, many Indians were recruited to serve in the National Guard, which was based on the principle of the "armed citizen." Little scholarship exists on indigenous military service in Imperial Brazil, but Vânia Moreira has speculated that it became an important marker of indigenous citizenship, since only slaves and the poor with less than an annual income of 100 mil reis (a significantly low qualification) were ineligible to serve in the guard. More importantly, these Indians could also vote. Thus, by being able to participate in an institution that excluded the African-born and many Brazilian freedpeople, they were able to distinguish themselves as occupying a level of relative honor among the nation's lower classes.[81] The National Guard was, therefore, one of the few avenues through which Indians could claim citizenship rights that were clearly unavailable to enslaved people of African descent.

Through military service to the state and by settling on aldeias, Indians expected certain rights and privileges in return. Such expectations may have been formed during their former status as royal vassals of the Portuguese Crown. Maria Celestino de Almeida has documented a royalist political culture among aldeia Indians in the Rio de Janeiro captaincy who were well aware of their role as subjects and servants of the king and

---

[79] Ferraz, "Apontamentos," 429; Maria Hilda Baqueiro Paraiso, "Guido Pokrane, o imperador do Rio Doce," n.d.; Guido Marliere, "February 17, 1825," *RAPM* 10 (1906): 567.

[80] Paraiso, "Guido Pokrane." For native participation in the Paraguayan War, see Tracy Devine Guzmán, *Native and National in Brazil: Indigeneity after Independence* (Chapel Hill: University of North Carolina Press, 2013), 82–88.

[81] Moreira, "índio a guarda nacional," 135; Hendrik Kraay, *Race, State, and Armed Forces In Independence-Era Brazil: Bahia, 1790s–1840s* (Stanford, CA: Stanford University Press, 2004), 225. 100 mil reis was the qualification in rural areas, while urban areas required 200 mil reis.

asked for his protection – in their case, land recognition – in return for their loyalty.[82] Similarly, Botocudo living in aldeias in the Mucuri Valley knew they possessed certain privileges not enjoyed by autonomous Indians and frequently complained to authorities to have them recognized, especially those pertaining to land ownership.[83]

Pokrane utilized this royalist political culture to articulate a specific vision of indigenous citizenship.[84] Possessing a keen eye for imperial social hierarchy, he disdained those of lower social rank, preferring the company of persons of importance and even demanding a noble title in return for his pacification of hostile Indians. His adeptness in the rituals of patronage was proven in June 1840 when he traveled to the Court in Rio de Janeiro, where he became the talk of the town. Dressed in imperial military garb, Pokrane was escorted around various sites of the capital – the navy arsenal, blacksmith workshops, mills, factories – where he was dutifully impressed by the fruits of hard work. The high point of his visit was an audience with the Emperor Pedro II himself, which he realized through the mediation of a state-appointed engineer working in the Doce Valley. By calling Pedro *Pakiajú* (great chief), Pokrane astutely tapped into the Emperor's Indigenist sympathies. He framed his visit using the language of state-sponsored civilization, supplicating to Pedro II and the imperial government to provide the necessary objects – fabric for clothing, farming, and construction tools – without which his group would "fall back into the primitive state of savages." In response, Pedro gifted Pokrane with a silver-plated hunting rifle, gunpowder carrier, and machete from his personal collection, and later agreed to become his son's godparent. Emboldened by imperial patronage and laden with European tools, Pokrane then headed to Ouro Preto, Minas Gerais to complain to the lieutenant general about not being paid for three years of military service, adding ominously that Pedro II had given him a rifle, even though National Guard service in general was unremunerated.[85]

---

[82] Almeida, "Reflexões sobre política indigenista," 100.

[83] Mattos, *Civilização e revolta*, 122–23.

[84] Moreira, "índio a guarda nacional," 137–38; Moreira, "Guerra contra os índios," 75; Bieber, "Mediation through Militarization," 233.

[85] Ferraz, "Apontamentos," 430; *Diario do Rio de Janeiro*, July 15, 1840; July 10, 1840; "O índio Guido Pocrane"; Bieber, "Mediation through Militarization," 247. Pokrane was not the first Indian to travel to the Court to receive a personal audience with the Emperor, although he excited unusual press attention. Judy Bieber discusses the equally fascinating story of a Maxacalí Indian named Innocêncio, who in 1825 traveled from southern Bahia to the Court of Pedro I and, like Pokrane later, received many gifts in return, including, significantly, a portrait of the emperor that he was later caught

His star continued to rise after returning to Cuieté. It soon became evident, however, that Pokrane's surging power in the early 1840s profoundly destabilized already tense intra-Indian relations in the frontier and further aggravated the general turmoil engulfing the region. The 1840s were precisely the period of rising settler–Indian conflicts in southern Bahia; the increase in kuruka slavery; and the emperor-related slave emancipation rumor in São Mateus. Aldeia Indians residing in the Doce River Valley watched in envy and trepidation as royal gifts destined for Pokrane and his family arrived from Rio de Janeiro. They beseeched the Director of Indians of the Doce River to cease the gifts, arguing that Pokrane's group was using the weapons he received to "kill them and steal their women." The latter was a reference to the important role of women in Botocudo ethnopolitics; in intergroup combat, they migrated to the winning group in a ritual exchange of wives.[86] We do not know whether Pedro II was aware of the repercussions of his patronage on intra-Indian politics, but the Director of Indians, João Malaquias, had a sober assessment of shifting local power relations. While state officials from afar continued to praise Pokrane for his military might and loyal service, Malaquias openly doubted the benefits of his special treatment. If anything, it had only been a "huge ill." Perhaps a bit naively, Malaquias believed that save for occasional squabbles, the Botocudo had lived peacefully but were now in permanent turmoil. Taking advantage of powerful patronage, firearms, and lax political control in the disputed territory straddling Minas Gerais and Espírito Santo, Pokrane attacked the rival Puri whom he accused of witchcraft, and especially the Botocudo around São Mateus, who had united forces against him. Pokrane's military maneuvers undoubtedly contributed to his rivals' forced exile into southern Bahia and their high mortality.[87]

The Director of Indians tried to stem the escalating hostilities by requesting the provincial president to end Pokrane's special treatment and make him cease his military operations. Malaquias argued that royal gifts should be given to all Indians since "all deserve the same consideration of His Majesty the Emperor" and "all are brothers and with

selling (!). Innocêncio had a falling out with the state, in contrast with Pokrane, who remained a favorite.

[86] Mattos, *Civilização e revolta,* 169.

[87] João Malaquias dos Santos e Azevedo to José Manoel de Lima, July 12, 1844; July 18, 1841; August 12, 1844; October 10, 1841, Lata 346 Doc. 27, IHGB; Mattos, *Civilização e revolta,* 149.

equal rights." He was wrong. Pokrane was precisely the civilized Indian-turned-citizen the state desired: Christian, peasant, and loyal soldier in the service of state expansion. Yet in demanding his rights as a personal reward and privilege in return for his service, Pokrane articulated an indigenous citizenship modeled on the highly subjective criteria of civilization and patronage politics that rested precisely on the unequal distribution of rights. Such a subjective version of citizenship was possible precisely because Brazilian law was silent on the criteria by which "wild" Indians could qualify for citizenship. Malaquias was therefore incorrect in arguing that the "Botocudos of the North and South, as inhabitants of the same Empire, have the same rights to Imperial protection." Pokrane's rise took place as autonomous Indians remained unaccounted for in the Constitution; Indians emancipated from slavery were orphans; and even aldeia Indians had to petition to have their rights recognized. Malaquias himself seemed to recognize the inequality of indigenous rights when observing that "perhaps those who are more vulnerable due to their level of civilization deserve more attention, as they are defenseless before their enemies." The privileges and patronage Pokrane received as a loyal subject of the Brazilian state helped aggravate the inequalities of indigenous citizenship, enhancing his own and his group's power as a chief but leaving other Indians devoid of state protection.[88]

"God willing all Indians were like Pokrane!" exclaimed one Brazilian military commander upon visiting his aldeia. Pokrane had died soon after the aforementioned events, around 1844, by disease or poisoning, and was succeeded by his son, who was also named Guido. The elder Pokrane was remembered for his strong physique, shining black hair, and love for his godfather Guido Marlière. But Luiz Ferraz, President of Espírito Santo and author of a flattering memorial article on Pokrane, also recognized in him a perfect Indian who learned the rituals of patronage and loyal state service and was willing to subjugate hostile Indians on its behalf. His acts of violence were praised as military valor and spared the hate-filled language of savagery attributed to other Botocudo. Even his "bad" Portuguese and polygamy were overlooked. Clearly Pokrane was not a pawn but a deft negotiator in the politics of state consolidation. As a youth, he had recognized the opportunity that state expansion provided. He became an astute leader who knew how to elicit Indigenist sympathies and perform the role of a civilized Indian

[88] Azevedo to Lima, July 12, 1841, IHGB; Azevedo to Lima, August 12, 1844.

to subjugate his own enemies and further his ambitions. During a time when many Botocudo were forced into exile, enslaved, and massacred, and the possibilities of citizenship remained null or elusive for African and Brazilian-born slaves, Pokrane articulated a singular example of indigenous citizenship that further highlighted the inequality of citizenship as a whole.[89]

Black, Indigenous, and Multiracial Worlds

As slavery established itself in indigenous territory, black and indigenous people found themselves defining new relationships with each other, not just with state agents and settlers. The state's role in shaping these relations must be considered alongside those forged by and among black and indigenous people themselves. This means that we cannot presume solidarity based on a similar class position; nor was all antagonism the product of state engineering. Untangling black–indigenous relations poses a formidable challenge. While Brazil did not have an official caste system as in colonial Spanish America, the archives are shaped by a vested state interest in creating racialized tensions among blacks and Indians. Patrick Carroll recognized a similar circumstance in colonial Mexican sources resulting from Spaniards' efforts to protect their minority rule. By eschewing reporting on harmonious relations among blacks and natives, Spaniards sought to maintain a strict racial caste system and encourage subaltern hostilities.[90] The historian of Brazil must similarly contend with the state's emphasis of black–Indian hostilities and the archival separation of the two populations.

To establish their authority over the frontier, the state and settlers deliberately fostered animosity among hostile Indians and rebellious slaves whom they wished to control. A Caravelas judge clearly linked these twin threats in exclaiming that "[a]side from the invasions by barbaric heathens... we must put an end to the quilombos in the backlands!"[91] Subduing them often assumed the guise of "ethnic

---

[89] Ferraz, "Apontamentos," 430; "O índio Guido Pocrane"; Castro, "Expedição ao Rio Doce, November 9, 1832."

[90] Patrick J. Carroll, "Black-Native Relations and the Historical Record," in *Beyond Black and Red: African-Native Relations in Colonial Latin America*, ed. Matthew Restall (Albuquerque: University of New Mexico Press, 2005), 246–47. The archives are discussed in the epilogue.

[91] Antonio Jacintho da Silva Guimarães to Joaquim José de Vasconcellos, President of Bahia, February 11, 1843, Colonial/Justiça/Caravelas/Mc 3001-1, APEB.

FIGURE 2.2 While "ethnic soldiering" among indigenous groups, slaves, and quilombolas – including battles pitting "civilized" Indian soldiers against autonomous Botocudo – encouraged fissures that benefited settler society, some Indians and blacks also saw military service as an avenue for social mobility. *Source: Sauvages Civilisés, Soldats Indiens de Mugi das Cruzes (Province de St. Paul) combattant des Botocoudos*, from Jean Baptiste Debret, *Voyage pittoresque et historique au Brésil* (Paris: Firmin Didot fréres, 1834). Courtesy of the John Carter Brown Library at Brown University.

soldiering," a term coined by Neil Whitehead to signify the use of different racial or ethnic groups against each other, usually by pitting Indians against Africans, in formal and informal free and enslaved militias.[92] Although often the product of necessity in frontier regions where free white men were scarce, ethnic soldiering also served as a divide-and-rule tactic. Officials and settlers also employed it to foster tensions between aldeia and autonomous Indians, and slaves and quilombolas (Figure 2.2). In the late colonial period, for example, the ouvidor of Porto Seguro had established a farm-cum-military outpost manned by African slaves and Indians in Itaúnas, in the São Mateus interior. Other outposts soon sprang

---

[92] Neil Whitehead as cited in Stuart B. Schwartz and Hal Langfur, "Tapanhuns, Negros da Terra, and Curibocas: Common Cause and Confrontation between Blacks and Natives in Colonial Brazil," in *Beyond Black and Red: African-Native Relations in Colonial Latin America*, ed. Matthew Restall (Albuquerque: University of New Mexico Press, 2005), 85–96. For native and black militias see also Restall and Vinson's contributions in the same volume.

up along the Bahia–Espírito Santo borderlands, at Galvêas, Tapadinha, Agua Boa, and Santa Anna. While their original purpose was to prevent hostile Indians from reaching coastal settlements, the black and Indian soldiers serving them soon had to combat quilombolas as well.[93]

However, ethnic soldiering could sometimes go awry. This was particularly the case when masters armed their slaves to protect their properties. Though never a recommended practice, masters frequently did so in defiance of numerous laws prohibiting arms possession by slaves, and sometimes paid the consequences.[94] Slaves may have been merely serving their masters' interests or perhaps hoped that their service would lead to manumission, but arms possession gave them a sense of power that sometimes encouraged them to act on their own. Such was the case in June 1835, when slaves armed to combat the Botocudo in the vicinity of the Galvêas and Tapadinha outposts revolted, terrifying the outnumbered residents.[95] In the 1843 São Mateus emancipation rumor seen earlier, one of the first actions law enforcement took was to seize weapons in their slaves' possession. On the other hand, while some Indians saw military service as an opportunity to qualify for citizenship, arming Indians also entailed risks, as Guido Pokrane demonstrated in using his military might to subjugate his own enemies and destabilize intra-indigenous relations. Controlling free black and colored militias had also proven to be difficult for the Crown on the eve of independence, when many of the 400 black and mulatto foot soldiers who had been stationed throughout Espírito Santo to fight hostile Indians deserted to São Mateus, taking advantage of lax control.[96]

Beyond ethnic soldiering, black, Indian, and mixed-race people also developed their own interracial hostilities and solidarities. Attacks on settler properties and their black and indigenous workforce was a common way for Indians and quilombolas to inflict economic damage and terrorize the settler population. Quilombolas assaulted an Indian working for the São Mateus resident Manoel Monjardim, mutilating the Indian's face beyond recognition and brutally slashing his body with a machete. The gruesomeness of the act suggests that the quilombolas harbored a particular hatred toward the Indian or intended to frighten Monjardim

---

[93] Wied-Neuwied, *Viagem Ao Brasil*, 170–71.

[94] Kraay, "Arming Slaves in Brazil," 150–54.

[95] Joaquim da Silva Caldas to President of Espírito Santo, June 23, 1835, Governadoria Ser. 383 Liv. 48 Fl. 46, APEES.

[96] Auguste de Saint-Hilaire, *Segunda viagem ao interior do Brasil, Espirito Santo*, trans. Carlos Madeira (São Paulo: Companhia Editora Nacional, 1936), 32–33.

with spectacular violence.[97] Conversely, some Indians disdained and targeted slaves during their raids.[98] In a rare example of Brazilian Indians utilizing the legal system to express their grievances, a group of settled Indians in Viçosa petitioned the Justice of the Peace to punish a pardo suspected of murdering a member of their group. The Indians "awaited the results of the investigation with a hostile attitude."[99]

On the other side, rumors that Indians preferred black flesh also suggests that cannibalism fears were not limited to the white imagination. Two slaves in Espírito Santo told Saint-Hilaire about their participation in a reprisal against local Indians who had attacked their master and kidnapped a black child. The slaves claimed to have found the Indians roasting pieces of the child's body on a flame and decapitated one of them in response.[100] Later, while traveling in northern Minas Gerais, the Frenchman heard the story of two slaves who had fled their master and settled near a group of Botocudo. They began to cultivate the land and were initially on good terms with the Indians until the latter captured one of the slaves. The other fled, and on returning, found only his companion's bones.[101] These episodes again are difficult to verify (how, for example, did the slave know the bones were his companion's?), but do reveal how images of indigenous cannibalism also aggravated black–Indian hostilities.

The struggle to control the frontier could also engender multiracial solidarities and hostilities. Shared anti-indigenous sentiment united people of various races in a vigilante massacre of nearly 140 Botocudo in São Mateus less than two years after the official end of the Botocudo

---

[97] Reginaldo Gomes dos Santos to Police Chief of Espírito Santo, October 7, 1851, Polícia Ser. 2 Cx 14 Mc 59 Fl. 122, APEES.

[98] Troina to President of Bahia, September 24, 1846. Troina says the Botocudo called the slaves "Macacri" to show their disdain, but no translation is available.

[99] Alvaro Tiberio de Moncorvo Lima, President of Bahia, "Falla (BA)," 1856, 39, CRL.

[100] Saint-Hilaire, *Segunda Viagem*, 42–43; Pedro Victor Reinault, "Relatório da exposição dos rios Mucury e Todos os Santos, feita por ordem do Exm. governo de Minas Geraes pelo engenheiro Pedro Victor Reinault, tendentes a procurar um ponto para degredo," *RIHGB* 8 (1846): 361. A contrary depiction of Indian anthropophagy vis-à-vis blacks is found in the ethnographic research of a renowned German anthropologist who collected narratives from the surviving Botocudo of this region in 1939. According to one of these tales, a Botocudo chief censured his people for slaying a dark-skinned man whom they were preparing to consume, asking, "'Why did you kill him? He is a mulatto!' [He did not want his people to kill mulattoes, but only whites.]" Curt Nimuendajú, "Social Organization and Beliefs of the Botocudo of Eastern Brazil," *Southwestern Journal of Anthropology* 2, no. 1 (1946): 115.

[101] Saint-Hilaire, *Rio de Janeiro e Minas Gerais*, 135.

Wars. The perpetrators were sertão residents comprising whites, pardos, *curibocas* (offsprings of Portuguese-Indian *mamelucos* and black people), Africans, and a few slaves, with the nonwhites grouped together by informants, disparagingly, as "people of color." The group had been attempting to pacify the Indians with gifts and livestock and became enraged when the Botocudo killed one of their sons and destroyed their properties.[102] The massacre revealed the existence of anti-Botocudo sentiments among a wide racial spectrum of the population. Perhaps it was the same multiracial group that later led the nativist *mata-maroto* rebellions in São Mateus, demanding a reunification of the comarca with Bahia.[103]

These examples illustrate the plural, contingent nature of black–Indian and multiracial relations that eludes facile categorizations of race- or class-based solidarity or hostility. Religion was one potential space of exchange, as noted by Ana Lucia Araujo in her study of the French painter Auguste Biard. During his sojourn in Espírito Santo, the artist witnessed indigenous and black Brazilians together celebrating the Festival of São Benedito (Saint Benedict), a black Catholic saint popular among people of African descent.[104] Yet settler encroachment and slavery expansion stimulated complex relations between black and indigenous people, as we can see in the following incident from the Mucuri River Valley. In 1863, a group of slaves and Botocudo laborers working together on the farm of José Vieira de Lima fled to the forests to set up a quilombo. Traveling along a densely forested trail with only a machete, the men were alarmed yet relieved to meet a group of Indians from the nearby aldeia. Their leader, Albino, warned them of the dangers they faced, of foraging and hunting in unknown indigenous and settler territory. They could also be found by Pojixá, the leader of an autonomous Botocudo

---

[102] Municipal Chamber of São Mateus to José Francisco d'Andrade e Almeida Monjardim, Vice President of Espírito Santo, Oficíos Recebidos pelo Presidente da Provincia da Câmara Municipal de São Mateus, November 3, 1832, Governadoria Ser. Accioly Liv. 351 Fl. 271, APEES.

[103] José dos Santos Porto, Justice of the Peace of São Mateus to José Francisco d'Andrade e Almeida Monjardim, Vice President of Espírito Santo, January 3 and 22, 1833, IJ1–729-ES, AN; José Francisco de Andrade e Almeida Monjardim, Vice President of Espírito Santo to Reginaldo Gomes dos Santos, Captain of the National Guard, Registro da Correspondência do Governo com a Câmara [Autoridades Civis e Militares da Vila] de São Mateus, January 12, 1833, Governadoria Ser. 751 Livro 165 Fls. 65v-66, APEES.

[104] Ana Lucia Araujo, *Brazil through French Eyes: A Nineteenth-Century Artist in the Tropics* (Albuquerque: University of New Mexico Press, 2015), 166–69.

group reputed to target not only blacks and whites but also aldeia-residing Botocudo. The men gladly accepted Albino's invitation to follow him to his aldeia, where they were warmly regaled with food, drink, and dance. Full and a little tipsy, the black men sat in a circle, an Indian on each side, as larger circles of Indian women and men formed around them. They lent their machetes to the women who wanted to borrow them to cut some cane. Their spirits high, the men were confused when their Indian hosts suddenly seized them, mid-dance, and tied them up. The festivities were over. The men were marched back to their master, Lima, who rewarded Albino for his services with a few heads of cattle and clothing. A Maxacali Indian who now ruled a group of rival Botocudo, Albino was closely allied with the local Director of Indians, Augusto Ottoni, who had contracted him to hunt down the fugitive slaves.[105]

At first glance this incident is another example of ethnic soldiering. Remarkably, Albino succeeded not with force but by falsely offering solidarity and capitalizing on black and indigenous people's shared fear of Pojixá. As a survivor of intergroup warfare between the Naknenuk Botocudo and the Maxacalí, Albino clearly understood that his own prospects hinged on an alliance with the Ottoni family that had swiftly established itself in the region. He was similar to Guido Pokrane in his astute reading of shifting power relations brought about by greater state and settler presence. The Director of Indians was the brother of Senator Teófilo Ottoni, who had extensive business ventures in the region. From Albino's perspective, then, quilombolas fleeing into their territory further compromised an already diminished supply of land and resources, and were best removed. He thus chose to ally himself with the Ottonis in persecuting the quilombolas.

But what of the Indian laborers who had fled to freedom with the black men? They disappear from the record after the initial flight. They hailed from the Corsiumas aldeia, also administered by Ottoni, and worked for Lima for a modest salary. Aldeia Indians regularly fled these compulsory labor obligations, whose duration often outlasted the "customary" period of two to three months while rarely compensating them properly.[106] It is certainly plausible that the Indians had tricked the quilombolas and delivered them into Albino's hands. However, camaraderie may have also bourgeoned during their time spent together, helped by a shared disdain for Lima. The possibility is strengthened by their intent to set

---

[105] "O homem põe e Deus dispõe," *Correio Mercantil*, May 14, 1863.
[106] Ibid.; Moreira, "Guerra contra os índios," 66.

up a quilombo rather than flee to the Indians' aldeia since Corsiumas, controlled by the Director of Indians, would have expelled or reenslaved the quilombolas. For a short while, then, both groups may have shared their vision of the forest as a place of freedom from a cruel labor regime.

The violence of frontier incorporation, founded on the expansion of slavery and anti-indigenous violence, engendered new tensions between black and indigenous people. The sources are undoubtedly biased toward episodes of interracial violence and treachery. Nonetheless, even as the spaces for autonomous living were fast diminishing, cross-racial alliances forged from camaraderie, kinship, and the sharing of freedom dreams were also part of the region's history.

Conclusion

"As the territory is covered with settlements, and more sertões are exposed to them," predicted the jurist Perdigão Malheiro, "the beam of civilization will open a path, defeating the darkness of savagery." Malheiro was decrying the continuing violence against Brazil's Indians but did not doubt that civilization – that is, European-based culture – would triumph over the backwardness and disorder that the nation's frontiers represented. On the ground, however, frontier settlement was a far cry from this orderly vision.[107] The black slaves who had definitively replaced immigrants as the Atlantic frontier's labor source revolted and fled in droves, and by mid-century, some were ready to welcome a collective emancipation. The Botocudo and other indigenous groups frustrated settlers with their selective engagement with "civilization" and increasingly chose open conflict with the people whose land occupation threatened their very survival.

To say that nation-building was absent on the frontier is to disregard how much state expansion was shaped the very people whom it sought to exclude. Even though most of the time they did not frame their actions and ideas in terms of nation and citizenship, it is clear that slaves and Indians actively rejected, redefined, and claimed their terms of exclusion and inclusion. This does not mean citizenship was their universal goal nor was simply dictated from above, but was among a range of possibilities through which black and indigenous people contested their relegation to servitude, violence, and usurpation in the process of frontier incorporation. Citizenship moreover held variable meanings. For slaves in 1851, it

---

[107] Agostinho Marques Perdigão Malheiro, *A escravidão no Brasil, ensaio histórico-jurídico-social*, Vol. 2 (Rio de Janeiro: Typographia Nacional, 1866), 160.

became the framework for articulating their right to freedom. For many Botocudo, however, it was the elusive end goal of a forced "civilization" process that was fundamentally incompatible with and destructive to their way of life. Still, some like Pokrane understood its promise of social mobility, even as it aggravated the inequalities of Brazilian citizenship as a whole. Above all, flights to quilombos, visions of an African kingdom in the sertão, temporary settlement on aldeias, and open confrontations with settlers were, along with citizenship claims, ways in which black and indigenous people fought to assert their own meanings of the frontier territory. If the region appeared disorderly and backward to the state, it was precisely because black and indigenous people had repeatedly and tenaciously thwarted the imposition of what it called civilization.

3

Mestiço Nation

Indians, Race, and National Identity

"We will be quite a show in the boulevard cancans and the burlesque operettas, where Brazil is known as a country that imports Africans and exports Botocudos!" exclaimed an anonymous writer in a Bahian newspaper in December 1882. The author was sarcastically commenting on the recent embarking of five Botocudo Indians from Espírito Santo onto the ship *Ville de Bahia*, bound for Europe, by an opportunistic citizen intending to display them in an exhibition of primitive indigenous populations. The outraged public feared how the "refined nations" of the Old World would ridicule Brazil by mocking its export-oriented economy – a nation that shipped Botocudo Indians alongside coffee and jacaranda wood – and the steadfast stigma of African slavery that continued to haunt it. If the incident brought unwanted attention to the surviving "primitive" indigenous populations, the author feared that it ultimately exposed Brazilians' own barbarism, casting the nation's progress toward civilization into doubt. "We too deserve to be exported as objects of curiosity," he exclaimed. "Then *we* will be Botocudos."[1]

Beyond this melodramatic self-assessment, the incident encapsulated a central issue that Brazil, approaching the end of the nineteenth century, had yet to resolve: the search for the "*povo brasileiro*," or the Brazilian people.[2] Visiting French physician Louis Couty, a firm adherent of the

[1] *Gazeta da Bahia*, December 6, 1882; December 23, 1882; *A Folha da Victoria*, July 10, 1884.
[2] Celia Maria Marinho de Azevedo, *Onda negra, medo branco: o negro no imaginário das elites – século XIX* (Rio de Janeiro: Paz e Terra, 1987), 33–104; Jaime Rodrigues, *O infame comércio: propostas e experiências no final do tráfico de africanos para o Brasil, 1800–1850* (Campinas, SP: Editora da UNICAMP, 2000), 31–68; Seyferth, Giralda,

belief in the idleness of Brazil's black and mestiço population, drove this point home two years later when he observed that "Brazil does not have people, or rather, the people that it was given by race mixture and by the freeing of the slaves do not play an active and useful role."[3] These unsympathetic words deeply touched the nerve of the postcolonial Brazilian elite who, like their counterparts in neighboring Spanish American republics, were seeking to define a racialized national identity that celebrated their country's unique racial heritage while affirming its place among its "civilized" European peers.[4] As seen previously, Brazil's heterogeneity had already been a cause for consternation among its ruling class prior to independence, when the Portuguese royal family arrived in Rio de Janeiro and found themselves amidst a society with an elite white minority and an African- and indigenous-descended majority, many of them enslaved. The Brazilian people, many believed, could be forged only through homogeneity, in cultural, civic, and racial terms. An early promoter of homogeneity

"Construindo a nação: hierarquias raciais e o papel do racismo na política de imigração e colonização," in *Raça, ciência e sociedade*, ed. Marcos Chor Maio and Ricardo Ventura Santos (Rio de Janeiro: Editora FIOCRUZ, 1996), 41–58.

[3] Louis Couty, *O Brasil em 1884: esboços sociológicos* (Brasília and Rio de Janeiro: Senado Federal, Casa Rui Barbosa, 1984). Curiously, Couty was also a firm believer in the absence of racial prejudice in Brazil and believed that immediate abolition would compromise the harmonious transition from slave to free labor that he believed would take place only under gradual abolition. Claudia Santos, "French Travelers and Journalists Debate the Lei do Ventre Livre of 1871," in *New Frontiers of Slavery*, ed. Dale W. Tomich (Albany: SUNY Press, 2016), 237–41.

[4] The vast scholarship on this subject includes Nancy Stepan, *The Hour of Eugenics: Race, Gender, and Nation in Latin America* (Ithaca, NY: Cornell University Press, 1991); Doris Sommer, *Foundational Fictions: The National Romances of Latin America* (Berkeley: University of California Press, 1993); Ada Ferrer, *Insurgent Cuba: Race, Nation, and Revolution, 1868–1898* (Chapel Hill: University of North Carolina Press, 1999); Marisol de la Cadena, *Indigenous Mestizos: The Politics of Race and Culture in Cuzco, Peru, 1919–1991* (Durham, NC: Duke University Press, 2000); Darío Euraque, *Conversaciones históricas con el mestizaje y su identidad nacional en Honduras* (San Pedro Sula, Honduras: Centro Editorial, 2004); Nancy P. Appelbaum, Anne S. Macpherson, and Karin Alejandra Rosemblatt, eds. *Race & Nation in Modern Latin America* (Chapel Hill: University of North Carolina Press, 2007); Marixa Lasso, *Myths of Harmony: Race and Republicanism during the Age of Revolution, Colombia 1795–1831* (Pittsburgh: University of Pittsburgh Press, 2007); Rebecca Earle, *The Return of the Native: Indians and Myth-Making in Spanish America, 1810–1930* (Durham, NC: Duke University Press, 2007); Brooke Larson, *Trials of Nation Making: Liberalism, Race, and Ethnicity in the Andes, 1810–1910* (Cambridge and New York: Cambridge University Press, 2008); Barbara Weinstein, "Slavery, Citizenship, and National Identity in Brazil and the U.S. South," in *Nationalism in the New World*, ed. Don Harrison Doyle and Marco Antonio Villela Pamplona (Athens: University of Georgia Press, 2006), 248–71; and, *The Color of Modernity: São Paulo and the Making of Race and Nation in Brazil* (Durham, NC: Duke University Press Books, 2015).

was the Portuguese royal administrator, the Marquis of Pombal, who made Indian-Portuguese intermarriage an important element of Indian administration in Brazil. However, other early attempts to alleviate this problem of heterogeneity through European immigration failed miserably, as attested by the trajectory of Colônia Leopoldina and other early colonies.

The concern over defining a homogeneous nationality only intensified after independence. Brazil was a new political nation (*nação*) that had to contend with a variety of African and indigenous "nations" (*nações*) within its borders – whether Congo, Nagô, Benguela, or Botocudo, Tupi, Guaykuru – who were considered to exist outside of "good society" consisting of propertied white citizens.[5] Some feared that the trans-Atlantic slave trade was transforming Brazil into West Africa, the "pátria of Africans rather than Brazilians," and espoused radical solutions to Brazil's heterogeneity, such as the deportation of Africans or Indian extermination.[6] But the solution that would come to garner the most enthusiasm in Brazil was miscegenation – of the nation's indigenous, black, and white populations – in order to create a homogeneous *povo brasileiro*.

This embrace of miscegenation suggested a reinvigorated enthusiasm among the elite to include the nation's hitherto largely excluded African-descended and indigenous populations among the body of citizens, engendering a uniquely harmonious national racial identity. It was soon evident, however, that they intended much more. While scholars have documented the nineteenth-century origins of the idea of Brazilian racial democracy, based on the mixture of the "three races," much less is known about its practice.[7] This chapter shows that miscegenation was implemented as a

---

[5] Kaori Kodama, *Os índios no Império do Brasil: a etnografia do IHGB entre as décadas de 1840 e 1860* (Rio de Janeiro: Editora Fiocruz and São Paulo: EDUSP, 2009), 98–108. According to the author the term *nação*, especially in the plural form *nações*, was commonly used in Brazil and Latin America more broadly since the colonial period to refer to both African and indigenous groups, and often interchangeably with "*raça*." In the nineteenth century, Brazilian Historical and Geographic Institute (IHGB) authors, ethnologists, and naturalists interested in classifying indigenous peoples used expressions such as "*Nação Tupi*" or "*Nação dos Botocudos*," as if they were easily identifiable organizations with subgroups and branches.

[6] Kaori Kodama, "Os debates pelo fim do tráfico no periódico 'O Philantropo' (1849–1852) e a formação do povo: doenças, raça e escravidão," *Revista Brasileira de História* 28, no. 56 (2008): 407–30.

[7] Thomas E. Skidmore, *Black Into White: Race and Nationality in Brazilian Thought* (Durham, NC: Duke University Press, 1993); Ronaldo Vainfas, "Colonização, miscigenação e questão racial: notas sobre equívocos e tabus da historiografia brasileira,"

national racial project by becoming the central feature of Brazilian indigenous policy, finally realized on a national scale in 1845. Documenting the connection between the racial discourse of miscegenation and indigenous policy reveals that their collective objective was, in fact, to promote the opposite of racial inclusion: the erasure of living Brazilian Indians from the nation. This occurred precisely at a time when idealized Indians were elevated into national symbols in the Brazilian version of *indigenismo*.

Complementing the anti-indigenous violence seen in the previous chapters, a new discourse of indigenous extinction emerged in this period that invented, and subsequently transformed, the Indians' alleged "disappearance" into a fact. Extinction discourse, according to Patrick Brantlinger, was a "specific branch of the dual ideologies of imperialism and racism" that focused on the "'doom' of 'primitive races' caused by 'fatal impact' with white, Western civilization."[8] Brazil was part of a global phenomenon from the United States and Great Britain to Japan, Mexico, and Argentina, who all embraced extinction discourse to validate their internal and external expansionism and violence against indigenous populations. Its emergence in Brazil in the later nineteenth century was deeply rooted in the violent conquest and settlement of the nation's frontiers, where land reform laws were wreaking havoc on indigenous people's territorial claims.[9]

Between the frontier and "gentle" state policy, history and anthropology, literature and law, the promotion of miscegenation and the production of indigenous extinction went hand in hand in the second half of the nineteenth century, seamlessly uniting Indian inclusion and

Tempo. Revista do Departamento de História da UFF 8 (1999): 7–22; Vânia Moreira, "História, etnia e nação: o índio e a formação nacional sob a ótica de Caio Prado Júnior," *Memoria americana*, no. 16–1 (June 2008): 63–84; Paulina L. Alberto, *Terms of Inclusion: Black Intellectuals in Twentieth-Century Brazil* (Chapel Hill: University of North Carolina Press, 2011).

[8] Patrick Brantlinger, *Dark Vanishings: Discourse on the Extinction of Primitive Races, 1800–1930* (Ithaca, NY: Cornell University Press, 2003), 1.

[9] See, for example, Brantlinger, *Dark Vanishings*; D. W. Meinig, *The Shaping of America: A Geographical Perspective on 500 Years of History* (New Haven, CT: Yale University Press, 1986); Richard W. Slatta, *Gauchos and the Vanishing Frontier* (Lincoln: University of Nebraska Press, 1992); Walter Delrio and Claudia N. Briones, "The 'Conquest of the Desert' as a Trope and Enactment of Argentina's Manifest Destiny," in *Manifest Destinies and Indigenous Peoples*, ed. David Maybury-Lewis, Theodore Macdonald, and Biorn Maybury-Lewis (Cambridge, MA: Harvard University Press, 2009), 51–83; David L. Howell, *Geographies of Identity in Nineteenth-Century Japan* (Berkeley: University of California Press, 2005); Jason Ruiz, *Americans in the Treasure House: Travel to Porfirian Mexico and the Cultural Politics of Empire* (Austin: University of Texas Press, 2014).

exclusion. Living indigenous people were deliberately disappeared from Brazil's racialized nation-building project, whose powerful legacies we continue to live with today.[10] At the same time, these emerging racial discourses about Indians shaped racial ideas about Africans and African-descended Brazilians in surprising ways. While indigenous extinction discourse would be echoed in later scientific theories about black disappearance, the language of inclusion and racial assimilation employed in nineteenth-century Indian policy would also be reclaimed and reinvigorated by black Brazilians claiming a fuller citizenship during the heyday of abolitionism and in the decades that followed.[11]

From Infestation to Extinction

The shipping of the five Botocudo to Europe in 1882 generated such a scandal because their presence challenged the idea, assiduously produced by Brazilians and European and US observers alike, that they had virtually ceased to exist by the 1880s. In the span of nearly forty years since Guido Pokrane's death, the Botocudo had undergone a startling transformation in the national imagination. In the 1840s and 1850s, many settlers in the Atlantic frontier believed they were under siege by the Botocudo who "infested" the lands. At the same time, the Indian soldier and chief Guido Pokrane garnered accolades from the national elite as the model for other "wild" Indians to follow. By the 1870s, however, the Botocudo had become prominent in a completely different realm: the new racial science of anthropology. A crop of new scientists assiduously collected and measured their crania and uniformly concluded that the Botocudo were the most primitive race, unfit for civilization, and verging on extinction. What accounts for this startling change? How and why were the Botocudo, who "infested" the forests, reduced to a collection of skulls?

Tracing this transformation in the Botocudos' place in the national imagination allows us to understand how indigenous Brazilians fit into emerging ideas about the povo brasileiro. To do this we must begin in 1845, when the German naturalist Karl Philip von Martius published his winning essay for the competition held by the Brazilian Historical and Geographic Institute, inaugurated by Pedro II in 1838. In this famous work, "How to Write the History of Brazil," whose purpose was to define the "foundations of [Brazil's] existence as a nation," the author

---

[10] Moreira, "História, etnia e nação."   [11] Alberto, *Terms of Inclusion.*

proclaimed that the present-day Brazilian population possessed a unique character that resulted from the convergence of the "three races." While he did not doubt the superiority of the Portuguese, Martius recognized the importance of Indian and African "races" to the formation of Brazil's people and character. He also suggested that race mixture had created a "new and wondrously organized nation." By praising Brazil's racially mixed heritage and proposing that the three races had created order instead of disorder, Martius helped invent a "common mestiço past" while expertly assuaging elite anxieties about the present and future of the povo brasileiro.[12]

Miscegenation appealed to a surprisingly wide range of the political spectrum. Liberals such as José Bonifácio believed that through race mixture, Brazil's black and indigenous elements would be incorporated eventually into a whitening, ever-more homogeneous people who would constitute "one body of the nation," finally enabling national unity and true liberty.[13] Even the vehemently pro-Portuguese, staunchly conservative historian Francisco Adolfo de Varnhagen entertained the idea of miscegenation. Varnhagen abhorred the Brazilian population's racial profile, whose "heterogeneity is worse than its small numbers." In his vision, "We have Brazilian citizens; we have African and *ladino* (acculturated) slaves, who produce labor; we have wild Indians who are completely useless or even deleterious; and we have very few European colonists."[14] Shuddering at the idea of an Africanized Brazil, he encouraged European immigration and white labor above all to promote Brazil's economy. But while immigrants lacked, the next best option were "wild" Indians who, once subjugated, would become workers "less dangerous than blacks, because they would soon be mixed with us in color and all."[15] Such espousals of miscegenation placed Brazil's racialized nation-building in sharp contrast with the Unites States or the neighboring Andean republics with large indigenous populations. There the nineteenth-century creole elite

---

[12] Karl Friedrich von Martius, "Como se deve escrever a História do Brasil," *Revista de Historia de América* 42 (1956); John M. Monteiro, "Tupis, Tapuias e Historiadores: Estudos de História Indígena e do Indigenismo" (Campinas, SP: Tese de Livre Docência, UNICAMP, 2001), 130. Maritus' essay was originally published in the Institute's journal in 1845.

[13] José Bonifácio, *Projetos para o Brasil*, ed. Miriam Dolhnikoff (São Paulo: Companhia das Letras, 1998), 47–48, 119.

[14] Francisco Adolfo de Varnhagen, "Memorial orgânico – Offerecido á nação," *Guanabara: Revista mensal, artística, scientifica e litteraria* Tomo I (1851): 357.

[15] Ibid., 392.

abhorred *mestizaje* as both discourse and practice and actively espoused a stark racial binarism that both reinforced and marginalized Indianness.[16]

However, if this celebration of the African and indigenous contributions to Brazil propagated an image of racial harmony founded on a shared past, striking disjunctures of the present marked the chasm between Martius' essay's affirmative vision and the period of its publication.[17] 1845 was a time of hardening proslavery interests in the face of the impending cessation of the trans-Atlantic slave trade. Anti-indigenous violence and illegal Indian enslavement were at their height in the nation's frontiers. Finally, it was also the year in which the Brazilian government issued its only national indigenous legislation for the entire nineteenth century, a subject to which we now turn.

A Nation of Brandura

In July 1845, the Brazilian government under Pedro II issued the *Regulamento ácerca das Missões de catechese, e civilisação dos Índios* (Regulation concerning the Missions of Indian Catechism and Civilization) in an effort to centralize Indian legislation and administration. Its focus on Indian acculturation was based on the late colonial precedent established by the Marquis of Pombal's Directorate of Indians. Prior to expelling the Jesuits in 1759, Pombal had founded the Directorate in 1755, applied colony-wide in 1758, which outlawed Indian slavery and promoted Indian assimilation through tutelage by lay directors, and miscegenation with whites. The Directorate was dismantled in 1798 in Grão-Pará and Rio Negro, and colony-wide in 1822, which abrogated any special protections and rights the Indians possessed and made them equal to all other Crown vassals. Indigenous legislation was henceforth decentralized and left to local authorities. In Espírto Santo, for instance, the Directorate was locally reinstated in 1806 to facilitate the navigation of the Doce River and resettle autonomous Botocudo captured in what would be officially declared the Botocudo Wars two years later.[18]

Following independence, as we have seen in Chapter 1, José Bonifácio envisioned reintroducing Pombal-inspired assimilationist policies – known as brandura, or gentleness, to contrast with the ongoing

---

[16] Larson, *Trials of Nation Making*, 17, 63–68.   [17] Monteiro, "Tupis, Tapuias," 130.

[18] Vânia Moreira, "Índios no Brasil: marginalização social e exclusão historiográfica," *Diálogos Latinoamericanos* 3 (2001): 95; Patrícia Melo Sampaio, "Política indigenista no Brasil imperial," in *O Brasil imperial*, ed. Keila Grinberg and Ricardo Salles, Vol. 1, 1808–1831 (Rio de Janeiro: Civilização Brasileira, 2009), 181–84.

offensive wars – at the national scale in order to realize his vision of a homogenized nation. However, his proposal was dropped with the autocratic Pedro I's dissolving of the Constituent Assembly and received another blow during the tumultuous Regency Period (1831–40) when the Additional Act (1834) allowed greater provincial autonomy to return. Harsh indigenous laws were issued at the provincial level, including offensive wars in Ceará and Goiás.[19] The 1845 Regulation, issued by a more consolidated state under Pedro II, was therefore a reinstatement of the "gentle" acculturative policies advocated in previous periods, now promulgated as national policy. As we will see, however, the Regulation, combined with the 1850 Land Law and subsequent land legislation, would become foundational to the production of Indian "extinction" in the ensuing decades.

The Regulation's principal goal was to prepare autonomous Indians for their inclusion into the body of Brazilian citizens through Catholic instruction, intermarriage with non-Indians, primary education, and labor training. Creating a labor force out of the nation's indigenous population was especially pressing given the labor shortage aggravated by the impending cessation of the trans-Atlantic slave trade in 1850 and the general lack of a productive working population (a topic addressed in greater detail in Chapter 6). The Regulation purported to protect Indians from enslavement and required people hiring them to offer contracts, but this requirement, as we have seen, was regularly ignored. Many Indians were put to work on public works projects or loaned out to locals.[20]

---

[19] Manuela Carneiro da Cunha, "Legislação indigenista no sec. XIX," in *História dos índios no Brasil*, ed. Manuela Carneiro da Cunha (São Paulo: Companhia das Letras, 1992), 137–38; Mary Karasch, "Catechism and Captivity: Indian Policy in Goiás, 1780–1889," in *Native Brazil: Beyond the Convert and the Cannibal, 1500–1900*, ed. Hal Langfur (Albuquerque: University of New Mexico Press, 2014), 204–10.

[20] Henrique Lima and Joseli Mendonça have argued that, against the backdrop of slavery and abolition in nineteenth-century Brazil, contracts tended to protect the interests of the master-employer rather than the servant-employee, and some employees opted to avoid contracts. One may draw parallels between the "older practices of unpaid dependency" of domestic workers whom Lima documents and Indian wardship under the care of settlers, neither of which easily translated into free labor subject to legal contracts. However, at least in the case of Indians, contracts were framed as a means to prevent illegal enslavement, especially in the wake of the Botocudo Wars. Henrique Espada Lima, "Wages of Intimacy: Domestic Workers Disputing Wages in the Higher Courts of Nineteenth-Century Brazil," *International Labor & Working-Class History* 88 (2015): 11–29; Joseli Maria Nunes Mendonça, "Sob cadeiras e coerção: experiências de trabalho no Centro-Sul do Brasil do século XIX," *Revista Brasileira de História* 32, no. 64 (2012): 45–60.

Another equally important objective was land. The law reaffirmed the aldeia system that relocated "errant" Indians onto government-directed villages, and included numerous clauses concerning the demarcation and use of indigenous lands. The emperor appointed a General Director of Indians for each province under the aegis of the Ministry of Empire, who in turn appointed a Director for each of the aldeia*s*. These Directors were vested with the power to merge or reassign aldeia lands depending on their assessment of how much land the Indians needed, based on the faulty claims that Indians, many of whom subsisted on hunting and foraging, could derive their livelihood from settled agriculture, and that they were continuously decreasing in numbers.[21] The actual work on the frontlines of Indian catechism and education fell to Italian Capuchin missionaries. Capuchins began arriving in various corners of Brazil following an 1843 agreement between the government and the Holy See. Unlike the colonial-era Jesuits, who had amassed too much autonomous power over the Indians and were eventually expelled by the Portuguese Crown, Capuchins were directly incorporated into the Brazilian state structure.[22]

State and local settlers alike relied on the Capuchins to relocate Indians onto aldeias. Serving on the frontlines across Brazil "in the company of savages, tigers, reptiles, and erratic fevers," as one Director of Indians put it, the friars were often indistinguishable from explorers, engineers, or military captains.[23] The Bahian Director of Indians complained that the lack of Capuchins in the forested valleys of Porto Seguro and Caravelas was encouraging the Mongoiós, Kamakãs, and Botocudos to "commit

---

[21] John Hemming, *Amazon Frontier: The Defeat of the Brazilian Indians* (Cambridge, MA: Harvard University Press, 1987), 177–79; Manuela Carneiro da Cunha (ed.), *Legislação indigenista no século XIX: uma compilação, 1808–1889* (São Paulo: Comissão Pró-Indio de São Paulo, 1992), 191–99.

    For an in-depth discussion of the Regulation, see Sampaio, "Política indigenista." Sampaio contests the idea that there was a vacuum in Indian legislation between the Directorate's abrogation and the Regulation by noting how local legislations remained in effect and were strengthened by the 1834 Additional Act.

[22] There were a few present since 1840, but the official agreement took place in 1843. Jacinto de Palazzolo, *Nas selvas dos vales do Mucuri e do Rio Doce, como surgiu a cidade de Itambacuri, fundada por Frei Serafim de Gorizia, missionario capuchino, 1873–1952* (São Paulo: Companhia Editora Nacional, 1954), 38. Italian Franciscan (but not Capuchin) missions exercised a similar role in frontier settlement in the Andes during the postcolonial era. Erick D. Langer, *Expecting Pears from an Elm Tree: Franciscan Missions on the Chiriguano Frontier in the Heart of South America, 1830–1949* (Durham, NC: Duke University Press, 2009).

[23] Antonio Luiz de Magalhães Musqueira, "Relatório do Diretor dos índios de Minas Gerais," 1876, 137, CRL.

hostilities and murders" and quickly retreat into the forests.[24] Directing our attention to the Atlantic frontier shows how the state's acculturative indigenous policies were enforced on the ground. For example, in March 1845, a few months before the law's official promulgation, the Italian Capuchin Frei Caetano de Troina was sent to catechize the Botocudo near the dilapidated hamlet of São José de Porto Alegre at the mouth of the Mucuri River, notorious for its involvement in the illegal kuruka trade. The friar joined a seventy-four member expedition that traveled upriver to identify the locations for an aldeia and an accompanying military colony that was to provide protection. He erected a cross in the local mountains and settled in to spread the gospel among "savages and cannibals." He was certain that "catechism [would be] very easy" once a farm was up and running and a few men and a lingua were sent to keep him company.[25] In November he reported that the "savages, though a little ferocious, are very disposed to become civilized."[26] He was remarkably optimistic during his first year.

Missionary letters expose the fissures in the Regulamento's objectives that led to its swift disintegration, visible in the speed with which Frei Caetano's optimism surrendered to solitude, tropical fevers, and the disease-ridden climate. Over the course of a year, the friar had descended into a state of permanent rage and fear. He would "never settle the Mucuri Indians." At the root of his rage was a profound feeling of betrayal, born from the realization that his missionary work had not made the progress he had initially perceived. His anger was only heightened by the admiration he had developed for them. The Botocudo were endowed with "much vivacity, lightness, and intelligence. For this they are distinguished." And yet their wish to have a priest among them was an "absolute lie," he seethed, for why would they flee from him, who had been so kind to them?[27] The Botocudo of the Mucuri Valley, like those seen in Chapter 2, had probably joined Frei Caetano's aldeia only insofar as it supplemented

---

[24] Casimiro de Sena Madureira, Director of Indians of Bahia, "Relatório do Diretor Geral dos índios da Bahia," February 19, 1852, 1, CRL.

[25] Hermenegildo Antonio Barbosa d'Almeida, "Viagem ás vilas de Caravelas, Viçosa, Porto Alegre, de Mucury, e aos rios Mucury, e Peruípe," *RIHGB* 8, no. 4 (1846): 435, 442–45; Fr. Caetano de Troina to President of Bahia, August 24, 1845, Colonial/Justiça/Caravelas/Mc 2330, APEB.

[26] Fr. Caetano de Troina to Caetano Vicente de Almeida, Jr., November 30, 1845, Colonial/Justiça/Caravelas/Mc 2333, APEB.

[27] Fr. Caetano de Troina, March 20, 1846, Colonial/Justiça/Caravelas/Mc 2333, APEB; Fr. Caetano de Troina to President of Bahia, September 24, 1846, Colonial/Justiça/Caravelas/Mc 2333, APEB.

their hunting and foraging and left when it no longer met their needs. As one lay observer would succinctly note, "[a]s long as there are tools, trinkets, and food there is a semblance of an aldeiamento – but when these government supplies cease, the priests and Indians disappear!"[28]

The Indians' point of view was completely lost on Frei Caetano, however, who angrily accused them of arrogance and laziness and disparaged them for wasting their physical strength on ambush and murder instead of learning the ways of work. He also considered the "closed forest" in which they lived, with no visible roads, trails, nor agriculture, as evidence of their incapacity for civilization.[29] Ire, disappointment, and disgust ultimately led Frei Caetano to abandon the central tenet of catechism – brandura – and openly endorse the residents' anti-indigenous violence. Previously warring Puri, Botocudo, and Maxacali groups joined forces against the settlers in response. The friar withdrew to Salvador to convalesce and was subsequently transferred to another province. Sent to frontier indigenous territory to enforce the state's civilizatory policy, Frei Caetano was eventually driven to empathize with the settlers' culture of terror, exposing the ease with which agents of Indian "civilization" could transgress the blurry boundaries of brandura and violence.[30]

Gentle policies did survive in some quarters. Some of the most vocal advocates emerged among lay proponents of the region's economic development, who considered Indian settlement essential to its success. The most prominent among them was the senator Teófilo Ottoni (1807–69), a leading liberal and republican from a well-connected mineiro family who withdrew from politics after an 1848 Conservative victory at the polls. Ottoni began his own exploration of Botocudo territory in the Mucuri Valley the year after Frei Caetano's departure from the region, founding the Mucuri Company in 1851. Like his countless predecessors and successors, Ottoni's goal was to encourage agriculture in northern Minas and establish lucrative commercial routes linking the landlocked province with the Atlantic by opening navigation on the Mucuri River from Santa Clara inland to São José de Porto Alegre on the Atlantic.[31]

---

[28] José Candido da Costa, *Comarca de Caravellas. Creação de uma nova província, sendo capital a cidade de Caravellas* (Bahia: Typographia de Camillo de Lellis Masson & C., 1857), 17.

[29] Troina to president of Bahia, September 24, 1846.   [30] Ibid.

[31] For more on the company's history, see Teófilo Benedito Ottoni, *Condições para a encorporação de uma companhia de commercio e navegação do rio Mucury, precedidas de uma exposição das vantagens da empreza* (Rio de Janeiro: Typographia de J. Villeneuve, 1847); Teófilo Benedito Ottoni, *Notícia sobre os selvagens do Mucuri*

His early years among the Botocudo were chronicled in his "News on the Savages of Mucuri" (1858), published in the *RIHGB* and reprinted extensively in the newspaper *Correio Mercantil*. A great admirer of US republicanism and William Penn, Ottoni founded a town in northeastern Minas that he named Filadélfia (today Teófilo Otoni) along with a military outpost called Urucú. He also began a colony of German immigrants in their vicinity with the hopes of transforming the forests into cultivated land.[32]

As he made his way into Botocudo territory, Ottoni became "convinced that the savages' aggressions against the Christians was almost always incited by the latter's violence and provocations" and deemed that "a system of generosity, moderation, and brandura could win their benevolence." Ottoni was particularly critical of the rampant kuruka slavery taking place in the region and was determined to convince the Indians that the "new process of catechism" need not rely on violence. Whenever he traveled into Botocudo territory, Ottoni's party dispensed gifts of tools and food among the Indians to show that they were "tame" and disposed to win them over with kindness.[33]

Ottoni established a foothold among the Naknenuk Botocudo in the Mucuri Valley by working in a private–state partnership with his brother Augusto, who was the local Director of Indians. The brothers consolidated their position through patronage ties with local Indians. One such figure was Poton, one of the Botocudo *caciques*, who welcomed Ottoni as his own relative and encouraged him to invite his extended family into the region, as "the lands abounded and were enough for everyone."[34] The Ottonis obliged by clearing the forest and establishing three "magnificent

---

(Belo Horizonte: Editora UFMG, 2002); *Companhia do Mucury. História da empresa. Importância dos seus privilégios. Alcance de seus projetos.* (Rio de Janeiro: Typographia Imperial e Constitucional de J. Villeneuve e comp., 1856); Izabel Missagia de Mattos, *Civilização e revolta: os Botocudos e a catequese na província de Minas* (São Paulo: EDUSC ANPOCS, 2004), 104–9.

[32] Judy Bieber, "'Philadelphia' in Minas Gerais: Teófilo Otoni's North American Vision for Indigenous Brazil," paper presented at Linguistic and Other Cultural Exchanges across Brazilian History: The Indigenous Role, University of Chicago, Chicago, IL, October 2016.

[33] Ottoni, *Notícia*, 51. The immigrant colony project was a disaster and the object of a diatribe by the German Robert Avé-Lallemant, an avid opponent of European emigration to Brazil. Robert Avé-Lallemant, *Viagem pelo norte do Brasil no ano de 1859* (Rio de Janeiro: Instituto Nacional do Livro, Ministério da Educação e Cultura, 1961), 157–267; see also Santos, "French Travelers and Journalists Debate the Lei Do Ventre Livre of 1871," 228–29.

[34] Ottoni, *Notícia*, 62–63.

fazendas" worked by 150 black slaves, a point of pride for Ottoni, a vocal critic of kuruka slavery. They gathered the Botocudo onto aldeias and reparceled out the land they had been living on with titles. They also leased the Indians out to settlers. Many Indians fled these often unremunerated labor obligations, an example of which were the Botocudo discussed in Chapter 2, who fled the farm where they had been working with their enslaved co-workers. They hailed from the Ottoni-administered aldeia of Corsiumas. Ottoni appeared oblivious to such tribulations and claimed that all the Indians came to rely on Augusto, who won their confidence by dispensing "not only justice, but also benevolence" to resolve any conflicts.[35]

Paternalism's fusion of kindness and violence was familiar to Ottoni, whose benevolence assumed a chilling turn when the Indians did not comply with his vision of landownership. He disparaged the cacique João Imã and his group who "dared to appear in the military colony and talk to the director in an arrogant tone, not showing their thankfulness for the gifts they had received, and protesting against the Christians, who were taking their lands."[36] Ottoni included a conversion narrative in which he enlightened disobedient Indians. Two caciques, Timoteo and Ninkaté, had initially "declared with arrogance that the whites should be content with the land they had already taken!" Yet after receiving the Ottonis' gifts and kindness, they had a change of heart. The Director of Indians registered land titles for Timoteo's group and assigned the rest to Ottoni's Company. Timoteo and his people, now grateful, "would risk their lives to defend the property that the Company gave them." Like a loyal slave of planter fantasies, the cacique later proved his dedication by endangering his own life to defend the Ottonis from an ambush by other Botocudo, who had told Timoteo that the whites were taking their lands.[37]

Unlike Frei Caetano de Troina, Ottoni never came to advocate violence. Yet his utter conviction in the gentleness of his civilizing methods enabled him to expropriate indigenous lands and forcefully reorganize and destabilize intra-Indian relations. A keen critic of anti-indigenous violence, Ottoni kept himself dissociated from the violence he helped unleash, all in the name of brandura.

Vanishing Indians, Disappearing Pasts

Ottoni's success in establishing himself in the Mucuri River Valley – even as his Mucuri company and immigrant colony were headed toward

---

[35] Ibid., 64–65.   [36] Ibid., 84.   [37] Ibid., 62–69.

failure and liquidation by 1861 – inspired him and others to advocate for an even more ambitious goal: the creation of a new province that would unite the wealth of landlocked Minas Gerais with the Atlantic. In 1857 a Caravelas local named José Cândido da Costa proposed the creation of an independent province called Santa Cruz, comprising the southern Bahian comarcas of Porto Seguro and Caravelas, the Espírito Santense comarca of São Mateus, and the northern Minas comarca of Jequitinhonha. Costa argued that the region's economic development was harmed by its subordination to the interests of its distant provincial capitals and especially its "stepmother," the city of Salvador. By this he was referring to Salvador's blocking the creation of a customs house in Caravelas that would enable it to trade directly with foreign markets in the United States and Europe. Instead, all of its exports and imports were forced to go through either Salvador or Rio de Janeiro.

Although outwardly supporting Ottoni's ventures, Costa was wary of the senator's attempts to establish Filadélfia as the new provincial capital and contended that Caravelas, with its ample port and close proximity to Colônia Leopoldina and the mineiro city of Santa Clara, was uniquely qualified to lead the new province. He was eager to capitalize on the expansion of coffee production, which was already "dethroning" manioc with an annual production of 200,000 arrobas, three-quarters of which came from Colônia Leopoldina.[38] The coffee frontier would soon expand into the indigenous hinterland of São Mateus as well, where in the 1860s and 1870s, the region's wealthiest families, consolidating into a regional oligarchy, began amassing large land holdings to cultivate the crop.[39]

It was in the second half of the nineteenth century, as locals of the Atlantic frontier were advocating for a new province, that the discourse about Indians began to transform at the national and provincial levels. These changes were deeply entwined with issues of territorial control and would fundamentally impact the course of subsequent indigenous policy. Complaints about Indian "infestation" were increasingly overshadowed by a new phenomenon: the disappearance and extinction of Indians and their aldeias. Such was the transformation that by 1873 the Minister of Agriculture, Commerce, and Public Works (MACOP) remarked that the "[Bahian] aldeamentos ... can be considered virtually extinct." The

---

[38] Costa, *Comarca de Caravellas; Cia. do Mucury*, 26–28; Avé-Lallemant, *Viagem pelo norte do Brasil no ano de 1859*, 152–53.

[39] Anna Lucia Côgo, "História do Espírito Santo no século XIX: a região de São Mateus" (doctoral dissertation, Universidade de São Paulo, 2007), 165–89. Some of these figures, such as Major Antônio Rodrigues da Cunha and the Barão of Timbuhy, also occupied high positions in the National Guard.

degradation was so advanced that the aldeias were "in ruins, lacking support and no longer convenient for their residents to remain on the land."[40] Indian extinction had raised concerns and attracted advocates since independence, especially during and soon after the Botocudo Wars. Yet it was only in the 1860s that it increasingly began to assume the guise of incontrovertible fact.[41]

Because aldeias were at the heart of national Indianist policy, their extinction suggests the total failure of the 1845 Regulation, whose objective was to relocate Indians onto them in order to "civilize" them for national inclusion. The Regulation did have some very vocal critics, including Varnhagen, who ranted that "far from helping improve matters, all it did was legalize or increase abuses." He also attacked the Capuchins whose efforts he found "costly and useless."[42] A skeptic of brandura policy, Varnhagen continued to advocate brute force to subjugate Indians. "Over a half-century of experience has shown the insufficiency of gentle means, which are the most damaging for the state," he argued, later urging, "[w]ithout the use of force it is not possible to reduce the savages, just as it is not possible to have society without punishment for delinquents." His most outrageous proposal was to reinitiate a just war to capture and reduce Indians into "temporary captivity" in service of their captors, with the goal of eventually making them into "exemplary citizens and good Christians." Since Indians were foreign to the social pact, he claimed that "we have all the right to conquer them, with no right to conquest more just than that of civilization over barbarism."[43] Varnhagen's proposals caused an uproar among the liberal readership and editors of the Romantic *Guanabara* magazine, where his original article appeared in 1851 and that he unrepentantly reprinted in 1867.

---

[40] José Fernandes da Costa Pereira Junior, "Relatório do Ministério da Agricultura," 1873, 200–201, CRL. Italics mine.

[41] Manoel Vieira de Albuquerque Tovar, "Informação de Manoel Vieira de Albuquerque Tovar sobre a navegação importantíssima do Rio Doce, copiada de un manuscrito oferecido ao Instituto pelo socio correspondente o Sr. José Domingues de Athaíde de Moncorvo," *RIHGB* 1 (1839): 134–38. This article, which advocates Indian extermination in Minas and Espírito Santo, was originally written during the early years of the Botocudo Wars in 1810. That it was reprinted eight years after the Wars officially ended reveals the enduring popularity of the idea.

[42] Francisco Adolfo de Varnhagen, *Os Indios bravos e o sr. Lisboa, Timon 3: Pelo autor da "Historia geral do Brazil." Apostilla e nota G aos nos. 11 e 12 do "Jornal de Timon"; contendo 26 cartas ineditas do jornalista, e um extracto do folheto "Diatribe contra a Timonice,"* etc (Lima: Imprensa Liberal, 1867), 38, 43–56. Varnhagen also criticized the Jesuits for protecting the Indians during the colonial period in *História Geral*.

[43] Varnhagen, "Memorial orgânico," 396–97.

Yet if these differences between advocates of violent and gentle methods of Indian civilization seemed irreconcilable, in reality the twin pillars of brandura policy that the Regulation of Missions promoted – acculturation and miscegenation – were themselves designed to orchestrate Indian "disappearance." In this regard, the 1845 Regulation was a resounding success. Following its promulgation, in the second half of the nineteenth century, legal reforms, including those that purported to protect Indians, melded with discursive manipulations and cultural and biological ideas of race to legalize Indian expropriation and produce a convincing case of their disappearance from Brazilian soil.

Five years after the Regulation, the Brazilian government issued a landmark law that would have a devastating impact on the indigenous population: the Land Law of 1850. This law, followed by the transfer in 1861 of Indian civilization and catechism from the Ministry of the Empire to the Directory of Public Lands under the newly established Ministry of Agriculture, Colonization, and Public Works (MACOP), marked the state's definitive merger of indigenous and territorial interests. The incorporation of Indians into the national body as citizens thus became inseparable from the integration of frontier territory into the nation.[44] Brazil offered an early example of land reforms that would take place in postcolonial Spanish American nations where latifundia consolidation in frontier territories unleashed waves of violence on local populations. Executed nominally to reform colonial land tenure, these transformations eroded protections for the indigenous and other socioeconomically vulnerable groups in the decades following independence. This was a period, as Erick Langer has stated, "in which both Chile and Argentina launched their invasions of Araucanian territories to the south, Mexico attacked and beat the Yaquis, the Tarahumara in northern Mexico and the Mayas in Yucatán, and the Putumayo River scandal uncovered the horrendous labor conditions under which rubber workers were subjected in the Peruvian Amazon." In Brazil, the seizure of indigenous land fused with the production of indigenous extinction.[45]

---

44 Scholars who have argued for the explicit relationship between Indian administration and territorial colonization include Sampaio, "Política indigenista"; Kodama, *Os índios no Império do Brasil*; Cunha, *Legislação indigenista*.
45 Erick D. Langer, "The Eastern Andean Frontier (Bolivia and Argentina) and Latin American Frontiers: Comparative Contexts (19th and 20th Centuries)," *The Americas* 59, no. 1 (2002): 53. See, for example, John Womack, *Zapata and the Mexican Revolution* (New York: Vintage Books, 1970); Slatta, *Gauchos and the Vanishing Frontier*; Ligia Osorio Silva and María Verónica Secreto, "Terras públicas, ocupação privada: elementos para a história comparada da apropriação territorial na Argentina e no Brasil," *Economia e Sociedade* 8, no. 1 (1999): 109–41; Walter Mario Delrio, *Memorias de expropiación:*

The Land Law's primary objective was to reform chaotic land titles throughout Brazil. This had resulted from the absence of any regulations since independence, a situation that had encouraged individuals to claim land through possession. Article 5 of the Land Law legitimized "tame and peaceful" holdings acquired through primary occupancy. This suggests Indians' right to the land, but the latter had to be cultivated. Scholars have disagreed on whether the law recognized the Indians' original rights to their land. During the Pombaline era, allied and mission Indians on aldeias were given land grants (sesmarias), a condition that the Indians sometimes asserted in order to reaffirm their land rights. Although the sesmaria system was suspended in 1822, existing sesmaria holders nominally held onto their titles.[46] Individuals who affirmed Indian land rights included José Bonifácio, who declared in his 1823 "Notes" that they are the "legitimate *senhores* (of the land) that God gave them," and Guido Marlière, the French-born Director of Indians of the Doce River, who advocated demarcating Indian territories "in order to avoid confusing Indians' properties with those of sesmaria recipients, and avoid dissensions among them."[47] The enduring confusion over Indian land ownership was captured by a newspaper piece in 1871 that argued, "since the *lands that belong to the State*... [find] themselves in the hands of their *natural proprietors*, the creation of aldeias for the catechism of these same masters would be convenient." In characteristic fashion, Varnhagen denied the Botocudo their right to land by alleging that they were nomadic intruders and not original owners of the territories they inhabited.[48]

   sometimiento e incorporación indígena en la Patagonia, 1872–1943 (Bernal, Buenos Aires: Universidad Nacional de Quilmes, 2005).

[46] Cunha, *Legislação indigenista*, 19–20; Maria Regina Celestino de Almeida, "Reflexões sobre política indigenista e cultura política indígena no Rio de Janiero oitocentista," *Revista USP* 79 (2008): 94–105.

[47] Bonifácio, *Projetos para o Brasil*, 102; Leda Maria Cardoso Naud, "Documentos sôbre o índio brasileiro, 2a parte," *Revista de informação legislativa* 8, no. 29 (1971): 312. Marlière appears to have differentiated Indians from non-Indian *sesmeiros*. Manuela Carneiro da Cunha and Carlos Gileno contend that laws did explicitly recognize their right to land ownership, while James Holston argues it was ambiguous, with the Crown asserting "original possession" over all lands. For the relationship between late nineteenth century indigenous policy and José Bonifácio see João Pacheco de Oliveira, "'Wild Indians,' Tutelary Roles, and Moving Frontier in Amazonia: Images of Indians in the Birth of Brazil," in *Manifest Destinies and Indigenous Peoples*, ed. David Maybury-Lewis, Theodore Macdonald, and Biorn Maybury-Lewis (Cambridge, MA: Harvard University Press, 2009), 90–100; Manuela Carneiro da Cunha, *Antropologia do Brasil: mito, história, etnicidade* (São Paulo: Editora Brasiliense, 1986), 165–73.

[48] "S. Matheus," *O Estandarte*, July 30, 1871, italics mine; Varnhagen, "Memorial orgânico," 393.

Another important article in the Land Law regarding indigenous lands was Article 12, which stated that "the government will reserve *terras devolutas* necessary to the colonization of Indians." Under the Land Law, terras devolutas became part of the public domain and were differentiated from private lands. A deeply contested category, terras devolutas were, according to James Holston, "those holdings returned to Crown patrimony for violating their terms of concession. It was also common, though perhaps not technically legal, to use the expression to mean empty or unoccupied lands." By legalizing both the formal and common definitions, the law marked a turning point in the history of terras devolutas, fundamentally impacting Indians' rights to the land.[49]

While the Land Law suggested a great stride in the arena of indigenous land rights, in practice its enforcement was easily subverted. This was particularly the case when it was combined with the Regulation. First of all, although Article 5 implied that Indians had land rights by primary occupancy, it was contradicted by Article 12, which did not guarantee those rights, instead reserving terras devolutas that the state would allocate for Indian settlement. One scholar has argued that the Land Law thereby transformed the Indians' condition from natural owners of the land into that of the expropriated who depended on the State's largesse to possess something that used to be theirs.[50] Another related problem was the Land Law's vagueness about whom it considered to be Indian. A decree in 1854 stated that "terras devolutas will be reserved for the colonization and settlement of Indians in districts where there are savage hordes." Yet, in a striking parallel to the Constituent Assembly debates on Indian citizenship discussed in Chapter 1, the law was silent on mission Indians who already held titles to sesmarias and aldeia lands prior to 1850.[51] Second, the Regulation's practice of resettling Indians onto aldeias concentrated them onto small plots of land, leaving their original territories to be, in fact, classified as empty and hence, terras devolutas. Local Municipal Chambers who stood to profit from land sales were unsurprisingly at the forefront of Indian resettlement.[52]

---

[49] James Holston, *Insurgent Citizenship: Disjunctions of Democracy and Modernity in Brazil* (Princeton, NJ: Princeton University Press, 2008), 148, 337–38, n. 43; Ligia Osorio Silva, *Terras devolutas e latifúndio: efeitos da lei de 1850* (Campinas, SP: Editora da UNICAMP, 1996), 173–74; Vânia Moreira, "Terras Indígenas do Espírito Santo sob o Regime Territorial de 1850," *Revista Brasileira de História* 22, no. 43 (2002): 158–59.

[50] da Cunha, *Legislação indigenista*, 16; José Mauro Gagliardi as cited in Silva, *Terras devolutas e latifúndio*, 186.

[51] Moreira, "Terras Indígenas do Espírito Santo sob o Regime Territorial de 1850," 161.

[52] Cunha, *Legislação indigenista*, 18–22.

The effects of the two laws were soon evident. Reports of Indian extinction were seen in Ceará in the 1850s, and by the early 1860s the Espírito Santo provincial government deemed the São Mateus hinterland to be "entirely devolutas and without inhabitants," and therefore ideal for colonization.[53] Indian extinction was followed by aldeia disappearances. In the 1870s, Bahian officials noted a precipitous decline in aldeamentos from 1860, when there were twenty-nine, to a decade later when they were reportedly down to twenty-one, many of which "could not be considered as such." The chronic lack of information due to underfunding and administrative negligence made an accurate assessment of the aldeias difficult.[54] During the same period in northern Espírito Santo, more than 1,000 autonomous Botocudo Indians allegedly continued to inhabit the region spanning the hinterlands of São Mateus and the Doce River to the south.[55] Yet the São Mateus Municipal Chamber observed in 1878 that "nothing exists that proves that there were any lands belonging to the Indians."[56] In the 1870s a series of decrees were issued aimed at surveying and dismantling aldeias throughout the country. By the early 1880s, there was only one verifiable aldeamento remaining in the entire province, further south in Mutum by the Doce River. If the aldeias were deemed extinct, the lands were reverted to the state, and later, to the provinces, and were sold or leased to interested parties by the local Municipal Chamber. The Bahian president already had complained presciently, in 1847, that Indians' lands were "usurped by local powerholders. The Municipal Chambers and clergy who should attend to their needs, one in the temporal realm, the other in the spiritual, sometimes cause the harm."[57]

---

[53] André Augusto de Padua Fleury, "Relatório (ES)," 1863, 25, CRL.

[54] Paschoal Pereira de Mattos to Viscount of Sergimirim, Director of Indians of Bahia, October 20, 1870, Colonial/Agricultura/Índios/Mc 4614, APEB; Viscount of Sergimirim, Director of Indians of Bahia to President of Bahia, March 22, 1879, Colonial/Agricultura/Índios/Mc 4614, APEB.

[55] Antonio Dias Paes Leme, "Relatório (ES)," 1870, 20, CRL; Thomaz José Coelho de Almeida, "Relatório do Ministério da Agricultura," 1876, 178–79, CRL.

[56] Paço da Câmara Municipal de São Mateus (São Mateus, November 8, 1878), Governadoria Ser. Accioly. Liv. 353, Fl. 373, APEES.

[57] Pereira Junior, "Relatório do Ministério da Agricultura," 210; Ministério dos Negócios da Justiça to President of Espírito Santo, September 12, 1881, Polícia Ser. 2 Cx. 72 Maço 265 Fl. 134, APEES; Antonio Ignacio de Azevedo, President of Bahia, "Falla (BA)," 1847, 14, CRL. For examples of aldeia extinction, see Decision 272 – July 8, 1875; Decree 2672 – October 20, 1875; Decision 127 of March 8, 1878. For these and other legislations see Cunha, *Legislação indigenista*.

Along with legislation, racial thought and in particular miscegenation were equally essential to the invention of Indian extinction. Race and law fused seamlessly.[58] The Land Law incorporated aldeia lands into national territory if they were inhabited by "dispersed Indians living confused among the civilized masses."[59] This language was ominously echoed by the Minister of Agriculture, who in 1873 claimed that the extinct aldeias' "primitive inhabitants were *mixed up in the general population* of the country, such that having changed their habits and customs, *they forgot their ancestors' language and are Indians in name only.*"[60] Such words indicate how colonial constructions of race as defined by quality (habits, customs, language) continued to determine who was Indian – or no longer qualified as such – in the late nineteenth century. However, new ideas of biological determinism were also evident. The Regulation allowed for aldeia lands to be leased out to non-Indians and encouraged the general population to settle around aldeias in order to promote acculturation and miscegenation among Indians and non-Indians. This very practice encouraged Indians to become "mixed up" among the latter and thereby "lose" what officials deemed to be their Indianness via both cultural transformation and biological miscegenation. Capuchin missionaries believed that miscegenation would have a taming effect on "wild" Indians.[61] The Land Law, combined with the Regulation of Missions, thus created a facile means by which those coveting indigenous lands could make Indians disappear simply by claiming that they were no longer genuinely indigenous. Freedpeople and the poor were also displaced because of their inability to produce documentary proof of their rights of land occupation or pay the taxes to have their properties registered. Large landowners were the Land Law's primary beneficiaries.[62]

However, if miscegenation was the method by which the Brazilian elite hoped to incorporate black and indigenous people into a homogeneous povo brasileiro, not all miscegenation was deemed positive. For instance, the Bahian Director of Indians, Father Manoel Cunha, utilized evidence of miscegenation to validate Indian disappearance, but did so disparagingly. Speaking of the Aricobé mission in northern Bahia, the

---

[58] Moreira, "História, etnia e nação," 70–71.
[59] Manuela Carneiro da Cunha, "Legislação indigenista no séc. XIX,", 141, 145.
[60] Pereira Junior, "Relatório do Ministério da Agricultura," 200–1, italics mine.
[61] Mattos, *Civilização e revolta*, 347.
[62] Ilka Boaventura Leite, "The Transhistorical, Juridical-Formal, and Post-Utopian Quilombo," in *New Approaches to Resistance in Brazil and Mexico*, ed. John Gledhill and Patience A Schell (Durham, NC: Duke University Press, 2012), 257–58.

priest claimed that the aldeias there were extinct, since only mestiços and mamelucos inhabited the lands.[63] The mission had transformed into a refuge for vagabonds, assassins, and thieves, "supposed Indians" who were in fact "pardos, crioulos, mulatos and cabras." Rather than making racial progress toward a whitened homogeneity, he believed the Indians had degenerated toward blackness. He accused the largely black mixed-race residents of falsely claiming to be Indian in order to squat on mission land. In Father Cunha's vision, the preponderance of blackness among the miscegenated inhabitants converged with their moral degeneration to produce individuals who were "turbulent and rabblerousing, insubordinate; in sum, a horde of bandits."[64] Such qualitative definitions of race and miscegenation were not new; yet, it was in the later nineteenth century that they were used to validate indigenous extinction from the national territory. The irony of the Aricobé mission's racial transformation was that the Indians were disappearing, not by whitening toward civilization, but by blackening toward depravity. On the other hand, the same sources also suggest the increasing presence of African-descended free and freed-people on and around mission lands that engendered black–indigenous unions.[65]

As Ivana Stolze Lima has noted in her study of the transformations in the language utilized to describe color and race in Imperial Brazilian censuses, the 1872 National Census was the first time that Indians were

---

[63] Brazilian, and by extension Latin American, racial terminology is a tremendously complex and even byzantine topic that many scholars continue to grapple with. Although the significance of these terms varies somewhat depending on the location and period, in general, *mestiços* were people of mixed race who were often but not always Indian and white. *Mamelucos* were the offspring of an Indian and a white person, and are generally associated with the first generation of mixed-race Brazilians born in the early years of colonial settlement. As much as the Brazilian state promoted miscegenation, there was a pervasive suspicion of mixed-race people as being morally ambiguous, if not degenerate.

[64] Father Manoel Ferreira Santos Cunha, Director of Indians, "Report on the Old Aldeia Called Mission of Aricobé in the Old Parish of Sant'Anna, Termo of the Town of Campo Largo, Province of Bahia" August 16, 1869, Colonial/Agricultura/Índios/Mc 4614, APEB.

[65] A comparison of the registry of Aricobé mission Indians and the census for the parish indicates that the majority of the local residents were in fact of African descent by 1872 – an "unmarked" quality in the Director of Indian's report – probably rendering the two groups physically indistinguishable. Hence, in order to differentiate the black-miscegenated mission Indians from the other residents, described as "honest" folk who were in earnest need for the mission's land for cultivation, the Director resorted to descriptions of moral degeneration as evidence that these were ersatz Indians. Colonial concepts of race as "*qualidade*" thus remained effective even as scientific racism was supposedly coming to predominate in Brazilian racial thought.

included as *"caboclos,"* a term that generally signified the miscegenation of Indian and white or Indian and black, depending on the region.[66] This discursive alteration from Indian to caboclo implied not only the Indians' miscegenation but also their assimilation because, as we have seen, race mixture and cultural transformation were never cognitively distinct. Thus in using the census as a means to assert its centralizing power over its disparate and distant subjects, the Brazilian state expressed its deeply racialized vision of nationhood. By officializing the caboclo category, it affirmed that Indians were included in the nation only insofar as they were already on the path toward "de-Indianization." Counting Indians as caboclos projected an image of racial harmony and order while simultaneously disappearing them from the national territory, rendering increasingly possible the imagining of a Brazilian nationhood in which Indians and blacks were merely elements of an ever-whitening people.

Indigenismo, Africans, and the National Past

Protected and disappeared, praised yet detested, there was one area in which the Brazilian Indian was unquestionably beloved: the arts. Postcolonial Latin American elites seeking a unique and distinctly non-Iberian heritage for their new nations found a perfect symbol in the pre-Columbian or early colonial Indian. Just as the elite leadership of Spanish America who disparaged their indigenous populations saw no problem in claiming a neo-Inca or neo-Aztec genealogy, the Indian became a central trope of the Brazilian elite's postcolonial invention of a national identity.[67] Such contradictory assessments of the indigenous were assuaged by what John Monteiro has called a form of racial thought

---

[66] Ivana Stolze Lima, *Cores, marcas e falas: sentidos da mestiçagem no Império do Brasil* (Rio de Janeiro: Arquivo Nacional, 2003), 120.

[67] See, for example, Sommer, *Foundational Fictions*; Charles Walker, *Smoldering Ashes: Cuzco and the Creation of Republican Peru, 1780–1840* (Durham, NC: Duke University Press, 1999); Cadena, *Indigenous Mestizos*; Lilia Moritz Schwarcz, *The Emperor's Beard: Dom Pedro II and His Tropical Monarchy in Brazil*, trans. John Gledson (Hill and Wang, 2003); Mark Thurner, "Peruvian Genealogies of History and Nation," in *After Spanish Rule: Postcolonial Predicaments of the Americas*, ed. Andrés Guerrero and Mark Thurner (Durham, NC: Duke University Press, 2003); Earle, *The Return of the Native*; Darlene J. Sadlier, *Brazil Imagined: 1500 to the Present* (Austin: University of Texas Press, 2008); Laura Gotkowitz, *Histories of Race and Racism: The Andes and Mesoamerica from Colonial Times to the Present* (Durham, NC: Duke University Press, 2012); Tracy Devine Guzmán, *Native and National in Brazil: Indigeneity after Independence* (Chapel Hill: University of North Carolina Press, 2013).

in Brazil prior to the spread of racial science. Injecting new blood into the colonial dichotomy of Tupi and Tapuia, or "good" and "bad" Indians, the postcolonial elite romanticized the Tupi as the originators of Brazilian nationality located in a distant colonial past. The Tupi had, in this imagination, helped and mixed with the early colonists but had conveniently disappeared as a people. The Tapuia had, by contrast, refused to submit to colonial rule and for this reason had, unfortunately, continued to survive. In this imagined genealogy, the Botocudo were the Tapuia's modern-day heirs. Their hold on the present was, however, becoming increasingly tenuous.[68]

Literary and artistic representations are arguably the one area in which the study of nineteenth-century Brazilian Indians has thrived. The purpose of this section is therefore to provide an overview of this movement known as "Romantic Indianism" in order to demonstrate its inseparability from the larger context of postcolonial indigenous and land policy, citizenship debates, and anti-indigenous violence. Only then can we understand Romantic Indianism beyond the framework of elite nationalism and see its role in the production of indigenous extinction.

The Tupi were the stars of Romantic Indianism. Embodying the tropical noble savage, they served as a "mythified Indian" who "allowed the young nation to discover an honorable past and foretell a promising future." Helming the effort was Brazil's most prominent Indigenist, the Emperor Pedro II himself, who flaunted his knowledge of Nheengatu (the Tupi-Guarani *lingua geral* standardized by the Jesuits) and dispensed indigenous titles to his aristocratic entourage.[69] The Botocudo Guido Pokrane, as we have seen, knew very well how to tap into Pedro II's indigenist sympathies. The monarch encouraged the Imperial Academy of Fine Arts, the producer of "all the official images of the empire," to celebrate Brazilian nationhood by creating works inspired by early colonial chronicles that featured Romantic Indians. Frequently depicted near death or as recently deceased, these mythified Indians, always confined to the distant past, helped forge a narrative of the nation's indigenous origins while simultaneously reinforcing the idea of indigenous extinction in the present. For instance, Victor Meirelles' "Moema" (1866) (Figure 3.1) and Rodolfo Amoedo's "Last Tamoio" (1883) were French academic-style paintings that depicted nearly naked

---

[68] John M. Monteiro, "As 'raças' indígenas no pensamento brasileiro do império," in *Raça, ciência e sociedade*, ed. Marcos Chor Maio and Ricardo Ventura Santos (Rio de Janeiro: Editora FIOCRUZ, 1996), 16–17; Cunha, "Introdução a uma história indígena," 136.

[69] Schwarcz, *The Emperor's Beard*, 108–13; Oliveira, "'Wild Indians,' Tutelary Roles," 100–102; Monteiro, "As 'raças' indígenas," 16.

FIGURE 3.1 Victor Meirelles, *Moema*, 1866. Oil on canvas, 130 × 196.5 cm Inv. 267P. As in many nineteenth-century Latin American nations, Romantic Indianists in Brazil celebrated idealized Indians of the distant colonial past who assisted Portuguese colonization and paved the way for the eventual birth of the nation. Such depictions reinforced the belief in the "extinction" of indigenous people in the present, particularly the Botocudo. Courtesy of the Museu de Arte de São Paulo Assis Chateaubriand. Photo by João Musa.

Indians languidly drawing their last breath on Brazilian shores. In the "Last Tamoio," the Indian chief lay cradled in the arms of the Jesuit Father José de Anchieta as he received his last rites. Amoedo based his painting on Romantic author Gonçalves de Magalhães' *The Tamoio Confederation* (1857), a fictionalized account of a sixteenth-century battle between the Tamoio Indians and Portuguese forces.[70]

Literary authors also embraced the mythified Indian in their oeuvre. Along with the aforementioned Magalhães, poet Gonçalves Dias (an editor of the *Guanabara* magazine where Varnhagen published his diatribe) and novelist José de Alencar celebrated Brazil's indigenous heritage. Alencar's Indianist trilogy *O Guarani* (1857), *Iracema* (1865), and *Ubirajara* (1874), all set in the early colonial period, defined a distinctly Brazilian national history and culture through the mining of indigenous traditions. *Iracema* (an anagram for America), for example, celebrated the union of an Indian woman and a Portuguese man that engendered the first

---

[70] Schwarcz, *The Emperor's Beard*, 108–17; Kodama, *Os índios no Império do Brasil*, 108–18; Monteiro, "Tupis, Tapuias," 147–48.

Brazilian. In line with the promotion of mestiçagem in nineteenth-century indigenous policy, *Iracema* depicted mestiços, and not Indians, as the true Brazilians, reinforcing the prevalent idea that Indians existed outside of Brazilian society. Like the "Last Tamoio," Alencar depicted Iracema's death as the event that enabled the Portuguese man and their mestiço son to thrive and pave the way for Portuguese colonization and the spread of Christianity. Romantic Indianists promoted the idea that death was what allowed Indians to make their most important contribution to the founding of the Brazilian nation.[71] Not all Brazilian elites were won over by this celebration of Brazil's indigenous past, however. Adolfo Varnhagen, an unrepentant lover of all things Portuguese, scorned the movement and dismissed what he saw as Gonçalves Dias' and Magalhães' brand of "caboclo patriotism."[72]

If Romantic Indianism celebrated in such artistic production was a "cultural and political movement with profound links to nationalism" spearheaded by the emperor himself, extinction discourse was its evil twin.[73] Romantic Indianists complemented extinction discourse by consciously excising living Indians from their creations. Also excluded were blacks, slavery, and African influences, all considered extraneous to elite conceptualizations of Brazilian nationhood. These tendencies were also evident in the Brazilian Historical and Geographic Institute (IHGB), whose journal gave lengthy treatment to the ethnography of Brazil's indigenous populations. Producing knowledge about the indigenous while reinforcing the idea that they were on their way to extinction allowed the Institute to tie them to its construction of a national past. At the same time, the journal virtually excluded Africans as ethnographic subjects in its copious production (in spite of having awarded Martius' essay on the three races), which contrasted sharply with the great fascination with Africans of various ethnicities among foreign travelers and

---

[71] A rich scholarship exists on Brazilian Romantic Indianism. For a good introduction and overview of *Iracema* and Alencar's other Indianists works, see the introduction by Naomi Lindstrom in José Martiniano de Alencar, *Iracema: A Novel*, trans. Clifford E. Landers (New York: Oxford University Press, 2000). On the relationship between literary Indianism and nationalism, see Lima, *Cores, marcas e falas*, Chapter 3; David T. Haberly, *Three Sad Races: Racial Identity and National Consciousness in Brazilian Literature* (Cambridge and New York: Cambridge University Press, 1983); Sadlier, *Brazil Imagined*, 132–49; Dave Treece, *Exiles, Allies, Rebels: Brazil's Indianist Movement, Indigenist Politics, and the Imperial Nation-State* (Westport, CT: Greenwood Publishing Group, 2000); Schwarcz, *The Emperor's Beard*, Chapter 7. Doris Sommer offers an analysis of Alencar's *O Guarani* and *Iracema* in the context of a broader Latin American nationalist literature in *Foundational Fictions*, Chapter 5.

[72] Varnhagen, *Os Indios bravos*, 57.

[73] Schwarcz, *The Emperor's Beard*, Chapter 7.

scientists who came to Brazil. From the IHGB's perspective, the Africans' nonnative origins and their associations with slavery rendered them undesirable representatives of a national past.[74]

The IHGB's exclusion of Africans exposes the cracks in mestiçagem's image of racial harmony. José Bonifácio, who tirelessly promoted miscegenation, advocated "favoring, by all possible means, marriages between Indians and whites, and mulattoes," or "marriages of white men and men of color with Indian women." He even suggested offering a "financial reward for all Brazilian citizens, white or of color, who marry a heathen Indian woman." Although at first glance José Bonifácio appears to embrace the three races idea, he in fact excluded Africans from his racialized nation-building project by addressing only mulattoes and men of color (an expression reserved for the Brazilian-born). He thus gave a racial seal to the legal exclusion of Africans, whether slave or free. Of the Indians, only women were accounted for, with the implication that marriages with Brazilian men of other races would have a civilizing effect. Both African and indigenous men were excluded from this vision of a harmonious *povo brasileiro*, and from the national past as well as its future.[75]

Botocudos and the New Science of Anthropology

While elites in Rio de Janeiro celebrated the contributions of Romantic, long-deceased Indians, another kind of celebration was taking place on the Atlantic frontier. In November 1882, Caravelas residents were thrilled to see Brazilian and foreign dignitaries gather in their town for the inauguration of the Bahia–Minas Railroad. The shining US- and British-made train cars departed on their maiden voyage from Caravelas, passing by Colônia Leopoldina, traveling on modern Bessemer steel rails in a gradual ascent to the interior, crossing the provincial border and arriving at the town of Aymoré near Filadélfia, straight through the heart of Botocudo territory.[76] To those present the railroad signaled the long-awaited union of the Minas interior and the Atlantic, fulfilling the ambitions of countless individuals who had aspired to realize similar ventures since the late colonial period as the forbidden lands began to unravel. The Caravelas press celebrated the railroad as the harbinger of civilization and exalted

---

[74] Kodama, *Os índios no Império do Brasil*, 108–18; Monteiro, "Tupis, Tapuias," 147–48.
[75] Bonifácio, *Projetos para o Brasil*.
[76] On the railroad, see, for example, Bahian Provincial Presidential Report for 1882, delivered on April 3, 1883, Pedro Luiz Pereira de Souza, "Falla (BA)," 1883, 118, CRL.

"this gigantic railroad project" as the "most perfect expression of the progresses of modern society."[77] The project engineer explicitly compared the railroad to the Union Pacific Railroad of the United States, with its promise to unite "distant populations separated by virgin forests, still in the power of wild heathens, where it will implant civilization."[78] Or as a British observer put it in no uncertain terms, with serious development of the region, "the poor Indians would soon be swept aside... before the irresistible advance of the white man."[79]

Brazilians and foreigners shared a conviction in the inevitability of Indian extinction before the force of Euro-American modernity. Foreign explorers, artists, and scientists who came to Brazil eagerly sought out the Botocudo, whom they considered to be, at best, in the early stages of civilization and increasingly, the last holdouts of a primitive and dying race. Negative images of the Botocudo had circulated since the colonial period and continued to influence artists, who depicted them with a mixture of wonder and disdain. Among the most famous was the French painter Jean-Baptiste Debret, who resided in Brazil between 1816 and 1831 at the behest of the royal family, which had invited him and other European artists to found the Academy of Fine Arts in Brazil. Debret's resulting *Voyage Pittoresque au Brésil* was the historical portrait of a nation in the "progressive development of civilization" that placed it on par with the "most distinguished nations of the old continent."[80] Debret's interest in native people was ignited by his chance encounter with a group of Botocudo in Rio de Janeiro two days after his arrival. They had been brought from southern Bahia for an audience with João VI, from whom they received iron machetes, the emblems of civilization. The artist was struck by the sight of "savages" in the "center of a civilized capital" and described them as the "cruelest and fiercest" of Indians with the "most horrific and terrible" physiognomy. While he did not connect João VI to the Botocudo Wars, he did include the text of the decree abolishing indigenous slavery in São Paulo in 1830 as evidence

---

77 "Dois progressos." *O Precursor*, January 23, 1881; *O Precursor*, May 22, 1881, cited in M. de Teive e Argollo, *Memoria descriptiva sobre a Estrada de Ferro Bahia e Minas* (Rio de Janeiro: H. Laemmert, 1883), 44.
78 Ibid., 31. On Manifest Destiny in the Americas, see the essays in *Manifest Destinies and Indigenous Peoples*, ed. David Maybury-Lewis, Theodore Macdonald, and Biorn Maybury-Lewis (Cambridge, MA: Harvard University Press, 2009).
79 Wm. John Steains, "An Exploration of the Rio Dôce and Its Northern Tributaries (Brazil)," in *Proceedings of the Royal Geographical Society and Monthly Record of Geography* 10, no. 2 (February 1, 1888): 83. Comment by Colin Mackenzie.
80 Jean-Baptiste Debret, *Viagem pitoresca e histórica ao Brasil*, T.1 (São Paulo: Livraria Martins, 1954), 6.

FIGURE 3.2 This ethnographically inaccurate depiction of various indigenous groups, who appear to be consuming human flesh, shows Debret's classifying the Botocudo, Puri, Pataxó, and Maxacali among the least "civilized" of Brazilian Indians. *Source: Botocoudos, Buris, Patachos, et Macharis*, from Jean Baptiste Debret, *Voyage pittoresque et historique au Brésil* (Paris: Firmin Didot frères, 1834). From the New York Public Library.

of Brazilian legislators' commitment to Indian civilization and national progress.[81]

Debret dedicated the first of three volumes to Brazil's indigenous groups in what he considered progressive degrees of civilization. The Botocudo were among the early images. The first featured muscular Botocudo warriors and their family in the wilderness, followed by an image of a group of naked women, men, and children gathered in the forest, all of the adults wearing lip disks (Figure 3.2). One of them devoured what appeared to be a human limb. The artist entitled the image, "Botocudos, Puris, Pataxós, and Maxacalí or Gamelas" in error, as only the Botocudo wore lip disks, and described their "repugnant aspect" resulting from the "mutilations they inflict on themselves." Debret's ambivalence about these Indians' place in Brazilian civilization was evident in his alternating descriptions of them as civilized and savage. The volume would conclude with a contrasting image of "civilized" Guarani Indians, fully clothed in Western dress.[82]

---

[81] Ibid., 7.
[82] Maria Regina Celestino de Almeida, "Índios mestiços e selvagens civilizados de Debret," *Varia Historia* 25, no. 41 (June 2009): 95–99. For the Indians and progress argument,

Yet if Debret had celebrated Brazil's capacity to civilize "wild" Indians to become part of the nation, another French artist whose sojourn in Brazil coincided with the emergence of extinction discourse assumed a different view. Unlike Debret, François-Auguste Biard came to Brazil in 1858 actively seeking the opportunity to stay among indigenous peoples in Espírito Santo and the Amazon. Yet beyond affirming his interactions with the Botocudo and producing a few sketches, the painter displayed little interest in his subjects. Echoing Orientalist views of North African and the Middle Eastern people, Biard believed white civilization corrupted indigenous people, and considered Brazil's indigenous and African-descended population as evidence of the nation's savagery in comparison to France's civilization.[83] Biard's unsympathetic views may also have been influenced by the 1844 daguerreotypes of a somber Botocudo man and woman who had been taken to Paris the previous year. In the 1850s their partially naked, seated images were among the first photographs to be included in the collections of the Natural History Museum in Paris as some of the earliest specimens of physical anthropology.[84]

Scientific enthusiasts for the Botocudo continued to grow on both sides of the Atlantic. Among them was the US explorer, scientist, and avid Botocudo skull collector Charles Hartt, who dedicated an entire chapter of his expedition journal to the Botocudo. Hartt seamlessly combined culturalist and scientific race theories and displayed his familiarity with Brazil's Tupi–Tapuia dichotomy. The Botocudo "race is fast diminishing and in a few years will pass out of existence," he observed, because they had refused to civilize themselves like the Tupi, who conversely had become an "integral part of the Brazilian nation." In other words, it was the Botocudos' own fault.[85] A British geographer later commented that an encounter with the Botocudo was to witness the "deathbed of an expiring race." Yet their extinction had some positive results,

---

see Valéria Lima, *J.-B. Debret, historiador e pintor: a viagem pitoresca e histórica ao Brasil (1816–1839)* (São Paulo: Editora UNICAMP, 2007), 251–63. Ana Lucia Araujo has noted that in spite of his claims to visiting Indians in the "virgin forests," Debret did not base his paintings on direct observation but on the collections of the Royal Museum of Natural History at São Cristóvão palace in Rio de Janeiro, and on European travelogues. Ana Lucia Araujo, *Brazil through French Eyes: A Nineteenth-Century Artist in the Tropics* (Albuquerque: University of New Mexico Press, 2015), 142.

[83] Araujo, *Brazil through French Eyes*, xix–xx, 162–64.

[84] Marco Morel, "Cinco imagens e múltiplos olhares: 'descobertas' sobre os índios do Brasil e a fotografia do século XIX," *História, Ciências, Saúde* 8 (2001): 1039–58.

[85] Charles Frederick Hartt, *Thayer Expedition: Scientific Results of a Journey in Brazil, by Louis Agassiz and His Travelling Companions: Geology and Physical Geography* (Boston: Fields, Osgood & Co., 1870), 602.

particularly in the realm of territorial colonization. "As they were totally and completely alien to any advance towards civilization," he stated, "there was this compensation for the loss of the tribe – that it would open up a richly endowed region to the benefits of civilization and Christianity." Extinction advocates thus proposed that by becoming extinct, the Botocudo were finally able to make a positive contribution to Brazilian civilization.[86]

Anthropology's establishment in Brazil endowed Indian extinction theories with the seal of incontrovertible fact. Among the new class of anthropologists were João Baptista de Lacerda Filho and José Rodrigues Peixoto, who coauthored the article "Contribution to the Anthropological Study of the Indigenous Races of Brazil (1876)" in the inaugural journal of the prestigious National Museum. "Given the cranium's small capacity, the Botocudos should be considered . . . among the races most notable for their inferior intellectual level," the authors concluded. "Their aptitudes are effectively limited, and it is very difficult to make them join the path towards civilization."[87] Lacerda and Peixoto were eager to carve out a space for themselves in a field dominated by European and US scientists who flocked to their country, captivated by the Botocudos' "primitivism" and in particular, their skulls. Eagerly excavating burial sites of the recently deceased, they carefully sketched, inspected, and measured each cranium. They then compared their findings to other studies, always arriving at the same conclusion: the Botocudo were the most primitive race, unfit for civilization, and therefore, destined for extinction (Figure 3.3).

Lacerda and Peixoto's efforts were encouraged by the National Museum, which organized the Anthropological Exposition with the patronage of Pedro II in July 1882. The Exposition was dedicated almost exclusively to the history, ethnography, and anthropology of Brazilian Indians to the notable exclusion of Africans and the Portuguese. Like Romantic Indianists, the Exposition's organizers emphasized the "enormous contrast between the importance given to the nation's indigenous origins and the negative depiction of actual Indians."[88] Pedro II himself had seen no problem patronizing Romantic Indianists while facilitating the National Museum's export of Botocudo skulls and skeletons to renowned scholars in Berlin and Paris.[89] The Exposition's star attraction was a living group of Botocudo Indians, brought from an aldeia in

---

[86] Steains, "Exploration of the Rio Dôce," 80. Quote by Mackenzie.

[87] João Batista Lacerda and José Rodrigues Peixoto, "Contribução para o estudo anthropologico das raças indígenas do Brasil," *Arquivos do Museu Nacional* 1 (1876): 47–75.

[88] Monteiro, "As 'raças' indígenas," 15.

[89] Lacerda and Peixoto, "Contribuição para o estudo," 52.

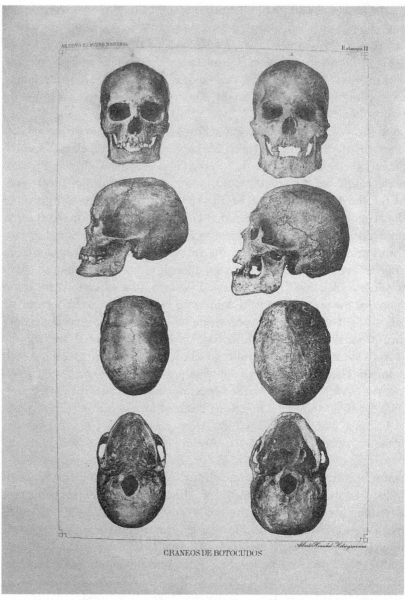

FIGURE 3.3 A new crop of anthropologists both Brazilian and foreign were keenly interested in collecting and measuring Botocudo cranea, always arriving upon the same conclusion: that they were biologically inferior and destined for extinction. *Source: Craneos de Botocudos*, from João Baptista Lacerda and José Rodrigues Peixoto, "Contribuição para o estudo antropológico das raças indígenas do Brasil." *Arquivos do Museu Nacional* 1 (1876). Photographed by the author.

Espírito Santo and exhibited amidst collections of Indian baskets, tools, ceramics, and bones. Visitors flocked to the exhibition in droves to be fascinated and repulsed by Brazil's "last savages," inspiring a famous satirist to report that it was the Botocudo who had to flee the visitors' savagery and seek refuge with the "great cacique" Ladislau Neto, the Museum's director.[90]

The terror of Brazilian settlers in the Atlantic frontier until mid-century, the Botocudo were now safely contained in the Exposition hall, reduced into anthropological specimens of a disappearing race. In contrast to the scandalous "export" of the five Botocudos, which took place outside of anthropological expertise, the Botocudos on display flattered the modernizing self-image that Brazil hoped to project to the world, since they were presented as evidence of their own impending extinction. The articles that Lacerda and Peixoto contributed to the Exposition's accompanying volume demonstrated their full embrace of the scientific racist theories taking hold across Latin America in the last quarter of the nineteenth century.[91] Utilizing the "truly scientific study" of anthropometrics, Lacerda "proved" the Botocudos' biological inferiority and their consequent inability to join the "path toward civilization." Whereas Varnhagen had clashed with brandura-advocates over the use of violent or gentle means to bring Indians into Brazilian civilization, anthropologists used their craniological data to prove that such a goal was impossible to begin with. Lacerda even utilized his expertise to close down the debate on the usefulness of Indian labor. The Botocudo Indians, he argued, were physically incapable of performing hard agricultural labor since their muscles were comparatively weaker than those of a white or especially a black worker. Because this was a physical defect, civilizing them could not remedy it.[92]

By making a biological argument, Lacerda effectively threw out the core tenet of postcolonial Brazilian indigenous policy. Brandura was based on the idea that through civilization and miscegenation, Indians could eventually be included into Brazilian society as citizens. Civilization hinged on their becoming a stationary, productive labor force that would serve the nation's interests. Lacerda argued that this was

---

[90] Angelo Agostini, *Revista Ilustrada*, No. 310, 1882.

[91] Lilia Moritz Schwarcz, *The Spectacle of the Races: Scientists, Institutions, and the Race Question in Brazil, 1870–1930* (New York: Farrar, Straus and Giroux, 1999).

[92] João Batista Lacerda, "A força muscular e a delicadeza dos sentidos dos nossos indígenas," in *Revista da Exposição Antropologica Brasileira*, 1882, 6–7; Monteiro, "As 'raças' indígenas," 20.

biologically untenable. "Now you see how we can deduce an economic and industrial problem from an anthropological one," he stated triumphantly. "It shows that anthropology is not merely a speculative science, but can have practical and useful application." Thanks to Lacerda's work, Brazilian Indians were now seen as not only unfit for survival, but completely useless to the nation.[93]

In the Shadows of Racial Harmony

At the end of the nineteenth century, the Botocudos' precarious existence contrasted with the potent union of extinction discourse and mestiçagem, which was reinvigorated during the First Republic (1889–1930). Unlike the monogenist ethnographers of the IHGB, in their study of the Botocudo, Lacerda and Peixoto had adopted the polygenist theories popular among US and European scientists such as Louis Agassiz, who believed that races were finished phenomena and therefore, that miscegenation was degenerative. These Brazilian anthropologists attributed the Botocudos' alleged racial inferiority to miscegenation, thereby contradicting the belief of brandura-advocates that race mixture would be a positive force.[94] However, Lacerda later completely reversed his views. As the sole Latin American representative at the "First Universal Races Congress" in London in 1911, Lacerda, now the Director of the National Museum, affirmed that miscegenation not only produced a healthy, mixed population, but also one that whitened over time. In his paper entitled "The Métis, or Half-Breeds of Brazil," he used his voice of scientific authority to argue for a new phase of extinction: within a century, mixed-race people would disappear, coinciding with the "parallel extinction of the black race in our midst." Now it was black people's turn.

Lacerda's "scientific" vision of Brazil's racial whitening had an eerily familiar tone. Since the abolition of slavery in 1888, blacks were "exposed to all kinds of destructive agencies." Now living "scattered over thinly populated districts," they "tend to disappear from our territory."[95] His language was identical to that of earlier claims discussed in this

---

93 Ibid., 7.
94 Lacerda and Peixoto, "Contribuição para o estudo," 75. For polygenism and social Darwinist theories in Brazil, see Schwarcz, *The Spectacle of the Races*, 49–63. Agassiz virulently disparaged the effects of race mixture or "amalgamation" in Brazil. Louis Agassiz and Elizabeth Cabot Cary Agassiz, *A Journey in Brazil* (Boston: Ticknor and Fields, 1868), 293.
95 Skidmore, *Black Into White*, 65–66.

chapter that "dispersed Indians living confused among the civilized masses" were evidence of their irreversible extinction.[96] Although his attention had shifted from the Botocudo to African-descended Brazilians, his new whitening thesis was clearly based on early discourses of indigenous extinction. In a trajectory that extended from Empire to the First Republic, indigenous extinction discourse, in harmonious partnership with the inclusivity of mestiçagem, laid the groundwork for racial theories that would later predict the disappearance of African-descended people. If its impetus was the wishful, whitening aspiration of the Brazilian elite, its implications were ominous. For whether the alleged cause was miscegenation or physical difference, extinction discourse erased the physical, legal, and discursive violence inflicted on black and indigenous Brazilians and made them, for being "inferior" races, responsible for their own disappearance.

Mestiçagem's entanglement with indigenous extinction discourse forces us to reconsider the image of racial harmony we often associate with race mixture. The suggestion that Portuguese colonialism and its heir, postcolonial indigenous policy, were benevolent because they promoted intermarriage and the Indians' incorporation as citizens seems less benign when we recognize that inclusion both produced, and was enabled by, indigenous extinction. Brazilian elites sought to bring the indigenous into the povo brasileiro through civilization and miscegenation, and in doing so deliberately closed down the possibilities of indigenous citizenship, or even national inclusion *as* Indians. To become a citizen, Indians had to be civilized, and once civilized, one was no longer an Indian. Johannes Fabian called this a "denial of coevalness" – the belief that "savages" belong in the past and have no place in the present or future.[97] And as Lacerda's new research revealed, the concept of extinction was easily transposed onto black Brazilians, who were headed toward their own vanishing point. Brazil's mestiço racial identity, celebrated by the elite and by proponents of "racial democracy" in the early twentieth century, was therefore remarkably exclusionary in both aspiration and practice.

Still, the image of racial harmony begotten by Portuguese and Indian miscegenation also created new political openings that demonstrated the idea's attraction and versatility. The famous mulatto journalist and abolitionist José do Patrocínio, for instance, lauded Portuguese colonizers for

[96] Cunha, "Legislação indigenista no séc. XIX," 141, 145.
[97] Fabian as cited in Brantlinger, *Dark Vanishings*, 2.

assimilating instead of destroying the "savage races," which he claimed had prepared Brazil to resist the "devastating invasion" of race prejudice. Other abolitionists and pro-immigrationists also intoned the absence of race prejudice in Brazil. Writing in 1887, it is impossible to know whether Patrocínio was acquainted with the Botocudo exhibition five years earlier, which would have clearly shown that the "savage races" were neither assimilated nor spared any racism. He nonetheless evoked an idealized indigenous precedent as a "paean to racial assimilation" which he used to make demands for fuller integration of African-descended Brazilians.[98] Indian miscegenation therefore served competing ideas, as a precedent for black extinction on one hand, and for black inclusion on the other.

Meanwhile, the search for a "future perfect" povo brasileiro continued. Lacerda's optimism about race mixture and whitening, which was inflected with black extinction discourse, was countered by literary scholar Silvio Romero, who recognized Brazil's unique racial mixture but was skeptical about the possibility of a whitened people.[99] It was the Indianist José Couto de Magalhães who energetically embraced the mixture of the three races as the source of not only a Brazilian but an American pride, with echoes of Cuban independence leader José Martí's Nuestra America. As if to counter Frenchman Louis Couty's claim that Brazil had no people, Magalhães enthusiastically asserted his vision of a povo brasileiro, stating that the "human race that currently inhabits Brazil is descended from three branches: the European white, the African black, and the American red. We are neither European nor African. In the colossal cauldron of South America, the blood of the three races have mixed and continue to mix, creating an American, Brazilian, race, that is large and powerful, because he is intelligent, strong, restrained, hardworking, and peaceful."[100]

---

[98] José do Patrocínio, "O grande projeto (May 5, 1887)," in Oito anos de parlamento, by Afonso Celso, Biblioteca básica brasileira (Brasília: Senado Federal, 1998), 116–17; as cited in Alberto, Terms of Inclusion, 9; Skidmore, Black Into White, 22–24; Azevedo, Onda negra, 76–77.

[99] Skidmore, Black Into White, 34–37, 69.

[100] José Vieira Couto de Magalhães, Anchieta, as raças e linguas indigenas (São Paulo: C. Gerke & Cia., 1897), 20.

4

Violent Terrains

Legal Regimes

In the predawn darkness of early July 1881, an entire village of Botocudo Indians from the Nok-Nok subgroup on the Pardo River, in southern Bahia, was massacred by a joint expedition of local residents and Kamakã Indians.[1] One of the participants described "killing caboclo like the devil" in the raid in which more than thirty Indians were murdered and four children captured.[2] Compelling witness testimonies gave the police confidence that a strong case could be made against the perpetrators. Yet by November, the case collapsed because of the lack of evidence. The local justice system concluded that no massacre had taken place, since no Indian bodies had been found. Then, in the summer of February 1884, another body disappeared in São Mateus. A slave named Seraphim, shot and bleeding, was dragged away by his master's family and never seen again. The family claimed that the slave had fled to the neighboring province of Minas Gerais. Few believed them, however. Law enforcement and locals alike were certain that the family had meted out its own

---

[1] The Nok-Nok, also known as Nek-Nek or, in the archival sources, Nocq-Nocq, were a Pojixá Botocudo group who first came into contact with Teófilo Ottoni in 1845. The sources consulted here record them as Nocq-Nocq, but I have modernized the orthography. Their location in 1881 suggests that with further territorial loss since the 1840s, they were forced north into the Rio Pardo Valley, an astonishing 187 miles (300 km) north of the Mucuri Valley. Maria Hilda Baqueiro Paraiso, "Guerra do Mucuri: conquista e dominação dos povos indígenas em nome do progresso e da civilização," in *Indios do Nordeste: temas e problemas: 500 anos*, ed. Marcos Galindo, Luiz Sávio de Almeida, and Juliana Lopes Elias (Maceió: EDUFAL, 2000), 139–40. The Kamakã also belong to the Macro-Gê linguistic group.

[2] Manoel do Bomfim Pereira Neto, "Nok-Nok Massacre Police Investigation" (Rio Pardo, September 15, 1881), Colonial/Polícia/Mc 6218, APEB.

justice against Seraphim, who had committed an intolerable transgression by impregnating the family's widowed daughter, Rita. The family, it was believed, had avenged Rita's honor by secretly castrating and executing the slave. They were charged with murder.

Through the cases of the Nok-Nok and Seraphim, this chapter examines the nexus of law, violence, and citizenship in the final years of slavery and imperial rule in Brazil, which would happen in 1888–89. It argues that comparing the collapse of the Nok-Nok investigation with the charges brought against Seraphim's suspected killers allows us to understand the diverging relationship of indigenous and enslaved people to the nation's body of laws, with the effective exclusion of the former mirroring the greater inclusion of the latter.

A central theme in this chapter is the ambiguous boundaries of legal and extralegal violence marking the cases through which we can perceive the presence of the state in the Atlantic frontier. Long disdained for its lawlessness owing to its sparse settlement, its distance from the centers of political and economic power, and its rebellious enslaved and indigenous population, the Atlantic frontier had, by the late nineteenth century, experienced decades of colonization, state expansion, and economic development. State-sanctioned Indian civilization projects fused with anti-indigenous violence to engender Botocudo extinction, while slave-based agriculture had given large slaveholders outsized political influence and few opportunities for the enslaved to gain their freedom through legal means.

Violence therefore did not signify state absence and frontier anarchy. Rather, it signaled the ways in which the state and local agents created uneven legal regimes of citizenship for indigenous and enslaved Brazilians during a critical moment in postcolonial Brazilian history when Indian "extinction" and abolitionism converged. The Nok-Nok massacre and its obfuscation by the legal system exposed the erosion of laws protecting indigenous Brazilians, particularly those who remained autonomous, effectively abrogating their ever-precarious right to citizenship and placing them outside the "body of the nation." On the other hand, although Seraphim's case was astonishing in its brutality against both him and Rita, his case echoed two important changes taking place across Brazil at large: the confluence of growing support for abolition among state institutions and the public, and the fraying of state support for masters' private domination of their slaves. Together these changes began to pry open spaces of greater legal inclusion for the enslaved, even in the proslavery Atlantic frontier.

Beyond serving as an indicator of state presence, violence also continued to shape the everyday lives of enslaved and indigenous people. This chapter closely examines the violence inflicted on the Nok-Nok and Seraphim, following Michael Taussig's contention that "far from being spontaneous, sui generis and an abandonment of what are often called the 'values of civilization,' such rites [of torture and institutionalized terror] have a deep history deriving power and meaning from those values."[3] Analyzing the violence itself, which was not only gruesome but also highly specific in its execution, shows the changing definitions of legitimate and illegitimate violence against enslaved and indigenous people in the final decade of the Brazilian empire.

The Nok-Nok Massacre

According to the initial police investigation conducted in September 1881, the massacre happened thus. Sometime in early July, two merchants in the town of Canavieiras, at the mouth of the Pardo River 110 miles to the north of Prado, offered a reward to several men to participate in an *entrada* – an invasion into an Indian settlement – on a group of "wild" or autonomous Nok-Nok Indians. A Pojixá Botocudo subgroup, the Nok-Nok were once under the leadership of Guido Pokrane in Manhuaçú (Chapter 3) but relocated to the Mucuri Valley after his death in the 1840s and had moved much farther north by the 1880s, likely pushed out by settler expansion and warfare.[4] The merchants' orders to the entrada members were to scatter the Indians, or kill them if they resisted. Several witnesses identified those merchants as Antonio Luiz de Carvalho and Antonio Peixoto Guimarães. A German immigrant named Georg Stolze and resident Manoel Cândido Moreira, soon to be the expedition's leader, recruited members, reassuring them that the entrada had government authorization. Canavieiras, home to a robust cacao plantation zone extending south from Ilhéus, had been jolted into frenzy with the recent discovery of new diamond mines along the Pardo River. An influx of mining prospectors from all corners of the state and beyond had nearly doubled the population to 6,000, increasing the contest for land and helping the spread of smallpox. By 1881, tensions between the

---

[3] Michael Taussig, "Culure of Terror – Space of Death: Roger Casement's Putumayo Report and the Explanation of Torture," in *Colonialism and Culture*, ed. Nicholas B. Dirks (Ann Arbor: University of Michigan Press, 1992), 164.
[4] Paraiso, "Guerra do Mucuri."

growing settler population and the Nok-Nok had already flared into physical confrontations.[5]

The Nok-Nok harbored a particular wariness toward their neighbor Georg Stolze, who as recently as March had, with another resident, urged the government to send a missionary.[6] Stolze had contracted with the Brazilian government to establish a new series of German and Polish colonies in the region in 1873. Although the colonies all failed by 1878, Stolze had in the meantime personally financed the opening of a road through indigenous territory, in what remained of the Atlantic forest between Vila da Vitoria in the interior and the Pardo River.[7] For the 1881 entrada, Stolze and Moreira assembled twelve residents and a group of six "tame" (*mansos*) Kamakã Indians. The Kamakã, originally from São Paulo hundreds of miles away, were now in Canavieiras after they too were exiled out of their own lands (Figure 4.1). A local who spotted Moreira purchasing a hefty cache of weapons asked what it was for, to which Moreira responded, "to kill the Nok-Nok Indians."[8] He was resolved to remain in the area for another six months after the assault in case any surviving Indians attempted to return.[9]

The expedition made its way to the aldeia under the cover of the predawn darkness, taking every precaution to conceal their presence. As participant Manoel Ramão Mendes recounted, their stealthy entry was abruptly announced by a rifle shot at around 4 a.m. A barrage of shooting followed, sending the panicked Indians into flight. The expedition followed the screams and further shooting ensued. A few men fired their rifles at an Indian aiming at them with his bow and arrow; the Indian fled. As the sun gradually appeared over the horizon a few hours later, traces of "a great carnage" were exposed. Blood was splattered everywhere. From the number of shots fired and the trail of blood in the nearby woods, the participants surmised that they had killed more than

---

[5] Durval Vieira de Aguiar, *Descripções praticas da provincia da Bahia com declaração de todas a distancias intermediarias das cidades, villas e povoações* (Bahia: Typographia do "Diario da Bahia," 1888), 273–74.

[6] Augusto Federico de Vasconcellos de Souza Bahiana to President of Bahia, May 3, 1880, Colonial/Polícia/Mc 2971, APEB; Police Chief of Bahia to President of Bahia, March 2, 1881, Colonial/Polícia/Mc 2971, APEB; Manoel Innocencio da Luis (Rio Pardo, February 8, 1881), Colonial/Polícia/Mc 2971, APEB.

[7] Francisco Vicente Vianna and José Carlos Ferreira, *Memoria sobre o estado da Bahia* (Bahia: Typographia e encadernação do "Diario da Bahia," 1893), 195–96; 209–10. Today, there is a small street named after Stolze in the aptly named Vitória da Conquista in southern Bahia.

[8] Manoel do Bomfim Pereira Neto, September 15, 1881

[9] Carlos José Warnaux, "Nok-Nok Massacre Police Investigation" (Rio Pardo, September 24, 1881), Colonial/Polícia/Mc 6218, APEB.

FIGURE 4.1 The Kamakã Indians were themselves persecuted by settler expansion into the Atlantic Frontier. In the 1881 Nok-Nok massacre, the investigation presented them as the settlers' collaborators, and increasingly, the main perpetrators, but they were never allowed to testify. *Source:* Auguste Seyffer, *Danse des Camacans.* From the New York Public Library.

thirty Indians.[10] The assailants saw "pretty dead caboclas" strewn about the ground.[11] Mendes told another local after returning from the entrada that the deaths were undeniable, even though his companions claimed the contrary. Moreira, the entrada leader, later boasted about how he shot a cabocla. As she crumpled to her death, a child came running to him, clung to his machete, and begged for his protection. Moreira obliged by hacking the child to death and leaving him "awash in his own blood." A witness, Carlos Warnaux, expressed his horror at the news of "such ferocity."[12]

Four Indian children, one still breastfeeding, were seized by the expedition and brought back as captives along with a stash of bows and arrows

---

[10] Augusto Frederico de Vasconcellos de Souza Bahiana Jr., "Nok-Nok Massacre Police Investigation" (Rio Pardo, September 15, 1881), Colonial/Polícia/Mc 6218, APEB; Manoel Ramão Mendes, "Nok-Nok Massacre Police Investigation" (Rio Pardo, September 15, 1881), Colonial/Polícia/Mc 6218, APEB.

[11] Warnaux, September 24, 1881. Here it appears that the term "cabocla" was used to refer to the Nok-Nok instead of to people of mixed-indigenous ancestry or their "acculturation." Perhaps it indicates a lexical shift from índio to caboclo.

[12] Ibid.

and were distributed among Moreira and two others. One of the children soon died from the bullet wounds in his leg. Although kuruka slavery had declined since its heyday in the 1840s, Indian children remained desirable. One of the expedition members had offered to procure a "little Indian girl" for a local resident.[13] Another wanted some sort of Indian souvenir from the entrada. Both requests were denied by Georg Stolze, who warned that they would compromise the entrada, perhaps concerned with dispersing too much evidence.[14] Meanwhile, Moreira received his payment from the two merchants, from which he paid Mendes and two other participants. He was arrested for his part in the expedition but was soon released upon filing a habeas corpus petition.[15]

Matar uma aldeia: A History of a Killing

The barrage of shooting, the screaming Indians, the trails of blood, the seized children – all this suggests frontier anarchy, where the rule of law has collapsed and the assailants' savagery is unleashed. But the Nok-Nok massacre followed a distinct history with a specific pattern of violence in spite of its apparent "absence of order and meaning."[16] The violence even had a name: *matar uma aldeia*, or to kill an Indian village. As chronicled by the mineiro senator Teófilo Ottoni in his memoirs about his early years among the Botocudo in the Mucuri River Valley, the practice had a long list of precedents dating back at least half a century. To understand the Nok-Nok massacre in relation to these historical precedents allows us to comprehend both the specificity of the violence and the transformations in how this brutal anti-indigenous violence was interpreted by both its perpetrators and critics.[17]

Ottoni's first mention of matar uma aldeia dated from 1830 amidst the escalation of indigenous–settler conflicts in the region.[18] An anti-Botocudo expedition was formed in Minas Gerais, led by two Indian

---

[13] Bahiana Jr., September 15, 1881.

[14] Felix Marques do Espírito Santo, "Nok-Nok Massacre Police Investigation" (Rio Pardo, September 16, 1881), Colonial/Polícia/Mc 6218, APEB.

[15] Mendes, September 15, 1881.

[16] Neil L. Whitehead, "Introduction," in *Violence* (Santa Fe: School of American Research, 2004), 5, 8–10.

[17] I follow Stephen Ellis, according to whom violence "draws on a range of symbols concerning power that are widely understood and historically rooted." "Interpreting Violence: Reflection on the West African Wars," in *Violence*, ed. Neil L. Whitehead (Santa Fe: School of American Research, 2004), 108–13.

[18] Prince Maximilian also lists an earlier example from the 1810s during the Botocudo Wars. Maximilian Wied-Neuwied, *Viagem ao Brasil nos anos de 1815 a 1817* (São Paulo: Companhia Editora Nacional, 1958), 312.

FIGURE 4.2 Settlers engaged in anti-indigenous expeditions, known as *matar uma aldeia* (to kill a village), which were often surprise attacks. Perpetrators massacred entire settlements and sometimes enslaved the children. *Source: Guerrilhas*, from Johann Moritz Rugendas, *Voyage pittoresque dans le Brésil* (Paris: Engelmann & Cie., 1835).

soldiers of the imperial militia named Cró and Crahy. This was the last year of the Botocudo Wars. The mineiro government itself provided the weaponry and manpower against the "wild" Botocudo. As would happen in the Nok-Nok massacre, the expedition surrounded the aldeia at night. They began their assault at dawn, seizing the Indians' bows and arrows. The victims disarmed, the aldeia became a "slaughterhouse, not a place of combat." The elderly, women, and children were indiscriminately targeted. Some children were separated to be sold into kuruka trafficking, along with some attractive Indian girls, while the rest were killed save some adults who were enslaved by their assailants (Figure 4.2).[19]

The practice of matar uma aldeia remained vigorous in the aftermath of the Botocudo Wars. The Indian soldiers Cró and Crahy continued as key players, leading several other raids, one on an Indian military deserter in the 1830s who had become the leader of a large indigenous

---

[19] Teófilo Benedito Ottoni, *Notícia sobre os selvagens do Mucuri* (Belo Horizonte: Editora UFMG, 2002), 46–47.

group, and another in 1854, along the Jequitinhonha River in southern Bahia. More aldeias were attacked throughout the borderlands of Bahia, Espírito Santo, and Minas Gerais along the Mucuri, Doce, and Jequitinhonha Rivers.[20] The Ottoni family had meanwhile established itself in the Mucuri Valley in the heart of Botocudo territory and would remain, undeterred by the eventual failure of their Mucuri Company and the catastrophic demise of an affiliated European colony in 1861.[21] Convinced of the righteousness of their "benevolent" relations with the Indians, the Ottonis did not perceive their role in engendering the very violence they decried, which culminated in another matar uma aldeia that took place in 1862.

Pojixá, the feared captain of an eponymous Botocudo group (the Nok-Nok were also Pojixá Botocudo), had become the Ottonis' nemesis in their quest to dominate the Mucuri Valley. After a temporary ceasefire collapsed, Teófilo's brother and the Director of Indians, Augusto Ottoni, ordered Pojixá's capture in 1862. A local police officer named Joaquim Fagundes assumed the task. Fagundes recounted that his expedition to capture the "criminal Indians" reached Pojixá's aldeia, near the São Mateus River, in mid-August. The aldeia surrounded, the participating official of justice ordered the Indians to turn themselves in. They responded by shooting arrows at the expedition, continuing to do so after a warning shot was fired. The expedition's commander concluded that surrender was unlikely and ordered an attack. "I did not stop him," Fagundes stated, "as the law orders us to repel, with force, any resistance to arrest." Like Georg Stolze and Manoel Moreira, who in 1881 would recruit members by assuring them the entrada had government authorization, Fagundes emphasized the legality of the attack. In his final tally they arrested seven Indians, while many others fled. Seventeen died.[22]

The Ottonis vehemently contested Fagundes' narrative, claiming that what in fact transpired was a "war of extermination." Ottoni insisted that Fagundes had concealed the participation of none other than Cró

[20] Ibid., 45–48.

[21] "Mucury Company Inventory" (Filadélfia, MG, June 20, 1861), IA6–141, AN; Teófilo Benedito Ottoni, Breve resposta que ao relatório da liquidaçõ da companhia do Mucury por parte do governo (Rio de Janeiro: Typographia de M. Barreto, 1862). Robert Avé-Lallemant, Viagem pelo norte do Brasil no ano de 1859 (Rio de Janeiro: Instituto Nacional do Livro, Ministério da Educação e Cultura, 1961), 157–267, delivers a diatribe against Ottoni and his failing ventures.

[22] Teófilo Benedito Ottoni, "Mucury," Correio Mercantil, November 12, 1862.

and Crahy, probably in order to hoard any rewards. He believed it was these two Indians who, returning to their "old habits," had launched the horrific carnage on the aldeia. Ottoni was skeptical that Pojixá's group would have resisted an armed siege, since Indians were aware of the superiority of firearms over their bows and arrows. He was also certain that the expedition was in reality a surprise attack. Indians were very alert and "do not let themselves be surrounded, save when they are sleeping from midnight until day break," something Cró and Crahy would have known and exploited. Pojixá barely escaped, with casualties far exceeding what Fagundes had reported. Of his two sons taken prisoner, one was privately given to a settler and the other died in Fagundes' hands. His large group of nearly 200 was decimated, leaving only eight survivors. The entrada members were as ruthless as Manoel Moreira would be in 1881 and included a soldier who shot an unarmed Indian woman who ran toward him asking for protection.[23] Ottoni later revised his account, conceding that prior to the attack, Cró and Crahy had been murdered by their own family members, who had replaced them in the entrada.[24]

The similarities between these earlier examples of matar uma aldeia to the Nok-Nok massacre are obvious, from the mixed Indian and non-Indian composition of the expedition to the claims of the act's legitimacy, the surprise dawn attack, the annihilating carnage, and the seizure of children as slaves. Together they point to a practice of violence that followed a specific transcript, rather than a breakdown of order in a state of frontier anarchy. Key to these examples is the uneasy presence of "acculturated" Indians, those paradoxical beings whose existence was made impossible by the tenets of Indian civilization. Ottoni repeatedly highlighted Cró and Crahy in his narratives as the authenticating factors of the expeditions. As loyal Indian intermediaries between "wild" Indians and settlers and the state, like Guido Pokrane, they provided the necessary knowledge of the terrain and indigenous customs that made the entradas possible.[25] Cró and Crahy were soldiers who made their services available to the state for over three decades, just like the "tame," Christianized Kamakã

---

[23] Letter from Augusto Ottoni to the Director of Indians of Minas Gerais, September 15, 1862, included in ibid.

[24] "Notícias do interior," *Correio Mercantil*, January 30, 1863.

[25] Judy Bieber provides several fascinating biographies of these "transculturated" natives in the first half of the nineteenth century, who served the Brazilian military but also maintained ambiguous loyalties. Judy Bieber, "Mediation through Militarization: Indigenous Soldiers and Transcultural Middlemen of the Rio Doce Divisions, Minas Gerais, Brazil, 1808–1850," *The Americas* 71, no. 2 (2014): 227–54.

who participated in the Nok-Nok massacre. Yet Ottoni simultaneously distrusted the sincerity of Cró and Crahy's acculturation, attributing the principal responsibility of the 1862 Pojixá massacre to them and their "old habits."

These Indians intermediaries were what rendered the violence of *matar uma aldeia* intelligible to its witnesses. If, as Neil Whitehead has argued, violence must be "judged appropriate in order to be considered legitimate and credible," placing Indians at the center of the massacres fulfilled this need, while attributing it to non-Indians rendered the violence inappropriate.[26] To prove what he saw as Crahy's innate savagery, Ottoni insisted that the Indian had murdered his own mother-in-law during an *entrada* to demonstrate his loyalty to the expedition. It was these Indians who, in Ottoni's view, contaminated non-Indians with both their knowledge and savagery.[27] He recounted with horror the story of an esteemed military commander in São Mateus who "attacked [an] aldeia, exactly following Cró and Crahy's methods. He returned to São Mateus with the disgusting trophy of 300 ears which he ordered amputated from the murdered Indians."[28] Without this narrative of indigenous contamination, non-Indian savagery was neither legitimate nor credible.

Needless to say, *matar uma aldeia* was illegitimate. No Indian massacre was legal under Brazilian law. Just war was over in 1831, and the state officially embraced a "gentle" indigenous policy in 1845. More importantly, the 1862 and 1881 massacres (and probably others) were largely perpetrated by non-Indians, including several representatives of the state whose very presence obscured their illegality. Fagundes, a state agent, was aware of the Pojixá massacre's illegitimacy. He asserted the contrary by calling it a legal action in response to their resisting arrest. Neither he nor Ottoni denied the brutality but deflected responsibility for it, Ottoni by blaming Indian contamination, Fagundes by emphasizing legality. It was a discourse that would reemerge in 1881, when the *entrada* leader, Manoel Moreira, told another that the assault on the Indians "had

---

[26] Whitehead, "Introduction," 5.

[27] They seem akin to the *muchachos* in Taussig's analysis of the Putumayo report, whom he describes as "mediating as civilized or rational Indians between the savages of the forest and the whites of the rubber camps." The muchachos "wrought to perfection all that was horrifying in the colonial mythology of savagery ... Not only did they create fictions stoking the fires of white paranoia, they embodied the brutality that the whites feared, created, and tried to harness to their own ends." Taussig, "Culture of Terror," 162.

[28] Ottoni, "Mucury."

guarantees, given that Captain Peixoto, Diogo Filho, and others, told him that they had requested and obtained government orders to this end." Manoel Mendes claimed that he had "joined the troop, deceived by their guarantee of a government order, which they read to him." In other words, they understood the seal of legality as exonerating them of accountability.[29]

Ottoni, Fagundes, and the assailants of 1881 were all governed by the same lexicon of violence formed in the crucible of indigenous conquest. They reproduced the fantasy of indigenous savagery that had sanctioned just wars since the late colonial period and continued to fuel anti-indigenous violence in their long aftermath. Even as he denounced the massacre, Ottoni uttered that "we here in Mucuri fear being devoured by the savages."[30] In the ambiguous frontiers of legality and extralegality, enduring colonial fantasies rendered the massacres of entire Indian villages necessary and legitimate.

The Unraveling

On completing their initial witness interrogations, on September 27, 1881 the police officer appointed by the Bahian president to investigate the Nok-Nok massacre concluded that it was "vehemently demonstrated . . . that the Nok-Nok Indians suffered a terrible attack within their own aldeia in early July of this year." He spoke in the language of nineteenth-century Brazilian indigenism. The Indians were "indubitably victimized" by their assailants, who had "unloaded their weapons on the unhappy Nok-Nok Indians resting in their forests, of which they are the children and true masters." He identified as the instigators the two Canavieiras merchants, Antônio Guimarães and Antônio de Carvalho, along with the German Georg Stolze and another named Diogo Filho. Six "tame" Kamakã Indians named Gregorio, Joaquim Antônio, Jeronimo, Militão, Manoel Joaquim, and Francisco and twelve other residents, including the entrada leader Manoel Moreira, were identified as representatives. There were twenty-two total suspects.[31]

If the testimonies seemed clear and the case against the assailants strong, the case collapsed spectacularly within a matter of months. Perhaps one of their witnesses, Manoel Pereira, had already foretold

---

[29] Bahiana Jr., September 15, 1881; Mendes, September 15, 1881.
[30] Ottoni, "Mucury."
[31] Firmino Ribeiro de Souza, Police Lieutenant, "Nok-Nok Massacre Police Investigation" (Rio Pardo, September 27, 1881), Colonial/Polícia/Mc 6218, APEB.

what would transpire when he told his interrogators in September that locals had joined forces to obstruct and even demoralize the government-appointed authorities sent to inquire about the massacre. The residents disdained the central government forces, whom they considered "ignorant of the forests and easy to deceive." He warned the police that the investigators would give up on reaching the site of the massacre.[32]

Two months later, in November, the accused assembled an aggressive legal team that focused their arguments on two points: the defendants' reputations, and the lack of a corpus delicti (concrete evidence for a crime, i.e., a body). In a glaring suggestion of backdoor dealing or intimidation, the witnesses, including those who had initially made incriminating testimonies against the two Canavieiras merchants, Stolze, Moreira, and others, revised or even denied their earlier statements, sometimes contradicting themselves. The defendants' reputations replaced the careful examination of evidence. Carvalho and Guimarães decried the accusations as a personal vendetta by the former prosecutor who had co-conducted the original police investigation, while a chorus of witnesses now affirmed that the four suspected orchestrators were "peace-loving" men whose renown and wealth made them incapable of crime. Only Stolze lived close enough to the Nok-Nok to have any conflicts, they added (we have seen that the Indians were wary of him); yet Stolze was not questioned even once. At the same time, less prestigious defendants were smeared. The presiding Justice of Law and public prosecutor concluded that the allegations of Manoel Cândido Moreira's and participant Manoel Ramão Mendes' being drunks and liars rendered the multiple incriminating testimonies against them unworthy of further investigation. In September Mendes had offered the single most graphic and detailed account of the massacre. He was noticeably excluded from the November proceedings, in spite of having had no obvious motive to invent the massacre with such vivid detail. Also missing were Stolze, Diogo Filho, the Kamakã Indians, and many of the entrada participants.

With each passing day, responsibility for the massacre shifted. First came an inversion of accountability. While the same twenty-two suspects remained, by November 5 they had switched places: now the eighteen Kamakã Indians and residents were the "authors," and the four alleged instigators were "accomplices." The latter were acquitted a month later. Then, similarly to how Ottoni had shifted responsibility for the *matar uma aldeia* onto the Indians Cró and Crahy, the incident's narrative

[32] Pereira Neto, September 15, 1881.

transformed from an anti-Indian *entrada* into an intra-Indian conflict, the Kamakã thrust from an auxiliary into a principal role. In a markedly leading question, the new public prosecutor asked one of the witnesses if he was "not aware that there is an old hatred between the Kamakã and Nok-Nok Indians, as the latter often invade the others' fields, causing trouble?" The witness, Carlos Warnaux, merely agreed.[33] Moreira seemed nonplussed by the personal attacks against him and soon joined in, claiming the *entrada* was entirely a Kamakã affair in which he had no part. His Kamakã pals had told him that "the Nok-Nok fled as soon as they saw them, and none of them fired their weapons." As to having been seen with several Indian children after the alleged massacre, Moreira explained that the Kamakã had given him the "abandoned" children whom he had intended to baptize.[34] He did not explain how one of them had died. By the time he made these statements in November 1881 and June 1882, nearly a year after the massacre, Moreira – originally described as having macheted a child to death with "such ferocity" and having "killed caboclo like the devil" – had safely removed himself from the center to the periphery of the case.[35]

A Massacre without Bodies, a People outside the Law

The fog thickened over the massacre. The defense harped on the lack of physical evidence to crush the massacre into nonexistence. "It is said that there was as great carnage, many Indians were killed," said the defendants' lawyer. "However, in all this massacre, not a single victim has appeared."[36] He was correct: there had been no *corpus delicti*, a point the defense repeatedly emphasized. No crime scene investigation had taken place, because the locals had likely affirmed Manoel Pereira's earlier prediction and ensured that the government agents, "ignorant of the forests," never made it to the *aldeia*. (Since Stolze's property neighbored it, it would not have been difficult to reach with his assistance.) The two Canavieiras merchants' representative argued that they could not

33 Carlos José Warnaux, 2nd Testimony, November 7, 1881, 29v, Processo Crime 21/853/05, APEB.

34 Luiz Federico Warnaux, 2nd Testimony, November 7, 1881, Processo Crime 21/853/05, APEB; Ivo Rodrigues do Espírito Santo, 2nd Testimony (Rio Pardo, November 21, 1881), Processo Crime 21/853/05, APEB.

35 Manoel Cândido Moreira, 1st Testimony, November 16, 1881, Fl. 65v–66v, Processo Crime 21/853/05, APEB; Manoel Cândido Moreira, 2nd Testimony, June 5, 1882, Fl. 90, Processo Crime 21/853/05, APEB.

36 Manoel do Bomfim Pereira Neto, 2nd Testimony, November 7, 1881, Fl. 32v, Processo Crime 21/853/05, APEB.

be punished for a crime "when there is not even the lightest, remotest proof of the existence of the crime." Because there were no bodies, they posited, no massacre had taken place.[37] They insisted that the absence of a corpus delicti invalidated the case on procedural grounds. However, the assertion that there was "not a single witnesses who has seen at least a bone of these many victims made in this entrada" was incorrect.[38] Manoel Ramão Mendes had seen blood splattered all over the forests in the wake of the entrada. Others said they had seen the corpses of dead caboclas. Another participant named Theodorico Britto said that they had killed many Indians, and several other witnesses had heard about Moreira's violent exploits. These testimonies were simply discarded.[39]

Was there no matar uma aldeia? The case is as distinguished by its horrific violence as by the concerted effort that followed to disappear the massacre as well as the Indians involved. From the first police investigation in September 1881 until the last acquittal in May 1893, not a single Indian voice was heard throughout the entire process, be that of Nok-Nok survivors or the Kamakã perpetrators. Indians remained invisible throughout the entire case. No Kamakã were interrogated, even though their residence and names were known since the beginning of the investigation, and even after they had been identified as the entrada's leaders. Nor was there any police effort to find any evidence of the massacre. They ensured that not a single bone was unearthed.

In spite of these silences, however, several factors strongly support the massacre's reality. The Nok-Nok massacre followed a specific transcript of violence, whose very similarities with a preceding half-century of matar uma aldeia may suggest that it was just a narrative trope, a story. However, the detail in the original testimonies defies that possibility. Those who testified to the police in September 1881 spoke with a specificity and vividness of detail never again seen in their later statements, which became a farce of character assessments and self-contradiction.[40] If anything, the

---

[37] Statement of Antônio Carvalho and Antônio Guimarães, November 22, 1881, 63v, Processo Crime 21/853/05, APEB.

[38] Warnaux 2nd Testimony, November 7, 1881, Fl. 26v.

[39] Theodorico was later acquitted, but there are no traces of an interrogation. After acquitting the two merchants, the Justice of Law maintained the homicide charges against the others. Yet one by one, they too were acquitted, including Moreira, Carlos Themer, Theodorico, and Antonio José dos Santos. Nobody, not once, bothered to go to the aldeia or question the Kamakã.

[40] For instance, Augusto Bahiana Jr. claimed that Moreira had said Stolze ordered the entrada, and later in the same testimony claimed he never heard of anybody ordering an entrada.

similarities point to the routinization of extravagant anti-indigenous violence by the hands of settlers, state agents, and their Indian allies. Second,
land was clearly at stake. As seen earlier, Stolze was a central player in the
region's colonization in addition to financing road construction through
indigenous territory. The Nok-Nok aldeia, neighboring his own land, was
probably an obstacle to his territorial ambitions. Finally, a disturbingly
similar murder of Indians had taken place just two months before the
Nok-Nok massacre that suggested a more widespread, troubling relationship linking anti-indigenous violence and the legal system.

In May 1881 a Botocudo Indian named Antônio Impó was murdered
by a wealthy farmer named Antonio Pereira de Abreu in the town of
Alcobaça, near Colônia Leopoldina. Impó and nine family members had
been harvesting timber for Abreu. After Impó's death, Abreu hired several
men to poison his surviving family. When that failed, the men shot the
Botocudo, hacked the women with machetes, and attacked the children.
Their corpses were then weighted with stones and thrown into a river.
Abreu and his relatives were soon suspected of ordering the massacre
and hiring the assassins, but the Justice of Law obstructed due process by
automatically granting them habeas corpus. The judge was involved in
the timber business with Abreu, whom he had already helped acquit of
Impó's murder by inventing a story of self-defense.[41] Countless obstructions of justice, probable witness intimidation, and mistrials allowed the
case to drag on. Four years after the incident the Municipal Judge rue-
fully recalled the "murder of three innocent children, three unfortunate
women, and three inoffensive youth, who constituted a family of peaceful
and civilized Indians."[42] The accused walked free.

In both these massacres, the violence was brutal and the punishment
null. Yet it would be erroneous to understand these outcomes as evidence
of frontier lawlessness, where the Brazilian state ceased to exist. What
these cases reveal is precisely how the state produced itself in the obscured
boundaries between the legal and extralegal. To understand why the Nok-
Nok massacre happened and why there were no consequences for the
perpetrators, we need to examine how the laws governing anti-indigenous
violence in postcolonial Brazil allowed the incident to be "exposed to the

---

[41] Manoel Soares da Silva Gomes to Municipal Justice of Alcobaça, June 10, 1881; and
Municipal Justice of Alcobaça to unknown recipient, June 26, 1881, Colonial/Justiça/
Alcobaça/Mc 2230, APEB.
[42] Municipal Justice of Alcobaça to President, June 19, 1885, Colonial/ Justiça/Alcobaça/
Mc 2230, APEB.

light and then allowed to fall back into the dark . . . how it came to happen and how it came to be denied."[43]

No Brazilian law in 1881 explicitly allowed Indian murder or enslavement. Yet their continuation – with the victims receiving no legal protection and their killers facing no consequences – was not a sign of anarchy. Rather, it was evidence of the Indians' state of exception. Poole and Das, in discussing Agamben's *Homo Sacer*, argue that the state of exception – whose classic example is war – may create "new categories of people included in the political community but denied membership in political terms." They elaborate, "the issue is not that membership is simply denied but rather that individuals are reconstituted through special laws as populations on whom new forms of regulation can be exercised." Expanding on *homo sacer*, a human life that is "included in the juridical order solely in the form of exclusion (that is, of its capacity to be killed)," Poole and Das argue that the law actively produces "killable bodies" who are "positioned by the law itself as prior to the institution of law."[44] Likewise, the Nok-Nok massacre exposes how Indians in postcolonial Brazil were placed outside the law and made into killable bodies.

Brazilian Indians' state of exception began under war. Portuguese Prince Regent João VI had declared the offensive wars in 1808 after recognizing the "futility of all humane means." Botocudos' purported savagery had given the king the "just motives" to "*suspend* the effects of Humanity." Under this state of exception, indigenous slavery was relegalized, land seizure permitted, and violence in general encouraged as a way to terrorize the Indians into submission.[45] The violence of the

---

43 Mark Danner, *The Massacre at El Mozote: A Parable of the Cold War* (New York: Vintage Books, 1994), 10.

44 Giorgio Agamben, *Homo Sacer: Sovereign Power and Bare Life* (Stanford, CA: Stanford University Press, 1998), 12; discussed in Veena Das and Deborah Poole, eds., *Anthropology in the Margins of the State* (Santa Fe: School of American Research Press; Oxford: James Curry, 2004), 11–13.

45 Manuela Carneiro da Cunha, ed., *Legislação indigenista no século XIX: uma compilação (1808–1889)* (São Paulo: Comissão Pró-Indio de São Paulo, 1992), 57–60, italics mine. The Brazilian Constitution of 1824 also describes the state of emergency in which individual liberties could be suspended: "XXXV. Nos casos de rebellião, ou invasão de inimigos, *pedindo a segurança do Estado, que se dispensem por tempo determinado algumas das formalidades, que garantem a liberdade individual*, poder-se-ha fazer por acto especial do Poder Legislativo. Não se achando porém a esse tempo reunida a Assembléa, e correndo a Patria perigo imminente, poderá o Governo exercer esta mesma providencia, como medida provisoria, e indispensavel, *suspendendo-a immediatamente que cesse a necessidade urgente*, que a motivou; devendo num, e outro caso remetter á Assembléa, logo que reunida fôr, uma relação motivada das prisões, e d'outras medidas

Botocudo Wars long outlasted the period's official end in 1831, with matar uma aldeia being the most gruesome example. Many of these acts of violence were private, yet often enabled by a state that embedded possibilities for them in its "gentle" indigenous policies and its pursuit of territorial conquest, and now, in its production of Indian "extinction." The full effects of the 1824 Constitution's silence on indigenous citizenship were now evident: for "wild" Indians, their state of exception was without end. They were simultaneously part of, yet outside, Brazilian laws.

The making of "killable" Indians occurred in the nebulous frontiers of the legal and extralegal. At first glance the state appeared to be in conflict with the Rio Pardo residents, perpetrators of extralegal violence who had obstructed its representatives – the police lieutenant and public prosecutor – from fulfilling their duty to the Bahian president to investigate the massacre.[46] By November both these men had been removed from the case and replaced by others who discredited their initial investigation and helped destroy the case. However, this transition did not signal the exit from state authority into the realm of the extralegal; for those who derailed the investigation, in particular the new public prosecutor and Justice of Law, were also agents who embodied the state. They simultaneously represented, like the Peruvian *gamonales* (strongmen) studied by Poole, *both* personalized, private power *and* the supposedly impersonal authority of the state, crossing and blurring the distinctions of public and private, legal and extralegal.[47] Just as the judge in Alcobaça helped acquit the Botocudos' murderers to satisfy his private interests, the officials involved in the Nok-Nok proceedings used their authority in the court of law to absolve the accused, to whom they were clearly partial. At the same time they ensured that the Indians would have no place in that same court – for no corpus delicti was found, no survivors were sought out, and no Kamakã testified.

These men used their position as state agents to legitimize acts of private, extralegal violence, and in doing so reinforced the "killability" of indigenous Brazilians, particularly those for whom "wild" status

de prevenção tomadas; e quaesquer Autoridades, que tiverem mandado proceder a ellas, serão responsaveis pelos abusos, que tiverem praticado a esse respeito."

[46] João Lustosa da Cunha Paranaguá, "Relatório (BA)," 1882, 24, CRL.

[47] Deborah Poole, "Between Threat and Guarantee: Justice and Community in the Margins of the Peruvian State," in *Anthropology in the Margins of the State*, ed. Deborah Poole and Veena Das (Santa Fe: School of American Research Press; Oxford: James Curry, 2004), 14, 42–51.

prevented their national inclusion. Through them the state reproduced itself on the frontier by specifically placing Indians outside its body of laws. Most disturbing, however, was the fact that the state and its agents did not stop at legitimizing extralegal violence. They went so far as to render the massacre's legitimacy irrelevant by disappearing the Indians' bodies and the massacre all together, as if driving a final nail in the coffin of extinction.

Mastery Unraveled: The Case of Rita and Seraphim

Shots detonated outside Olimpio Leite de Amorim's home in São Mateus on the afternoon of February 5, 1884. A slave named Seraphim staggered in, desperately seeking Olimpio's protection. His arms, pierced by shotgun pellets, were bathed in blood. Soon three more men forced their way in, two with shotguns and another with a club. One of them reloaded his weapon while telling Olimpio that he was killing the slave for money. Olimpio implored the men not to murder Seraphim, promising to turn him over to the authorities or to his master, José Vicente de Faria. Faria was São Mateus' alderman in the Municipal Chamber and his father, Vicente José de Faria, the patriarch of a large local family of some importance. The Farias' patronage ties with Dr. Raulino, a major slaveholder, President of the Municipal Chamber, and leader of the local conservative faction, further cemented their position among the São Mateus slave-owning oligarchy.[48] Vicente Faria himself soon arrived with his sons and dependents in tow. The Faria men, totaling nine, secured a rope around Seraphim's hands, waist, and back so that the bleeding slave was tightly bound. Olimpio watched in silence as the Farias, all on horseback, dragged the slave away to their plantation, located four leagues from the town center.[49]

Seraphim was never seen again. In the ensuing police investigation, the Faria men uniformly claimed that he had slipped out of his rope and fled. Vicente Faria himself presumed the slave had gone to Minas; none of the men bothered to explain how a severely injured slave was able to undo the rope and outrun nine men on horseback. Their account convinced no one. A local policeman was certain that the Farias had meted out their own

[48] *Almanak* (Espírito Santo), 1884, CRL.
[49] Traslado do inquérito policial referente sobre o assassinato do escravo Seraphim de propriedade de José Vicente de Faria (1884). Auto de perguntas feitas a Olympio Leite de Amorim, March 10, 1884, Polícia/Delegacias/22: Inquéritos/Cx 706/Processo 815, APEES. The file is hereafter referred to as Seraphim Inquérito.

justice by brutally castrating and murdering Seraphim, after which they buried him in secrecy. Others' testimonies made clear that the Faria men, though they maintained their ignorance, believed Seraphim guilty: he had impregnated Vicente Faria's widowed daughter, Rita, whose honor they sought to avenge.[50]

The sexual union and reproduction between a black slave and a white woman was a flagrant violation of social mores.[51] Rita and Seraphim's relationship and its tragic end show how the case transgressed multiple legal and social boundaries at the heart of slaveholding society – of race, gender, and status – while exposing the confinements of female honor. Yet Seraphim's execution was clandestine, and its perpetrators, powerful slaveholders, *denied* their involvement. The Farias' secrecy and denial contradicts the predominant understanding of slave punishment, mutilation, and execution throughout the Americas, which have emphasized their public, spectacular nature. Private punishment of one's own slaves did occur behind closed doors in Brazil and other slaveholding societies. But punishment was most effective when it was public, for its purpose was to affirm mastery over one's slaves and instill fear and submission through example.

Since the colonial period, the Brazilian state had maintained an ambiguous stance on private master–slave relations and punishment. Sometimes it intervened, but most often abetted masters' authority or simply abstained from interference. Seraphim's case thus allows us to witness an important political shift in the realm of private master–slave relations beginning to take place in the Atlantic frontier, echoing larger transformations across Brazil. His execution happened amidst a growing public support for abolition, whose most palpable evidence in Espírito Santo was the 1883 founding of the Domingos Martins abolitionist society by prominent liberals.[52] Seraphim's violent death and aftermath, marked by public censure of the Farias, tore open an intensifying struggle over slaves' and masters' rights. Increasing state intervention on behalf of the enslaved

---

[50] Luiz Antonio dos Santos, Police Lieutenant of São Mateus to Police Chief, February 17, 1884, Polícia Ser. 2 Mc 287 Fl. 176–77, APEES.

[51] Seraphim's racial identity is based on his sales record according to which, on May 25,1880, a "slave by the name of Serafim, *preto* (black)" was sold to José Vicente de Faria. Tabelionato Liv. 11 Fl. 168v, CPSM. As for Rita, it is unlikely that her brother would have occupied the position of alderman if he were not white, so I have deduced that she too was white.

[52] See Chapter 6 for more on the society. A leading figure was Affonso Claudio, the author of a highly regarded study of the 1849 Queimado slave insurrection and soon to be the first president of Espírito Santo in Republican Brazil.

accelerated the erosion of slaveholder power and created more openings for the enslaved to exploit. Yet much has been written on the laws of slave punishment and executions in Brazil and the Americas.[53] This section assumes a different perspective. Rather than focusing on slave punishment per se, it juxtaposes Seraphim's case with the Nok-Nok massacre. Doing so reveals the simultaneity of expanding citizenship opportunities for enslaved people and the total legal exclusion of Indians, which challenges liberal narratives that have shaped our understandings of slavery and citizenship in postcolonial Latin American history.

Economic Downturn and Gradual Emancipation

The 1870s and 1880s were a precarious time in São Mateus. The later decades of the nineteenth century were a boom for the wealthy planters of the south-central coffee regions in Rio de Janeiro, São Paulo, and Minas Gerais whose political power expanded along with their economy. As the coffee frontier spread east from Rio de Janerio's Paraíba valley into southern Espírito Santo, economic ties strengthened between Rio and Vitória, Espírito Santo's provincial capital, facilitated by the latter's inclusion into the Brazilian Steamship Company's coastal route in 1874. São Mateus was excluded from the shipping route because of its interior location and the local river's limited navigability. Still, a local steamship service allowed it to maintain its manioc trade with Rio as well as with Bahia and Pernambuco further north. That same year, the first street lamps were illuminated, cobblestones began paving some of its streets, and new telegraph lines connected São Mateus to other coastal cities.[54]

Still, these infrastructural improvements could not shield it or the larger province from the economic impact of the 1871 Free Womb Law. With its perennially small slave population further diminished, São Mateus' manioc exports of nearly 7.5 million liters in 1870 plummeted to 4.9 million liters by 1874 and would fall to 4.5 million liters by 1884.[55] However, this decline was also due to its slow shift to coffee cultivation, a change led from around the 1860s by an emerging rural oligarchy extending its landholdings into the city's hinterland. This oligarchy, bound through ties of family and slaveownership around the coronel Antonio Rodrigues da Cunha and his son of the same name, came to occupy seats in the

---

53 They are referenced in this chapter.
54 Anna Lucia Côgo, "História do Espírito Santo no século XIX: a região de São Mateus" (doctoral dissertation, Universidade de São Paulo, 2007), 116–25.
55 Domingos Monteiro Peixoto, "Falla (ES)," 1875, 60, CRL; Antonio Joaquim Rodrigues, "Relatório (ES)," 1885, 7, CRL.

Provincial Assembly. As representatives of the Conservative party, they gave a loud voice to São Mateus' slaveocratic interests.[56]

In 1872 the combined population of São Mateus and its neighboring parishes of Barra de São Mateus and Itaúnas was 8,170, including 2,793 slaves, 2,728 free blacks and pardos, 141 caboclos, and 2,488 whites. The slave population fell to 2,500 in 1876, the last year before abolition for which there are statistics.[57] These diminishing numbers did not appease the enslaved. In 1865 and 1866, the Paraguayan War (1864–70) sparked insurrection fears in São Mateus, Barra, and the towns of Cariacica and Serra further south. According to the police chief, "some slaves, believing that the war against the Republics of Plata will bring freedom to all Brazilian slaves, were ready for an insurrection in parts of the province."[58] The Free Womb Law triggered several insurrection rumors again in 1871. In São Mateus, fugitive slaves believed that a general emancipation was underway. The city's enslaved were aware that changes were afoot.[59]

Interracial Sex and the Limits of Female Honor

Rita Faria was visibly ill when she arrived to Vitória in October 1883. Accompanying her from São Mateus was her former slave, Magdalena. Already widowed at thirty years old, in February of that year she had aborted a seven-month-old fetus conceived with Seraphim by ingesting various herbal potions, and was still struggling to recover. She later recounted to police chief Antonio Pitanga that the abortion had taken place in order to "hide her shame." Magdalena and another female slave buried the fetus in her flower garden. Rita had come to Vitória under a

---

[56] Maria do Carmo de Oliveira Russo, "A escravidão em São Mateus, ES: economia e demografia (1848–1888)" (doctoral dissertation, Universidade de São Paulo, 2011), 27–36, 108–13.

[57] For the 1872 statistics: Brazil and Directoria Geral de Estatística, *Recenseamento da população do Imperio do Brazil a que se procedeu no dia 1°. de agosto de 1872* ([Rio de Janeiro]: [A Directoria], 1873). For 1876, see Vilma Paraíso Ferreira de Almada, *Escravismo e transição: o Espírito Santo (1850–1888)* (Rio de Janeiro: Graal, 1984), 118. A precise population count for São Mateus in the 1880s is unavailable; the total slave population of Espírito Santo in 1884 was 20,216, the largest concentration in the southern sugar-producing areas of the province. Source: Robert Edgar Conrad, *The Destruction of Brazilian Slavery, 1850–1888* (Berkeley: University of California Press, 1972), 291.

[58] Eduardo Pindahiba de Mattos to José Joaquim do Carmo, President of Espírito Santo, February 22, 1865, IJ1–437-ES, AN; Manoel da Silva Rego to Carlos da Cerqueira Pinto, January 12, 1866, Governadoria Ser. 383 Liv. 276 FL. 423, APEES.

[59] Francisco Ferreira Corrêa, September 1, 1871, IJ1–440-ES, AN.

false name to recuperate and escape from her disapproving relatives. She was mortified to be exposing her most intimate details to the police.[60]

In marked contrast to the reticent Rita was Magdalena, an eager witness. Magdalena had won her freedom from the Farias by entering a deal to assist the abortion, bury the fetus, and accompany Rita to the capital. Perhaps emboldened by her newly won liberty, Magdalena was not shy about recounting lurid details, shedding light on the startling intimacy that bound free white and enslaved black women in the same private sphere.[61] She told Pitanga that she had been aware of the relationship because she "sometimes found traces in her mistress's clothing." It was only when her pregnancy was no longer concealable that Rita told Magdalena, adding bitterly that she was suffering because the "author of her disgrace" was very satisfied with what had happened.[62]

Noticeably absent in this scandalous affair between an upper-class white woman and her family's slave is the allegation of rape. For although Rita and several witnesses mentioned her "shame" and "dishonor," at no point, either from herself, her family, the witnesses, or the police, was there any suggestion of forced sexual relations. According to Magdalena, her mistress had told her that she was in the relationship willingly, a revelation that instantly abrogated any possibility of rape. Meanwhile, even the Farias refused to acknowledge that they were hunting Seraphim for having had sexual relations with, and impregnated, their daughter and sister. The patriarch Vicente Faria claimed had Rita told him that her misfortune had been committed by a free person whose identity she refused to divulge. He asserted that the family was hunting down Seraphim only because he was a fugitive slave. One of his sons, Vicente Jr., stated that while he first believed Seraphim was simply disobedient, he later heard rumors that "he had dishonored someone in [his] family," but did not elaborate. Even when pressed by the police about whether his family did not want to punish the slave after discovering what had happened, he remained elusive, stating "no, because we

---

[60] Auto de perguntas feitas a Rita Rosa dos Santos (Faria), March 6, 1884, Seraphim Inquérito.

[61] See, for example, Sandra Lauderdale Graham, *House and Street: The Domestic World of Servants and Masters in Nineteenth-Century Rio de Janeiro* (Cambridge and New York: Cambridge University Press, 1988). In the US South, such proximity among enslaved and white women first came to light in Harriet Jacobs, "Incidents in the Life of a Slave Girl," in *The Classic Slave Narratives*, ed. Henry Louis Gates (New York: New American Library, 1987), 437–668.

[62] Auto de perguntas feitas a Magdalena liberta, February 20, 1884, Seraphim Inquérito.

weren't certain."[63] But how were a slave and a mistress able to maintain a sexual relationship under household vigilance? The lack of evidence notwithstanding, it is possible that at least some family members had tacitly allowed the relationship, with Rita's pregnancy being the real problem.

Whatever the Farias thought in private, publicly, the relationship was completely unacceptable. The racial and gender hierarchy of slave societies across the Americas was founded on masters' entitlement to the bodies and reproductive capacities of enslaved women, a hierarchy upended by black male prowess and reproductive power exercised on the bodies of white women.[64] The fear of black masculinity was evident in the feverish emergence of the black rapist trope – allegations of black men raping or coveting children and white women – in São Mateus soon after Seraphim's execution. As a growing abolitionist movement threatened slaveholder power, the latter retaliated by equating black freedom with sexual violence. In this growing climate of paranoia, the absence of rape accusations in this case was therefore all the more striking.

Rita's predicament revealed the narrow field in which a white woman with social standing could defend her honor. A white (married, now widowed) woman from an established family and the sister of the city alderman, Rita had enjoyed a significant degree of honor prior to her relationship with Seraphim. Her sexual relationship with a slave destroyed it. The terms "shame" and "dishonor" haunt her throughout this investigation. Brazilian women did have the means to restore their honor legally, as stipulated in the Brazilian criminal code's crimes against honor; yet her uniquely vulnerable position denied her these means. As a widow she did not have her husband's protection, nor was she a virgin who could defend her honor on the basis of her deflowering, through marriage. Marriage,

---

[63] Auto de perguntas feitas a Vicente de Faria Jr., March 13, 1884, Seraphim Inquérito.

[64] On white-on-black rape after reconstruction in the US South, see Hannah Rosen, *Terror in the Heart of Freedom: Citizenship, Sexual Violence, and the Meaning of Race in the Postemancipation South* (Chapel Hill: University of North Carolina Press, 2009). During slavery in the United States, see Saidiya V. Hartman, *Scenes of Subjection: Terror, Slavery, and Self-Making in Nineteenth-Century America* (New York: Oxford University Press, 1997), Chapter 3. As is well known, Gilberto Freyre recast this violent relationship as the celebration of Brazilians' propensity toward race-mixing in his *Masters and Slaves*. While Brazil may have been more tolerant of interracial unions than the United States, as Peter Beattie has suggested, I contend that the "policing of the color line" was applicable to unions of black men and white women. Peter M. Beattie, "'Born Under the Cruel Rigor of Captivity, the Supplicant Left It Unexpectedly by Committing a Crime': Categorizing and Punishing Slave Convicts in Brazil, 1830–1897," *The Americas* 66, no. 1 (2009): 52.

which may have been a possibility had her relationship been with a free white man, was out of the question with a slave.[65] In essence, a consensual relationship was not a crime. Criminalizing sexual relations between free and enslaved people would have caused an uproar among slaveholders. The absence of rape accusations (or of attempts to frame the case as such) suggests that even her family, to a certain degree, acknowledged the consensual nature of their relationship, which was dishonorable nonetheless. The Farias ultimately forced Rita into exile and began hunting down the slave.

However, if the disgraced Rita struggled to hide her relationship and her pregnancy, Seraphim had no qualms. Magdalena recounted that "everyone knew" about their liaison since he had bragged about it in public. That included Olimpio, who had heard that "the slave had illicit relations with one of the young Faria mistresses." Rita resented Seraphim for being "very satisfied [with her disgrace], and it was she who suffered." Youthful swagger undoubtedly goaded Seraphim to flaunt his sexual adventures with his white mistress, allowing him to scandalize and impress his fellow slaves. But his bragging signified much more than recklessness. By publicizing his sexual relationship with a white mistress, Seraphim defied what was permissible for an enslaved male and threatened to upend the image of barbarism associated with black male sexuality. In doing so, he committed what a slave was never permitted to do: smear his master's family name and absolute authority. Perhaps suddenly realizing the danger he had stepped into, Seraphim went into hiding when news of their relationship reached the family.[66]

Punishment and Mastery Reconsidered

The Farias found Seraphim and subjected him to brutal violence. Violence, exercised through physical discipline, fused with paternalism to form the foundation of slave societies. In his best-selling *Manual do Agricultor Brasileiro* (1839), the French-born, Brazilian transplant Carlos Augusto Taunay drew a direct relationship between slave discipline and increased productivity by highlighting the importance of "fear, and only fear" to subject slaves to a "rigorous discipline and their inevitable

---

[65] The Brazilian Imperial criminal code's section on crimes against women's honor – rape and kidnapping (*rapto*) – can be consulted in Part 3, Title II, Chapter 2, Articles 219 to 228. On the relationship between deflowering and female honor in Rio, albeit in the early Republican period, see Martha de Abreu Esteves, *Meninas perdidas: os populares e o cotidiano do amor no Rio de Janeiro da belle époque* (Rio de Janeiro: Paz e Terra, 1989); Sueann Caulfield, *In Defense of Honor: Sexual Morality, Modernity, and Nation in Early-Twentieth Century Brazil* (Durham, NC: Duke University Press, 2000).

[66] Magdalena; Olimpio Leite de Amorim, Seraphim Inquérito.

FIGURE 4.3 Public slave whippings, which disciplined and terrorized the slave and onlookers alike, became scarce by the later nineteenth century as it became difficult to reconcile slavery with Brazil's claims to be a modern nation. *Source: L'Exécution de la Punition du Fouet,* from Jean Baptiste Debret, *Voyage pittoresque et historique au Brésil* (Paris: Firmin Didot frères, 1834). From the New York Public Library.

punishment."[67] The most common methods included the wooden paddle, the stocks, and various kinds of whips and lashes, the last two exclusively reserved for slaves. Brazilian law limited the daily maximum to fifty lashes.[68] Corporal punishment was elevated into spectacle with the *pelourinho,* or whipping-post, placed centrally in city and town squares in full public view (Figure 4.3). Slaves witnessed the back of the punished turning into raw flesh and heard their agonizing screams. The Portuguese penal code had made clear that the objective of punishment was to set a public example, not to correct individuals. Similarly, Taunay emphasized that punishment be "executed with regard to all the slaves, with

---

[67] Carlos Augusto Taunay, *Manual do agricultor brasileiro,* ed. Rafael de Bivar Marquese (São Paulo: Companhia das Letras, 2001), 55–56; Rafael de Bivar Marquese, *Feitores do corpo, missionários da mente: senhores, letrados e o controle dos escravos nas Américas, 1660–1860* (São Paulo: Companhia das Letras, 2004), 270–71.

[68] See Title II (on punishments), Chapter 1, Article 60 of the criminal code. On slave punishment, see Leila Mezan Algranti, *O feitor ausente: estudo sobre a escravidão urbana no Rio de Janeiro* (Petrópolis: Vozes, 1988); Emília Viotti da Costa, *The Brazilian Empire: Myths & Histories* (Chapel Hill: University of North Carolina Press, 2000), 138; Peter M. Beattie, "Slaves, Crime, and Punishment in Imperial Brazil," *Luso-Brazilian Review* 45, no. 2 (2009): 191–93; Beattie, "'Born Under.'"

the greatest solemnity, so that [it] serves to teach and intimidate the rest."[69]

When punishment did not suffice, masters called on the spectacle of death. The public execution of rebellious slaves and the mutilation of their corpses became powerful means to demonstrate slaveholder power. Slaves' bodies were publicly displayed as specific place and memory markers of crime and punishment. Public executions took on special significance in slave societies as masters employed slave cadavers, or sometimes pieces of their bodies, as a terrifying method of domination. In a practice that Vincent Brown has called necromancy, slave masters harnessed the affective power of the dead to "transmute their legal mastery into sacred authority" to subjugate both the bodies and souls of the enslaved.[70] Corporal mutilation was similarly a finely calibrated act. In eighteenth-century Jamaica, removed body parts were often accompanied by specific instructions as to their display and were nailed to cotton trees, the gallows, and other public sites that "extended the spectacular effect of the punishment beyond the brief moment of its actual infliction."[71] The Farias similarly understood the power of corporal mutilation. Although Peter Beattie has contended that "ritualized lynching was not a prominent part of Brazil's cultural grammar of popular justice," slave castration was exactly this: a ritualized act of violence against black masculinity.[72] The Farias punished Seraphim's intolerable violation of order within a slave society through sexual mutilation and murder.

Yet if the potency of punishment and execution was realized through spectacle, secrecy and denial nullified that power.[73] Why were Seraphim's torture and mutilation, his execution and burial, all clandestine? A public display of Seraphim's mutilated cadaver or testicles would have provided the ideal opportunity for the family to terrorize the enslaved. Instead, Seraphim was disappeared. A Faria family associate had informed

---

[69] Algranti, *O feitor ausente*, 195; Taunay, *Manual do agricultor brasileiro*, 66–67.

[70] Vincent Brown, *The Reaper's Garden: Death and Power in the World of Atlantic Slavery* (Cambridge, MA: Harvard University Press, 2008), 129–31.

[71] Diana Paton, "Punishment, Crime, and the Bodies of Slaves in Eighteenth-Century Jamaica," *Journal of Social History* 34, no. 4 (2001): 940.

[72] Beattie, "'Born Under,'" 47.

[73] Aside from the other works mentioned in the foregoing, see João José Reis, *Slave Rebellion in Brazil: The Muslim Uprising of 1835 in Bahia* (Baltimore: Johns Hopkins University Press, 1993). Significantly, although some of those involved in the Malê uprising were sentenced to death by gallows, Reis notes (p. 217) that it did not take place because nobody was willing to be the executioner, which reinforces the fact that executions were effective only when there was public participation in the spectacle.

Seraphim's mother, Dulce Maria da Conceição, that the Farias had taken her son to the forest, where they killed him and discarded his body in a hole dug in the ground. She was "certain that her son was murdered" since, although he had frequently come to visit her while he was hiding from the Farias, the visits had ceased the day after the Farias dragged him away. She believed the Farias had "removed [his body] out of fear that it would be discovered."[74] She would be unable to see her son again or give him a proper burial.

The Farias erected a wall of silence and denial. The disgrace brought upon their family was perhaps too great to warrant a public spectacle. They probably also understood that rumors about Seraphim's fate could sufficiently discipline other slaves. But it was the awareness of the illegality and illegitimacy of their actions that really drove their silence. The Brazilian public's opposition to and discomfort with public disciplinary violence was already evident by the 1830s, when pelourinhos were dismantled throughout Brazil and public hangings sparse. By the second half of the nineteenth century, various sectors of Brazilian society, most prominently Pedro II himself, began challenging slave punishment and executions in general. Such transformations steadily eroded the slaveholders' mastery over their human property.

A murky relationship between the state and individual masters had arbitrated slave punishment in the colonial era. The Portuguese state paid little attention to slave administration compared to the Caribbean colonies, generally avoiding interfering in masters' domestic slave governance except to encourage general good treatment.[75] After independence, Brazilian law remained notoriously permissive of private punishment. According to Article 14 of the Criminal Code, issued in 1830, punishment was a "justifiable crime" when consisting of a "moderate punishment that fathers give their children, slaveowners their slaves, and masters their disciples." Moreover, "slaveowners should abstain from excessive punishment, and in punishing their slaves should limit

---

[74] Dulce Maria da Conceição, March 11, 1884, Seraphim Inquérito.

[75] Marquese, *Feitores do corpo*, 189–90. There are certainly variations to this relationship. In the case of Jamaica, the unison of the state and the slaveholders seems to have been clear. By contrast, in St. Domingue, Laurent Dubois argues that masters employed private and illegal acts of violence against their slaves in defiance of the state, since intervention on the part of the state into slave-master relations would shatter the entire plantation system. For Jamaica and Brazil, see texts cited in this section; for St. Domingue, see Laurent Dubois, "Avenging America: The Politics of Violence in the Haitian Revolution," in *The World of the Haitian Revolution*, ed. David Patrick Geggus and Norman Fiering (Bloomington: Indiana University Press, 2009).

themselves to means informed by justice and humanity." Such loose language gave masters significant leeway in interpreting what constituted just and humane punishment.[76] Private slaveholder power and the public state authority clearly aligned in state-run slave jails, of which Rio de Janeiro's Calabouço was the best known, where masters could bring their slaves to be whipped.[77]

Greater interest in slave administration, including punishment, arose after 1831 with the law abolishing the trans-Atlantic slave trade. Although ineffective, the law sparked concerns about the maintenance of Brazil's enslaved workforce after African sources were cut off. Agricultural manuals from this period encouraged moderate and effective slave punishment as a means to encourage their productivity and reproduction. They also promoted a paternalist ethos, that masters, as members of "good society" of the Brazilian nation, should view slavery as a civilizing mission.[78]

The state began asserting itself more fully in the private sphere of slave discipline with Law 4 of June 10, 1835, passed in the aftermath of the Malê Revolt. This law mandated the death penalty for slaves who murdered their masters, family, or overseers, or were involved in an insurrection. The accused were denied the usual avenues of appeal. In addition, a slave guilty of "gravely injuring or committing any other physical offense to his master, his wife, or his descendants or ancestors" was punishable by the lash, or death. The state thus affirmed its right to intervene in slave discipline, sometimes against the masters' own wishes, for the sake of maintaining public order and economic productivity.[79] The law ironically coincided with a growing public distaste for public punishments and executions.

---

[76] On the practice of slave holders claiming this law to curtail state intervention, see Ricardo Alexandre Ferreira, *Senhores de poucos escravos: cativeiro e criminalidade num ambiente rural, 1830–1888* (São Paulo: Editora UNESP, 2005), 91–92.

[77] Thomas H. Holloway, *Policing Rio de Janeiro: Repression and Resistance in a 19th-Century City* (Stanford, CA: Stanford University Press, 1993), 55. Owners also had to pay for the holding and whipping of their slaves, which sometimes led them to abandon their slaves when costs mounted.

[78] Miguel Calmon du Pin e Almeida Abrantes, *Ensaio sobre o fabrico do açucar*, ed. José de F Mascarenhas, Waldir Freitas Oliveira, and José Honório Rodrigues (Salvador: Federação das Indústrias do Estado da Bahia, 2002), 63–64; Taunay, *Manual do agricultor brasileiro*; Marquese, *Feitores do corpo*, 268–98.

[79] Alexandra K. Brown, "'A Black Mark on Our Legislation': Slavery, Punishment, and the Politics of Death in Nineteenth-Century Brazil," *Luso-Brazilian Review* 37, no. 2 (December 1, 2000): 95–121. A full study of this law is found in Ricardo Figueiredo Pirola, "A lei de 10 de junho de 1835: justiça, escravidão e pena de morte" (doctoral dissertation, UNICAMP, 2012).

However, the state could also intervene on the slaves' behalf. Chapter 2 discussed how the enslaved believed the emperor and government had freed them by placing their interests above masters' private property rights; such ideas were partly founded on the actual practice. Slaves sometimes ran to the police to request protection from their masters. Taunay argued that the master–slave relationship was akin to a contract in which the state was the guarantor with the right to intervene on behalf of both parties. He assuaged masters' fear about state intervention by stating that both would benefit from it. "The law that regulates slavery becomes especially useful for the wealthy and for their slaves," he stated, "sparing them the fatigue of legislating their own fazendas, and the latter from superfluous cruelties and irregularities of treatment." To this end, he recommended that the law decide what was moderate and effective punishment, be it the iron collar, jail, or fifty lashes.[80]

Yet if state intervention in slave discipline was deemed necessary for the maintenance of public order, and agricultural manuals claimed slavery was a "civilizing mission" in the first decades after independence, such ideas had lost much ground by the time of Seraphim's murder. As seen in Chapter 3, well into the 1880s, many Brazilian elites remained preoccupied with the stain of slavery and an enduring indigenous population, which they saw as impeding Brazil's civilization and the realization of a povo brasileiro. Pedro II, a vocal critic of slavery and capital punishment, was keenly aware of his nation's pariah status as the last independent nation in the Western Hemisphere with slavery after the US Civil War, and he sought to prove Brazil's civilization to the outside world. Recognizing, however, that slavery was entrenched and required Parliamentary action to abolish, he focused his efforts instead on ending the death penalty for slaves, which his Moderating Power enabled. Pedro II began phasing out capital punishment in the 1850s, and the last slave execution took place in 1876.[81] Meanwhile in 1873, two years after the Free Womb Law, the Minister of Justice declared public slave whippings to be an anachronism. The Calabouço jail was closed the following year and

---

[80] Taunay, *Manual do agricultor brasileiro*, 67–68. Marquese states that what made Taunay's, and Brazilian, ideas about slave management unique was the emphasis on the union of discipline and paternalism. Marquese, *Feitores do corpo*, 279–97. Speaking of pre-independence-era, urban Rio de Janeiro, at the heart of the Court and state institutions, Algranti argues that the state's rights clearly superseded masters' rights over their slaves. As she concedes, however, in more rural regions, landowners likely had more control over the justice system. Algranti, *O feitor ausente*, 196–98.

[81] Peter M. Beattie, *Punishment in Paradise: Race, Slavery, Human Rights, and a Nineteenth-Century Brazilian Penal Colony* (Durham, NC: Duke University Press, 2015), 208.

punishment was henceforth administered only with the permission of the police, out of public view.[82] The growing recognition among Brazilians of the incompatibility of slavery and civilization subsequently contributed to the 1886 parliamentary ban on public authorities from flogging slaves all together. Although the law did not curtail private violence, its scope was expanded by the enslaved, who defied their masters more openly. Thus, state retrenchment from slave punishment directly impacted the ability of masters to inflict it privately.[83]

This recognition of slavery's incompatibility with civilization delegitimized the prerogative of masters to disciplinary violence. It was the Farias, and not the slave who impregnated his mistress, who stood accused of a "barbaric" act.[84] The family knew that their exercise of violence was illegitimate in the eyes of both the law and the public, which stood "opposed to this occurrence."[85] The emergence of a local abolitionist movement later the same year, violently shut down by São Mateus slaveholders, testified to this intensifying clash between slaveholders, the public, and the state at the local and national levels.[86] By 1884 abolition was already underway in three Brazilian provinces. Slavery's hold on São Mateus was daily weakened by the coalescing of abolitionism with slave insurrection rumors and quilombola agitation. In these rapidly shifting terrains of slavery and freedom, a slave who dared to transgress his legal, racial, and sexual boundaries garnered public sympathy instead of being

---

[82] Holloway, *Policing Rio de Janeiro*, 229–30.

[83] Beattie, *Punishment in Paradise*, 201; Brown, "A Black Mark on Our Legislation," 111.

[84] This was even though, according to Law 4 of June 10, 1835, Seraphim could likely have been considered guilty of "gravely injuring or committing any other physical offense to his master, his wife, or his descendants or ancestors," an offense punishable by the lash. For the full text of the legislation, promulgated in the aftermath of the 1835 Malê uprising, see http://presrepublica.jusbrasil.com.br/legislacao/104059/lei-4-35. On the repression and aftereffects of the Malê uprising, see Reis, *Slave Rebellion in Brazil*, 189–230. More recently, Peter Beattie stated in his review of João Luiz Rebeiro's work on slave punishment and the Brazilian legal system that this law had been in debate in the Parliament much prior to this date, inspired by the less famous 1832 Carrancas revolt in Minas Gerais, but was expedited by the Malê revolt. Beattie, "Slaves, Crime, and Punishment in Imperial Brazil," 193.

[85] Luis Antonio dos Santos, Police Lieutenant, to Police Chief, March 18, 1884, Polícia Ser. 2 Mc 287 Fl. 176–77, APEES; Emília Viotti da Costa, *Da senzala à colônia* (São Paulo: Editora UNESP, 1997), 344–54. Such attitudes contrasted sharply with the widespread public support for vigilantism against freedpeople practiced by night riders in the US South during Reconstruction. Rosen, *Terror in the Heart of Freedom*, 182–83.

[86] This conflict is discussed in Chapter 6.

branded a rapist. And families whose power and wealth was founded on their slaves found their supremacy endangered.

A trial was held in July 1884 in which an abolitionist, Olavo Henrique Baptista, served as prosecutor. This time, the São Mateus slaveholding class prevailed. A sympathetic jury and presiding judge unanimously acquitted all the Farias, who were tried as accomplices, and one of the hired killers.[87]

If these outcomes seemed to affirm the Farias' victory, however, their worst fears were also realized. In his annual report delivered the same year, the Minister of Justice stated that "it was proven that a daughter of Vicente José de Faria had illicit relations with the slave." In forceful language he continued, "There are strong indications that Vicente and his sons killed the slave in order to avenge her honor."[88] The Farias were publicly condemned by the highest legal organ of the nation. Worse, even though they were acquitted, their shame and dishonor had now entered the permanent public record – a catastrophic outcome for a family that had gone out of its way to avenge its honor.

Still, the violence could not be undone. Seraphim paid the price for daring to claim a freedom unpermitted to enslaved black men. His body was buried somewhere in São Mateus, as was the fetus of the unborn mulatto child, whose fate exposed the bitter underside of the Law of the Free Womb (1871). Although the law had initiated the slow process of de-biologizing enslaved status by granting freedom to the children of enslaved women, the child of a free white woman and an enslaved man was legally free but forbidden to exist.[89] Rita, although alive, lost her honor and even her name. She was as good as dead to her family, a disgraced woman with nowhere to go and no means to restore her honor. All three were victims of violence, disappeared in their own

---

[87] Secretary of Police of Espírito Santo to Police Chief of Minas Gerais, March 19, 1884, Polícia Ser. 2 Liv. 257, APEES; *A Província do Espírito Santo*, July 2, 1884.

[88] Francisco Prisco de Souza Paraízo, "Relatório do Ministério da Justiça," 1883, 39–40, CRL. The actual report was delivered on May 13, 1884, more than three months after Seraphim's death in early February 1884.

[89] On the process by which the condition of slavery became biologized through the bodies of enslaved black women, see the classic work by Kathleen M. Brown, *Good Wives, Nasty Wenches, and Anxious Patriarchs: Gender, Race, and Power in Colonial Virginia* (Chapel Hill: University of North Carolina Press, 1996); Jennifer L. Morgan, *Laboring Women: Reproduction and Gender in New World Slavery* (Philadelphia: University of Pennsylvania Press, 2004).

For the law's implications in Brazil, see Martha Abreu, "Slave Mothers and Freed Children: Emancipation and Female Space in Debates on the 'Free Womb' Law, Rio de Janeiro, 1871," *JLAS* 28, no. 3 (1996): 567.

way. Finally, after all the physical and psychological suffering she had to endure, Rita, along with Magdalena, was charged with the crime of abortion.[90]

A Spectacle of Subversion

Peace would not return to the region. Just two months after Seraphim's disappearance, on April 25, 1884, the planter José Antonio Venerote was found clubbed to death on his plantation in Colônia Leopoldina. His skull had been shattered, his forehead caved in, his scalp split. A dark splotch spread over his swollen torso, suggesting severe bruising or the onset of decomposition. Next to his cadaver, which lay splayed out on a path leading to his coffee fields, was a cracked club caked with blood on both ends. Four more blood-stained clubs were discovered in a nearby thicket. In what could hardly seem accidental, the perpetrators had left a whip – the most hated symbol of slave punishment – under Venerote's nose, adorning his mangled head with a shriveled leather whisker.[91] Venerote was returning from out of town business when he was ambushed at the edge of his property and clubbed to death. Seven of his male slaves who had run away on Easter Sunday, less than two weeks before the murder, were soon brought before the police as suspects. Another group of female fugitive slaves who had fled with them was released. First maintaining their innocence, the male slaves later amended their statement to say that they had been contracted to kill Venerote by another Colony resident. Two years later the slaves would recant their testimonies again and claim that they were forced to make a false confession, but were left to languish in prison, where at least one eventually died.[92]

The paternalist ethos had eluded Venerote. In late 1882 he helped suppress two slave uprisings on Colônia Leopoldina, one involving nearly 200 slaves, whom he had denounced for being "extraordinarily disobedient and rebellious."[93] Three weeks before his death he had purchased

---

[90] Antônio Pitanga, March 14, 1884, Seraphim Inquérito.

[91] Henrique Hertzsch to Police Chief of Bahia, May 2, 1884, Colonial/Polícia/Delegados/Mc 6221, APEB.

[92] "José Venerote Murder Investigation" 1890, Processo Crime 17/1604/10, APEB.

[93] José Antonio Venerote (Colônia Leopoldina, September 4, 1882), Colonial/Polícia/Delegados/Mc 6219, APEB; Firmino Bernardo da Motta (Vila Viçosa, September 20, 1882), Colonial/Justiça/Viçosa/Mc 2638, APEB; Pedro Luiz Pereira de Souza, "Falla (BA)," 1883, 63, CRL.

a staggering forty-seven adult slaves and thirteen children, ballooning his total slave ownership to ninety-seven, making his workforce equal to that of the largest coffee plantations in the nation's Center-South. At the time of his death he possessed 291,000 coffee plants.[94] In addition to owning slaves, Venerote was also a slave trader who stood to profit from any transactions he conducted on behalf of third parties. He therefore may have intended to resell his attackers to an unknown owner and uncertain future, thereby subjecting them to the cruel separation from kin and the loss of hard-won customary rights.[95]

Such was the slaves' dislike for Venerote that even in asserting his innocence, the slave Cristiano stated acerbically that "if they had any intention to kill their master because of the bad treatment they received on the fazenda and here in the Caravelas prison where they had been punished, they would have done so a long time ago."[96] Although none of them admitted to harboring murderous intent, they unanimously expressed their desire to be freed of his ownership. Still, whether they had actually murdered him or not, his gruesome death is distinguished by being precisely what the deaths of the Nok-Nok and Seraphim were not: a spectacle.[97] A friend of Venerote's who rushed to the scene described

---

[94] Teodora Flores Venerote, "Inventory of José Venerote" (Colônia Leopoldina, July 8, 1884), 9v–19v; 20v–21v; 104–105, Inventários 5/2135/2604/01, APEB. A few comparative statistics from the center of coffee production in Campinas, São Paulo: in 1872, Robert Slenes has found plantations with 50–99 or more than 100 slaves as being relatively few, counting only 5 or 6 among a total of 103. Robert W. Slenes, *Na senzala, uma flor: esperanças e recordações na formação da família escrava, Brasil Sudeste, século XIX* (Rio de Janeiro: Editora Nova Fronteira, 1999). In the Bahian Recôncavo, Walter Fraga has shown a steady decrease in slave ownership among the holdings of the Baron of Pirajá's six plantations between 1871 and 1887, from 379 to 196 (–48%). Walter Fraga Filho, *Encruzilhadas da liberdade: histórias de escravos e libertos na Bahia, 1870–1910* (Campinas, SP: Editora UNICAMP, 2006), 284. It is unclear how Venerote was able to "purchase" the children, who would have been born free by this point. They may have been treated as *ingênuos* (children born to enslaved women after the Free Womb Law in 1871) to be placed under his so-called tutelage. Regarding the scale of coffee cultivation, between 1883 and 1887 an average coffee plantation in Campinas had 102,500 coffee plants, while in Cantagalo, Rio de Janeiro, the average was 173,268. This shows the magnitude of Venerote's plantation, whose numbers were closer to the average in Valença, Rio de Janeiro, of 286,939.

[95] On Venerote's slave trading activities see Alane Fraga do Carmo, "Colonização e escravidão na Bahia: a Colônia Leopoldina (1850–1888)" (M. A. thesis, Universidade Federal da Bahia, 2010), 78–79. Carmo argues that this fear of resale alone may have been the slave's motive for killing him.

[96] "José Venerote Murder Investigation," 317.

[97] "José Venerote Murder Investigation."

finding him "dead on the ground, the head smashed by clubs, the front split in two from where his brains spilled out, and his body purple and swollen from being clubbed."[98]

Mutilated slavemaster bodies were the single greatest sign of their eroding dominion over their slaves. A similar incident had taken place in September 1882 on a sugar mill in the Bahian Recôncavo, where the slaves mutilated and murdered their master, a Carmelite friar, with scythes, hoes, and other implements regularly used to harvest cane. As recounted by Walter Fraga, the friar had meted out brutal punishments and abrogated their hard-won customary rights.[99] Both murders are distinguished by the specificity of the violence. The whip and agricultural implements were the very tools intended to foster slave obedience and productivity, and by utilizing them against their masters, the attackers subverted the lexicon of subjugation. They allow us to glimpse into how the enslaved utilized violence to express their impatience with a slaveholding class that refused to recognize their customary rights and ignored the growing abolitionist tide.

On the other hand, violence silenced the Nok-Nok and Seraphim. The Nok-Nok massacre was the killing and erasure of people trapped in a "state of exception." The specific violence of matar uma aldeia was the greatest testament to the endurance of wartime anti-indigenous violence in postcolonial Brazil. As autonomous Indians and quasi-citizens whose rights to citizenship the Constitution never affirmed, the Nok-Nok were trapped in the ambiguous frontiers of the legal and extralegal. With the mantle of state authority and in the court of law, perpetrators and state representatives actively produced and took advantage of this blurring in order to place Indians outside the law. Such acts of extravagant violence signified not a condition of anarchy brought about by the breakdown of the state, but the active joining of state and private interests to enable such violence against its own citizens made "killable." In this sense the Brazilian constitution was not "inclusively inegalitarian" but allowed for exclusion within the very parameters of inclusion. Rendering the tragedy more devastating was the erasure of the massacre itself, which further burnished Indian "extinction" with the patina of fact. The Nok-Nok, in the official record, had never even existed.

---

[98] Pedro Cusandier, Ibid., 34.
[99] These slaves were also in communication with abolitionists in Salvador. Fraga Filho, *Encruzilhadas da Liberdade*, Chapter 2.

If Indians were citizens placed outside the law, what of slaves? As people unequivocally excluded from Brazilian citizenship, are they not too in a state of exception? Their legal regimes examined together reveal the striking contrast between the numerous laws governing slave punishment and masters' authority, and the absence of an indigenous equivalent. Although the 1845 Regulation of Missions had encouraged "gentle" means, none specifically regulated Indian treatment. Tellingly, an increasing number of Indian-related laws from the 1870s and 1880s – when most gradual emancipationist laws were issued – concern not treatment or rights, but surveys that evaluate whether the lands were abandoned due to indigenous extinction and could be reverted to the government for redistribution.[100] The very absence of laws on Indian treatment thus rendered them vulnerable to the violence born from the problematic overlap of state and private, legal and extralegal, ultimately producing the de facto legalization of anti-indigenous violence.

The laws governing slave treatment and punishment tell a different story. State intervention in masters' private domination of their slaves was irregular and motivated mainly by the desire to foster economic productivity and promote the social order of "good society." As slavery's compatibility with civilization became difficult to defend, however, the state began limiting masters' power over their slaves through gradual emancipationist laws and other laws curtailing and abolishing harsh punishment and the death penalty. Black people, like Indians, continued to be held in illegal or quasi-captivity, as Chapter 6 discusses. Yet public opinion was growingly, if cautiously, sympathetic to the enslaved. Legal changes, joining with a growing abolitionist movement and the slaves' own political actions, were diminishing the legal separation between citizens and slaves. Already in 1870 a twenty-one-year-old Joaquim Nabuco, speaking of the white and black races, had argued that "the law of one race does not have power over another.... The sons of the same soil are citizens of the same fatherland, and as citizens, they have immutable rights."[101] Similarly, Ricardo Pirola has contended that the abolition of the whip in 1886, accompanied by a proposal to abolish the 1835 law on capital punishment, demonstrated the struggle to expand slaves' guarantees in the imperial judiciary, which was moving toward equaling rights

---

[100] For example, see several laws between 1875 and 1889 in Cunha, *Legislação indigenista*, 282–304.

[101] Joaquim Nabuco as cited in Beattie, *Punishment in Paradise*, 208–9.

between free people and slaves.[102] With the expansion of slaves' rights, masters' disciplinary violence became evidence of barbarism. The Farias chose silence.

But if such developments signaled ampler citizenship opportunities for the Brazilian-born enslaved in the 1880s, this chapter has demonstrated that slave punishment and executions alone, an object of significant scholarship, offer only a partial view of the shifting relations between law and citizenship. To study the Nok-Nok massacre and Seraphim's murder together reveals very different trajectories for two groups excluded from citizenship, implicitly and explicitly, since the nation's inception. Accompanying the lessening legal separation of slaves and citizens was the effective exclusion of Indians from the body of laws, even though all were, as Nabuco stated, "sons of the same soil." The two cases from the Atlantic frontier thus provide a way to consider how racialized hierarchies were constructed on the ground, shaping the differential access to power among people of African and indigenous descent.

To recognize the divergence is not to diminish the horror inflicted on Seraphim or the suffering imposed on Rita and their unborn child. However, a haunting question remains: why are entire villages of Indians massacred, over and over again, while there is no equivalent violence unleashed on the enslaved? Material explanations, that slaves were valuable property, unlike Indians, or that Indians occupied lands, are important but unsatisfactory. Perhaps our answer lies in the very reasons that slavery became anathema to Brazil. As people condemned to extinction by the unassailable authority of science, Indians, too, became irreconcilable with Brazil's quest for civilization.

---

[102] Pirola, "A lei de 10 de junho de 1835," 426.

5

Fleeing into Slavery

Geography

On July 26, 1880, four years before Seraphim's disappearance, a major prison break scandalized São Mateus. Benedito, the town's most notorious *quilombola*, disappeared from the public prison in a flamboyant escape.[1] After his drunken guards fell asleep, Benedito placed a cleaning bucket on top of his cot and employed it as a steppingstone in tandem with a rope made from his bedsheet to scale the back wall enclosing the cell. He leapt to the other side, opened the back door, and slipped out noiselessly. Rendering the situation even more preposterous to those who discovered him gone were the handcuffs that lay on the floor smeared with sheep fat, which he had used to help slip his hands out without forcing the locks. The slave of a female landowner from one of the town's wealthiest families, the twenty-four-year-old had fled from his mistress's family years before, becoming a quilombola with a growing list of well-publicized activities under his belt, including homicide.[2] The police officer investigating the incident grimly acknowledged that rearrest would be difficult. Not only was there a chronic lack of officers, but the quilombolas rarely acted alone. He was certain that Benedito would be impossible to

---

[1] On Benedito in oral history, see Maciel de Aguiar, *Os últimos zumbis: a saga dos negros do Vale do Cricaré durante a escravidão* (Porto Seguro: Brasil-Cultura Editora, 2001); for the 1884 insurrection rumor, see Robson L. M. Martins, "Em louvor a 'Sant'Anna': notas sobre um plano de revolta escrava em São Matheus, norte do Espírito Santo, Brasil, em 1884," *Estudos Afro-Asiáticos* no. 38 (2000): 67–83.

[2] The sources vary as to his exact age. The estimate of twenty-four is based on the record of his sale on January 22, 1872, which states that he was "more or less 16"; he would have been twenty-four or twenty-five in July 1880. Tabelionato Liv. 4 Fl. 90, CPSM.

capture because he was likely protected by a local quilombo in the city district – and possibly by many others.[3]

Chapter 4 showed how political transformations in the 1870s and 1880s began curtailing masters' power and offering more legal protections for the enslaved. Much more remarkable than these changes, however, were the actions taken by the enslaved themselves, who asserted their own ideas about freedom and national inclusion that were far more expansive than any law could conceive. The method they chose was flight, through which they made claims on the spatial and political geography of late-nineteenth-century Brazil.[4]

Exploring the quilombolas' uses and ideas of space highlights the theme of geography, the competing visions of which have been a central theme in this book. From a web of indigenous territorial claims, to the subjugation of the Atlantic frontier and its black and indigenous people in an expanding nation-state, the conquest of indigenous territories, slavery expansion, and marronage, overlapping and often clashing claims over the geography have revealed the multiple epistemologies shaping Brazil's postcolonial history. This chapter is based on the unusually rich body of documentation on the quilombolas of São Mateus in the 1880s. The events here overlap with the Nok-Nok massacre, the shipping of the five Botocudo to Europe, and the anthropological exhibition in Rio de Janeiro. During a period in Brazilian history that cloaked

---

[3] Aglinio Requião to Police Chief, August 2, 1880, Polícia Ser. 2 Cx. 436 Mc 666 Fl. 38, APEES.

[4] Early studies by "New World Negro" scholars emphasized the quilombos' counter-acculturative force, in which they represented a total rejection of slaveholding society that made them guardians of a more "African" culture, with Palmares as the prime example. Marxist historians including Clóvis Moura, *Rebeliões da senzala: quilombos, insurrecicoes, guerrilhas* (Rio de Janeiro: Conquista, 1972), rebuffed these culturalist interpretations but still argued that only by placing themselves outside the structures of a slave-based economy could quilombos exert any influence on its transformation and undoing. More nuanced analyses emerged with Stuart B. Schwartz's landmark discovery of a list of demands authored by a group of marooned slaves: "Resistance and Accommodation in Eighteenth-Century Brazil: The Slaves' View of Slavery," *HAHR* 57, no. 1 (February 1977): 69; and "Rethinking Palmares: Slave Resistance in Colonial Brazil," in *Slaves, Peasants, and Rebels: Reconsidering Brazilian Slavery* (Chicago: University of Illinois Press, 1996), 103–36. João José Reis and Flávio dos Santos Gomes, eds., *Liberdade por um fio: história dos quilombos no Brasil* (São Paulo: Companhia das Letras, 1996) is an essential multipdisplinary collection on quilombo scholarship. See also Gomes' *A hidra e os pântanos: mocambos, quilombos e comunidades de fugitivos no Brasil (séculos XVII–XIX)* (São Paulo: Editora UNESP, 2005), among others. While he engages with the idea of quilombolas and quasi-citizenship, however, gender does not figure prominently in his analyses.

Botocudo extinction in the mantle of racial science, it is no coincidence that the Botocudo, prominently highlighted as specimens in anthropological texts, are virtually absent from the police and justice-related archival sources in which they were ubiquitous until the mid-century. By the 1880s they seldom appear in any sources from São Mateus and southern Bahia, a testament to their forced migration, assimilation, and of course, mortality. The quilombolas' geographies overlapped, shaped, and collided with indigenous geographies under siege, reminding us that black freedom and indigenous persecution could uncomfortably converge. For the Botocudo, their territory that once stretched from Porto Seguro to the Doce River was now reduced to a corner of northern Minas, around the mission of Itambacuri. Their stories will be told in the next and final chapter.

So far we have seen how quilombolas, many of them African-born, and "hostile" Indians were already stymying settler colonization in the Atlantic frontier in the early post-independence period. By the 1840s, quilombolas were also feared for their ability to carry dangerous information across provincial borders, including slave emancipation rumors. Numerous anti-quilombo expeditions proved fruitless, however, and quilombos continued to flourish into the 1880s. The free African-descended population far outnumbered the enslaved by this time in Brazil overall. But opportunities for manumission were much fewer in the Atlantic frontier because of the perennial labor shortage, staunch proslavery interests, and few avenues for self-purchase. The quilombolas thus decided to flee *into* São Mateus, rather than away from it, by living as de facto free people within the social and spatial geography of the region in which they were legally enslaved, in a practice I call "insurgent geographies."

The political dimension of this practice within the context of Brazil's postcolonial territorial colonization can best be understood in light of Edward Saïd's idea of a "rival geography," which describes the geographical practices of colonized people in their opposition to imperial conquest. Stephanie Camp adapted Saïd's concept to examine how enslaved people in the antebellum South of the United States creatively reconfigured the spaces of the plantation and slave society.[5] Camp's method resonates

---

5 Edward W. Saïd, *Culture and Imperialism* (New York: Knopf, 1993); Stephanie M. H. Camp, *Closer to Freedom: Enslaved Women and Everyday Resistance in the Plantation South* (Chapel Hill: University of North Carolina Press, 2004), 7. According to Camp, geographers have utilized Saïd's concept to describe resistance to colonial occupation.

with Flávio Gomes' *campo negro* (black field), a network of quilombolas, slaves, and free people in Rio de Janeiro in which a kaleidoscope
of social actors engendered an alternate claim on a geography defined
by slavery.[6] By understanding the quilombolas' flight in terms of what
Jonathan Crush has called the "hidden spaces occupied, and invested
with their own meaning, by the [post]colonial underclass," this chapter
argues that their insurgent geographies were a political practice through
which they reimagined their lives as free people within the very geography
in which they were intended to remain enslaved. And in the context of
an antislavery struggle that was daily challenging the division of slaves
and citizens, marronage signified not only an act of slave resistance, but
also a political expression of citizenship.[7] In 1851, the enslaved of São
Mateus had learned that the Brazilian government was unwilling and
unable to grant what they considered their right to freedom. Now, three
decades later, they claimed it themselves. Their stories reveal how the
Atlantic frontier, marked by anti-indigenous violence and slavery expansion throughout the nineteenth century, became the very battleground
over the possibilities of black freedom and citizenship.

The first part of the chapter focuses on events between 1880 and 1881
as told through the lives of the eleven female and male quilombolas who
were Benedito's peers and their more than 50 suspected collaborators and
neighbors. The quilombolas' highly complex and contradictory social and
economic networks bound them with slaves, freedpeople, and slaveholders and were essential to their insurgent geographies. Quilombos were also
contingent communities created by individuals with a variety of motivations and internal tensions that belied their apparent unity, who had to
negotiate between individual goals and a larger maroon politics. Particular attention will be given to quilombola women, whose experiences

---

She defines rival geography as "alternative ways of knowing and using plantation and
southern space" and its fundamental characteristic as the "movement of bodies, objects,
and information."

[6] Gomes employs this concept, defined as the "social and economic, beyond the geographic,
territory in which different social actors who are not limited to blacks or slaves, circulate,"
frequently in his works. A good place to start is Flávio dos Santos Gomes, "Quilombos
do Rio de Janeiro no século XIX," in *Liberdade por um fio*, ed. Flávio dos Santos Gomes
and João José Reis, 1996, 19.

[7] Ana Lugão Rios and Hebe Maria Mattos de Castro, *Memórias do cativeiro: família, trabalho e cidadania no pós-abolição* (Rio de Janeiro: Civilização Brasileira, 2005), 49–50.
The quote, to which I have added the "post," is from Anne Godlewska, Neil Smith, and
Jonathan Crush, eds., "Post-Colonialism, De-Colonization, and Geography," in *Geography and Empire* (Oxford: Blackwell, 1994), 336–37.

have not been sufficiently recognized. We will subsequently fast-forward to 1884, the year of Seraphim's death, when an antislavery insurrection rumor emerged in São Mateus in which the suspected leader was none other than Benedito. Through a dizzying array of rumors, quilombola attacks, and police chases, we will see how the quilombolas' insurgent geographies forged an antislavery politics.

The Entangled Worlds of Free, Slave, and Quilombola

On July 5, 1881, nearly a year after Benedito's dramatic prison break, a young enslaved woman from São Mateus named Marcolina was on horseback en route to her master's farm just south of the town center, when she was startled by the sudden appearance of a black man in the road. Dressed in denim pants and a coarsely woven shirt with a rifle in hand, he approached Marcolina with "libidinous ends," threatening to kill her if she did not comply. Marcolina attempted to flee but collapsed when a bullet pierced her upper left arm. Her pained gaze captured the sight of two other men dressed and armed similarly to the first. Alarmed by her screams for help, the men ran toward her master's farm and disappeared. Although she stated to the police the next day that she did not recognize her assailants, Marcolina was certain that they were quilombolas. As news of the attack spread, the townsfolk began uttering the name of the most notorious quilombola in town: had Benedito struck again? Investigation into the attack on Marcolina brought into relief the highly complex networks constituting São Mateus society. The presumed social divisions between slave and slave-owning, slave and free, were exposed for their remarkable ambiguity; residents began whispering and pointing fingers at free individuals who were rumored to be helping fugitive slaves.

Marcolina had good reasons for identifying her attackers as quilombolas rather than common outlaws. She stated, as many others eventually would, that it was widely known by both free and enslaved people in the town that her master's neighbor, Francisco Pinto Neto, tolerated the presence of a quilombo on his very grounds that counted about eleven male and female members. Corroborating her testimony was an employee of the municipal council, according to whom the existence of the quilombo on Pinto Neto's grounds had in fact been public knowledge for years.[8]

---

[8] "Auto de inquirição sumaria do Alferes Antonio José de Oliveira Pinha" (hereafter Antonio Pinha), August 6, 1881, AN/CA, Fl. 21. Unless otherwise noted, all documents marked AN/CA are derived from the Appellate Court Ser. 20, #24, Cx 23, Gal. C.

Marcolina's master, Bernardino d'Araujo, added that the quilombolas had established themselves on Pinto Neto's grounds at least eight years before; just a few years back, he had encountered two of them on the road heading toward his farm.[9] The slaves on this quilombo were notorious for stealing livestock, manioc, and other property.[10] Equally striking was the fact that such quilombos were hidden in plain view on the town's properties, and that the quilombolas themselves opted to create a settlement within the easy reach of local law enforcement. Why had nobody said or done anything for all these years? These quilombos were realized through a complicit network of enslaved and free people – a network that enabled the quilombolas to exercise freedoms that eroded their legal status as slaves.

Arguably, the most problematic aspect of this case for the police was not merely the rumor that the quilombolas had been residing on Francisco Pinto Neto's property for years, and with tacit public knowledge, but that they also received his protection, and some goods, in exchange for the labor they provided in his fields.[11] These so-called "slave-hiders" (*acoitadores de escravos*) were a constant source of headache for the authorities. Individuals who were discovered giving shelter, aiding, or employing the labor of fugitive slaves were aggressively investigated, and yet slave-hiders were hardly eradicated, much like the quilombolas themselves. The practice had a long history in Brazil, having persisted and even flourished in spite of its prohibition in the Philippine Ordinances of 1603.[12] In fact, three men aside from Pinto Neto would also be accused of aiding the quilombolas in the same police investigation.

---

[9] "Auto de perguntas feitas a Bernardino Alves d'Araujo" (hereafter Bernardino d'Araujo), September 20, 1881, AN/CA Fl. 102.

[10] "Auto de exame e corpo de delicto na pessoa de Marcolina escrava de Bernardino Alves Pereira d'Araujo," July 6, 1881, Polícia, Ser. 2 Cx. 71 Mc 264, Fls. 174–177, APEES; copy with slight alterations in AN/CA, Fls. 14v–18v; "Auto de perguntas feitas à informante Marcolina" (hereafter Marcolina), August 6, 1881, AN/CA, Fls. 22v–23.

[11] Antonio Pinha, AN/CA, Fl. 20; "Auto de perguntas feitas a Josepha, escrava de Americo Assenço de Barcellos" (hereafter Josepha), August 5, 1881, AN/CA Fls. 12–12v; "Auto de inquirição sumária de Liberato da Silva Catarina" (hereafter Liberato Catarina), August 6, 1881, AN/CA Fl. 23v.

[12] On this widespread practice in Brazil, see José Alipio Goulart, *Da fuga ao suicídio: aspectos da rebeldia do escravo no Brasil* (Rio de Janeiro: Conquista, 1972), 55–64; Gomes, *A hidra e os pântanos*; João José Reis, "Escravos e coiteiros no quilombo do Oitizeiro, Bahia 1806," in *Liberdade por um fio*, ed. Flávio dos Santos Gomes and João José Reis, 1996. Kathleen J. Higgins, *"Licentious Liberty" in a Brazilian Gold-Mining Region: Slavery, Gender, and Social Control in Eighteenth-Century Sabará, Minas Gerais* (University Park: Penn State University Press, 1999), 191–92, demonstrates that in eighteenth-century Minas, many free people engaged in commerce with fugitive slaves.

FIGURE 5.1 Manioc flour, São Mateus' most important product, was exported to various Brazilian markets. Enslaved and quilombola women and men were employed in manioc cultivation and its transformation into flour. *Source: Préparation de la racine de mendiocca*, from Johann Moritz Rugendas, *Voyage pittoresque dans le Brésil* (Paris: Engelmann & Cie., 1835).

Slave-hiding was a problematic practice that blurred the borders separating slave owners from slaves, free from unfree, citizen from outsider. Although a slaveowner himself, Francisco Pinto Neto reaped financial gain by colluding with the quilombolas, who were legally others' property. In doing so he gained an expanded work force that he did not have to purchase or fully maintain. Pinto Neto was a small-scale slaveowner who had only three slaves and was likely among the small property owners who constituted 70 percent of the town's landowners. Quilombola labor exercised a powerful allure for such individuals with little economic girth. João Reis has noted a similar utilization of fugitive slave labor by manioc farmers in southern Bahia in the early nineteenth century, which contributed to tensions with other residents (Figure 5.1).[13] Slave-hiding was

[13] Inventory of Dona Maria Francisca Leite da Conceição, wife of Francisco Pinto Neto, Processos Box 96 (1886), Fl. 21, CPSM. By June 21, 1886, Pinto Neto's slave inventory contains only one individual, Ignacio, who appears in this chapter. He manumitted a woman named Marcolina in 1885; the last of his three slaves was João Carretão, who

also akin to the use of Indians by local residents. As seen in Chapter 1, these labor arrangements, often made privately, existed in a murky zone that rendered them hardly distinguishable from slavery, leading residents and aldeia directors to clash over the control of and access to Indian laborers.

Equally convenient to Pinto Neto was the quilombolas' partial self-sufficiency, based on hunting and regular thefts of manioc and occasionally livestock from neighboring farms. There is no evidence that the quilombolas were allotted land on which to practice cultivation. Since frequent relocations did not permit them to grow their own food, let alone build a surplus, they offered their labor in exchange for shelter, munitions, and food.[14] This reciprocal arrangement is evidence that the quilombolas, while not economically independent, did not lead an entirely "parasitic" existence, either. They enjoyed freedom from their masters' control and a greater mobility than plantation slaves. At the same time, their semi-itinerant lifestyle and consequent lack of access to cultivable land obliged them to create labor-exchange arrangements with slave-hiders, offering

soon joined the maroons. Concerning such "senhores de poucos escravos" (masters of few slaves), typical among manioc farmers in the Bahian Recôncavo, Bert Barickman has argued that the ownership of few slaves helped reduce, but not free, a farmer and his family from house and field work. See B. J. Barickman, *A Bahian Counterpoint: Sugar, Tobacco, Cassava, and Slavery in the Recôncavo, 1780–1860* (Stanford, CA: Stanford University Press, 1998), 152–53; on small-scale slaveholding, see Ricardo Alexandre Ferreira, *Senhores de poucos escravos: cativeiro e criminalidade num ambiente rural, 1830–1888* (São Paulo: Editora UNESP, 2005). For slave hiders who used quilombola labor in Rio das Contas, southern Bahia, see Reis, "Escravos e coiteiros," 350–51. For São Mateus landownership patterns, see Anna Lucia Côgo, "História do Espírito Santo no século XIX: a região de São Mateus" (doctoral dissertation, USP, 2007).

[14] A good overview on slave provision grounds can be found in the essays in *The Slaves' Economy: Independent Production by Slaves in the Americas*, ed. Ira Berlin and Philip D. Morgan (London: Frank Cass, 1995). For the Caribbean, see, for example, Sidney W. Mintz, *Caribbean Transformations* (New York: Columbia University Press, 1989), 131–250; Dale W. Tomich, *Through the Prism of Slavery: Labor, Capital, and World Economy* (Lanham, MD: Rowman & Littlefield, 2004). For Brazil, see Flávio dos Santos Gomes, "Roceiros, mocambeiros e as fronteiras da emancipação no Maranhão," in *Quase-cidadão: histórias e antropologias da pós-emancipação no Brasil*, ed. Olivia Maria Gomes da Cunha and Flávio dos Santos Gomes (Rio de Janeiro: Editora FGV, 2007), 147–70; B. J. Barickman, "'A Bit of Land, Which They Call Roça': Slave Provision Grounds in the Bahian Recôncavo, 1780–1860," *HAHR* 74, no. 4 (1994): 649–87; Walter Fraga Filho, *Encruzilhadas da liberdade: histórias de escravos e libertos na Bahia, 1870–1910* (Campinas, SP: Editora UNICAMP, 2006). For the US South, see Dylan C. Penningroth, *The Claims of Kinfolk: African American Property and Community in the Nineteenth-Century South* (Chapel Hill: University of North Carolina Press, 2003).

us perspective into a different kind of maroon economy than one based on independent cultivation and sales of their products.[15]

Yet collaborating with quilombolas was a risky choice, for several reasons. First, although hiring them probably garnered Pinto Neto some security against depredation, he had literally armed fugitive slaves who resided in close proximity, making himself and his family easy targets in the event of an uprising. We have seen how settlers in the region armed their own slaves in order to defend their property *against* maroons and hostile Indians, but arming maroons was an entirely different matter.[16] Second, by protecting others' slaves, Pinto Neto was pitting himself against other slaveholders, although it was self-interest and not abolitionist sympathy that lay at the root of his actions. In fact, none of the testimonies reveal any antislavery sentiment, even as late as 1881. Regardless of intent, however, his actions menaced the basic division of slave and slaveholder, a threat that could not be ignored in light of surging antislavery activity throughout Brazil. Later we will see how slave-hiding would indeed acquire new meaning in three years' time, when a burgeoning group of local abolitionists would be accused of protecting quilombolas, including Benedito. These relationships, initially formed as opportunistic labor-exchange agreements between the quilombolas and their employers, thus harbored the capacity to transform into explicitly antislavery movements in this turbulent decade.

Third, the quilombolas negotiated and were remunerated for the labor they provided in Pinto Neto's fields, whether in cash, shelter, goods, or arms, a practice that destabilized their legally enslaved status. This was not the only situation in Brazil in which slaves received pay for extra work. In his study of the Bahian Recôncavo, Walter Fraga has shown that the enslaved regularly performed extra work on their days off, especially in the 1870s and 1880s, either in their own gardens or for hire. They considered such labor their right and took advantage of the opportunity

---

[15] The argument of a "parasitic" maroon economy relies on a presumed antagonism between maroons and planters and implies an overall economic damage maroons are assumed to have inflicted on their so-called victims. See Stuart B. Schwartz, *Slaves, Peasants, and Rebels: Reconsidering Brazilian Slavery* (Chicago: University of Illinois Press, 1996), 108–9, although Schwartz himself recognizes the mutual economic relationships practiced in Palmares on p. 24. On the other hand, quilombos' independent economy and their commercial practices in Brazil are discussed in Schwartz, "Resistance and Accommodation"; Reis, "Escravos e coiteiros"; Gomes, "Roceiros, mocambeiros."

[16] It is not known where Pinto Neto acquired these weapons. On arming slaves, see Chapter 2.

to accrue the funds to purchase their freedom.[17] The practice was also present in São Mateus, where slaves customarily took their Saturdays off. What the quilombolas did was stretch this customary right until every day of the week became available for extra work, leaving no days left for their own masters. Since they were not owned by their hiders, the quilombolas were able to negotiate their labor conditions in ways that were antithetical to their legal status as slaves, who by law were "things" that did not possess the capacity to negotiate labor relations.[18] For example, one of the quilombola women recounted that she left her hider because of disagreeable work for what she considered too little pay, a clear example of what she understood to be her rightful share.[19] By performing remunerated labor exclusively for their own gain, the quilombolas, though legally enslaved, were working as de facto free people.[20] Finally, one of Pinto Neto's slaves testified that he had seen Benedito on the grounds. Harboring the city's most notorious fugitive slave and criminal may have won accolades from some of the enslaved, but certainly did not make Pinto Neto popular among authorities and other slaveholders.[21]

Enslaved collaborators were also essential to the quilombolas' insurgent geographies. The perilous nature of his endeavor made Francisco Pinto Neto eschew direct interaction with the quilombolas and relegate the task to one of his own slaves, João Carretão, who acted as a go-between to provide them with goods and shelter.[22] A fellow slave on the plantation, Ignacio, recounted that João Carretão was universally recognized by Pinto Neto's slaves to be the quilombolas' supplier of goods, gunpowder, and shot. João Carretão would eventually make

---

[17] Fraga Filho, *Encruzilhadas da liberdade*, 42–46.

[18] Keila Grinberg, *Código civil e cidadania* (Rio de Janeiro: Jorge Zahar, 2008), discusses the conundrum posed by the existence of slaves hired out by their masters (*escravos de ganho*) – who were not the same as slaves who hired themselves out for extra work, but similar nonetheless in their capacity to negotiate and work for others – and its incompatibility with the liberal Civil Code.

[19] For more on *escravos de ganho*, see João José Reis, "'The Revolution of the Ganhadores': Urban Labour, Ethnicity and the African Strike of 1857 in Bahia, Brazil," *JLAS* 29, no. 2 (May 1997): 355–93. For the practice in rural areas see Barickman, "A Bit of Land," 670–71. Moreover, as Sidney Chalhoub has argued, an essential aspect of slaves' ideas of freedom was the right to their savings (*pecúlio*) that was included in the 1871 Free Womb legislation. See Sidney Chalhoub, *Visões da liberdade: uma história das últimas décadas da escravidão na corte* (São Paulo: Companhia das Letras, 1990).

[20] "Auto de perguntas feitas a Rufina, escrava de José Joaquim de Almeida Fundão Jr." (Rufina hereafter), September 3, 1881, AN/CA, Fl. 81v.

[21] "Auto de perguntas feitas a Ignacio, escravo de Francisco Pinto Neto" (Ignacio hereafter), July 30, 1881, AN/CA Fl. 7v.

[22] Bernardino d'Araujo.

the decision to cross over the elusive barrier of slave and quilombola entirely, joining the latter, fathering a child with one of the quilombola women, and deserting the farm, to his owner's likely dismay.[23] Ignacio also purchased goods for the quilombolas on occasion and had visited the quilombo twice, once to see his friend. There were many arms, he recalled. But rather than transporting the goods to the quilombo directly, Ignacio delivered them on a road connecting the town to the outlying fields. When asked why he had not informed the police of the quilombo, Ignacio responded that although he told his master, he did not tell the authorities out of fear of the quilombolas.[24]

From the stories of João Carretão and Ignacio, a complex map of the networks tying the enslaved and the quilombolas begins to emerge. Since the latter worked for Francisco Pinto Neto on his fields, they must have spent the day side by side with his slaves on a regular basis. If they had not previously known each other, interaction in the fields would have generated – if not friendship or camaraderie – at least some sort of familiarity. As such, we must allow for the possibility that Ignacio's stated "fear" of the quilombolas was actually a subterfuge. Among the slaves of the fazenda were individuals who did not escape themselves, but willingly aided those who had, while others like João Carretão made the decision to join the quilombolas themselves. With limited access to foodstuffs, weapons, and other essential items, these go-between slaves – and the masters who allowed or willingly participated in such interactions – were essential in ensuring the quilombolas' survival. At the same time, daily interaction with the quilombolas gave slaves a tangible experience of life away from the master's control. Such fluid interactions attest to the porousness of the boundaries separating slaves and quilombolas as they were negotiated in daily interactions.

However, Ignacio's expression of fear, if he is taken at his word, insinuates that there were also tensions among slaves and quilombolas. Precisely because the latter were so close by and armed, slaves may have faced dangerous consequences for noncompliance with their demands. Marcolina's assault was the most telling example. Although she claimed that she was unable to identify her assailants, the close-knit nature of the enslaved–quilombola community may have compelled her to lie out of

---

[23] Ignacio; "Auto de perguntas feitas a Manoel da Silva do Espírito Santo, conhecido por Curandor," August 5, 1881, AN/CA Fl. 12v; "Auto de perguntas feitas a Manoel Bahiano, escravo de Dona Maria Benedita Martins" (Manoel Bahiano hereafter), August 8, 1881, AN/CA Fl. 25v.

[24] Ignacio, Fls. 6v–7v.

fear of vengeance.[25] (The attempted sexual assault on her illuminates the gendered conflicts shaping enslaved and quilombola women's lives, a topic that will be addressed in depth later in this chapter.) Meanwhile, some of the slaves themselves suspected Benedito. Another quilombola named Rufina recalled that Marcolina's own brother had expressed doubts about Benedito's innocence in the matter.[26] Even some of Benedito's fellow quilombolas suspected him, believing he "had a bad attitude and was a rabble rouser."[27] Such manifestations of fear and suspicion are a reminder that the ties that bound slave and quilombola, while possessing the power to threaten slaveholding society from within, simultaneously harbored a smoldering discord.

In his own defense, Francisco Pinto Neto admitted that he was aware of the quilombo and some of its members but made no admission of collusion, opting to cast the blame on other suspected slave-hiders. Reluctance to give up a lucrative situation and the fear of reprisal were his likely motivations.[28] Some of the quilombolas that came to live on his grounds had in fact previously established a very similar arrangement with another farmer named Manoel Curandor, who did not own any slaves. The quilombola Vicentino observed that "given [Curandor's] crops and the time he spends hunting, it's clear that he wants the labor of fugitive slaves."[29] The quilombolas were fully aware of the demand for their labor and leveraged it when seeking protectors. Like Pinto Neto, Curandor denied the allegations. These slave-hiders clearly knew that slaveowners would not look kindly upon their illegal activities, so neither of them openly embraced their practice.[30]

Opportunism was not the only reason that some provided shelter to fugitive slaves. Pinto Neto's neighbor in Ribeirão, the African freedperson Manoel Chagas, known as Cabinda, admitted to having aided the quilombolas in the past. He regretted not reporting his actions but revealed that "if he were to tell, he would have fallen into disfavor with the slaves'

---

[25] Only later does a witness, Manoel Antonio de Azevedo (brother of Maria Benedita Martins, Rogerio and Manoel Bahiano's owner), say that according to Josepha, Benedito himself had said that day, on leaving the quilombo with Lucindo, that he had shot Marcolina. "Testemunha jurada de Manoel Azevedo," September 20, 1881, AN/CA Fls. 107–107v; Marcolina.

[26] Rufina, Fl. 82v.   [27] Manoel Bahiano, Fl. 26.

[28] "Auto de perguntas feitas a Francisco Pinto Neto," August 22, 1881, AN/CA Fls. 61v–62v.

[29] "Inquirição sumária do réu Vicentino, escravo de José Antonio Faria" (Vicentino hereafter), August 13, 1881, AN/CA Fl. 50v.

[30] "Interrogatório do réu Manoel Curandor," September 24, 1881, AN/CA Fl. 131.

relatives and with the slaves themselves."[31] Cabinda's words express a sense of obligation to help the quilombolas who came to him, in a mixture of both solidarity and fear of censure similar to Ignacio's, if only because he had close ties with the enslaved community. Cabinda's awareness of the ties binding slaves and quilombolas led the former slave to open his doors to others in flight from captivity. Through his and others' stories we have seen so far, there emerges a picture of the complex social networks to which the quilombolas belonged, in which slave-hiders, go-between slaves, neighboring residents, and sometimes even the very authorities (who, in Pinto Neto's case, knew about his arrangement but did nothing for years) were willing or reluctant accomplices. The handful of slave-hiders arrested by the police in August 1881, then, may have been the tip of the iceberg.

As Flávio Gomes has argued, quilombos were historically dynamic communities forged not outside of but within slavery, communities that simultaneously transformed the world in which they all lived.[32] The insurgent geographies as a social practice, embodied by the relationships Benedito and his fellow quilombolas established with enslaved and free people in the early 1880s, were clearly based on existing communal ties and economic practices forged under slavery, whether motivated by camaraderie, fear, or opportunism. In 1881, none of them explicitly expressed any antislavery ideology undergirding their actions, but their very actions destabilized slavery from within. For the quilombolas to desert their masters and work as free people before their very eyes amounted to a rejection of their enslavement. While their arrangements with slave-hiders did not represent the independent peasantries associated with post-emancipation societies, their forging of free labor relations from the very social fabric of slave society was a political act through which they asserted their own terms of inclusion, long before legislation could dictate the terms. Steeling themselves against such challenges to their power, São Mateus' large slaveholders would violently suppress the burgeoning abolitionist movement three years later, probably horrified upon realizing that abolitionism had grown out of the very networks that slave, free, and quilombola had forged under slavery.

---

[31] "Auto de perguntas feitas a Manoel das Chagas, conhecido por Cabinda," August 18, 1881, AN/CA Fl. 61.
[32] Flávio dos Santos Gomes, *Histórias de quilombolas: mocambos e comunidades de senzalas no Rio de Janeiro, século XIX* (São Paulo: Companhia das Letras, 2006), 36.

Fleeing into Slavery

The quilombolas' social networks, though extensive, included many who were loath to admit their complicity. That stood in striking contrast to the actions of the quilombolas themselves, who made little effort to conceal their existence. Their settlement on Francisco Pinto Neto's property first became known to his slaves because they heard voices singing sambas in the middle of the night, drifting across the dark sky to their master's house. Pinto Neto's son had also crossed paths with the quilombolas, including Benedito, on several occasions on his way to the fields. The quilombolas had settled about a kilometer from the farmer's residence, not so close as to be in the immediate reach of his vigilance, but still within a short walking – and hearing – distance. This made it convenient for the quilombolas, go-between slaves, and even Pinto Neto himself on at least one occasion to interact directly, sometimes in the farmer's house.[33]

How do we explain this carefree behavior? Marronage has been generally understood as flights of considerable distance to faraway, inaccessible locations, or to urban centers, where a growing free black population allowed fugitive slaves to blend in and pass as free. Such flights are contrasted with temporary escapes to nearby locations, commonly known as *petit marronage*, to see loved ones or as a negotiatory tactic with their masters. The São Mateus quilombolas included those who had intended only a short flight, but the resulting group became something quite distinct. With little interest in secrecy, these quilombolas set up camp on Pinto Neto's property for months or even years, acting as free people. In other words, they deliberately collapsed the distance that separated quilombos from the space of slavery by fleeing *into* it.[34] This reconfiguration of the geographies of slavery and freedom is at the heart of the

---

[33] "Auto de perguntas feitas a Isidio, escravo de Bellarmim Pinto Neto," July 30, 1881, AN/CA Fls. 8v–9v; Ignacio; Liberato Catarina; Antonio Pinha, Fl. 20v.

[34] Many works have addressed the relationship between marronage and geography, although the ideas of distance, inaccessibility, and isolation remain predominant. Aside from the aforementioned work by Camp, see, for example, Jane G. Landers, *Black Society in Spanish Florida* (Urbana: University of Illinois Press, 1999); Gabino La Rosa Corzo, "Subsistence of Cimarrones: An Archaeological Study," in *Dialogues in Cuban Archaeology*, ed. L. Antonio Curet, Shannon Lee Dawdy, and Gabino La Rosa Corzo (Tuscaloosa: University of Alabama Press, 2005), 163–80; Flávio dos Santos Gomes and Carlos Eugênio Líbano Soares, "Sedições, haitianismo e conexões no Brasil: outras margens do atlântico negro," *Novos Estudos* 63 (2002): 131–44. A preliminary discussion of flight away from and into slavery in Brazil can be found in João José Reis and Eduardo Silva, *Negociação e conflito: a resistência negra no Brasil escravista* (São Paulo: Companhia das Letras, 1999), 71.

quilombolas' insurgent geographies. Their spatial claims and social networks were overlapping layers of the same map, whose richness and com-
plexity reveal the ways in which enslaved people reimagined their ways
of belonging in Brazilian society. Although their choices were shaped by
the region's geopolitics, their flight became a transformative force that
destabilized these very configurations.

No clearer evidence of how the quilombolas gave new meaning to
their geography of enslavement existed than the locus of their settlement.
Living daringly close to Pinto Neto's residence, the quilombolas felt com-
fortable enough to make loud music at night and crisscross the grounds
in broad daylight. They were undoubtedly not strangers to the fact that
sambas and *batuques*, the music of choice of the African-descended community, were regularly persecuted by authorities who feared they bred
public disorder.[35] Making loud music – whether to praise a higher power
or simply for enjoyment – was their way to stake their claims not just
on the landscape but also the soundscape of the property. Although they
were outside the immediate vigilance of the Pintos, their singing trespassed
the invisible boundary drawn between slave and slaveowner, encroaching
upon the latter's space. Even more brazen was walking across the fields
before the eyes of Pinto Neto's son. In doing so, the quilombolas made a
mockery of what was in truth an invisible distinction between slave and
free, claiming the geography for themselves.[36]

At the same time, the quilombolas could not disregard the precariousness of their position. Perhaps their masters tolerated the occasional
flight as long as their slaves returned and their property was not dam-
aged. The attack on Marcolina, however, upset the delicate balance upon
which the quilombolas' protective network rested, prompting her master, Bernardino d'Araujo, to seize the opportunity to speak out after a
long-standing disgruntlement. Back in April of that year, his farm had
been attacked and his livestock stolen by three quilombolas whom he
identified as Benedito and two of his fellows, Lucindo and Rogerio.
The morning after the attack, Bernardino followed their trail, which
led back – he claimed – to the gates of Francisco Pinto Neto's property. He proceeded to notify the slaves' respective owners to join him

---

[35] This was particularly the case in São Mateus, where *batuques* were a regular object of
complaint by the police in the 1880s. For example, the law of April 1883 expressly prohibited batuques within the city, likely built on existing frustration over such gatherings.
Manoel Vasconcellos to Felintro de Moraes, September 22, 1887, Processos Box 97,
CPSM.

[36] Penningroth, *The Claims of Kinfolk*, 98–108, 144–50.

in their capture, but was unable to participate himself due to a "sudden illness."[37]

The intimacy of the town allowed Bernardino to recognize his assailants. Although his relationship with Benedito and Rogerio is unknown, we do know how he was able to identify Lucindo: Bernardino was his former master.[38] The farmer had purchased Lucindo from his previous owner around 1872, when the latter was a nine-year-old child. Lucindo would invoke this fact of his past to contest accusations that he was an accomplice in the attack on Marcolina. They grew up together and had a good relationship, he stated; he had no reason to kill her.[39] The restless Lucindo was sold in June of 1877 and again in July 1880 to new owners, two local slave traders, but ran away again.[40] For Bernardino the most infuriating aspect of Lucindo's proclivity to flight was that the he did not bother to escape beyond his former master's reach but was residing right next door with a group of fellow quilombolas on the grounds of his neighbor, Francisco Pinto Neto. Four years after his sale he was still there, living as a free person, and to add insult to injury, had the audacity to steal Bernardino's livestock.[41]

The proximity of Lucindo's destination, combined with the duration of his flight, shows the remarkable workings of an insurgent geography in practice. The quilombolas not only claimed Pinto Neto's property for themselves, but also chose to flee extremely short distances from their owners. Indeed, none of the quilombolas fled far from São Mateus. This apparently counterintuitive flight pattern was a carefully deliberated choice, shaped by their awareness of regional geopolitics and founded on their conceptualizations of freedom. Safety was one of the main reasons the quilombolas fled into the town and its environs, owing to a network of other quilombolas, slaves, and known slave-hiders. Such knowledge about spaces of freedom even within the overall confines of slavery, which Philip Troutman terms "geopolitical literacy," was fundamental to the decisions they made about where to go and who to include in

---

[37] Bernardino d'Araujo, Fls. 102–102v. This may be what we call an opportunistic illness. It was also a common excuse in rural northeastern Brazil for not having done something.

[38] Lucindo had previously been owned by Caetano Bento de Jesus Silvares, who presented the slave for registration on August 8, 1872; Lucindo sales record, AN/CA Fls. 186–186v.

[39] "Interrogatório ao réu Lucindo," March 2, 1882, AN/CA Fl. 175v.

[40] Lucindo was sold in absentia to the slave-trading company Fonseca, Rios & Cia on June 27, 1877 and after its dissolution, to Domingos and Manoel Rios on July 15, 1880. Tabelionato Liv. 7 Fl. 304 and Liv. 11 Fl. 175, CPSM.

[41] Bernardino d'Araujo.

their networks.[42] Within São Mateus their knowledge enabled them to possess a mental map of potential settlements and their nearby water and food sources, not to mention slave-hiders and collaborating slaves, all vital knowledge for these women and men who were often mandated to relocate on a moment's notice.[43] The quilombolas' testimonies indicate that they never wandered about aimlessly, a practice that would have threatened their chance at survival. When they relocated, they headed to specific *ranchos* that they chose for their relative safety and proximity to food and water, repeatedly utilizing them during transit. Benedito frequently crisscrossed the Bahia–Espírito Santo provincial border, displaying a remarkable knowledge of the local topography and a vast network of protectors that enabled him to elude large expeditions for years. However, he too always remained in proximity to the coast, cognizant of the potential dangers of the interior.

Indeed, venturing outside of São Mateus without extensive knowledge of the surrounding geography entailed high risks. It is essential to situate these slaves' flights in their particular geopolitical context in order to understand why the sertão was not an obvious safe haven. The flourishing of quilombos in the 1840s and 1850s was partly enabled by the forced migration of the Botocudo and other indigenous groups from São Mateus to southern Bahia. In the following decades, however, the city's hinterland had become increasingly inhospitable to fugitive slaves. While São Mateus' economy remained based predominantly on small-scale manioc production, in the 1860s and 1870s some of the wealthiest families began purchasing large tracts further inland to cultivate coffee. Among those who had aggressively expanded their landholdings was Rita Maria da Conceição Cunha, Benedito's late mistress. The wealthiest of these new coffee planters was her son, Major Antonio Rodrigues da Cunha, the future Baron of Aimorés and one of São Mateus' biggest slaveholders. He possessed both the motive and resources to capture the able-bodied fugitive slave.[44] Further inland in Minas Gerais, the Itambacuri mission's

---

[42] Philip Troutman, "Grapevine in the Slave Market: African American Geopolitical Literacy and the 1841 Creole Revolt," in *The Chattel Principle: Internal Slave Trades in the Americas*, ed. Walter Johnson (New Haven, CT: Yale University Press, 2004), 203–33.

[43] The quilombola Francisca, for example, states that their various settlements were always made in places close to vegetable gardens, where they could steal manioc. "Interrogatório da ré Francisca," September 27, 1881, AN/CA Fl. 143v.

[44] Côgo, "História do Espírito Santo," 170–89; Maria do Carmo de Oliveira Russo, "A escravidão em São Mateus, ES: economia e demografia (1848–1888)" (doctoral dissertation, USP, 2011), 27–28.

founding in 1873 near Filadélfia was enticing settlers with newly available lands. By the early 1880s, infrastructural development had integrated the region more than ever before into the national economy. The most salient of these transformations was the Bahia–Minas railroad, linking the mountain town of Aimorés (near Filadélfia) with the Atlantic at Caravelas, whose construction was near completion by 1881. The railroad ushered in a new population of railroad workers and colonists into the region, and by the mid-1880s, more than 900 farmers had settled in the São Mateus hinterland. The sertão was thus a far cry from the sparsely settled "forbidden lands" of the independence period; by this time, uncharted long-distance flight was extremely risky.

Flight into the interior also converged quilombola and indigenous geographies with unpredictable consequences. Nobody knew the territory of the Atlantic frontier better than the native population. Chapter 2 discussed the tremendous importance the Botocudo gave to territorial claims, since their survival as hunter-foragers depended on their access to important watersheds, hunting grounds, and seasonal fruit-bearing trees. Settler colonization, land privatization, aldeia relocation, and forced migration wreaked havoc on their way of life. Paltry archival evidence of Indian–settler interactions in coastal cities and towns by the 1870s and their greater visibility near Filadélfia and Itambacuri in northern Minas suggests both the forced confinement of the Botocudo to the interior and further north in Bahia and the diminishing spaces for strategic negotiations with expanding settler society. A few months before Marcolina's attack, a group of Pojixá Botocudo had ambushed and killed a settler and a team of construction workers clearing roads from São Mateus to northern Minas, prompting the chief engineer to demand their extermination.[45]

In this volatile territorial contest, a slave's flight to freedom could directly threaten Indian survival by occupying indigenous territory, competing for already scarce resources, and attracting expeditions. Nor was the African-descended population immune to rumors of Botocudo ferocity. Indian–quilombola alliances most likely existed. For instance, the Itambacuri missionaries claimed that "amidst the terrible Pojixá are some black fugitive slaves who give the Indians bad advice, rule over them, and gather them in the nearby forest of São Mateus."[46] An oral history

<hr>

[45] Lucrecio Augusto Marques Ribeiro to Manoel Buarque de Macedo, May 27, 1881, Polícia Ser. 2 Cx. 72 Mc 265 Fls. 152–53, APEES.

[46] Fr. Angelo de Sassoferato and Fr. Serafim de Gorizia to Police Lieutenant of Teófilo Ottoni, March 5, 1885, 20-III-51, ACRJ; Fr. Angelo de Sassoferato and Fr. Serafim de

recounts the story of a fugitive slave who fled his master in northern Minas. The slave killed a jaguar in the forest, which "led him to be called Captain Grande by the Indians. In his prestigious position, the fugitive slave incited the Indians to invade the fazenda Liberdade to kill [his master], captain Leonardo, and steal his five daughters."[47] Both examples accuse quilombolas of manipulating Indians into resisting missionaries and settlers and show the latters' inability to comprehend indigenous resistance. At the same time, they provide fleeting yet suggestive examples of black–Indian collaboration forged in the context of slavery and settler encroachment. Such alliances, however, were far from guaranteed nor should be presumed.[48]

Given these risky conditions, the quilombolas' familiarity with the terrain and people was essential. By carefully navigating among familiar places and faces, they enjoyed a notoriety that gave them leverage over their potential enemies; by venturing farther afield, a quilombola would become just another fugitive slave, vulnerable to multiple hostilities. In other words, it was safer to be among people one knew, whether friend or foe. Capitalizing on the residents' fear, or need, of quilombolas like Benedito, Lucindo and his peers could brazenly flee to another part of town for months, if not years. That said, safety was not the only reason for their flight into São Mateus. The importance of maintaining kinship ties, access to land, and other hard-won customary rights was the fundamental reason that freedpeople often remained in locations where they had only recently been captives – moving away could signify the loss of those things. Their idea of freedom was not defined by moving afar (which is not to be confused with freedom of movement) but by the ability to live together with family and community in the

Gorizia to Police Lieutenant of Teófilo Ottoni, March 8, 1885, 20-III-51, ACRJ; Fr. Angelo de Sassoferato and Fr. Serafim de Gorizia to MACOP, March 15, 1885, 20-III-52, ACRJ; Fr. Angelo de Sassoferato and Fr. Serafim de Gorizia to MACOP, March 20, 1885, 20-III-50, ACRJ.

47 Cléia Schiavo Weyrauch, *Pioneiros Alemães de Nova Filadélfia* (Caxias do Sul: Editora da Universidade de Caxias do Sul, 1997), 90; cited in Izabel Missagia de Mattos, *Civilização e revolta: os Botocudos e a catequese na província de Minas* (São Paulo: EDUSC ANPOCS, 2004), 356.
48 There are snippets of evidence suggesting that maroons and Indians sometimes did join hands in attacking settlers, but the regularity is difficult to assess. Manoel da Silva Mafra, Relatório ao Ministério da Justiça, 1881, 26, CRL; Ministry of Justice to the President of Espírito Santo, July 26, 1881; and Marcellino d'Assis Fortes to Police Lieutenant of the Capital, August 8, 1881, Polícia Ser. 2 Cx. 72 Mc 265 Fls. 152–156, APEES. See Chapter 2 for quilombolas and Botocudo sharing their fear of the Pojixá.

location of their choice, a choice that had all but vanished for the region's indigenous.[49]

Just as the quilombolas working as free laborers destabilized the legal definition of slavery, their flight into the terrains of São Mateus began to erode the geographies of enslavement. Their flight was undeniably shaped by their awareness of the diminishing opportunities for freedom in the hinterlands. Freedom for the quilombolas, however, was meaningful only insofar as it was realized among their own community and on their own terms, and that was precisely why they remained. A bird's-eye view of São Mateus and its environs allows us to appreciate the larger impact of their insurgent geographies. Tucked throughout a landscape ruled by powerful proslavery interests and reaching as far as southern Bahia were safe havens among which the quilombolas lived and moved about as free people, assisted by a network of slave-hiders and slaves. The very existence of these spaces within the terrains of slavery weakened slavery's grip on the region. The quilombolas utilized marronage not to isolate themselves from Brazilian society but as a way to reimagine their terms of inclusion within the very same geography. We will now see why and how this remarkable community came together.

Quilombos as "Contingent Communities"

In August 1881, approximately a month after Marcolina was attacked and a year after Benedito's dramatic prison break, an anti-quilombo expedition nearly captured Benedito, who almost killed the expedition leader with a machete in a fierce tussle before disappearing among the trees. He later told a fellow quilombola in his only recorded words, "[m]y friend, I threw a stone at the devil; they surrounded me. I used my machete, but in the end they got me in the fight."[50] Benedito had been traveling with four others, three of them women. They had been living with eight others on Francisco Pinto Neto's property until tensions between Benedito and his fellow quilombola Rogerio split the group in two. Traveling on their own, Benedito's group was soon attacked and disbanded, after which it was partially reconstituted, and again reconfigured.

---

[49] Important works addressing the value given by freedpeople to kinship and land owner-ship include Penningroth, *The Claims of Kinfolk*; Fraga Filho, *Encruzilhadas da liber-dade*, 245–60; Rios and Castro, *Memórias do cativeiro*. Fraga also discusses how freed-people, whose new status was precarious, faced increased risk of police repression and criminalization the farther away they moved.

[50] Lucindo, AN/CA Fl. 174v–175v.

These fleeting and frequently self-reinventing social arrangements oblige us to question what constitutes a quilombo or maroon community. Must it have a minimum size or duration? A unified political intent? Quilombos did not adhere to any paradigm but were what Walter Johnson calls "contingent communities," constantly renegotiated through personal decisions, daily interactions, and changing material conditions.[51] These communities in the making were brought together by family ties, friendships, and hopes of a better life, while simultaneously contending with internal dissonances born from the clash of individual needs and aspirations.[52] Failure to recognize these contingencies risks rendering quilombos as ahistorical, and the women and men who made them as prototypes of resistance, rather than human beings with varied aspirations and foibles. The São Mateus quilombolas, even as late as 1881, were not inevitably drawn together through a shared antislavery ideology but had a variety of motivations for flight, rooted in their daily experiences under slavery. These disparities make their decision to create a community together all the more remarkable; it is precisely this experience that allowed the quilombolas, with their individual goals and aspirations, to begin forging a larger maroon politics that challenged slavery from within.

Not every slave who fled her or his master to join others was driven from the outset by the explicit intention of rejecting or challenging the institution of slavery. For many, it was a negotiatory tactic, whereas others fled to visit loved ones or to protest punishment. Goals were also contingent: living with fellow quilombolas could engender aspirations that were hitherto implausible for a slave who had intended to run away only briefly.[53] Individual flight and marronage belonged to the same continuum.[54]

---

[51] This expression comes from Walter Johnson, *Soul by Soul: Life Inside the Antebellum Slave Market* (Cambridge, MA: Harvard University Press, 2009), 72–77.

[52] Robin D. G. Kelley, *Race Rebels: Culture, Politics, and the Black Working Class* (New York: The Free Press, 1996), Chapter 2, especially 39–40.

[53] The idea of freedom as a moving target, first proposed by Barbara Fields in *Slavery and Freedom on the Middle Ground: Maryland during the Nineteenth Century* (New Haven, CT: Yale University Press, 1987), has had a profound impact on studies of slavery, resistance, abolition, and freedom.

[54] Barbara Bush makes a pronounced distinction between these two forms, arguing that marronage (in the British Caribbean) was primarily the practice of male, "unseasoned" plantation slaves who ran away to establish "free, autonomous communities." Making autonomy the benchmark for a maroon community, however, obscures their much more fluid realities. Barbara Bush, *Slave Women in Caribbean Society: 1650–1838* (Kingston: Heinemann, 1990), 63.

The quilombolas whose paths converged on Francisco Pinto Neto's property were brought together by a remarkably diverse array of "push" and "pull" factors, rather than any semblance of a common cause – except for the desire to put an end to their current circumstances. They ranged in age from twenty to fifty and consisted of six women, seven men, and at least one infant (not all of them testified). One group, led by Rogerio, had first come together at the farm of another slave-hider and relocated to Pinto Neto's after a disagreement broke out with the farmer. They included Manoel Bahiano, a slave of the same mistress as Rogerio, who fled to join his friend.[55] Gertrudes had escaped with her toddler son close to six years prior in the hopes of finding a new owner, a plan that was never realized. After some tremendous hardship, much of it in solitude, she arrived at the slave-hider's, where she was eventually joined by the other quilombolas.[56] Sheer exhaustion led to Hortência's decision to leave her master nearly two years prior and arrive at the same farm.[57] Vicentino had been put up as collateral for his master's debt and fled a few weeks afterward, probably for fear of being sold.[58]

Others soon joined the quilombo at Pinto Neto's, guided by rumors that fellow escaped slaves had founded a settlement there. Rufina, age twenty-two, ran away from her master, the São Mateus police lieutenant. After spending several months with other quilombolas, she went her own way, but eventually rejoined them.[59] More than a year and a half into her flight, her mother Josepha, an African-born woman of around fifty, decided to join Rufina and was led to Pinto Neto's by Lucindo, whom she ran into during her wanderings. Her decision points to the importance enslaved women gave to maintaining mother–daughter relationships even when the latter was no longer a child, and was likely motivated by their belonging to different owners.[60] Lucindo, who would be accused of participating in the attack on Marcolina, was in the midst of one of his

---

[55] Manoel Bahiano, Fl. 25.

[56] "Interrogatório feito à ré Gertrudes" (Gertrudes interrogation hereafter), September 24, 1881, AN/CA Fls. 140–41.

[57] "Auto de perguntas feitas a Hortência, escrava de Dr. Raulino Francisco de Oliveira" (Hortência hereafter), September 3, 1881, AN/CA Fls. 78v–80v.

[58] Vicentino's owner, José Antonio de Faria, put him up as collateral for debt twice in May 1880 and again on February 8, 1881, to creditor Major Cunha, and the slave fled sometime around March. Ironically, Francisca and Ricarda fled with hopes to be purchased by the same man. Tabelionato Liv. 12 Fl. 8v and 11; Liv. 15 Fl. 24, CPSM.

[59] Rufina, Fls. 81–82.

[60] Josepha, Fls. 10–11. Generally the literature that does discuss fugitive slave mothers describes them with small children.

habitual flights. He joined his fellow quilombolas at Pinto Neto's after fleeing in fear from his latest, demanding owner. Another mother and daughter pair, Francisca and Ricarda, had escaped their master together and come to town with the hopes of being purchased by Major Cunha, São Mateus' most powerful planter and a central figure of the local conservative oligarchy.[61] While their flight was not a rejection of slavery itself, like Rufina and Josepha's, what mattered to these women was to stay together. Unsuccessful in encountering their potential buyer, Francisca and Ricarda were trying to regain their bearings when they were found by Rogerio, who the women later claimed had "tricked" them into joining the quilombolas at Pinto Neto's with the promise that he would take them to their destination.[62] Their statement conflicted with Lucindo's testimony that every quilombola had joined the quilombo of his or her own volition, rather than through seduction or force, as the authorities presumed.[63] Júlio probably joined a group here as well, while Benedito was somewhere on his own.

What is remarkable about the processes that brought these women and men together is precisely the lack of a common motivation. In spite of that, they created a community, albeit a fluctuating one, with the power to further erode slaveholder power. We may be inclined to perceive an overarching and preexisting antislavery ideology that united these quilombolas against slaveholders. This is not at all unreasonable given the strengthening antislavery climate of the 1880s discussed in Chapter 4. However, their testimonies reveal a wide variety of reasons, some conflicted but none of them *explicitly* aimed at rejecting the institution of slavery (although it is possible they simply chose not to mention it). Benedito or Rogerio may have spoken more explicitly against slavery, but they did not testify. The closest instance to an assertion of freedom involved two quilombolas who attempted to "pass" as freedpeople (*forro/a*) in first presenting themselves to their slave-hiders.[64]

Still, all of the quilombolas were contesting their captivity in one way or another. In recognizing the diversity of flight-inducing factors, it is

---

[61] Searching for another owner was a common motivation for slave flight. Reis, "Escravos e coiteiros"; Marcus J. M. de Carvalho, *Liberdade: rotinas e rupturas do escravismo no Recife, 1822–1850* (Recife: EDUFPE, 1998), 271–310.

[62] "Auto de perguntas feitas a Ricarda, escrava de José Rodrigues de Souza Flores," August 9, 1881, AN/CA Fl. 32; "Auto de perguntas feitas a Francisca, escrava de José Rodrigues de Souza Flores" (Francisca hereafter), August 9, 1881, AN/CA Fl. 45v.

[63] "Interrogatório ao réu Lucindo," April 26, 1882, AN/CA Fl. 201v.

[64] They are Vicentino and Rufina.

essential not to privilege clearly discernible antislavery motivations as being "more political" than the desire to join friends and family or to seek better conditions under a different owner. These apparently quotidian claims expressed the quilombolas' ideas about freedom and were made at tremendous risk to their personal safety. While the quilombolas certainly had a network of people to protect them and acted as free agents whenever possible, they also confronted daily the harsh reality of persecution. Anti-quilombo expeditions escalated in the months following the attack on Marcolina, making all the more striking the fact that the quilombolas still remained in São Mateus. This was because the quilombolas' politics did not exist outside of their lives under slavery but were formulated within it. Their desires to live with kin, to protect their children, or to ameliorate their working conditions within the very terrain that enslaved them were in themselves political acts through which quilombolas asserted their lives as free women and men, not property that could be beaten or sold, even if they did not articulate those ideas in the language of antislavery. Their insurgent geographies were expressed in their striving to realize these aspirations exactly where they lived and on their own terms.[65]

Crisis befell the Francisco Pinto Neto quilombola settlement soon after Benedito joined the group, followed by Pinto Neto's slave, João Car-retão, who brought their total number to thirteen. Just five months later, the precarious symbiosis of farmer, slave, and quilombola was compromised when Benedito attempted to shoot Júlio, sending a fissure through the group. Tensions and internal divisions among the quilombolas had become evident, with some openly skeptical of Benedito's character. Manoel Bahiano blamed Benedito and Lucindo for rampant livestock thefts.[66] Vicentino was confident that Benedito would be "ready to do anything bad because he's lost."[67] Rogerio disapproved of the disorder Benedito caused in their settlement, given its potential to invite hostility. On concluding that reconciliation was impossible, Rogerio gathered seven of the quilombolas and an infant and left Pinto Neto's to relocate to another property.[68] In Josepha's alternate retelling, the rift was caused by Benedito and Rogerio's battle over her daughter, Rufina.[69]

The actual causes of the parting of ways may have been manifold. This incident illuminates that the quilombo community cannot be taken

[65] Kelley, *Race Rebels*, Introduction and Chapter 1.
[66] "Interrogatório feito ao réu escravo Manoel Bahiano," September 26, 1881, AN/CA Fl. 135. As we may recall, he and Rogerio also believed Benedito to be guilty of the attack on Marcolina.
[67] Vicentino, Fls. 49–52.   [68] Manoel Bahiano, Fl. 25v.   [69] Josepha, Fl. 11.

for granted, given the fragility of such an endeavor in the face of individual differences and suspicions manifested under strained conditions. Benedito's threat to shoot Júlio was the last straw in a brewing factionalism. The quilombolas' criticism of Benedito's risky behaviors stemmed from a code of behavior they had devised for each other as they related to the outside world, cognizant that survival on their own was impossible. By attempting to murder a fellow quilombola, Benedito delivered a severe blow to the unity of the precarious settlement where the thirteen of them had come together. All of the quilombolas committed thefts outside the settlement in order to survive, but those who sided with Rogerio in his contest for leadership against Benedito perceived the latter's thievery as reckless and as menacing to their survival. Once past the tipping point, their networks could no longer protect them, and persecution would follow, exposing the entire group to grave dangers and a life on the run. Exerting leadership among the quilombolas was also an act of masculine self-assertion, partly defined by the access to women, the possession of weapons, and at least for Benedito, a performance of bravado. Significantly, all of Benedito's critics were men. Sexual rivalries and tensions, then, may have contributed in bringing the two men to blows, and were thus another factor that would have threatened group cohesion.[70]

Violence awaited after the group had parted ways. Multiple anti-quilombo expeditions, constant relocations, and scarce resources resulted, as we will see, in Rogerio's murder and the arrest of many others in August 1881. Such travails suggest the downside of what Clóvis Moura, in his seminal work on quilombos, argued to be their lifeline: mobility. Landlessness granted versatility but was simultaneously grounds for vulnerability.[71] Yet such instability did not negate the quilombo's significance. As we have seen, each quilombola had distinct motives for fleeing into the terrains of São Mateus. While they were not united by an explicit antislavery ideology at the outset, the most striking outcome of these events was that *none* of them returned to slavery until they were coerced, even if doing so would have saved them from further instability and persecution. A second notable outcome was that they strove to maintain a community despite all the odds. Fleeing in order to protect

---

[70] Richard Price, *Maroon Societies: Rebel Slave Communities in the Americas* (Baltimore: The Johns Hopkins University Press, 1996), 18–19, noted the struggle over women in maroon communities.

[71] Moura, *Rebeliões da senzala*, 227–31.

what was important to them, the quilombolas experienced firsthand a life beyond slavery. They forged a consciousness of freedom by creating a community and sharing their lives as quilombolas; going back seemed no longer a viable option. Freedom, then, became a collective political practice through which they remapped their lives onto the terrains of São Mateus. Even so, women living in enslaved and quilombola communities confronted unique challenges in their struggles for individual and collective freedom.

Women Quilombolas and Gendered Tensions

Benedito's flamboyance threatens to overshadow some of the most valuable information these testimonies provide about the lives of quilombola women.[72] Beyond the lack of sources, our limited knowledge of women quilombolas stems from the male gendering of marronage. Enslaved women are often considered incapable of withstanding the harsh living conditions of marronage, and to tend toward truancy rather than permanent flight because of the emotional difficulty of leaving children behind or the physical hardship of fleeing with a child. In short, many have concluded that family largely bound women to the realms of their masters.[73] Yet the quilombola women of São Mateus fled in order to be with, or to gain a better life with, their children. Their stories help illuminate maroon politics as a gendered practice shaped by the specific ways in which women were denied, and struggled for, freedom in late-nineteenth-century Brazil.[74]

---

[72] For literature on Brazilian quilombos, see n. 5 above. Women do not figure prominently in these studies, and when they do, they are generally depicted as kidnapping victims or noted only in passing. Maria Lúcia de Barros Mott, _Submissao e Resistência: a mulher na luta contra a escravidão_ (São Paulo: Editora Contexto, 1991), offers a brief discussion of women quilombolas on pp. 42–48.

[73] Such views have been posited, for example, by Camp, _Closer to Freedom_; Deborah G. White, _Ar'n't I a Woman?: Female Slaves in the Plantation South_ (New York: W. W. Norton, 1999); Bush, _Slave Women in Caribbean Society_.

Bush also discusses female maroons, but as fighters and spiritual leaders categorically separate from runaways. In their introduction to _Women and Slavery_, 2 Vols., ed. Gwyn Campbell, Suzanne Miers, and Joseph Calder Miller (Athens, OH: Ohio University Press, 2008), 8–9, the editors cogently criticize the implicitly male nature of ungendered slaves and consequentially of the common categories of slave resistance (submission, flight, revolt) but reinforce the idea that enslaved women rarely fled.

[74] Works that have specifically focused on female flight and marronage include Sally Price, _Co-Wives and Calabashes_ (Ann Arbor: University of Michigan Press, 1993), which highlights the gendered tensions among Saramaka women and men; Hilary Beckles, _Natural_

The ties binding mother and child were often not a deterrent but rather a powerful motivating factor in women's decisions to flee, regardless of a child's age. It is difficult to know whether it also factored into men's decisions, since none of the men mentioned kin as a motivation. Earlier we saw that Josepha and Francisca fled to be with their respective adult daughters, Rufina and Ricarda. The story of Gertrudes, who fled with her toddler son, highlights women quilombolas' particular struggles for freedom as embodied by their willingness to risk their lives for a better life with their children, even while suffering devastating losses.[75] Gertrudes' ordeal typifies the separations endured by enslaved people despite later nineteenth-century Brazilian laws that increasingly recognized slaves' rights to have and remain with their own families, and the extraordinary lengths to which these quilombola women went in order to keep their families together.[76]

Rebels: A Social History of Enslaved Black Women in Barbados (New Brunswick, NJ: Rutgers University Press, 2000), 164–69; Barbara Krauthamer, "A Particular Kind of Freedom: Black Women, Slavery, Kinship, and Freedom in the American Southeast," in *Women and Slavery*, Vol. 2, ed. Gwyn Campbell, Suzanne Miers, and Joseph Calder Miller (Athens, OH: Ohio University Press, 2008), 100–27.

[75] Hortência was also pregnant while in flight, but the child she gave birth to died soon afterward. Rufina gave birth in May 1881, also as a quilombola, just a few months before her arrest. The fate of her child is unknown. "Interrogatório feito à ré Hortência," September 24, 1881, AN/CA Fl. 124; "Autos de perguntas feitas a Tereza Maria de Jesus," August 6, 1881, AN/CA Fl. 53v. Of all the male quilombolas, we know only that João Carretão had a child, with Gertrudes. Since he was not questioned, we do not know whether his child or relationship with Gertrudes (her story that follows suggests they did not stay together) was a motivating factor.

[76] As noted by Mahony and Slenes, after 1869, separating legally married couples and their children under fifteen (later twelve) became illegal. The Free Womb Law of 1871 declared the legal freedom of children born to enslaved mothers. Known as *ingênuos*, these children were placed under the "protection" of their mothers' owners, and often the latter opted to keep these children's "services" until they were twenty-one. Mary Ann Mahony, "Creativity under Constraint: Enslaved Afro-Brazilian Families in Brazil's Cacao Area, 1870–1890," *Journal of Social History* 41, no. 3 (2008): 643; on the Free Womb Law, see Camillia Cowling, "Debating Womanhood, Defining Freedom: The Abolition of Slavery in 1880s Rio de Janeiro," *Gender & History* 22, no. 2 (2010): 286. Other important works on enslaved women, families, and strategies for freedom in Brazil include Robert W. Slenes, *Na senzala, uma flor: esperanças e recordações na formação da família escrava: Brasil Sudeste, século XIX* (Rio de Janeiro: Editora Nova Fronteira, 1999); Rios and Castro, *Memórias do cativeiro*; Fraga Filho, *Encruzilhadas da liberdade*; Júnia Ferreira Furtado, *Chica da Silva: A Brazilian Slave of the Eighteenth Century* (Cambridge: Cambridge University Press, 2009). Mary Karasch, "Slave Women on the Brazilian Frontier in the Nineteenth Century," in *More than Chattel: Black Women and Slavery in the Americas*, ed. David Barry Gaspar and Darlene Clark Hine (Bloomington: Indiana University Press, 1996) is a rare and important study of enslaved women in frontier regions (Goiás) in the postcolonial period.

A thirty-five-year-old woman who had spent more than half a decade in flight, Gertrudes survived for years in the sole company of her toddler son by hunting and foraging in the forests. Her escape was motivated by the urgency to protect herself and her child from her master's punishments, and the hope for better conditions under a new owner. While not an outright rejection of slavery in the beginning, her decision was founded on the resolute determination to remain together with her child and break free of the circumstances that bound their lives to violence. However, being a quilombola denied her the legal protection to keep her family intact. Gertrudes' hopes for the possibility of a collective purchase of mother and son were dashed when a local resident illegally purchased only her son, a legally free *ingênuo*, thereby separating him from his mother.[77] As Mary Ann Mahony has noted, individuals who were not large plantation owners had little incentive to obey the 1869 law to keep slave families intact, since they relied more than others on the purchase and sale of individual slaves. As a quilombola, Gertrudes was even more vulnerable to such legal transgressions, since losing her son appears to have resulted from direct, unregistered transaction between her and the buyer.[78]

We can understand the depth of Gertrudes' struggle to stay with her son in light of an earlier experience. Prior to the sale of her son, a pregnant Gertrudes gave birth to a second child alone at an apparently abandoned manioc flour mill. She did so at tremendous risk to her own and her infant's life in the mill's ill-equipped and unsanitary environment. After giving birth, the quilombola temporarily left her newborn, only to discover on her return that the infant had disappeared. The mill, as she soon discovered, was in fact not abandoned but belonged to one of São Mateus' well-known slave-hiders who had found the infant, whom he then refused to return to his mother. Gertrudes' child, unlike his mother, should have been legally free since he was born after the 1871 Free Womb Law – but then the child lost his freedom to a stranger. The tragedy that befell Gertrudes revealed the risks of treading the geopolitics of São Mateus society; although she happened upon a slave-hider, the latter was no guarantor of shelter and aid. As such, Gertrudes' decision to remain on

---

[77] "Auto de perguntas feito a Gertrudes, escrava de Francisco José de Faria" (Gertrudes hereafter), August 9, 1881, AN/CA Fls. 33v. See previous note for ingênuos.
[78] Mahony, "Creativity under Constraint," 643. Slenes has also noted that larger plantations in the Paraíba Valley tended not to sell off their slaves, so slave families had a greater opportunity to stay intact. *Na senzala, uma flor*, 107–9.

the slave-hider's farm in spite of his open hostility to her presence signaled her commitment to stay close to her child by fleeing *into* São Mateus. Gertrudes' resolve not to have and raise her children on her master's property, and her long-term decision not to return to slavery in spite of terrible losses, demonstrate how quilombola women understood their freedom as a right to motherhood. Freedom meant the control over their own bodies and reproduction – not just the freedom of the womb – and the ability to be with their own children. Gertrudes' actions thus bear out what Camillia Cowling has stated with regard to enslaved women in Rio: "[t]he struggle for custody of children as part of the struggle for emancipation was first and foremost women's battle." Gertrudes eventually decided to cast her lot with the other quilombolas. She was found with a third child at her breast when an expedition arrested many of them in early August 1881. Even after losing two children, then, she fought to keep this hard-won right to motherhood as a quilombola who chose not to return to slavery (Figure 5.2).[79]

Escaping the masters' control over their bodies and families was an important determinant in women quilombolas' quest for freedom. However, living with fellow quilombolas, while providing these women with a new "family" with whom to share their experiences, was not free of its own gendered tensions. A closer examination of gender relations among the quilombolas reveals an important side of the little-understood inner workings of maroon communities, and how women's freedoms could be circumscribed not only by their masters but also by fellow male quilombolas.[80] Labor was one example. All of the quilombolas worked, whether for a slave-hider or for themselves, setting traps and gathering or stealing manioc. Women drew water while men served as lookouts. Gertrudes and Rogerio, for instance, planted cane and made baskets and other goods (Figure 5.3). However, when it came to stealing larger items like livestock, it was tacitly agreed to be the exclusive task of the men. Hortência testified that she had no idea where the animals came from.[81]

---

[79] Gertrudes, Fls. 33v–34v, and Gertrudes interrogation, Fls. 140–41v. It is unclear which child she had with João Carretão. For the quote, see Cowling, "Debating Womanhood," 296.

[80] Even scholars who have recognized the importance of women maroons have noted the lack of work documenting gender relations among maroons; see, for example, Flavio Gomes, *Palmares: escravidão e liberdade no Atlantico Sul* (São Paulo: Editora Contexto, 2005), 81; Hilary Beckles, *Centering Woman: Gender Relations in Caribbean Slave Society* (Kingston; Oxford: Ian Randle; James Currey, 1999), 167.

[81] Hortência, Fl. 79. The contention that the hard work associated with being part of a maroon community acted as another deterrent for women to flee seems not to have been

FIGURE 5.2 The lives of quilombola women like Gertrudes show that the desire to remain with, and have a better life with, one's children was an important motivation for women to flee their masters. *Source: Black woman with a child*, c.1869. Alberto Henschel / Instituto Moreira Salles – Leibniz-Institut für Laenderkunder. Reproduced with permission.

FIGURE 5.3 Quilombolas were employed by town residents in need of extra labor. In addition to working as fieldhands, the quilombolas Rogério and Gertrudes made these *samburá* baskets. *Source: Marchand de sambouras* (detail), from Jean Baptiste Debret, *Voyage pittoresque et historique au Brésil* (Paris: Firmin Didot frères, 1834). From the New York Public Library.

Thus, while women and men often performed separate tasks for their masters under slavery, the quilombolas themselves also created and maintained their own gendered divisions.[82] The male quilombolas deliberately kept certain information from the women. Nowhere was this practice more salient than in the acquisition and possession of weapons. The men never left the quilombo without a rifle, which was probably the visual marker that allowed Marcolina to identify her assailants as quilombolas in the first place. While certainly important for self-defense,

an issue here. The only related complaint was lodged by Rufina, as seen earlier, who was more discontented by the compensation than the labor itself. This labor-as-deterrent argument is made by editors Gwyn Campbell, Suzanne Miers, and Joseph Calder Miller in their introduction to *Women and Slavery*, 10.

[82] On labor and gender under slavery see Jennifer L. Morgan, *Laboring Women: Reproduction and Gender in New World Slavery* (Philadelphia: University of Pennsylvania Press, 2004). Stuart Schwartz's analysis of the quilombolas of Sant'Anna, mentioned in n. 5, also demonstrates their gendering of labor. Schwartz, "Resistance and Accommodation."

weapons possession was also a way for male quilombolas to assert their masculinity and bravado. For although the women faced equal if not greater dangers, they were prohibited from possessing weapons, let alone knowing where they came from. Francisca clearly remembered that "the *negros* would return with gunpowder and arms," but "she did not know how they obtained them, because they were extremely reserved about it."[83] Gertrudes and Rufina were equally kept in the dark. Vicentino's remarks plainly reveal the attitude behind such measures. The women were not allowed to know what was going on, he recounted, because Rogerio did not in the least bit trust them with any information.[84] Apparently secrecy was more important than allowing women greater control over their own safety. The male quilombolas' tight control over vital information on where to acquire certain sources of nourishment and weapons – information that would have allowed women more self-protection and mobility – limited the women's access to resources necessary for their survival and made them dependent on men. This may have enhanced the male quilombolas' sense of themselves as providers, expanding their own sense of freedom and measure of control over their environment (even though they may have fought for control among themselves, as seen earlier), but at the expense of female quilombolas' freedom.

If the male quilombolas found the women so unreliable, why were they incorporated into the quilombos? The quilombola men viewed women with condescension while actively seeking them. Both Francisca and Ricarda squarely placed the responsibility on Rogerio for bringing them into his community. According to their testimonies he had deceived them, "feeding their hope" that he was going to help them to their destination but luring them to the quilombo instead. Yet the women stayed for months. Of course, mother and daughter may have been attempting to downplay their own agency before the police. A more obvious reason for the incorporation of women was to meet the men's – and women's own – sexual needs, the most brutal example being Marcolina's attempted rape by her unidentified quilombola assailants. The sources are reticent regarding sexual relationships among the quilombolas. Gertrudes had a child with João Carretão, which we could ostensibly consider a quilombola family, but we do not know whether they stayed together. Hortência and Rufina also gave birth as quilombolas, but the fathers' identities are not revealed. Benedito and Rogerio allegedly clashed over Rufina, but the testimonies do not hint at any tensions among the women regarding their

---

[83] Francisca, Fl. 46v.   [84] Vicentino, Fls. 51v–52.

access to men. Francisca and Josepha were twenty to twenty-five years older than the men and therefore sexual partnerships may have been less likely, although certainly not impossible. Still it is worth emphasizing that none of the women claimed they were kidnapped or otherwise brought by force. Rather, each woman clearly had her own reasons to flee.[85]

Gender shaped the quilombolas' experiences under slavery and in flight. Enslaved women's freedoms were curtailed in very specific ways, first in their right to motherhood under slavery, and second in their relations with quilombola men, forcing us to recognize women's unique experiences in a practice that has been overwhelmingly masculinized. Family and children were far from deterrents but rather the very factors that shaped the political consciousness of women like Gertrudes, who decided to claim her right to motherhood by taking matters into her own hands. At the same time, living with male quilombolas revealed that their own masculinized ideas of freedom sometimes curtailed the women's own opportunities to live as fugitive and, eventually, free people. These tensions did not in any way negate the import of the quilombolas' conceptualizations of freedom, but they do oblige us to recognize the very real conflicts between quilombola women and men as they sought to forge a collective maroon politics.

"Siege! Siege!" Rogerio shouted to his fellow quilombolas. "Everyone, let's go! The expedition is coming!!"[86] It was still dark in the predawn hours of August 8, 1881 when a police raid startled the quilombolas who had accompanied Rogerio to a settlement on Campo Redondo farm – four men, three women, and an infant. The panicked women broke into flight as the sound of bullets echoed among the trees. Hiding themselves behind a tree, they saw the men exchange fire with the expedition.[87] Rogerio sprang forward and stabbed an expedition member in the chest. His victory was only temporary, however, as he was soon showered with bullets. It was only moments later that Francisca, Ricarda, and Gertrudes, the latter clutching her infant son to her breast, were discovered by the expedition and arrested. Some were subsequently sold for punishment. The remaining men, João Carretão, Júlio, Vicentino, and Manoel Bahiano, fled through the woods in various directions. Vicentino was hit by

---

[85] A full discussion of Marcolina's case falls outside the scope of this chapter. She may have been a potential kidnap victim, but that does not explain why the quilombolas tried to kill her when she resisted. Perhaps Marcolina was hiding something from the police about her involvement with her attackers. Alternately, the quilombolas may have intended to spread terror among enslaved and free people.

[86] Rogerio as quoted by Manoel Bahiano, AN/CA Fl. 27v, 135v–136v.

[87] Gertrudes, AN/CA Fl. 24v.

a total of fifteen bullets, while Manoel Bahiano was shot by an ex-slave who had joined the expedition; both survived. They hid in the forest until they decided to give themselves up to the authorities.[88] João Carretão and Júlio succeeded in escaping entirely. Benedito, who was not in the siege, vanished into thin air.[89]

Between Rumor and Action: The Santana Slave Insurrection

Three years passed before anything was known of Benedito. News of his whereabouts surfaced only on July 9, 1884, just a week after the Farias were acquitted of Seraphim's murder. Approaching was the annual Festival of Santana (Saint Anne), a popular holiday among the region's enslaved. However, this year a rumor began circulating that "on the 27th of this month during the Santana festivities, the [slaves] want to unite and unleash an insurrection in order to be freed." A similar rumor was reported by the town's police lieutenant, according to whom the enslaved were expecting their emancipation on the saint's day and were poised to rise to the cry "Long live liberty!" Although he did not suspect an insurrection, he was worried by a series of festival game competitions that brought together slaves from the city and countryside and gave them a troubling degree of autonomy.[90]

As these rumors circulated, a group of twenty to thirty armed quilombolas from São Mateus, Barra de São Mateus, and southern Bahia had joined forces to attack travelers and farmsteads. Soon the police chief of Espírito Santo, Antonio Pitanga, fused these two separate incidents (for

---

[88] They did so after securing patronage protection, a common practice for slaves facing the possibility of punishment. According to Walter Fraga, this practice of "*tomar padrinho*" (taking patronage) exemplified the customary ways in which slaves complained about injustices by adhering to social hierarchies. However, by the 1880s such customary practices became overwhelmed by the slaves' expectations of freedom. Fraga Filho, *Encruzilhadas da liberdade*, 47.

[89] Gertrudes, AN/CA Fl. 141, and Emilio Domingues Gomes de Almeida, Head of the Police Forces of Rio de Janeiro, August 9, 1881, AN/CA Fl. 42.

[90] The slaves competed in two groups named Primos and Sornamby. Their origins are unknown; however, Sornamby is probably Sernamby, a neighborhood in the center of São Mateus. A description of festivities in the São Mateus region (but not the Feast of Sant'Ana) can be found in Hermógenes Lima da Fonseca and Rogério Medeiros, *Tradições populares no Espírito Santo* (Vitória: Departamento Estadual de Cultura, Divisão de Memória, 1991). Bento de Jesus Silvares, Police Lieutenant of São Mateus to Antonio Pitanga, July 9, 1884, Polícia Ser. 2 Cx. 77 Mc 288 Fls. 97 and 117, APEES; José Antonio de Souza Lé, Police Sublieutenant of São Mateus to Antonio Pitanga, July 9, 1884, Polícia Ser. 2 Cx. 77 Mc 288 Fls. 97 and 117, APEES.

reasons that remain unclear) and unleashed a new rumor: that twenty to thirty quilombolas from the two provinces were planning an antislavery insurrection, headed by none other than Benedito. He informed the provincial Vice President that the quilombolas had gathered on the property of Barra planter José Guedes, and urged the local police to destroy their settlements.[91] Was the speculation of Benedito-led insurrection a police invention, or was there substance to the rumor?

Insurrection scares were nothing new in São Mateus. Emancipation rumors had triggered such fears in 1843 and 1851, and the Paraguayan War and the Free Womb Law inspired others in 1866 and 1871.[92] By 1884, however, the political climate had changed dramatically. Ceará, Rio Grande do Norte, and Amazonas had already abolished slavery in their provinces. Closer to home, two slave uprisings on Colônia Leopoldina in 1881 and 1882 culminated in the violent murder of the planter José Venerote by his own slaves in 1884. In São Mateus, slaveholders knew that the Farias' innocent verdict for Seraphim's murder could not protect them transformations in law and public opinion that were eroding their authority. Soon, a local abolitionist movement would plunge them into panic and frenzy.

The enslaved and quilombolas were, of course, acutely aware of these transformations. Why else would they expect a general emancipation in July 1884? We have seen how the quilombolas, through their insurgent geographies, asserted their own terms of national inclusion. Foundational to these geographies were the complex social and economic networks that tied them with the enslaved and free, as well as their intricate knowledge of the terrain that allowed them to find spaces of freedom within a geography of captivity. In the three years since their arrest, much had changed. In 1881, no quilombola expressly spoke against slavery, and nobody in the vast network of slave-hiders and collaborators demonstrated abolitionist sympathies. General emancipation was not explicitly part of the public discourse in São Mateus, and nobody considered Benedito the leader of an antislavery insurrection. That such ideas gained so much traction in 1884 revealed the new set of possibilities on the horizon, and the emergence of a new insurgent geography of antislavery.

---

[91] Antonio Pitanga to Vice President of Espírito Santo, José Camillo Ferreira Rebello, July 12, 1884, Governadoria, Liv. 243 Fl. 217, APEES; President of Espírito Santo to Minister and Secretary of Justice, Francisco Maria Sodré Pereira, July 16, 1884, Ibid Fl. 219; and Vice President Rebello to Antonio Pitanga, July 16, 1884, Polícia Ser. 2, Cx. 77, Mc 288, Fl. 96, APEES.

[92] See Chapters 2 and 4.

The archival documents allow us to trace how the police chief's new rumor about a quilombola-led insurrection became increasingly burnished with a patina of fact with every apparently routine exchange between him, the provincial vice president, and eventually the Minister of Justice. The rumor's evolution certainly suggests the workings of paranoid men who saw a slave conspiracy in every corner, and of officials neatly aligned with slaveholding interests.[93] Such possibilities nonetheless cannot overshadow the fact that the original rumor – of a general slave emancipation on the Festival of Santana – had emerged among the enslaved; the police only expanded on it. If rumors are, as Steve Hahn has argued, a "field and form of political struggle" that allowed the enslaved to participate in and shape political debate, the enslaved of São Mateus staked their claims in the politics of abolition through this emancipation rumor. In the turbulent climate of 1884, the rumor signaled that emancipation was both plausible and desirable for the enslaved. That the police increasingly validated and embellished it shows that not only did they too find it plausible, but that they also saw the quilombolas, ever more explicitly, through the lens of antislavery.[94] For their part, the quilombolas used action to assert, deliberately and publicly, their own stakes in this political debate.[95]

Benedito's reappearance fortified the rumor with substance. Only on July 22 an expedition ordered by the provincial vice president departed the town of Barra for José Guedes' property on which the quilombo presumably existed.[96] Commanded by Second Lieutenant Manoel Souza from Vitória, the party included five planters, among them Guedes himself. After two days of fruitless searching, Souza continued solo, venturing into a forested area outside of Barra amidst an evening rain. He was startled by two gunshots. Turning to the source, Souza discerned the figure of Benedito standing only a few yards away, pointing a rifle straight in his direction. Souza shot back but was impaired by the deepening night, allowing Benedito to slip away, his silhouette swallowed by the trees.

---

[93] On "white paranoia" regarding insurrection scares and the need to look beyond them, see Steven Hahn, "'Extravagant Expectations' of Freedom: Rumour, Political Struggle, and the Christmas Insurrection Scare of 1865 in the American South," *Past & Present* no. 157 (1997): 122–58.

[94] Ibid., 133.

[95] I thank Greg Childs for forcing a reconsideration of black politics from the lens of conspiracy (with the presumption of secrecy) to sedition (which was public).

[96] José Rebello, Vice President of Espírito Santo to Antonio Pitanga, July 16, 1884, Polícia Ser. 2 Cx. 77 Mc 288 Fls. 96, APEES.

The shots alerted the rest of the expedition, which followed Souza and arrested six quilombolas, while others escaped. The quilombolas had prepared for raids by arranging their settlement into three separate ranchos. The expedition destroyed what remained of the quilombo infrastructure to prevent them from returning there.[97]

The police were elated by the results. The expedition also arrested eight suspected slave hiders. Also captured was Júlio, who had successfully eluded capture since the Campo Redondo shootout. Interrogations revealed that the quilombo had been founded about a month earlier and included at least nine individuals, both men and women, most of them belonging to a wealthy slaveowner named Gothardo Esteves.[98] Júlio and another quilombola named Venancio Camundá affirmed that the settlement had ties with Benedito, who had visited on several occasions, always heavily armed with rifles and machetes. He had supplied the quilombo with the bulk of their necessities and firearms, probably as a way to gain admission.[99] These revelations seemed to reinforce Pitanga's alarm about a Benedito-led insurrection.

The subsequent police investigation of this quilombo is odd, however. Although the interrogations took place between July 26 and 31, the dates of which encompassed the Festival of Santana, *not a single question is asked regarding the insurrection,* as if the rumor never existed. The interrogator was Bento de Jesus Silvares, the police lieutenant who had reported on July 9th about the quilombola depredations and the slaves' expectations of liberty on the saint's day. Silvares questioned Júlio about his whereabouts since 1881 and about Benedito, but focused his interrogations almost entirely on a separate murder investigation for reasons that remain unclear.[100] The bizarre proceedings did not stop the police from celebrating their success in averting disorder on the Festival of Santana, even though they had discovered no evidence either substantiating or refuting the insurrection, or establishing its connection to the

---

97 Bento de Jesus Silvares to Antonio Pitanga, August 6, 1884, Governadoria Ser. 383 Liv. 243 Fls. 296–98, APEES.

98 Júlio interrogation in "Diligências para a destruição de quilombos," July 21,1884, Processos Box 94, fls. 11–13v, CPSM. Júlio also named the following male and female maroons: Faustino, Brandino, Adolpho, José, Leopoldina, Monica, Andreza, belonging to Esteves, and Felisdoro, the slave of Matheus Cunha (another son of D. Rita Maria da Conceição Cunha, Benedito's mistress).

99 Venancio Camundá interrogation in ibid, fls. 14–14v.

100 The police investigation inexplicably focuses on the murder of a São Mateus resident named Antonio Bambolâu and includes the interrogations of several suspected slave hiders and Júlio, among others. Processos Box 94, CPSM.

quilombolas and Benedito.[101] Such behavior suggested that the police had merely invented the link between the rumor, Benedito, and the quilombolas as a pretext for arresting the latter. The case seemed closed.

Their satisfaction was short lived. The illusion of police control and public order was obliterated by the quilombolas' dramatic actions in the immediate aftermath of the Festival day. Just as the insurrectionary fears seemed to dissipate with the arrests, Benedito reappeared on July 30 heading a group of quilombolas, who embarked on a string of guerrilla-like attacks on São Mateus and Barra properties over the next few days. The redeployed expedition was no match. By the time it reached the areas with the quilombolas sightings, they had already fled, forcing the frustrated pursuers to return empty-handed.[102] Locals feared that police failure was stoking a "daring" attitude among the enslaved and encouraging them to join the quilombolas.[103] Their attacks abruptly ended any semblance of peace, generating a climate of fear and breathing new life into the insurrection rumor.

That the quilombolas were orchestrating a spectacle of terror against slaveholders and the police became increasingly evident on August 6, when they sacked and destroyed Gothardo Esteves' fazenda. This was no random attack. Esteves owned most of the recently captured quilombolas and had participated in the expedition to capture them. He was a politically well-connected slaveowner who had previously murdered one of his slaves with impunity, but now the quilombolas' vengeance left him fearing for his life.[104] The following day, any trace of confidence Barra residents had in their law enforcement was finally shattered when the quilombolas, again under Benedito's lead, appeared in the neighborhood of São Domingos near their recently destroyed settlement, shooting their weapons and robbing properties.[105] While such attacks would have engendered fear at any point, uncertainty about the insurrection rendered their actions much more ominous.

---

[101] Telegram from Police Lieutenant of São Mateus Bento de Jesus Silvares to Antonio Pitanga, July 29, 1884. Polícia Ser. 2, Cx. 77, Mc 288, Fl. 103, APEES.

[102] Bento de Jesus Silvares to Antonio Pitanga, August 6, 1884, Governadoria Ser. 383 Liv. 243 Fls. 296–98, APEES.

[103] Interim Justice of the Law of São Mateus Lopes d'Oliveira to Antonio Pitanga, August 3, 1884, Polícia Ser. 2, Cx. 77, Mc 288 Fl. 107, APEES.

[104] Police Lieutenant of São Mateus Bento de Jesus Silvares to Antonio Pitanga, August 8, 1884, Ibid. Fl. 110. Police Chief of Espírito Santo, June 21, 1876, IJ1–442-ES, AN.

[105] Municipal Justice of Barra de São Mateus Manoel Tobias to Antonio Pitanga, August 9, 1884, Ibid. Fl. 115.

A month after the Feast of Santana, Pitanga was forced to acknowledge police incompetence in capturing the quilombolas, although he remained confident that the insurrection would not materialize.[106] New anti-quilombo efforts began under Manoel Vasconcellos, an enthusiastic Second Lieutenant of the Company of Police, also sent from Vitória.[107] On September 11, Vasconcellos received a tip that Benedito was hiding on a local farm named Santa Isabel. The lieutenant and his men headed swiftly to the property but found no one on arrival. He made a female slave named Anna, reputed to be Benedito's girlfriend, confess his whereabouts. It was true, she admitted, Benedito had been there until yesterday. But thanks to his extensive contacts, he was tipped off about the expedition and promptly departed to the hinterlands of Caravelas in southern Bahia to seek the protection of his mother and relatives.

Vasconcellos immediately telegraphed the police in Caravelas to prevent Benedito from escaping again. Eight days passed without any news, when he finally received word that Benedito was seen crossing a swamp and was heading back south toward the hinterlands of São Mateus. The lieutenant hurriedly led a sizeable expedition of more than sixty men toward the swamp. Standing aghast at the vast and forbidding expanse stretching before them, "it [was] admirable that Benedito crossed it," he recounted later, "when none of us were able to do it."[108] Another two weeks passed with no news until a laborer encountered Benedito in the forests of São Mateus. To avoid advertising his arrival, Vasconcellos renewed his quest with only eight men this time. They soon found themselves facing the same, impossible swamp. Vasconcellos candidly acknowledged, "I realized that only a lot of will power could spur Benedito to cross that swamp, where we would have all lost our lives, drowning in its depths." After three full days to struggle across it, supplies and morale were running low, and assistance scarce. The fifty foot soldiers who joined Vasconcellos from Barra soon began complaining about the lack of supplies, obliging him to pay out of his own pocket for their maintenance. The expedition combed the woods in the São Mateus hinterland without success and returned empty-handed on October 4.[109]

During his exhausting expedition, Vasconcellos had gained remarkable insight into Benedito's extensive insurgent geography spanning the

---

[106] Antonio Pitanga to Vice President of Espírito Santo José Camillo Ferreira Rebello, August 25, 1884, Governadoria Ser. 383 Liv. 243 Fl. 302, APEES.

[107] Manoel Vasconcellos to Antonio Pitanga, October 22, 1884, Polícia Ser. 2 Cx. 73 Mc 271 Fl. 31–33, APEES.

[108] Ibid.   [109] Ibid.

borderlands of Bahia and Espírito Santo. A high-profile criminal he may
have been before the law, but networks of family, friends, and others
spanning these cross-provincial territories provided him with invaluable
protection and resources. With a remarkable capacity to navigate forbidding terrains, he frequently fled to Caravelas, where he could rely on
his mother and kin. Another who protected him was the slave Anto-
nia Colota, who, like Anna, told Vasconcellos that Benedito had fled
to Caravelas. The exasperated lieutenant concluded, "I don't believe we
should give full credence to these slave women. That criminal is protected by many." But women were not his only protectors. There were
male slaves, and a farmer who sometimes employed Benedito. Most ominously for slaveholders, he was also believed to be in contact with the
abolitionist lawyer Olavo Henrique Baptista, who had tried to prosecute the Farias in Seraphim's murder. Vasconcellos dryly concluded, "I
think that he won't be found in any of these places."[110] Meanwhile
the anti-Benedito campaign raged in Barra, where the police lieutenant
had dramatically declared that "Benedito today is the terror of various
inhabitants in this district, and his arrest [will] ensure the public good and
individual safety."[111] Until early November there were intermittent sightings of the quilombola around Colônia Leopoldina but with no arrests.
He always slipped away, ever just out of reach.[112]

What was Benedito thinking? What did he and the quilombolas want?
Their mercurial movements confound the historian today as they did their
pursuers in 1884. We will never know whether they were definitively
tied to the emancipation rumor, although they very likely knew about it
through their grapevine. Still, to reduce their actions to random violence
only replicates the discourse of the police who, after disseminating the
rumor that Benedito was leading an insurrection, sought to cover their
failures by reducing the quilombolas to the status of common criminals.
Such smear campaign tactics became evident when rumors drifted in from
Barra during a police investigation that Benedito had seized an eleven-
year-old girl from her parents and "barbarously" raped her, leaving her
in a "horrible state." Indignation and widespread panic ensued.[113] That

[110] Ibid.
[111] Police Lieutenant Anthero José Vieira de Faria to Antonio Pitanga, September 19, 1884,
       Polícia Ser. 2, Mc 287, Fl. 33, APEES.
[112] Police Chief of Bahia to Police Chief of Espírito Santo, November 6, 1884, Polícia Ser.
       2 Cx. 77 Mc 293 Fl. 24, APEES.
[113] Municipal Justice of Barra de São Mateus Manoel Tobias to Antonio Pitanga, August
       12, 1884, Governadoria Ser. 383 Liv. 243 Fl. 300, APEES; and Francisco Maria Sodré

the alleged victim was a child torn from her parents' protection depicted Benedito as a violator of innocence and honor as well as the safety of the domestic sphere, which would have horrified not only whites and free people but also the enslaved. The black rapist trope was a common tactic employed by slaveholders to depoliticize black freedom by equating it with the rape of white women (and children, in this case). As greater number of Brazilians began adhering to the abolitionist cause, proslavery interests in São Mateus reached for this low-hanging fruit as a way to turn public opinion against emancipation and Benedito's association with it.[114]

But to imagine how the enslaved perceived the quilombolas' actions opens up a different world of meanings, one that helps shift our focus away from a discourse of crime to a much richer world of antislavery politics. It is certainly plausible that many slaves were as fearful as the free residents of the depredations and rape rumors. For those who had excitedly anticipated their liberation on the Festival of Santana but did not see it materialize, however, knowing that Benedito and the quilombolas repeatedly thwarted a much larger group of slaveholders and police in the aftermath of the Festival must have kept their hopes alive. After all, the original emancipation rumor expressed what the enslaved themselves considered both plausible and desirable in the turbulence of 1884. Such expectations were not easily dispelled just because they were not realized on a particular date.

Timing and deliberation marked the quilombolas' seemingly random acts of violence. If anything they were far more attuned to – and more often carried – circulating news and rumors than the police. Benedito had disappeared in August 1881 after his escape from the police expedition, his whereabouts unknown until July 1884. Mere happenstance cannot explain his reappearance on the police radar specifically in the days preceding the Festival of Santana. The quilombolas' dramatic actions in the days following the Festival embroiled slaveholders and the police in a spectacle of terror while continuing to breathe life into an emancipation struggle. Benedito's continued ability to elude arrest attested to the extraordinary networks of protection he enjoyed. Why did people protect

Pereira, "Relatório do Ministério da Justiça," 1884, CRL. No further details on this incident are available.
[114] Because there is no documentation on this alleged rape of the girl, unlike the attack on Marcolina, which led to a police investigation, I am inclined to believe it was a fabrication. Recall also that what distinguished the Seraphim–Rita case was the absence of rape allegations given the evidence of the black rapist trope in São Mateus.

him? Of course more than a few were afraid of him, or simply wanted to employ him as a farmhand. But fear and opportunism alone cannot explain his presence in the lives of so many. To conclude this chapter, we will briefly reflect on what we know of his short life.

Looking for Benedito

The man who came to be known as the *"celebre criminoso"* (famous criminal) was a Brazilian-born slave who, at about age sixteen, was sold as a fieldhand from Vila Viçosa near Colônia Leopoldina to his late mistress Rita Maria da Conceição Cunha of São Mateus, in January 1872.[115] By 1878 Benedito was sentenced to a lifetime of hard labor for homicide and made a flamboyant prison break in Barra de São Mateus in July 1880 while his drunken guards slept. A year later he was accused of the attempted murder of Marcolina; lived with a group of quilombolas until they had a falling out; grappled with a fugitive slave hunter; and again disappeared until three years later in July 1884, when he reemerged along with the Santana insurrection rumor, before vanishing again.

Benedito was ubiquitous. Multiple individuals in the vast stretch of territory from northern Espírito Santo to southern Bahia attested to having seen him in this or that location; in that sense he was a very public figure. This fame allowed him to elude a massive government expedition against him for years on end while never seeming to leave the region, whose geography he knew like the back of his hand. To be a well-known fugitive seems risky. Yet he remained hidden in plain view, precisely owing to his extensive and diverse network of collaborators and protectors who would shelter him, supply him with weapons and food, or warn him of a coming expedition.

As someone so widely recognized, what did Benedito look like? None of his numerous witnesses ever expressed any doubt about whom they had seen. They included people who were not even locals, such as Second Lieutenant Manoel Souza of Vitória, who had been nearly shot by Benedito in a dark, rainy forest. But how did they know? In an era with limited dissemination of photographs, fugitive slave advertisements resorted to colorful verbal descriptions including the name, age (missing) teeth, their "nation" and scarification patterns if they were African-born, hair texture, facial features, supposed personality traits such as "lazy" or "haughty," skin color, clothes, and often specified skills such as a cook or

[115] Tabelionato Liv. 4, Fl. 90–91, January 22, 1872, CPSM.

carpenter, which the fugitive slaves would have utilized in order to survive. The following is the only police-generated description of Benedito I have found among the substantial documentary trail he left behind:

Slave of D. Rita Maria da Conceição Cunha, about twenty-seven years old, single, native of Caravelas, regular height, *fula* (yellowish; neither very dark nor very light) color.[116]

It is astonishingly generic. Any number of young black men could fit this description, its utility in an interprovincial manhunt being highly doubtful. Short of announcing himself every time he made an appearance, it is unclear how he, even with the usual accoutrements of a quilombola – the hat, the shirt, and above all, the weaponry – could have been uniquely recognized by so many.

Certainly many knew him in person. But many others probably did not. Collectively, the act of witnessing Benedito and speaking about it became a way to participate in the political debate over antislavery and emancipation. By circulating in various places at once and assuming multiple meanings among his witnesses, Benedito was a human in flesh and bone who simultaneously became a vessel for people to express their own stakes in the debate. Variously considered an insurrection leader, quilombola, bandit, laborer, boyfriend, rapist, son, and abolitionist protégé, Benedito was a remarkably protean figure embodying people's fears and hopes in this volatile time. Slavery's unraveling, projected through Benedito, signified the collapse of social order for some, the promises of freedom for others. And by moving – physically and discursively – among these various personalities and locales of the Atlantic frontier, Benedito wove together enslaved people's demands for freedom with an emerging abolitionist movement, creating a new geography of antislavery politics.

Benedito would make a final appearance. After leading some mayhem in Alcobaça in June 1885 and nearly shooting and killing a Colônia Leopoldina resident in October, he vanished again.[117] Then in the first days of January 1886, a brief telegram arrived from Colônia Leopoldina

---

[116] Antonio Pitanga to Police Chief of Bahia, October 24, 1884, Polícia Ser. 2 Liv. 257 Fl. 334, APEES. According to Michael Gomez, the term "fula" likely derives from the Fulbe/Fula/Fulani of West Africa, who were a very distinct looking group with atypical features, often called the "red men" of West Africa for their lighter complexions. Personal communication.

[117] Henrique Hertzsch to Police Chief of Bahia, Telegram (June 8, 1885); Processo Crime (Viçosa, 1885), 18/1728/04, APEB.

to the Police Chief of Espírito Santo, who had requested his Bahian counterpart's help in his capture. It reported:

When arrest announced offered tenacious, armed resistance, ferocious struggle waged resulting death criminal.[118]

He was discovered and killed in Colônia Leopoldina, near the site of his birth and close to his mother and relatives. When the police finally caught up with him in early 1886, he probably knew, like others in the region, that emancipation would be coming soon. Still, he chose not to turn himself in and await that day, which was only two years away. He decided to put up a good fight and died among his kin, in the land of his birth.

Quilombos have occupied a central place in Brazilian historiography ever since Palmares, but largely under the rubric of slave resistance.[119] The quilombolas of São Mateus certainly contested their enslavement, but that was not all. They employed marronage not in order to flee slave society but in order to challenge it from within, by living as free people in its very midst. In doing so, they expressed the terms by which they wanted to live in Brazilian society. Excluded from citizenship by the 1824 Constitution for being "outside of the social pact," now, as the nation faced the reality of abolition, enslaved people continued to confront a horizon of limited freedoms. Inclusion into the povo brasileiro was premised on their continued subjugation. Prevailing discussions about their preparedness for freedom centered on their comparative inferiority – as citizens and laborers – to white immigrants and Indians, a topic to be discussed in Chapter 6. Amidst these very narrow definitions of black freedom imposed from the state as well as their own masters, the quilombolas' asserting their own terms of national belonging was a powerful rebuke.

As settlers and new plantations spread into the sertão, seizing the last of Botocudo lands and persecuting those who remained, the São Mateus quilombolas saw little opportunity to gain freedom through manumission or long-distance flight. Instead, they collaborated with a network of slaves, slaveowners, and free people to flee into São Mateus to forge their own, insurgent geographies. Rather than originating as a community of individuals united under a common political intent, their opposition to

---

[118] João Falcão Metzker to Police Chief of Espírito Santo, Telegram (January 5, 1886), Polícia Ser. 2 Cx. 436 Mç 668 Fl. 98, APEES.

[119] For more on Palmares, see n. 4.

slavery and their political claims to freedom evolved over time. They endured tensions born from differing motivations for flight and experienced constant reconfigurations in their quest to establish a community. Freedom in turn was not a vague concept but rooted in real experiences under slavery, which enabled the quilombolas to elucidate how they would live as free people. They did this by controlling and negotiating their own labor with free residents, remaining in São Mateus in order to be safe and remain close to their community, and claiming their right to motherhood and family. Here was the basis of another vision of citizenship born from experience and aspirations, one that was far richer and more urgent than the vague notions of the "great Brazilian family" proposed by the authors of the Constitution.

By the time three years had passed, their insurgent geographies had further evolved and acquired a new dimension. The quilombolas and enslaved asserted their demand for emancipation by forcing it to the center of political debate. Their political voice emerged amidst a growing abolitionist movement at the national and grassroots level. Slaves' demands for emancipation, quilombola activity, local abolitionism, and public opinion thus converged to forge a new insurgent geography of antislavery. The contest over the meaning of black freedom – as subservient, quasi-citizens or as women and men able to define citizenship on their own terms – would only intensify. With slavery's future hanging in the balance, the quilombolas and the enslaved claimed their place in the center of the political debate as never before.

6

Unfinished Emancipations

Labor and Abolition

The growing abolitionist tide across Brazil in the 1870s and 1880s brought competing visions of black and indigenous citizenship to the fore. The impending end of slavery and fears of a labor shortage reignited old tensions and engendered unlikely new affinities on the Atlantic frontier. One conflict centered on the Itambacuri mission, founded in 1873 in northern Minas Gerais under the leadership of the Italian-born Capuchin missionaries, Serafim de Gorizia and Angelo Sassoferato. Itambacuri's main purpose was to resettle and catechize one of the region's last autonomous Botocudo Indian strongholds. In late 1882, however, the local senator Cristiano Ottoni accused the friars of bringing the "Indians to aldeias to profit from their work" which in his view was "not catechism, it [was] slavery." The senator denounced the friars as being "two useless priests" who, instead of pacifying hostile Indians to aid the area residents, were relocating already "tame" Indians to the mission for their own gain. The centuries-old tensions between missionaries and laypeople over the access to Indian labor reemerged, now aggravated by the impending end of slavery.[1]

Equally rattled by abolition were the slaveholders of São Mateus and Colônia Leopoldina. Their authority already eroded by laws, public opinion, and quilombola activity, they soon had to contend with a new threat: grassroots abolitionism. In November 1884, with Benedito still at

---

[1] *Anais do Senado do Império do Brasil. 2a sessão da 18a legislatura*, Vol. IV (Rio de Janeiro: Typographia Nacional, 1882), 276; cited in Jacinto de Palazzolo, *Nas selvas dos vales do Mucuri e do Rio Doce, como surgiu a cidade de Itambacuri, fundada por Frei Serafim de Gorizia, missionario capuchino, 1873–1952* (São Paulo: Companhia Editora Nacional, 1954), 156–59.

large after the Feast of Santana, nineteen prominent São Mateus planters decided to take preemptive action by accusing a local farmer named Cosme Francisco da Motta of deceiving their slaves into believing they were free and fomenting a violent uprising against their masters.[2] Never one to suffer in silence, Motta rose to his own defense. He told authorities he was no instigator but a "Protector of Africans" and described his struggles to establish an abolitionist movement in São Mateus. Motta would soon find his southern Bahian counterpart in the Vicar Father Geraldo, who exasperated Colônia Leopoldina planters with his thunderous and sometimes questionable abolitionism. If the prospect of black freedom was the essence of the planter-abolitionist conflict, it was also, as with the Itambacuri missionaries, a struggle to control their labor after slavery.

The end of slavery signaled new possibilities and profound anxieties for the enslaved, the free, and those caught in between. Abolition would finally "free the nation," allowing Brazil to stand proud before its American and European peers. Some even hoped that "within a century [of abolition]...the black stain on the bosom of Brazilian society [would] be erased."[3] Yet beneath any optimism about the liberation from slavery was a steadfast uncertainty on two fronts: who would replace the enslaved workforce? And on what terms shall these newly emancipated women and men join society? This chapter contends that both black and indigenous histories are essential to addressing these central questions in the history of abolition in Brazil and the Atlantic World. Chapter 1 demonstrated how a reinvigorated indigenous slavery and an expanding African slavery converged in the Atlantic frontier in the decades after independence, creating people who existed "outside of society" even as the 1824 Constitution extended citizenship to many. This chapter examines how the process of abolition created new forms of inequality for black and indigenous people. Scholars have noted how the 1881 electoral law drastically reduced the electorate by raising minimum income requirements and making literacy mandatory, disproportionately affecting the poor and those of African and indigenous descent.[4] However,

---

[2] Telegrams between Miguel Bernardo d'Amorim and Antonio Pitanga, November 12, 1884, Polícia Ser. 2 Cx 77 Mc 291 Fl. 52–53, APEES.

[3] Celso Thomas Castilho, *Slave Emancipation and Transformations in Brazilian Political Citizenship* (Pittsburgh, PA: University of Pittsburgh Press, 2016), 174; *O Espírito Santense*, May 5, 1888, 4.

[4] It fell from 1 million in 1872 to only 100,000 by 1886. José Murilo de Carvalho, *Cidadania no Brasil: o longo caminho* (Rio de Janeiro: Civilização Brasileira, 2001),

new servile labor regimes became another means to exclude black and indigenous people from citizenship. Such similarities become visible only when we understand the struggle for black freedom taking place in the ambiguous aftermath of indigenous emancipation in 1831.

The Atlantic frontier became the theater of virulent anti-abolitionism and labor disputes in the 1880s. Mid-century indigenous policy and the Land Law had accelerated the seizure of indigenous territory that had long been happening through slavery expansion and anti-indigenous violence, paralleling the dispossession of vulnerable populations all over Latin America from Argentina and Chile to Bolivia, Colombia, and Mexico.[5] Now, with the prospect of black freedom and indigenous autonomy becoming inseparable from the issue of land scarcity, the battle to control black and indigenous labor and land converged, the right to the territory overlapping with the right to citizenship. Abolitionists and missionaries became a lightning rod for these conflicts, clashing with slaveholders and settlers over the future of the nation's freedpeople and Indians. Notwithstanding their disagreements, these groups revealed themselves to share a racialized vision of servile labor through which they attempted to reinscribe a severely limited vision of black and indigenous citizenship. Black and indigenous people's own interpretations of freedom, citizenship, and "civilization" radically rebuked these racialized and exclusionary ideas of liberal nationhood with repercussions lasting into the Republic.

The End of Slavery and the Indian Worker

Indian labor and slavery abolition had been deeply intertwined since the early nineteenth century. The trans-Atlantic slave trade and Indian slavery shared the ignominy of continuing brazenly after their respective abolitions in 1831. With the actual abolition of the trans-Atlantic trade approaching in 1850, the fear of a labor shortage helped propel Indian slavery and trafficking to their height in the 1840s. The coming of 1850 also spurred the issuance of the 1845 Regulation of Missions, whose plan for Indian civilization focused heavily on transforming Indians into a settled workforce by training them in applied arts, agriculture, and military service. The clamor for Indian labor surged once again in the 1870s

38–39; Sidney Chalhoub, "The Politics of Silence: Race and Citizenship in Nineteenth-Century Brazil," *Slavery & Abolition* 27, no. 1 (April 2006): 83–84. Castilho, however, argues that such closures also engendered new forms of political participation. Castilho, *Slave Emancipation*, 16. Women, children, and the infirm continued to be excluded.
5 See Chapter 3.

and 1880s with the promulgation of the Free Womb Law in 1871 and successive abolitionist laws. Few seemed to recognize the contradictions of this last phase, which coincided with the consolidation of indigenous extinction discourse.

Some individuals had perceived the ties between abolition and Indian labor since the eve of Brazilian independence. Maciel da Costa, a vocal critic of the trans-Atlantic slave trade, claimed in 1821 that the inundation of "barbaric African slaves" and their labor had led Brazilians to neglect Indian civilization and considered Indians an agricultural workforce in the making.[6] Costa's views were followed in 1839 by Brazilian Historical and Geographic Institute (IHGB) co-founder Januário Barbosa, who published an essay in the institute's journal with the lengthy title of "If the Introduction of African Slaves in Brazil Hinders the Civilization of our Indigenous, Exempting them from Work, which was Entirely Turned over to Blacks. In that case, How Does it Compromise Brazilian Agriculture." Barbosa was likely eyeing the ineffectiveness of the 1831 abolitions and argued similarly that African slavery obstructed Indian civilization, making a farce of Indian "freedom" and compromising Brazil as a whole. Treated well, Indians would be a good "working class" that would render African slaves unnecessary.[7] While Barbosa highlighted themes that the journal's subsequent authors would largely avoid – slavery and the slave trade – he was not alone in linking their abolition to the possibilities of Brazil's indigenous workforce. José Bonifácio had similarly raised these interrelated goals as being fundamental to the "future prosperity of this Empire." Civilizing Indians into becoming productive laborers would abrogate the need for African slaves, a condition without which "Brazil will never affirm its national independence." Together these themes penetrated problems both practical – labor self-sufficiency – and epistemological – a Brazilian nationhood and the povo brasileiro, liberated from the stain of slavery.[8]

---

[6] João Severiano Maciel da Costa, *Memória sobre a necessidade de abolir a introdução dos escravos africanos no Brasil: sobre o modo e condiçõis com que esta abolição se deve fazer; e sobre os meios de remediar a falta de braços que ela pode ocasionar* (Coimbra: Imprensa da Universidade, 1821), 60.

[7] Januário da Cunha Barbosa, "Se a introdução dos escravos africanos no Brasil embaraça a civilização dos nossos indígenas, dispensando-se-lhes o trabalho, que todo foi confiado a escravos negros. Neste caso qual é o prejuizo que sofre a lavoura Brasileira," *RIHGB* 1, no. 3 (1839): 127–29.

[8] José Bonifácio, *Projetos para o Brasil*, ed. Miriam Dolhnikoff (São Paulo: Companhia das Letras, 1998), 45–46, 82; Leda Maria Cardoso Naud, "Documentos sôbre o índio brasileiro, 2a parte," *Revista de informação legislativa* 8, no. 29 (1971): 317–18.

Guido Pokrane's adulation by the national elite in the 1840s was similarly shaped by anxieties about the impending cessation of the trans-Atlantic slave trade. The Botocudo Indian's successful adoption of agriculture appeared to embody the promise of Indian labor and helped assuage fears of a labor crisis. Having assiduously aided his benefactor Guido Marlière in "[spreading] among the indigenous people the love for work, in order to leave their errant life," Pokrane went on to cultivate a bounty of crops – rice, manioc, maize – on his own aldeia. One Pokrane enthusiast urged the imperial government to give him all the accouterments of civilization that he requested since "the necessity of free labor is so keenly felt."[9]

The 1870s were a particularly volatile period for the future of Brazilian labor. The nation had only recently emerged from the Paraguayan War (1864–70), which had taken a toll on the nation's able-bodied free and enslaved male population. The Free Womb or Rio Branco Law of September 1871 ended the unlimited biological reproduction of Brazil's enslaved workforce, further affirming the end of slavery and opening up means for slaves to obtain their manumission by legally recognizing their right to their *pecúlio* (personal earnings). Meanwhile, the internal slave trade had been transporting massive numbers of African and crioulo slaves from the Northeast to the coffee plantations of the Center-South. The planter-elite there was in turmoil over the relative merits of the "free national" (*nacional livre*) and libertos vis-à-vis European immigrants, with many skeptical that the former possessed the discipline and labor capacity of more "advanced" Europeans.[10] Discourses about slaves' and libertos' vagrancy circulated; for example, it was thought that the typical slave was "lazy, and if he desires liberty . . . it is because he would like to do nothing," and that "all libertos are lazy vagrants . . . because they are tired of forced labor and accustomed to frugality, so with an hour of work per week [they make enough food to be] freed from further work."[11] The Northeast, by contrast, experienced a relatively quiet

---

[9] *Diario do Rio de Janeiro*, July 10, 1840.

[10] Celia Maria Marinho de Azevedo, *Onda negra, medo branco: o negro no imaginário das elites – século XIX* (Rio de Janeiro: Paz e Terra, 1987); Giralda Seyferth, "Construindo a nação: hierarquias raciais e o papel do racismo na política de imigração e colonização," in *Raça, ciência e sociedade*, ed. Marcos Chor Maio and Ricardo Ventura Santos (Rio de Janeiro: Editora FIOCRUZ, 1996), 41–58.

[11] Louis Couty, *L'esclavage au Brésil* (Paris: Librairie de Guillamin, 1881), 6, 73; *Correio Paulistano*, May 19, 1885, 3; for a general discussion about these ideas, see Walter Fraga Filho, *Mendigos, moleques e vadios na Bahia do século XIX* (São Paulo: Editora Hucitec, 1996).

abolition due to the abundance of cheap free labor, which in turn damp-
ened the planters' enthusiasm about immigration.[12] Neither of these
examples reflected the situation of regions that had been largely unsuccessful in attracting and sustaining immigrants while enjoying neither the
influx of slaves nor an abundance of cheap free labor.[13] Amidst this labor
shortage, Indians, in spite of their longstanding reputation for laziness
and violence, seemed more attractive an option than ever. Their population accordingly bounced back from extinction when their services were
needed.

Just a year after the Free Womb Law, the Bahian Director of Indians,
the Viscount of Sergimirim, addressed the labor crisis assailing the nation.
"[I]f the key to all large problems to be resolved in Brazil, especially in its
agricultural provinces, is population – because if it exists in abundance,
there is work, wealth, and well-being," he began, "it is remarkable how
we allow thousands of Indians to be lost to brutality and barbarism,
when they are the free workers of the country." Indian laborers were
"accustomed to the climate but devoid of the colonists' demands and
the slaves' danger during a time when salaries are rising as slave labor
diminishes, and colonists do not appear."[14] It was no coincidence that the
man who made these remarks was also the scion of a major planter family
of the Bahian Recôncavo and the President of the Imperial Bahian Institute
of Agriculture. In 1880 Sergimirim would found the first mechanized
sugar processing plant in Santo Amaro (the Engenho Central do Bom
Jardim), only to see it fail, in no small part due to the declining slave
labor force and failure to attract immigrants.[15]

Sergimirim specifically presented Indians favorably in comparison to
colonists and slaves and argued that an aldeia was akin to a "fazenda
worked by Indians who, tame and peaceful, should not produce much
less than the slaves, as long as they are given good direction and

---

[12] For these debates in São Paulo, see Azevedo, *Onda negra*. For Pernambuco see Peter L.
Eisenberg, *The Sugar Industry in Pernambuco; Modernization without Change, 1840–
1910* (Berkeley: University of California Press, 1974); Castilho, *Slave Emancipation*.

[13] Barickman has documented a similar labor scarcity in the sugar-growing Bahian
Recôncavo in the aftermath of emancipation. B. J. Barickman, "Persistence and Decline:
Slave Labour and Sugar Production in the Bahian Recôncavo, 1850–1888," *JLAS* 28,
no. 3 (October 1996): 581–633.

[14] Viscount of Sergimirim, Director of Indians of Bahia, "Relatório da Directoria Geral
dos Indios (Bahia)," February 15, 1872, 3, CRL.

[15] Eul-Soo Pang, *O Engenho Central do Bom Jardim na economia baiana: alguns aspectos
de sua história, 1875–1891* (Rio de Janeiro: AN/IHGB, 1979); Barickman, "Persistence
and Decline."

permanence."[16] An Espírito Santo newspaper shared his enthusiasm, arguing that "it is a crass error to consider the Botocudo as resistant to domestication; a prejudice to suppose him so proud of his independence that he couldn't get used to someone else's direction." The writer believed that the "thousands of lazy individuals wandering in the sertões of São Mateus and the Doce River could, with patience, be made into hardworking men to substitute slaves." He too was wary of the coming labor shortage, "given that the acquisition of foreign labor is doubtful, or slow in coming."[17]

Such views reflected the reality that while slave prices had risen sharply since the cessation of the trans-Atlantic slave trade, immigrants had failed to fulfill expectations. By the 1850s the Colônia Leopoldina immigrants had lost their luster because of their dependence on slavery and their failure to encourage more immigration, and in the 1860s Ottoni's European colony was all but abandoned.[18] A joint public–private venture by the Leão and Moniz Company to establish a few German and Polish immigrant colonies in southern Bahia in the early 1870s failed after only five years.[19] Labor shortages and mounting worker disobedience thus bequeathed urgency to the Indian labor question. Slaves all over Brazil acted upon new possibilities opened up by the Rio Branco Law to demand concessions and even manumission from their masters.[20] In the months surrounding the law's promulgation in 1871, Espírito Santo alone was the site of four insurrectionary rumors. Residents of São Mateus feared that slaves inspired by news of the law had marooned themselves on several properties in town to hatch an uprising.[21] The slaves' impatience only

---

[16] Sergimirim, "Relatório da Directoria Geral dos Indios (Bahia)," 3; italics mine.

[17] "S. Matheus," *O Estandarte*, July 30, 1871.

[18] Azevedo, *Onda negra*, 123–24; Warren Dean, *Rio Claro: A Brazilian Plantation System, 1820–1920* (Stanford, CA: Stanford University Press, 1976), 97–98; Emília Viotti da Costa, *The Brazilian Empire: Myths & Histories* (Chapel Hill: University of North Carolina Press, 2000), 105–8; Robert Avé-Lallemant, *Viagem pelo norte do Brasil no ano de 1859* (Rio de Janeiro: Instituto Nacional do Livro, Ministério da Educação e Cultura, 1961), 157–66.

[19] Bernardo Augusto Nascentes de Azambuja, *Relatório sobre as colônias ao sul da província da Bahia, apresentado ao Ministério da Agricultura, Commércio, e Obras Públicas* (Rio de Janeiro: Typographia Nacional, 1874). See also Homem de Mello, "Falla (Bahia)," 1878, 43, CRL.

[20] Azevedo, *Onda negra*, Chapter 3; Sidney Chalhoub, *Visões da liberdade: uma história das últimas décadas da escravidão na corte* (São Paulo: Companhia das Letras, 1990), 151–67.

[21] Francisco Ferreira Corrêa to Francisco de Paula de Negreiros Saião Lobato, June 1, 1871; September 1, 1871; September 6, 1871; and November 6, 1871, IJ1-440-ES, AN.

seemed to grow in subsequent years. In February 1875 the slave Ignacio shot his master who refused to put him up for sale.[22] The following year a slave of a Swiss Colônia Leopoldina planter returned after fleeing for nine months with money in hand to purchase his freedom, a legal right since 1871. Although the local municipal judge deemed the funds insufficient, he opened up the slave's manumission proceedings, sending his owner into panic. The planter's Swiss representative accused the judge of being a "partisan of emancipation" and sought to impede him from meddling in private property rights.[23] Several months later a slave in São Mateus named Victor, an electrician, stabbed his neighbor for dishonoring him in public. Significantly, what had set Victor off was the neighbor's taunting flicker of a whip, reminding Victor of his bondage.[24]

Such news of ubiquitous slave disobedience spawned a new discourse about Indian docility that overrode images of savagery and placed Indians at a distinct advantage over slaves and even immigrants. Had brandura succeeded? Work training was enthusiastically promoted through the language of citizenship. Sergimirim argued that Indians resided on the land with other Brazilians but did not "share the duties and rights of citizens with us, because the barbarism in which they live does not allow it."[25] Labor discipline would place Indians on the path to becoming "useful citizens" and achieving national inclusion; without it such goals would be impossible, since Indians were considered, like libertos and free blacks, to be "naturally indolent, resistant to work, with no other need than the freedom of the forests and the hunt."[26] Once disciplined into productivity, Indians would "be distributed among rural establishments as free laborers, prepared to work in the fields through practical instruction in managing the plough and other agricultural implements."[27] Sergimirim believed that a well-managed aldeia could become a "*vivarium*," or animal farm, for agricultural laborers.[28]

Others argued that aldeias were too removed from reality and Indians would receive more practical job training by working on public works

---

[22] Tribunal do Jury, Homicidio (São Mateus, February 12, 1875), Processos Cx 76, CPSM.
[23] Swiss Consul of Bahia to President of Bahia, January 4, 1876, Colonial/Justiça/ São José de Porto Alegre/Mc 2540, APEB.
[24] Tribunal do Jury, Summario de culpa – Ferimentos (São Mateus, June 12, 1876), Processos Cx 79, CPSM.
[25] Sergimirim, Director of Indians of Bahia, "Relatório da Directoria Geral dos Indios (Bahia)," 2.
[26] Antonio Dias Paes Leme, "Relatório (ES)," 1870, 20, CRL.
[27] Sergimirim, 4.   [28] Sergimirim, 4.

projects or directly for individuals under government supervision. In this view, direct contact with residents would help attenuate their "instinct for savage liberty and passion for the forests."[29] Never did the advocates of Indian labor regimes discuss the possibilities of their attaining other hallmarks of citizenship, such as the vote, the right to hold office, or even the right to property. Nor was the goal to create an independent peasantry. The objective of Indian labor advocates was to produce a subservient class of free labor to fill the void left by slaves. Indian labor regimes thus became a means to reinforce their limited citizenship, whose terms would be reproduced in discussions about libertos.

The Itambacuri Mission

While provincial presidents and Indian directors debated the possibilities of Indian labor, Capuchin missionaries remained at the frontlines to dedicate themselves to the actual task. As we have seen, in the 1840s, the missionary Caetano de Troina was sent to the Mucuri River Valley to catechize the Botocudo. Quickly disillusioned, he joined the settlers to advocate anti-indigenous violence. Subsequent Indian missionary work had largely failed in the region and many aldeias were declared extinct, allowing a substantial, autonomous Botocudo population to maintain control of the verdant forests and watersheds near the source of the São Mateus River. Among the most numerous were the nearly eight hundred Mucuri and Nhãnhãn Indians under the leadership of Captain Pohóc, who had defended their hunting and foraging grounds through alliances with other indigenous groups. Such alliances were affirmed during times of bounty, especially of green maize, when Pohóc organized feasts to commemorate the ancestors.[30]

Settler interest in the region's lands initiated a large-scale reconfiguration of territorial control. The local Director of Indians and Leonardo Ottoni, a powerful long-time settler in the region and brother of Teófilo, began approaching Captain Pohóc's people in 1871 with the aid of the indigenous interpreter Felix Ramos, who had married Captain Pohóc's daughter. Probably as a result of this contact, which led to the loss of important foraging grounds, the Indians relocated up a local stream.

---

[29] Leme, "Relatório (ES)," 20–21.
[30] Domingos Ramos Pacó, "Hámbric anhamprán ti mattâ nhiñchopón? 1918," in *Lembranças da terra: histórias do Mucuri e Jequitinhonha*, ed. Eduardo Magalhães Ribeiro (Belo Horizonte: CEDEFES, 1996), 198–99.

Meanwhile, the Minas government ordered the founding of five central aldeias in parts of the province where autonomous Indians still remained, principally in the north. Two Italian Capuchin missionaries, Friars Serafim de Gorizia and Angelo Sassoferato, were charged with establishing what would become the most important of these new aldeias. The friars first began surveying the land along the São Mateus River. However, another group of Indians called Potón, with their own territorial claims along the river, deflected the friars by urging them to explore the territory controlled by Captain Pohóc instead, enticing them with images of bountiful rivers and lands that would yield endless supplies of fish and grains.

Perhaps it was the recognition of territorial loss and the need to ensure the survival of his large group that led Pohóc to collaborate with the friars. In 1873 Frei Serafim and Angelo inaugurated the aldeia of Itambacuri on Pohóc's territory, 38 km southwest of Filadélfia, near the head of the Mucuri and São Mateus Rivers. Pohóc's group was the first to settle on the aldeia, soon followed by his Indian allies living on the aldeia's fringes. The friars assiduously set to work in their catechism and civilization, placing the Indian children in school; encouraging mestiçagem through intermarriage with the general population; teaching them agriculture through the cultivation of aldeia lands; and opening up roads around Itambacuri, which came to comprise a vast territory equivalent to the modern state of Sergipe (15,190 km²). While some Indians remained on the aldeia among their kin, however, others came and went. By official count, 570 Indians had settled on Itambacuri by 1878.[31]

Partners in theory in the opening of one of the last remaining areas of Atlantic forest, missionaries and settlers soon found themselves locked in an acrimonious struggle over Indian labor and land. "There would be many more [Indians] settled [on Itambacuri]," remarked the Minister of Agriculture, who oversaw Indian catechism and infrastructural development, "if it were not for the efforts of the neighboring residents and *fazendeiros* to employ Indians in their own service."[32] Many settlers continued to engage in illegal Indian slavery and other informal, often exploitative labor arrangements, such as paying the Indians with *cachaça*. Among

---

[31] José Fernandes da Costa Pereira Junior, "Relatório do Ministério da Agricultura," 1874, 296, CRL; Jacinto de Palazzolo, *Nas selvas dos vales*, 61; 92–94; Pacó, "Hámbric anhamprán," 198–202; Izabel Missagia de Mattos, *Civilização e revolta: os Botocudos e a catequese na província de Minas* (São Paulo: EDUSC ANPOCS, 2004), 271–74; and "Educar para dominar," *RAPM* 1, no. 100 (2011): 98–109.

[32] Pereira Junior, "Relatório do Ministério da Agricultura," 297.

them were local fazendeiros who had been confident of their ability to survive the end of slavery by subjugating Indians in their stead. They suspected the friars of stealing Indians away and even accused them of slavery – allegations that Senator Cristiano Ottoni (another brother of Teófilo) clearly referenced. Ottoni sarcastically claimed the friars were "attracting only the most tame, to make them work in their fields, whose products they sell for the greater glory of God." The friars responded with a counteraccusation of illegal slavery.[33]

Indian slavery was not a merely rhetorical device. As recently as 1875, the Director of Indians of Minas Gerais had decried its endurance. Indians were "incited to steal the children of their companions and sell them to the settlers in exchange for any object of little value, so that they are raised in subjection, and later serve as slaves." He mentioned unspecified measures he had taken "to put an end to this ignominious traffic of our Indians' flesh in the service of agriculture."[34] Illegal practices nonetheless continued, including the seizure of several kurukas in the 1881 Nok-Nok massacre. Such realities exposed the grave faults in optimistic arguments about the complementarity of slavery abolition and Indian civilization. While the fates of African-descended slaves and Indians were clearly linked, the prospect of black freedom was encouraging Indian exploitation.

In the early 1880s, during the cat-and-mouse chase between São Mateus police and the quilombolas, an estimated two thousand autonomous Botocudo (Pojixá, Jiporok, Krenhé, Urucú, Pampan) still remained in the interior in the vicinity of Itambacuri. While some came to settle on the aldeia, their tenacious resistance to the new wave of incursions plunged northern Minas into a reinvigorated territorial battle.[35] Botocudo Indians attacked the engineers and construction workers of the Bahia–Minas railroad, which cut right through their territory. The Pojixá nearly killed a boy from Philadelphia on his way to the railroad's inaugural ceremony in 1882. At times they inflicted economic damage on settlers that may also have been a symbolic attack against agriculture, such as when they set fire to settlers' grain reserves, killed their

---

[33] *Anais do Senado 1882*, IV:276; Jacinto de Palazzolo, *Nas selvas dos vales*, 139; Maria Hilda Baqueiro Paraiso, "O tempo da dor e do trabalho: a Conquista dos Territórios Indígenas nos Sertões do Leste" (doctoral dissertation, Universidade de São Paulo, 1998), 711.

[34] Antonio Luiz de Magalhães Musqueira, "Relatório do Diretor dos índios de Minas Gerais," 1875, 5, CRL. Mattos cites an abridged and somewhat different version of this text in *Civilização e revolta*, 85.

[35] João Ferreira de Moura, "Relatorio do Ministério da Agricultura," 1884, 42, CRL.

livestock and slaves, and assailed their fazendas.[36] Nor were their targets limited to settlers. The Botocudo also attacked settled Indians, such as in March of 1884 when they murdered two Indians and their livestock. Proceeding to Itambacuri, they attacked the aldeia's residents and killed eight people including two children, a "civilized" female Pojixá, and two linguas.[37] Domingos Pacó, a mestiço former teacher and lingua of Itambacuri, described a similar incident involving a group of Pojixá who had been on Itambacuri for a few months. During their stay the Pojixá married the mission's Indians whose relatives they later invited to come hunt and spend time on their territory. Yet as soon as the group passed the mission's threshold, "they surrounded the civilized Indians and killed all of them, taking the women and only allowing one Indian . . . to escape."[38]

Amidst worsening relations between settlers, mission, and autonomous Indians, in March 1885 Frei Serafim and Angelo learned that several São Mateus residents were planning to attack the Pojixá, whom the settlers particularly feared and reviled. The friars convinced the Pojixá residing near São Mateus to relocate to Itambacuri for their safety. However, during the relocation they were ambushed by a group of youth, leading the Pojixá to believe that the friars had framed them. They murdered eight linguas and nearly killed the friars in retaliation. The friars believed that this act of sabotage had ruined the "decisive moment" in the Pojixás' relocation to Itambacuri. They further alleged that this incident (as mentioned in Chapter 5) had driven the Indians to join hands with fugitive slaves.[39] Hostilities remained unabated in October when the Pojixá kidnapped a slave of Leonardo Ottoni. The slave escaped to the town to seek help from the authorities. Rumors of a Pojixá attack spurred more than 100 people to join Ottoni to protect his property. The Pojixá, painted red for war, kidnapped two of Ottoni's daughters and lay siege to his property. The settlers ultimately prevailed, however, resulting in the massacre

[36] "Vítima dos Pojichas," *Gazeta da Bahia*, November 22, 1882; João Ferreira de Moura, "Relatório do Ministério da Justiça," 1882, 63–64, CRL.
[37] Affonso Augusto Moreira Penna, "Relatório do Ministério da Justiça," 1884, 92.
[38] Pacó, "Hámbric anhamprán," 208.
[39] Fr. Angelo de Sassoferato and Fr. Serafim de Gorizia to Police Lieutenant of Teófilo Ottoni (Filadélfia), March 5, 1885, 20-III-51, ACRJ; Fr. Angelo de Sassoferato and Fr. Serafim de Gorizia to Police Lieutenant of Teófilo Ottoni, March 8, 1885, 20-III-51, ACRJ; Fr. Angelo de Sassoferato and Fr. Serafim de Gorizia to MACOP, March 15, 1885, 20-III-52, ACRJ; Fr. Angelo de Sassoferato and Fr. Serafim de Gorizia to MACOP, March 20, 1885, 20-III-50, ACRJ.

of forty Indians. The incident drove frightened German immigrants to flee the region.[40]

The friars were keenly aware that the impending abolition of slavery was driving a new escalation in anti-indigenous violence. In a letter to the Minister of Agriculture they defended the Indians as victims, not perpetrators, and requested greater state support for their missionary work. Imperial government support was essential especially after the mineiro provincial government, and Cristiano Ottoni in particular, representing local advocates of the emancipation of mission lands, defunded all the aldeias. The friars took special care to present their work as both a solution to the labor crisis and a patriotic act. They challenged Brazilian statesmen to live up to their own professed ideals of civilization and progress. "If the noble and great Brazilian nation declares itself today to be in favor of the freedom of captives and favors foreign colonization," they insisted, "with more reason it should be interested in the civilizing, useful, and beneficial cause of thousands of still-savage Brazilians." They emphasized how the Indians, "once transformed into moral, hard-working men by good missionaries," could serve the state's objectives of territorial conquest and economic development by "opening unknown forests for the flourishing of the country's agriculture, industry, and commerce."[41] Once again, Indian civilization was framed in terms of their labor utility to the state, implying that only in those terms were indigenous citizenship and national inclusion both desirable and feasible.

The friars assiduously reconfigured land use and occupation in northern Minas. By 1884 Botocudo territory was limited to the area bounded by the Doce, Mucuri, Saçuí Grande, and São Mateus Rivers.[42] In two years' time, more than 1,000 Botocudo from various subgroups including the Pojixá, Naknenuk, Puruntum, Jiporok, Poton, Catolé, Krenhé, and Aranã came to Itambacuri. Coffee and maize became the mission's staple crops

---

[40] Joaquim Delfino Ribeiro da Luz, "Relatório do Ministério da Justiça," 1885, 44, CRL; Cléia Schiavo Weyrauch, *Pioneiros Alemães de Nova Filadélfia* (Caxias do Sul: Editora da Universidade, 1997), 90; as discussed in Mattos, *Civilização e revolta*, 355–56; *Liberal Mineiro*, October 29, 1885. Chapter 5 addresses this incident from an alternate, oral history perspective collected by Weyrauch, according to whom locals remembered the incident quite differently: a fugitive slave who had fled Ottoni killed a jaguar and became a captain among the Indians, whom he incited to attack Ottoni and kidnap his daughters. The fate of the latter is unknown.

[41] Fr. Angelo de Sassoferato and Fr. Serafim de Gorizia to Antonio da Silva Prado, Minister of Agriculture, January 10, 1886, 20-III-57, ACRJ; Mattos, *Civilização e revolta*, 265.

[42] Maria Hilda Baqueiro Paraiso, "Os Botocudos e sua trajetória histórica," in *História dos índios no Brasil*, ed. Manuela Carneiro da Cunha (São Paulo: Editora Schwarcz, 1992), 420.

as the Indians learned to practice settled agriculture in place of hunting and foraging.[43] This massive Botocudo relocation to Itambacuri opened up indigenous territories around the mission to colonists, enticing hundreds of small-scale farmers to move onto newly available lands between Filadélfia, Urucú (also in northern Minas), and São Mateus. More than 800 poor Brazilian nationals, whom the friars called "caboclo pioneers" and were likely people of mixed white, African, and indigenous descent, had come to reside on the mission lands the same year, in 1886. The friars encouraged these settlers to intermarry with the Indians as a means to "civilize" the latter through miscegenation and acculturation – both practices, as we have seen, designed to engender Indian extinction.[44]

The friars' years of toil finally appeared to bear fruit in 1888, when the Pojixá arrived in Itambacuri en masse. The friars were thrilled to witness the formidable entry of the nearly two hundred Pojixá men carrying their bows and arrows. The Indians' bodies were painted bright red with *urucum* berry "the color of blood," just as when they had attacked Leonardo Ottoni.[45] The friars placed the new arrivals, who eventually reached nearly 2,500, in a separate settlement 30 km south of Itambacuri at a place called Santo Antônio in order to protect the aldeia's "civilized" residents from the still "uncivilized" new arrivals.[46]

Itambacuri's apparent success, however, exacerbated already embattled relations with area residents who criticized the aldeia for blocking their access to Indian labor and land. As more Botocudo arrived, Itambacuri's adversaries saw in its very growth the seeds of obsolescence. The same year as the Pojixá's arrival en masse, less than a month before the May 1888 abolition of slavery, local strongmen related to the Ottonis lobbied to emancipate the mission lands for general colonization. Missionary efforts, they argued, should be redirected to areas with hostile Indians. It was part of a wide-reaching, aggressive land occupation taking place in the region.[47] In the face of such unabated settler antagonism, Frei Angelo maintained his optimism, projecting that with the death of the elderly Indians, the distinction between Indians and non-Indians would

---

[43] Fr. Angelo de Sassoferato and Fr. Serafim de Gorizia, "Statistical Report," January 10, 1886, 20-III-57, ACRJ.

[44] Jacinto de Palazzolo, *Nas selvas dos vales*; Affonso Augusto Moreira Penna, "Relatório do Minstério da Agricultura," 1883, 124, CRL.

[45] *Urucum* (Tupi), Latin *bixa orellana*, also known as *achiote*, is a plant indigenous to the tropical regions of the Americas. Its bright red seeds are used for body paint and a derivative, annatto, is still used as food coloring in many Latin American dishes.

[46] Jacinto de Palazzolo, *Nas selvas dos vales*, 211–13; Mattos, *Civilização e revolta*, 355.

[47] Jacinto de Palazzolo, *Nas selvas dos vales*, 216–17.

soon disappear. He entertained the prospects of cultivating an ever-larger area around the mission through domestic and immigrant labor. For a time, all seemed well on Itambacuri.[48]

Abolitionism on the Frontier

Closer to the Atlantic, another labor conflict pitted slaveholders in São Mateus and Colônia Leopoldina against their dreaded foe: abolitionism. In early November 1884, nineteen prominent São Mateus slaveholders preemptively accused resident Cosme Francisco da Motta, a forty-three-year-old farmer and merchant, of fomenting a violent uprising by deceiving their slaves into believing they were free.[49] In his defense, Motta identified himself as a "Protector of Africans" to draw attention to his leadership in São Mateus' burgeoning abolitionist movement. Rather than receiving accolades or winning more supporters, however, he was thrown in prison. Then, a year after Motta's release, in April 1886 slaveowners across the provincial border in Colônia Leopoldina were alarmed by the fiery sermons of their local vicar, Father Geraldo, who incited the slaves to rise against them. Father Geraldo's feverish mix of religious doctrine, abolitionist fervor, and disinformation forced the question of abolition onto the table but also cast doubt on the priest's intentions.

The battle over black and indigenous labor in the Atlantic frontier united sertão and coast. While the access to Indian labor pitted missionaries against settlers, the impending end of slavery fueled an astonishingly acrimonious battle between abolitionists and slaveowners in the movement's frontiers. In spite of slaveholders' virulent opposition to anti-slavery efforts, however, closer inspection of the abolitionists' political programs reveals that they and their foes did not radically differ in their ideas about how best to keep freedpeople under control once slavery was over. Such limited visions of black freedom and citizenship conflicted and at other times uneasily resonated with freedpeople's own aspirations for life after slavery.

"Protector of Africans": Cosme Motta's Popular Abolitionism
Seeds of the allegations against Motta had already been planted in January, when Motta, then a police sublieutenant, angered São Mateus

---

[48] Ibid., 250.
[49] Telegrams between Justice of Law Amorim and Antonio Pitanga, November 12, 1884, Polícia Ser. 2 Cx 77 Mc 291 Fl. 52–53, APEES.

slaveholders by trying to take a census of the local free and enslaved population. As with the Indians, the issue was illegal enslavement. Motta suspected his fellow residents of illegally enslaving adults and unregistered children born after the Free Womb Law.[50] He was dismissed in July after questioning his superior's authority and competence.[51] In a town where slaveholding families intermarried and patronage ties ran deep, Motta, who came from a modest background, stood out for his lack of ability to navigate – or disinterest in – patronage politics. The insurrectionary accusation followed in November. The town's leading slaveholders alleged that Motta had incited their slaves to abandon their masters and resort to theft and murder if necessary, and that his true intention was none other than to "win the slaves' favor, to have them as his workers on his 'Three Islands' property." They were basically calling him a slave hider. Privately, Justice of the Law Miguel Amorim and Police Chief Pitanga were skeptical; Pitanga was more concerned about capturing Benedito. Still, powerful proslavery interests could not be easily dismissed.[52]

It was in response to these allegations that Motta penned an impassioned letter identifying himself as "Cosme Motta, Protector of Africans in this District." The document is replete with spelling errors and run-on sentences sometimes lasting nearly two pages, vividly evoking a man whose head was swirling with thoughts he could barely rein in.[53] Motta's abolitionism had a specific cause: the emancipation of Africans who had been illegally imported in violation of the Law of November 7, 1831, the flagrantly ignored legislation banning the trans-Atlantic slave trade. Close to 760,000 Africans were illegally transported to Brazil between 1830 and 1856 as contraband slaves. Only a handful, officially recognized as illegally enslaved, were classified as *emancipados*.[54] It was those who

---

[50] Cosme Francisco da Motta to Antonio Pitanga, February 28, 1884, Polícia Ser. 2 Cx. 77 Mc 289 Fl. 88–89, APEES.

[51] José Pinto Homem Azevedo to Chief of Police, July 19, 1884, Polícia Ser. 2 Cx. 77 Mc 289 Fl. 3, APEES; Luis Antonio dos Santos to Antonio Pitanga, July 8, 1884, Polícia Ser. 2 Cx. 77 Mc 290 Fl. 175–176, APEES.

[52] Telegrams between Justice of Law Amorim and Antonio Pitanga, November 14, 1884, Polícia Ser. 2 Cx 77 Mc 291 Fl. 54–55, APEES.

[53] Cosme Francisco da Motta to Antonio Pitanga, November 15, 1884, Polícia Ser. 2 Cx. 77 Mc 293 Fl. 30–31, APEES.

[54] Beatriz Gallotti Mamigonian, "O direito de ser Africano livre: os escravos e as interpretações da Lei de 1831," in *Direitos e justiças no Brasil: ensaios de história social*, ed. Silvia Hunold Lara and Joseli Maria Nunes Mendonça (Campinas, SP: Editora UNICAMP, 2006), 130; Robert Conrad, "Neither Slave nor Free: The *Emancipados*

lacked this official recognition whom Motta advocated for and suspected the slaveholders of hiding during his census taking. Defending Africans enslaved in violation of the 1831 law – instead of pressing for general emancipation – was a specific strategy of many abolitionist movements gaining strength in the 1880s.[55]

Proslavery political interests had subverted the 1831 law for decades. As late as 1874 the Council of State discouraged its application, claiming it would disrupt the rhythm of gradual emancipation established by the 1871 Free Womb Law and be tantamount to "insurrectionary propaganda." By the 1880s, abolitionist societies and newspapers, including those led by Joaquim Nabuco, Rui Barbosa, and Luiz Gama, began to openly criticize the 1874 declaration.[56] Their demands for the emancipation of all Africans illegally imported after 1831 created panic among slaveholders, since by the 1880s the majority of Brazil's enslaved population was composed of those who entered after 1831 or their descendants.[57]

Motta harshly criticized São Mateus' rejection of abolitionism. While "all corners of the Empire are raising a nearly unanimous cry" in its favor, he stated, São Mateus "erred in becoming ever more slaveocratic, waging a cruel war against all those who dared support this great movement of the age: abolitionism."[58] Indeed, already in the late 1860s, at least two dozen new abolitionist associations had appeared throughout

---

of Brazil, 1818–1868," *HAHR* 53, no. 1 (1973): 50–70. Illegally enslaved Africans intercepted on their way to Brazil after 1831 were classified as *emancipados* and occupied the ambiguous category of persons who were neither slave nor free. They were obliged to await eventual full freedom under the "tutelage" of individuals or the state in the form of service or public works projects for what could amount to several decades. The *emancipados* were administered by the Justice of Orphans in a legal category shared by recently emancipated Indians, under the premise that neither group was capable of responsible judgment.

[55] See the works in Beatriz Gallotti Mamigonian and Keila Grinberg (eds.), "Dossiê: 'Para inglês ver? Revisitando a lei de 1831'," *Estudos Afro-Asiáticos* 1–3 (2007), which also focus on Africans' own uses of the law since many decades prior.

[56] Sidney Chalhoub, *A força da escravidão: ilegalidade e costume no Brasil oitocentista* (São Paulo: Companhia das Letras, 2012); Tâmis Parron, *A política da escravidão no Império do Brasil, 1826–1865* (Rio de Janeiro: Civilização Brasileira, 2011); Robert Edgar Conrad, *The Destruction of Brazilian Slavery, 1850–1888* (Berkeley: University of California Press, 1972), 139–40; 154–55; Elciene Azevedo, "Para além dos tribunais: advogados e escravos no movimento abolicionista em São Paulo," in *Direitos e justiças no Brasil: ensaios de história social*, ed. Silvia Hunold Lara and Joseli Maria Nunes Mendonça (Campinas, SP: Editora UNICAMP, 2006), 214–17.

[57] Costa, *The Brazilian Empire*, 164–65.

[58] Cosme Francisco da Motta, "Habeas Corpus Petition" (Processos, São Mateus, November 26, 1884), Box 94, Fl. 1, CPSM.

Brazil.[59] Motta drew his own inspiration from an abolitionist society established in 1883 in Vitória, the provincial capital of Espírito Santo, where the local Justice of the Law had recently freed all illegally imported Africans and their descendants. Calling itself "Domingos Martins" after a Espirito Santense hero of the Pernambucan revolution of 1817, it counted among its founders some of the most prominent liberals of the province including Affonso Claudio, who would soon become Espírito Santo's inaugural president in the First Republic (1889).[60] The society appointed representatives throughout the province to advance its cause. The lawyer Olavo Henrique Baptista, the prosecutor in Seraphim's murder case and one of Benedito's suspected protectors, was appointed to São Mateus. Instead of being able to promote his project, however, Baptista was denied official recognition for his society in São Mateus and received death threats.

These obstructions of the Domingos Martins Society in São Mateus inspired Motta to found his own society. In late September 1884, a month and a half before the insurrectionary accusation and during the chaotic anti-Benedito expeditions, Motta began recruiting several individuals interested in his cause, including, significantly, two of the police officers who had initially reported on the Santana emancipation rumors. Also present was Baptista, who had just a few days prior defended the quilombola Júlio in court (he was on trial as Benedito's accomplice in Marcolina's murder attempt).[61] The group drafted a document delineating their agenda with the plan to collect supporting signatures. However, in the final hour, Motta's companions were overcome by fear of slaveholder retaliation and backed out, while Motta, like Baptista, received death threats. He thus undertook the task of proving the freedom of two "clients," the Africans Laurino and Francisco, on his own. The men belonged to a powerful planter with nearly 100 slaves named

---

[59] Angela Alonso as cited in Castilho, *Slave Emancipation*, 39.

[60] Domingos Martins was an important freemason who was instrumental in revitalizing the English branch of the order in the 1817 Pernambucan revolution. Evaldo Cabral de Mello, *A outra independência: o federalismo pernambucano de 1817 a 1824* (São Paulo: Editora 34, 2004), 36–38. For the society, see Maria Stella de Novaes, *A Escravidão e a abolição no Espírito Santo: história e folclore* (Vitória, ES: Instituto Histórico e Geográfico, 1963), 118–22.

[61] While the majority-slaveholding jury would find Júlio guilty in December 1884, a surprising turn came when the presiding Justice of the Law Amorim clashed with the jury's decision on grounds that it was based solely on circumstantial evidence and took the case to the Appellate Court in Rio de Janeiro. Given these judgments, Amorim was likely listening to these fazendeiros' complaints about Motta in November with a large grain of salt.

João Gomes dos Santos. On discovering that Motta had obtained their slave registration documents and proof of their ages from the local vicar, Santos punished the two Africans ruthlessly, beating, strangling, hand-cuffing, and locking them up in a pitch-dark shed where they nearly starved.[62]

Motta reported the incident to the local authorities, and from there matters became increasingly hysterical. Through a barrage of accusations the slaveholders concocted out of Motta an insurrectionary mastermind. They said he was harboring more than a hundred slaves on his own property who were armed and trained to assault, rob, and murder.[63] They also alleged that Motta was rousing the "rude" slaves to commit violent crimes and plotting to rob Santos for the funds to procure their letters of manumission.[64] Seeing how his efforts on behalf of illegally enslaved Africans were perverted into an incitation for a bloody slave uprising, Motta responded that his only weapons were the laws of 1831 and 1871 and the Constitution. He emphasized the Africans' docility, calling them helpless beings who were resigned to the "tortures of captivity" while patiently awaiting their day of redemption.[65] His words fell on deaf ears. His detractors deposed under oath that Motta was threatening the social order by "inciting an insurrection against [the slaves'] masters to obtain their liberty," and should the slaves lack the courage to carry it out, "he would come in person to help them," advising murder as the easiest means to achieve their "desideratum" (ominously underlined in the document).[66] The black rapist trope emerged once again. The slaveholders asserted that once the revolt was unleashed come December 2, the slaves would burst into their "domestic space and dishonor them, because 'all are equal and the wives were born to that end.'" Included as a quotation in the original source, it is not clear whether the latter phrase was imputed to a particular individual or was an idea that planters imagined the slaves nourished in their minds. Whichever the case, they envisioned black freedom in terms of sexual violence against white women; otherwise the enslaved figured into these allegations only as Motta's puppets, their own demands for emancipation rendered irrelevant.[67]

---

[62] Motta, Protector.   [63] Motta to Pitanga, November 15, 1884, Fl. 31.
[64] São Mateus Planters to Justice of Law of São Mateus, November 11, 1884, Box 94, CPSM.
[65] Motta, "Habeas Corpus Petition," Fl. 4v.
[66] Joaquim Vicente Lopes de Oliveira to Antonio Pitanga, November 27, 1884, Polícia Ser. 2 Cx. 77 Mc 293 Of. 37 Fl. 21–23, APEES.
[67] Ibid., 22v.

Meanwhile Baptista was arrested after the police discovered him sheltering five presumed slaves in his residence. Motta's own arrest followed on November 20, on charges of authoring a slave conspiracy.[68] In his habeas corpus petition feverishly written in his prison cell, Motta emphasized that his efforts to free illegally enslaved Africans were "authorized by the Law that gives citizens the right" to do so. He had never advised slaves to disobey their masters nor advocated criminal activity, he stated, and described his abolitionist work and the resistance he had faced. Freemasonry had inspired him. A prince within his order, Motta felt compelled to advocate for the Africans in order to defend "Liberty, Equality, and Fraternity," since "a man's conscience is everything." Given the presence of freemasons among Brazilian abolitionists, including Rui Barbosa and Luiz Gama, it is likely that Baptista and other members of the Domingos Martins Society were also members.[69]

Motta's plan was logistically straightforward. His two-step process was founded on an amalgam of slaves' customary rights. The first step was to have the Africans earn the necessary funds ($5,000 reis) to purchase the documentation proving their illegal captivity. This they would accomplish by working for someone other than their masters on their day off, their rights to a portion of the earnings (pecúlio) guaranteed by the 1871 law. As in many regions across the Americas, in São Mateus it "was customary for planters to give slaves [Saturdays] so that they could return to the fazendas on Sunday." Motta instructed the Africans to avoid raising their masters' suspicion by resisting theft and workplace absence.[70] Thus, in his vision, illegally enslaved Africans brought after 1831 could legally accrue the amount of money needed to purchase their paperwork, with which they could petition for their lawful freedom. The Africans would earn this money through work performed during their free time. It was hardly an insurrectionary vision.[71]

However, the second part of Motta's plan, which he called a "*plano de trabalho*" (labor program), exposed the contradictory, limited vision

[68] Miguel Bernardo Vieira Amorim to Antonio Pitanga, November 16, 1884, Governadoria Ser. 383 Liv. 243 Fl. 399–399v, APEES; Aglinio Jard de Magalhães Requião to Antonio Pitanga, November 16, 1884, Governadoria Ser. 383 Liv. 243 Fl. 400, APEES; Police Lieutenant of São Mateus, November 28, 1884, Polícia Ser. 2 Liv. 258 Fl. 171, APEES.

[69] On Brazilian abolitionists and Freemansonry, see Celia Maria Marinho de Azevedo, *Maçonaria, anti-racismo e cidadania: uma história de lutas e debates transnacionais* (São Paulo: Annablume, 2010). Many freemasons were also involved in the illegal slave trade.

[70] Motta, "Habeas Corpus Petition," Fl. 4v–5.

[71] Questions for Cosme Francisco da Motta, November 27, 1884, Ibid., Fls. 12v–13.

of black freedom common even among its proponents. As it turned out, the slaveowners' earlier allegation – that Motta was planning to incite the slaves with the ultimate goal of using them as laborers on his own property – was not entirely groundless. Motta openly admitted to having told the Africans that, once freed, they would enter into a contract with him to lend their services on his Three Islands farm. In his view, this would prevent their falling into the throes of vagrancy.[72] Motta believed directed labor to be the most effective means of preparing Africans for freedom, if not full citizenship.[73] Although clearly opposed to slaveholders on the institution's future, he reiterated the racialized discourse shared by Indian labor proponents, abolitionists, and even slavery advocates. In their view, freedpeople (whether African or Brazilian) and Indians were naturally susceptible to vagrancy and required disciplinary labor regimes to prepare them for freedom and ensure their place in Brazilian society.

Meanwhile, in spite of his elaborate and peaceful appeals, Motta's habeas corpus petition was denied. He was charged with inciting a slave insurrection and conniving to use their labor. He was finally acquitted by a jury in June 1885.[74]

"Evil of All Evils": Father Geraldo's Rowdy Abolitionism

Subtlety was not among the qualities that Father Geraldo, the vicar of Our Lady of the Conception of Villa Viçosa who also served Colônia Leopoldina, was known for. In April 1886, a few months after Benedito's death on the colony, the priest stood before a majority-slave congregation and began making a few remarks on slavery that soon escalated into the dramatic declaration that there were no more slaves. The Justice of Orphans present at the church – whose responsibilities included manumissions – was horrified when the priest admonished him, before a room full of slaves, to declare their freedom. Father Geraldo then accused the Judge

---

[72] Ibid., Fl. 12.

[73] For the control of freedpeople and the relationship to vagrancy discourse, see, for example, Azevedo, *Onda negra*; George Reid Andrews, *Blacks & Whites in São Paulo, Brazil, 1888–1988* (Madison: University of Wisconsin Press, 1991); Thomas C. Holt, *The Problem of Freedom: Race, Labor, and Politics in Jamaica and Britain, 1832–1938* (Baltimore: Johns Hopkins University Press, 1992); Mimi Sheller, *Democracy after Slavery: Black Publics and Peasant Radicalism in Haiti and Jamaica* (Gainesville: University Press of Florida, 2000).

[74] Penna, "Relatório do Ministério da Justiça," 43–44; Sabino José Oliveira, July 6, 1885, Polícia Ser. 2 Cx. 79 Mc 299 Fl. 100, APEES.

of being opposed to emancipation, since he had not recognized the manumission of 180 sexagenarian slaves on the colony whom the law had freed in 1885. A diatribe against slave masters, local authorities, and even the monarch followed, topped with a warning that God would deliver punishment on Viçosa.[75]

With abolition still two years away, Father Geraldo's declarations potentially signaled the emergence of a radical abolitionism in a region where proslavery interests still stood firm. Was the Brazilian Catholic church, historically indifferent to slavery, finally changing course? From his shocking words to dubious political maneuverings, Father Geraldo's mercurial, even messy abolitionism lacks the clarity of narrative hindsight enjoyed by the likes of elite abolitionists such as Joaquim Nabuco. While his colorful sermons jolted slaveholders into reckoning with the reality of abolition, his plans for freedpeople were similar to Motta's, expressing racialized ideas about black vagrancy that again echoed the language of indigenous labor regimes and disregarded freedpeople's own aspirations for life after emancipation. As we will see, Father Geraldo's abolitionist vision was also explicitly tied to the battle over landownership.[76]

Abolition did not bode well for Colônia Leopoldina's planters. The colony's coffee, though threatened by rivals, was reputedly the best in all of Bahia. While its dependence on the crop made it vulnerable to price fluctuations, the colony remained the lone economic engine of the province's south while Caravelas and Viçosa stagnated, with the 1882 opening of the Bahia–Minas Railroad generating negligible profits.[77] In 1884 the combined districts of Caravelas, Viçosa, and São José de Porto Alegre had 2,217 slaves (aside from 713 *ingênuos*), with 786 in Caravelas and 1,131 in Viçosa and San José, most of them likely on Colônia Leopoldina.[78] The colony had done remarkably well compared to the rest of the region in maintaining its workforce after the 1850 cessation of the slave trade, which they managed by encouraging high reproduction rates

---

[75] José Machado de Pedreira to Teodoro Machado Freire Pereira da Silva, President of Bahia, May 5, 1886, Colônia/Justiça/Viçosa/Mc 2638, APEB; Alane Fraga do Carmo, "Colonização e escravidão na Bahia: a Colônia Leopoldina (1850–1888)" (M. A. thesis, Universidade Federal da Bahia, 2010), 77.

[76] Jailton Lima Brito, *A abolição na Bahia, 1870–1888* (Salvador: EDUFBA, 2003), 237.

[77] Durval Vieira de. Aguiar, *Descrições Práticas da Província da Bahia: com Descrições de Todas as Distâncias Intermediárias das Cidade, Vilas e Povoações* (Rio de Janeiro: Livraria Editora Câtedra, 1979), 284–93.

[78] Antonio Vicente da Costa, "Alfândega na comarca de Caravellas (Relatório ao Senador Dantas)," *Gazeta da Bahia*, December 17, 1884. Costa does not account for the remaining three hundred slaves.

among their slaves. Many children continued to be born after 1871, a considerable number of whom the planters kept illegally by falsifying their birthdates or not registering them at all, as Motta had suspected among slaveholders in São Mateus.[79] Given this reliance on slave labor and an ongoing failure to attract immigrants, the planters would witness their coffee production become "extraordinarily diminished" with abolition.[80] Some of the colony's slaves who were unwilling to await emancipation had taken drastic action. Laurindo, a slave of Luiz Bornaud (who would later manumit his sexagenarian slaves), was driven by desperation to kill his own sons Pamphilio and Gregorio in 1883 after their mother Firmina was whipped for missing work to care for them. Laurindo stated that he had acted to "end Firmina's great suffering, and prevent the two of them from seeing their children suffer later."[81] The following year seven enslaved men clubbed their master José Venerote to death. Then, in early 1886, Benedito chose death over capture on the colony's grounds.

The fall of the Baron of Cotegipe's conservative cabinet (August 1885 to March 1888), whose repressive tactics had helped radicalize the abolitionist movement, and the ascent of João Alfredo de Correia to prime minister, marked the coming of abolition.[82] Sambas, parades, and fireworks celebrated the Golden Law abolishing slavery on May 13, 1888. In São Mateus law enforcement was relieved to witness abolition and the days following it pass without any mayhem, with the Domingos Martins Society announcing the end of slavery to its associates throughout the province.[83] Festivities were far less peaceful in southern Bahia, however. Starting on the evening of the 12th, the streets of Caravelas became a battleground for the town's Conservative and Liberal factions whose celebrations were entangled with mutually hurled insults aimed at

---

[79] Carmo, "Colonização e escravidão," 106–12.

[80] Aguiar, *Descrições Práticas da Província da Bahia*, 290–92. In 1884 Bahia as a whole still counted 132,822 slaves. Even with a sharp decrease there were still at least 76,838 in 1886–87, making it the fourth largest slaveholding province. Conrad, *Destruction of Brazilian Slavery*, 285; Moura, "Relatorio do Ministério da Agricultura," 372.

[81] Manoel José de Figueredo, August 6, 1883, Colonial/Polícia/Mc 3000, APEB; Ricardo Tadeu Caires Silva, "Os caminhos da abolição: escravos, senhores, e direitos nos últimas décadas da escravidão (Bahia, 1850–1888)" (doctoral dissertation, Universidade Federal do Paraná, 2007), 284–85.

[82] Jeffrey D. Needell, "Brazilian Abolitionism, Its Historiography, and the Uses of Political History," *JLAS* 42, no. 2 (2010): 231–61; Castilho, *Slave Emancipation*, Chapter 5.

[83] C. Vasconcellos, Telegram (São Mateus, May 18, 1888), Polícia Cx. 436 Maço 669 Fl. 40, APEES; Paço da Câmara Municipal de São Mateus (São Mateus, June 8, 1888), Liv. 353 Fl. 512, APEES; *A Província do Espírito Santo*, May 16, 1888.

convincing the libertos that the other faction had opposed abolition.[84] If Father Geraldo's detractors believed the priest had quieted down with abolition, they were mistaken. First, the priest had shown he was not above worldly politics by becoming elected to the provincial assembly on the Liberal party ticket. Nor was he above partying. The priest was at the forefront of rowdy celebrations on the 19th and 20th, leading a group of libertos and others around town who gave cheers to him, the Liberal party, and the republic. The group headed over to the house of a local prostitute and designated it their "republic," after which they wandered the streets armed with knives and clubs, shooting rifles and pistols, and singing unwholesome songs to the cacophonous beat of an improvised drum. "Let the samba roll, everything is over!" they shouted. "Long live Father Geraldo, Long Live the Liberals! Die, Conservatives!" A local policeman observing his extravagant behavior called the priest the "evil of all evils."[85]

Father Geraldo's reasons for courting libertos would become evident with time. On May 15, the newly minted politician-priest had barged onto the fields of several Colônia Leopoldina plantations. Standing before nearly 500 of the colony's newly emancipated women and men, he held aloft a statuette of St. Benedict, a black Catholic saint venerated by black Brazilians. The freedpeople stood as the priest incited them to destroy the chains of captivity and leave their work. Reminding them of the punishments they had endured under slavery, he beseeched them to abandon their masters, roaring, "The time of vengeance has arrived! Vengeance is proof of your sentiment!" Should they return to the ex-masters' plantations, he warned, they would be reenslaved. The police officer witnessing the sermon, whose antagonism toward the priest clearly shaped his report, complained that Father Geraldo was dressed as a servant of God but spoke the words of Satan. As with the slaves supposedly under Motta's sway, the officer feared that the libertos, whom he considered mired in ignorance and easily provoked, would resort to violence against their ex-masters.

---

[84] Francisco Antonio de Carvalhal, Public Prosecutor of Viçosa and S. José de Porto Alegre to Police Chief of Bahia, June 9, 1888, Colonial/Polícia/Chefes de Polícia/Mc 2986, APEB.

[85] In Portuguese, *república* signifies not only the political configuration but also a student dormitory, and sometimes is used to suggest a state of lawlessness. Angelo Domingues Monteiro (Vila Viçosa, June 1, 1888), Colonial/Polícia/Chefes de Polícia/Mc 2986, APEB. Iacy Mata Maio has read this incident as evidence of the libertos' political gains, in that rather than being coopted by the town's political factions, they were openly rejecting their subjection; see her "'Libertos de treze de maio' e ex-senhores na Bahia: conflitos no pós-abolição," *Afro-Ásia* 35 (2007): 163–98.

But whereas Motta assiduously refuted such fears (if in vain) by speaking of his lawful methods, Father Geraldo fanned the flames by encouraging the former slaves of the planter Ludovico Avellar to tear down the remaining slave quarters and slap him around should he obstruct them. The Leopoldina planters were supremely irked by the priest's intrusion. Expecting longstanding master–slave relations to remain unchanged after abolition, they accused Father Geraldo of persuading their former slaves, who had allegedly agreed to continue working for them, to demand a salary and food. They also complained that some libertos had abandoned the plantations and were now wandering like vagrants, becoming a nuisance.[86]

Many aspects of Father Geraldo's abolitionism would raise eyebrows. For instance, he informed the libertos he had personally freed them, since the government had forgotten them in their remote corner of the province. He told them he had martyred himself for their cause by confronting their despised masters, and only through his battles had they been freed. He also demanded that the emancipated men and women each pay him 1,000 and 500 reis, respectively, for his work on their behalf. The exasperated police officer criticized Father Geraldo for "calling himself an abolitionist, when abolition is already accomplished."[87] However, if he were indeed an opportunistic, after-the-fact abolitionist, he was not alone. Liberals and conservatives, priests and slavemasters alike scrambled to side with abolitionism once it was a fait accompli. Even the colony's European planters jumped on the bandwagon, writing to the *Diario da Bahia* that the "great fact of general emancipation in the country ties us ever more intimately to the Brazilian family." Eliding Colônia Leopoldina's ignominious past as an immigrant-colony-turned-slave-plantation, the planters added, "[w]e nourish the hope that, with the government's protection, our colony can serve to attract immigrants, who like us will undoubtedly enjoy the hospitality of the Brazilian lands."[88]

Father Geraldo's affiliations with abolitionist organizations remain unknown. He was not all talk; for instance, he did successfully force the Justice of Orphans to manumit 180 sexagenarian slaves. But opportunism cannot be discounted. The new Liberal party deputy likely had

---

[86] João Falcão Metzker to Police Chief of Bahia, May 28, 1888, Colonial/Polícia/Mc 2986, APEB. Maio has also documented instances of masters trying to force libertos into continued, unremunerated labor in this and other regions of Bahia after abolition in Iacy Mata Maio, "Os treze de maio: ex-senhores, polícia e libertos na Bahia no pós-Abolição (1888–1889)" (M. A. thesis, Universidade Federal da Bahia, 2002), 19–29.

[87] Metzker to Police Chief of Bahia, May 28, 1888.

[88] Manoel Machado Portella, "Relatório (BA)," 1889, 13, CRL.

an eye on the libertos' money and potentially, their votes, although new income requirements disenfranchised many freedpeople.[89] From another perspective, Father Geraldo may have represented a long-awaited end to the Catholic Church's historical indifference to the problem of slavery, in Bahia and Brazil in general. Many Brazilian abolitionists had denounced the Church for its deference to large landholders and slaveowners, and because the Church itself had owned slaves. It was only in the eleventh hour, when abolition was becoming an inexorable reality, that the Brazilian Church finally embraced the cause of abolition.[90] In light of this chronology we cannot say that Father Geraldo was exactly a harbinger, but he was denouncing slavery – in his own way.

Civilizing Vagrants

Cosme Motta and Father Geraldo opposed slavery; that much is clear. A closer look at their visions of black freedom, however, forces a more critical reevaluation of their abolitionist projects. Both men echoed the discourse of Indian administrators who instituted disciplinary labor regimes in the name of saving indigenous people from vagrancy and savagery. While presented as a preparation for their national inclusion that as slaves and "savages" many black and indigenous people did not yet enjoy, these labor regimes envisioned a citizenship that was fundamentally servile. Such ideas became particularly clear in their denying black and indigenous people access to land, which revealed how the unequal access to citizenship was inflected through the right to territory. Yet this was not the final word. Freedpeople negotiated the terms of these labor regimes to forge spaces of freedom even within their restrictive parameters. In this regard, they were similar to those Indians who chose negotiation with missionaries and settlers. In other cases, black and indigenous people contested the coercive nature of "civilization" and national inclusion, sometimes with catastrophic consequences.

In São Mateus, the indefatigable Cosme Motta set about realizing his "labor plan" after his release from prison. Among the participants was a

---

[89] On freedpeople and voting rights, see Hebe Maria Mattos de Castro, *Escravidão e cidadania no Brasil monárquico* (Rio de Janeiro: Jorge Zahar, 2000), 20; Manuela Carneiro da Cunha, *Negros, estrangeiros: os escravos libertos e sua volta à África* (São Paulo: Editora Brasiliense, 1985), 68–69.

[90] Robert Brent Toplin, *The Abolition of Slavery in Brazil* (New York: Atheneum, 1975), 117–19; 234. The Church's inaction regarding slavery was in fact the specific object of criticism by the Bahian abolitionist Luís Anselmo da Fonseca, outlined in his 1887 text, *A escravidão, o clero e o abolicionismo* (Bahia: Imprensa Economica, 1887).

fifty-one-year-old slave named Ludgero, who embodied the ambiguities
of freedom experienced by enslaved people in these new labor regimes.
A man with gray speckles in his hair, Ludgero was born into slavery in
São Mateus. In May 1887, after a half-century of captivity, he walked
away.[91] Much like the quilombolas, who had forged their own meanings
of freedom and citizenship by fleeing into São Mateus' geography of
slavery, Ludgero defined his freedom through place and community. He
chose to flee to Motta's nearby property and treasured his friendship with
other slaves, with whom he was rehearsing for a pageant to be performed
on the upcoming Festival of Santana, on a nearby farm.[92] His master
was the prominent local resident Captain Raulino Francisco de Oliveira,
whose son, a doctor also named Raulino, was the recent President of the
Municipal Council. The younger Raulino was allied with the nineteen
slaveholders who had accused Motta of fomenting an insurrection.[93]
Two months into relocating to Motta's, Ludgero was working in the
fields when he was approached by a man who had come to return him
to his master. His response was swift. "I will not give him the pleasure
(*gosto*) of taking me," he uttered, and stabbed himself with a knife.
Murmuring, "I've killed myself," he collapsed to the ground.

Death eluded Ludgero, as did the certainty of freedom. In a police
interrogation the following day, poignant contradictions interlaced his
claims of freedom. Asked why he chose suicide over returning to his
master, he replied it was because he "considered himself free, as Mr.
Cosme Motta had told him." He repeatedly expressed how he "feared
returning to the chains." Three freed sexagenarian Africans residing on
Motta's property who had transported Ludgero after the suicide attempt
recalled that he had claimed to be a freedperson (*forro*) or simply free
(*livre*). And yet, unlike the Africans who likely benefited from Motta's
abolitionist project and whose freedom was now all but guaranteed by
the 1885 Sexagenarian Law, Ludgero had no such guarantees.[94] The

[91] STR June 13, 1878, Liv. 11, Fls. 4–9, CPSM.
[92] "Police Investigation into Suicide Attempt by Ludgero, Slave of Captain Raulino Fran-
        cisco de Oliveira" (São Mateus, July 24, 1887), Box 97, CPSM.
[93] Inventory of D. Rita Adelia de Oliveira (wife of Capt. Raulino), February 14, 1887, Box
        99, Fls. 39–40, CPSM; *Almanak (ES)*, 1885, 189. Though not among the 19 accusers,
        Raulino joined some of them in complaining to the police that his life was threatened
        by Motta's alleged conspiracy. Miguel Bernardo Vieira Amorim to Antonio Pitanga,
        November 14, 1884, Polícia Ser. 2 Cx. 77 Mc 291 Fl. 54–55, APEES.
[94] Many slaveholders had fraudulently registered illegally imported Africans as being much
        older than their actual ages in order to avoid the consequences of the 1831 Law. As
        Conrad notes, a disproportionately large number of Africans were registered as being

precariousness of freedom now confronted a man who claimed to be free but was, legally, a fugitive slave who could be reenslaved at a moment's notice. His fear was realized.

Did Motta deceive Ludgero by telling him he was free? He was not interrogated in this incident. The idea of deception echoes Motta's accusers, however, denying significance to Ludgero's own ideas.[95] Ludgero probably came to Motta's property aware of the emancipated Africans working there under a contract and entered into a similar arrangement. Even though Motta's "labor plan" did not offer a clear break from slavery, for Ludgero it signaled a much better life than remaining with his dreaded master. Motta likely believed he was saving Ludgero from a life of vagrancy in addition to gaining another worker. However, self-interest alone cannot explain why he would risk reexposing himself to slaveholder vitriol and imprisonment. The Saraiva Bill of 1885 had made sheltering fugitive slaves a heavily punishable crime. By telling Ludgero he was free and offering him shelter, Motta likely knew he was breaking the law at great personal risk.[96]

If Motta and Ludgero had erred, it was through optimism. Both men presumed that by July 1887, São Mateus slaveholders would be finally ready to concede to the forces of abolition, a reasonable expectation given that even in Rio de Janeiro the Conservative forces were losing ground to an increasingly radical abolitionist movement, rendering abolition only a matter of time.[97] No matter how many quilombolas the São Mateus slaveholders chased or abolitionists they imprisoned, slavery would be abolished in Brazil in less than ten months. His cautious embrace of freedom shattered when his master came to reclaim him, Ludgero saw that suicide was the only way to deny him the perverse "pleasure," as he called it, of human possession.

---

age fifty-one or older in the 1872 Census, all of whom would have been freed by the Sexagenarian Law. The only other option was to acknowledge fraud. Conrad, *Destruction of Brazilian Slavery*, 215–16.

[95] For a critical analysis of the narrative of radical abolitionists urging and manipulating slaves to abandon plantations in São Paulo, see Elciene Azevedo, *Orfeu de carapinha: a trajetória de Luiz Gama na imperial cidade de São Paulo* (Campinas: Editora da UNICAMP, 1999), 133.

[96] According to the Bill, passed on September 28, 1885, the crime of sheltering runaways was brought under Article 260 of the Criminal Code regulating stolen property. The fine for hiding a fugitive slave was between 5 and 20 percent of the value of the slave, and the person found guilty of aiding a runaway slave was subject to imprisonment for as long as two years. Abolitionist Rui Barbosa compared it to the US Fugitive Slave Act. Conrad, *Destruction of Brazilian Slavery*, 223–24, 226.

[97] Needell, "Brazilian Abolitionism," 251–55.

Two years later, another conflict erupted over the definition of freedom. On July 5, 1889, more than 2,000 libertos revolted on Colônia
Leopoldina. The nearly 77 percent increase in the freed population since
1884 suggests that the vast majority of the colony's freedpeople remained
after abolition, while a significant number relocated there from Caravelas
and Alcobaça, staying close to the site of their captivity.[98] Such choices
made particular sense in Colônia Leopoldina, where generations of kin
resided together to help free each other from bondage and win important concessions, including small tracts of land, from their masters. Libertos who remained in their former site of captivity generally enjoyed
greater stability and growth in the post-emancipation years compared
to others who, by virtue of being itinerant, were unable to accumulate
wealth. An African man named Anacleto Flach, for example, who had
been freed by his half-brother, possessed a coffee farm of seven thousand trees and a manioc field at the time of his death in 1881 on the
colony, where his mother and half-brother had also resided (Figure 6.1).[99]
By the eve of abolition, however, soil degradation along the local
Peruípe River had already enticed away some wealthier residents to fertile lands further north.[100] The massive uprising therefore suggested that
the shortage of fertile land could endanger family and economic stability
after emancipation, sowing explosive discontent among the libertos who
remained.[101]

---

[98] Police Lieutenant of Viçosa and S. José de Porto Alegre to Police Chief of Bahia, July 5,
1889, Colonial/Polícia/Delegados/Mc 6226, APEB. Those who moved there probably
included libertos from the towns of Caravelas and Alcobaça, whose 300 libertos had
all but abandoned it by May 30, 1888. Vicente Ignacio de Sant'Anna, May 30, 1888,
Colonial/Justiça/Alcobaça/Mc 2231, APEB. The increase is based on the figure of 1,131
slaves in Viçosa and São José in 1884.

[99] Flach is clearly recorded as an "Africano liberto" in his inventory, which suggests that
he came with his mother as a child from Africa. Henrique Metzker, "Inventory of
Anacleto Flach" (Colônia Leopoldina, November 23, 1881), Inventários 08/3410/10,
APEB.

[100] Francisco Vicente Vianna and José Carlos Ferreira, Memoria sobre o estado da Bahia
(Bahia: Typographia e encadernação do "Diario da Bahia," 1893), 197–98.

[101] For the kinship networks among the colony's slaves and their strategies for emancipation, see Carmo, "Colonização e escravidão." Walter Fraga's study of slaves and
former slaves in the Recôncavo clearly demonstrates that many libertos stayed on or
near the fazendas where they were enslaved, where they had strong and intricate kinship networks. See also Ana Lugão Rios and Hebe Maria Mattos de Castro, Memórias
do cativeiro: família, trabalho e cidadania no pós-abolição (Rio de Janeiro: Civilização
Brasileira, 2005); Dylan C. Penningroth, The Claims of Kinfolk: African American
Property and Community in the Nineteenth-Century South (Chapel Hill: University of
North Carolina Press, 2003).

FIGURE 6.1 Familial ties and friendships formed under slavery would inform freedpeople's aspirations in post-emancipation Brazil. Many former slaves in Colônia Leopoldina remained there after abolition, which kept them close to their kin but also created land shortages. *Source: Slaves in the coffee harvest*, c.1882. Marc Ferrez / Gilberto Ferrez Collection / Instituto Moreira Salles. Reproduced with permission.

It was during this new phase of land conflicts that Father Geraldo's vision for the libertos became more explicit.[102] Two weeks after the revolt, the vicar filed a request for a land grant along the north bank of the local Pau Alto River to the Viçosa Municipal Chamber. The vicar's stated objective was the establishment of an agricultural colony, under his direction, composed of "ex-slaves freed by the Law of May 13." The priest recognized that the lack of cultivable land and the funds to

---

[102] Scholars who have written on Father Geraldo have tended to depict him as a politically connected, heroic radical abolitionist without sufficient critical analysis of his plans for libertos. His case is also subsumed under a general discussion of abolition-related unrest in Bahia without attention to the region's specific history. Wlamyra Ribeiro de Albuquerque, *O jogo da dissimulação: abolição e cidadania negra no Brasil* (São Paulo: Companhia das Letras, 2009), 134–39; Maio, "Libertos de treze de maio," 192–96; Silva, "Caminhos da abolição," 277–95; Carmo, "Colonização e escravidão," 75–78; Brito, *Abolição na Bahia*, 269–76.

purchase it were at the root of the unrest and argued that it was necessary to "animate those libertos who, lacking in resources within the first year [after emancipation], do not have the means for subsistence, medicine, farming tools, etc." He planned to settle about two hundred free families on terras devolutas along the river.

However, Father Geraldo's main objective was not to help the libertos realize their post-emancipation aspirations for independent land owner-ship. Employing the same language as Motta and Indian labor advocates, he described his "labor plan" as a disciplinary mechanism to prevent the "unhappy ex-slaves from hurling themselves on the path of vagabondage, theft, and crime" resulting from the "lack of work and someone to over-see them." His supporters in the Chamber enthusiastically agreed that uneducated freedpeople, "supremely ignorant and inclined to all sorts of vice," would need the vicar's guidance to stay on course. The Cham-ber praised Father Geraldo as a "perfect missionary" whom the libertos loved, since he, as an abolitionist, had always been their "defender and patron." Underlying this paternalist language about saving black people from their supposedly innate vagrancy was an interest in keeping them bound to the agricultural colony while denying them economic inde-pendence. Confining them geographically would prevent libertos from competing for scarce, fertile lands while maintaining a cheap, dependent labor force after emancipation. Perhaps the libertos no longer had to serve their Colônia Leopoldina masters, but their battle over the rights of black citizenship was only beginning.[103]

Crisis on Itambacuri

Just a few months after the Colônia Leopoldina revolt, a military coup forced Pedro II to abdicate the throne, on November 15, 1889, and sent the royal family into exile. The curtain was drawn on the Brazil-ian Empire and nearly four centuries of monarchical rule, ceding way to the First Republic (1889–1930). Among the many changes augured by the political transformation was the newly decreed separation of Church and State, casting the future of state-funded missionary work into doubt. Nestled in their corner of northern Minas, however, Frei Serafim and Angelo continued their work among the Indians. They and their suc-cessors would remain at the helm of Itambacuri until the Republican

---

[103] Câmara Municipal de Vila Viçosa to José Luiz de Almeida Couto, President of Bahia, July 23, 1889, Colonial/Câmaras/Viçosa/Mc 1458, APEB.

government's newly created Indian Protection Service (SPI) would take over in 1911.[104]

New challenges strained life on the aldeia. Catastrophic droughts in the Northeast in the early 1890s brought droves of desperate migrants from Ceará and northern Bahia to Itambacuri. With the area's population suddenly tripled, the aldeia's once bountiful food supplies were severely strained.[105] Starving people devoured tree bark and poisonous plants, abandoning their dead to the mercy of wild animals and vultures. These hardships were aggravated by a devastating smallpox epidemic in 1892 and 1893 that took the lives of nearly 400 Indians.[106]

Then, at nightfall on May 24, 1893, the friars were on their usual evening stroll of the aldeia when they were ambushed. A barrage of arrows pierced Fr. Serafim's forearm and Fr. Angelo's shoulder blade. Fr. Angelo instinctively shot his rifle toward his assailants, whom he recognized as the mission's Indians, painted red with urucum. They were led by Manoel Pequeno and Querino Grande, two Botocudo who had been living in Itambacuri since the mission's founding twenty years earlier. Manoel Pequeno was a skilled carpenter who had built the central church's magnificent lateral altar, and the friars had considered him among the most intelligent of the aldeia Indians. On hearing the sound of people approaching, the Indians swiftly released the twenty-three children being kept by the friars and, leaving behind a few others to keep watch, retreated south. The friars suspected Manoel and Querino of having lured other Indians to join them by lying that the friars had tried to poison their children. The friars thanked Divine Providence for sparing their lives. Manoel Pequeno and Querino Grande, as the friars eventually learned, were leading a staggering 700 to 800 Indians.[107]

Aid arrived from Filadélfia the following day, among them the Director of Indians of Mucuri, Antônio Onofri, who arrested sixteen Indians. The friars believed that only thanks to their arrival did Itambacuri avoid a massive assault. Their relief was short lived, however. The Indians

[104] Lilia Moritz Schwarcz, *The Emperor's Beard: Dom Pedro II and His Tropical Monarchy in Brazil*, trans. John Gledson (Hill and Wang, 2003), 326–332; Mattos, *Civilização e revolta*, 380; and "Educar para dominar," 101.

[105] Jacinto de Palazzolo, *Nas selvas dos vales*, 242–43.

[106] Fr. Angelo de Sassoferato and Fr. Serafim de Gorizia to Antonio Alves Pereira da Silva, August 22, 1893, 20-V-100, ACRJ; Mattos, *Civilização e revolta*, 357.

[107] Sassoferato and Gorizia to Silva, August 22, 1893. For the most complete and ethnographic account of the May 1893 "revolt," see Mattos, *Civilização e revolta*, Chapter 6.

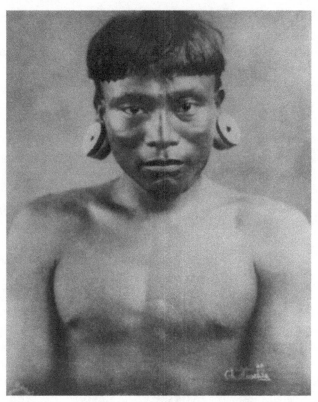

FIGURE 6.2 In the final years of of the Imperial period and the early Republic, settlers and missionaries considered "civilizing" the Botocudo as a solution to the labor and land shortage aggravated by the abolition of slavery. The Botocudo, however, radically criticized this vision of subservient citizenship. *Source: Brazil. 3 Botocudos Indian men with large ear and mouth rings* (detail). Retrieved from the Library of Congress.

reinitiated their attack soon after the reinforcements departed, sacking the aldeia for "one month and seven days." Once the friars' pride and glory, Itambacuri's symbols of civilization now lay in ruins. The Indians destroyed bridges, razed 120 km worth of fields, burned settler properties, and killed domestic animals, leaving behind a "truly horrific scene." Settlers fled. Additional help on June 29 finally put an end to the conflict. More than twenty Indians perished, including Manoel Pequeno. "We owe everything to [the friars]," Onofri observed, "and it is lamentable that after twenty years of dedication, they receive such perfidious ingratitude in return." The friars were particularly angered by what they perceived as the deception and ingratitude of Querino Grande, who "although on the aldeia for more than twenty years, maintained his false, indocile, and bad disposition." The friars decided to pardon the Indians who chose to return in hopes that they would help reconstitute Itambacuri's devastated population (Figure 6.2).[108]

Izabel Mattos' ethnographic reading of Querino Grande's actions prior to the attack provides important insight into the Botocudos' motivations. According to Mattos, the Botocudo considered the missionaries responsible for the general hardships on Itambacuri, hardships exacerbated by the catastrophic smallpox deaths. Querino Grande's leadership is particularly noteworthy. As noted by anthropologist Curt Nimuendajú, the Botocudo believed their leaders to possess *Yikégn*, or supernatural power. That Querino, a Botocudo leader, was seen as a shaman with such powers is strongly suggested by the friars' observation that in the days preceding the attack, he had been luring other Indians to the sort of "nocturnal meetings and savage dances that had ceased long ago." In Botocudo cosmology, these nocturnal meetings were a way to avenge the death of relatives, and the dancing a ritual preparation to attack against an enemy's witchcraft. Indeed, the Botocudo considered all death, physical pain, and illness to be the work of invisible, "poisoned" magical arrows launched by their enemies. A leader's role was to prevent these supernaturally transmitted attacks, or to avenge the deaths they caused.[109] Vengeance assumed the form of a carefully orchestrated attack on their enemies through the use of physical arrows. This may explain why Querino and Manoel began their offensive by shooting the friars with arrows when, as Onofri later witnessed, they owned firearms and could handle them expertly.[110]

Tellingly, the two groups differed entirely on their perceptions of the event. The friars called it a revolt by ungrateful Indians. The Indians, painted in red, were at war. Fr. Serafim and Fr. Angelo blamed the Indians' hygiene for their massive smallpox deaths and argued that they had attacked Itambacuri in order to "sell and live by the sweat of nationals, without having to work for two to three years." Once enraged to be slandered as Indian slavers, the friars belittled the Indians as vagrants interested only in exploiting settler labor.[111] While the Indians' wider motivations can only be surmised, their destruction of the symbols of

---

[108] Sassoferato and Gorizia to Silva, August 22, 1893; Antonio Onofri to Antonio Alves Pereira da Silva, June 10, 1893, 21-I-19, ACRJ.

[109] Guido Pokrane also accused his enemies of witchcraft.

[110] Mattos, *Civilização e revolta*, 137–38; 364; Curt Nimuendajú, "Social Organization and Beliefs of the Botocudo of Eastern Brazil," *Southwestern Journal of Anthropology* 2, no. 1 (1946): 98; Onofri to Silva, June 10, 1893.

[111] Mattos, *Civilização e revolta*, 363–64; Sassoferato and Gorizia to Silva, August 22, 1893; Jacinto de Palazzolo, *Nas selvas dos vales*, 253.

Christianity and agriculture – the church and fields – strongly suggests that they intended much more than economic damage. From the hundreds of smallpox deaths and pervasive hunger to destabilized kinship networks and territorial loss, such unparalleled suffering may have, in their view, originated in the friars' witchcraft.

Revisiting the events twenty-two years later, Fr. Angelo added details to the final confrontation that had been missing in his earlier account. He recalled that he and Fr. Serafim had faced the "difficult necessity of organizing an expedition of well-armed and equipped men to combat the Indians." The expedition was entrusted to a "loyal" lingua, an "exemplary user of the bow and arrow with perfect knowledge of all the places visited by the savages." The lingua traveled ahead of the expedition and secretly surveyed the forests. One morning, the troops assumed their positions, and the shooting began. Fr. Angelo recounted that the "savages, in spite of all their swiftness and capability, were unable to organize a resistance; many succumbed and others fled. This combat ended the Indians' revolt." The friars then gave the remaining Indians a generous pardon.[112]

Fr. Angelo's narrative may now be familiar to the reader: the Indian "revolt" of 1893 ended with a missionary-led *matar uma aldeia*. Twenty Indians perished. Such a conclusion lends greater significance to Onofri's ambivalence about the Indians in his 1893 letter to the Director of Indians of Minas Gerais. Although it was his denouncement of their "unheard-of ferocity" and apparent "return to their old, nomadic life" that would greenlight state support for the expedition, Onofri also allowed that the Indians could "no longer be considered savages, they who are already accustomed to civilized life." If the Indians' destruction of the very symbols of civilization cast its inexorable triumph over savagery into doubt, the missionaries' endorsing their massacre shook the very meaning of civilization to its core.[113]

The Times of Post-Emancipation

After May 13, 1888, there were no more slaves in Brazil. The long struggle to end slavery in Brazil began in 1831 and finally came to fruition in 1888, destroying the last slave society in the Americas.[114] In the

---

[112] Fr. Angelo de Sassoferato (1915) as cited in Jacinto de Palazzolo, *Nas selvas dos vales*, 260.

[113] Onofri to Silva, June 10, 1893.

[114] The trans-Atlantic slave trade was initially abolished north of the equator in 1815.

post-emancipation period, freedpeople would strive to realize their dreams of landownership or travel to the cities to look for new opportunities, seeking to define their own terms of citizenship as they confronted new racisms and inequalities.

This is a familiar narrative of abolition and post-emancipation in Brazil and the larger Atlantic World. It is an incomplete narrative. The struggle for black liberation in Brazil transpired in the long aftermath of another abolition that had already taken place in 1831. Indigenous post-emancipation, marked by illegal enslavement and unrelenting violence, cast a long shadow on black people's struggles for liberation in the nineteenth century, shaping racially tinged debates about their capacity for national belonging. Within the overlapping temporalities of indigenous post-emancipation and the gradual abolition of African-based slavery existed the liminal spaces between bondage and freedom, slavery and citizenship, existence and extinction, inclusion and exclusion. Theirs was a relationship of simultaneity that endangered the very meaning of abolition and the promise of life after slavery.

The prospect of abolition provoked anxieties about the nation's economic viability and violent slaveholder backlash. It also engendered hopes for Indian civilization and the liberation of the povo brasileiro from the stain of slavery. Yet by the 1870s and 1880s, Brazil's future increasingly relied on the creation of a subservient labor force, both black and indigenous. Missionaries, slaveowners, settlers, and state agents confined freedpeople and Indians geographically, by restricting land access, and discursively, through racialized intonations of vagrancy and limited citizenship capacities. Abolitionists and missionaries promoted disciplinary labor regimes that awkwardly coexisted with the alleged inexorability of Indian extinction. Even as evolving legal regimes marked the divergences of enslaved and indigenous people's place within the nation, their mirroring histories were exposed once again in the labor and land controversies of the late Empire.

In the lives of freedpeople and Indians, the battle over citizenship and geography converged. Freedpeople's aspirations for land, family, and self-sufficiency incited their former masters to confine them to landlessness and supervised labor. Such clashes over the right to the territory did not emerge in the process of slave emancipation. They had begun much earlier in the century, when João VI authorized the conquest of indigenous territories of the Atlantic frontier. At the end of the nineteenth century, their land reduced to a small corner of northern Minas Gerais, the Botocudo on Itambacuri declared war against the agents of their devastation.

   Indians and freedpeople powerfully condemned Brazilian liberal nationhood and its terms of black and indigenous inclusion. Marked by illegal slavery and equivocal citizenship, indigenous post-emancipation in postcolonial Brazil exposed the relentless violence of forced national incorporation and the impossibility of maintaining territorial control in the face of unequal power. The limited citizenship and racialized exclusions that shaped indigenous lives would cast a long shadow on the future of freedpeople, overlapping black and indigenous temporalities of abolition and an uncertain post-emancipation in the transition from Empire to Republic.

Epilogue

The journey from southern Bahia to Rio de Janeiro today follows a
highway through endless rows of eucalyptus whose monotony may be as
disorienting as the Atlantic forest that overwhelmed the early nineteenth
century traveler. This impassive landscape recounts little of the histories
of the Atlantic frontier.

My interest in this region originated in the fortuitous union of two circumstances. My original project on quilombos in late nineteenth century
Salvador and its environs had reached an early dead end. A new path
appeared when two Rio-based anthropologists told me about a former
European colony-turned-slave plantation in the extreme south of Bahia.[1]
Research into the history of Colônia Leopoldina revealed an extraordinarily rich world of slave resistance. My findings took me completely by
surprise, as the region had barely registered among historians of slavery,
most of whom have focused on major cities and plantation zones. As
my research took me further south into São Mateus, my interest was
also piqued by the curious overlaps and divergences between the archival
record and vibrant oral histories of slavery, recorded by a local historian
in the 1960s and 1970s. The quilombola Benedito in my archival findings
was killed around age thirty but in oral history met his violent end at an
old age. Rather than indicating the accuracy of one record over another,
this was a powerful testament to the legacies of slavery in the region and
Benedito's enduring significance in popular memory.[2] Clearly, the region
was no uneventful backwater in the history of Brazilian slavery.

---

[1] For this I am deeply indebted to Olivia Gomes da Cunha and Martin Ossowicki.
[2] Maciel de Aguiar, *Os últimos zumbis: a saga dos negros do Vale do Cricaré durante a
    escravidão* (Porto Seguro: Brasil-Cultura Editora, 2001), 221–29; *Brincantes & quilom-
    bolas* (São Mateus: Memorial, 2005).

Yet in another regard, my findings were deeply troubling. The archives were a treasure trove of slave uprisings, quilombos, and insurrection rumors. But document after document also mentioned local indigenous populations, often by the name Botocudo and almost invariably in violent conflict with settlers. Furthermore, these enslaved and indigenous people resided in the same geographic region where Bahia, Espírito Santo, and Minas Gerais met, but their lives barely overlapped in the archive, as if they inhabited mirroring worlds. Such a sense was reinforced by the few, important studies of the Botocudo, in which African-descended people appeared only fleetingly in the margins.

The plethora of indigenous sources in the nineteenth century posed a problem for a historian like me, who had approached Brazilian history through the framework of slavery and the African diaspora. This conventional approach is built on the widely established idea that Brazil's legacies of slavery and the "disappearance" of indigenous populations outside of the Amazon region have engendered Latin America's largest African-descended population. Archival evidence of postcolonial indigenous populations – on the Atlantic littoral, of all places – fundamentally contradicted this idea and bore little connection to the scholarly attention showered on Romantic Indians. For the historian of slavery, then, there was a simple and admittedly tempting solution to this conundrum: putting the evidence aside. Our archival investigation can continue uninterrupted by selecting only those sources that affirm the racial narratives that shaped our original research. Yet to see how indigenous people were deliberately erased from the nation in the nineteenth century raised the uneasy prospect that a historian's ignoring the indigenous was a parallel act of archival violence.[3]

I thus decided to view this conundrum as an opportunity to understand Brazil's postcolonial history in a new way, to see how those seemingly mirroring black and indigenous worlds were actually one and the same. This meant understanding the central issues in postcolonial Brazilian and Latin American history – slavery and abolition, the unequal access to citizenship, and constructions of racialized hierarchies and national identity – through the interrelated histories of black and indigenous people.

What I have learned is that such a practice is not only possible, but necessary. For only then can we recognize the formation of inequalities embedded in the very construction of Brazil's inclusive citizenship. These

---

[3] Trouillot, Michel-Rolph. *Silencing the Past: Power and the Production of History* (Boston: Beacon Press, 2015).

findings enrich our understandings of African diasporic and indigenous experiences across the Americas, as new nations similarly grappled with the legacies of slavery and the limitations of liberal nationhood. I explored the ways in which the Brazilian nation was formed simultaneously on the frontier and at the center, the Atlantic frontier being the very space in which the relationship between race, nation, and citizenship were daily tested and defined. The convergence of African and indigenous slavery on the Atlantic frontier gave concrete meaning to the Constituent Assembly debates happening in Rio, where the new Constitution's drafters were delineating the boundaries of the national community. Economic reliance on slave labor joined with racial discourses of savagery to create people who were "outside of society." In the mid-nineteenth century, the implementation of postcolonial indigenous policy on the Atlantic frontier revealed the ominous consequences of *mestiçagem* as a national racial project. Celebrated by elites as a union of the "three races" that would engender a povo brasileiro, mestiçagem seamlessly melded indigenous policy with the Land Law, artistic representations, and anthropological scholarship to disappear indigenous people from the nation. In the 1870s and 1880s, the prospect of abolition fed racialized debates nationwide about black people's fitness for citizenship based on their supposed labor capacity. On the Atlantic frontier, a vision of servile citizenship was shared by abolitionists and missionaries, who proposed strikingly similar labor regimes for black and indigenous people that denied them autonomy. The battle to control black and indigenous labor and land converged, the right to the territory overlapping with the right to citizenship. This conflict remains a central concern throughout Brazil into the present day.

At the same time, the interrelatedness of black and indigenous histories forces us to reconsider the relationship we draw between popular politics and citizenship. Black and indigenous people's interpretations of, and responses to, nation-building projects on the Atlantic frontier show that their politics were not always expressed as a demand for greater citizenship. If enslaved people from the 1820s to the 1880s increasingly claimed greater rights, protection, and inclusion within the Brazilian nation on their own terms, for indigenous people, national inclusion was a coercive process whose ultimate objective was their extinction. Certainly there were those like Guido Pokrane who manipulated imperial patronage politics and Indians who strategically allied with settlers and missionaries. They did not, however, alter the fundamental terms of indigenous national inclusion: territorial loss and the impossibility of remaining indigenous. The years surrounding abolition again revealed black and indigenous people's radically different criticisms of their servile citizenship. At the heart of the freedpeople's uprising on Colônia Leopoldina were frustrated post-emancipation aspirations for a fuller citizenship to be realized in land ownership and self-sufficiency. The Botocudo on Itambacuri, on the other hand, waged war against the mission and the friars whose methods of Indian civilization, intended to bring them into the fold of citizenship, wreaked havoc on their very existence.

This book also questions the well-established narrative of the nineteenth century as the Atlantic World's "Age of Emancipation" that began with the Haitian Revolution and concluded with the abolition of Brazilian slavery in 1888. To recognize the struggle for black freedom taking place in the ambiguous aftermath of indigenous post-emancipation and ongoing illegal enslavement forces us to reconsider this liberatory trajectory. The age of antislavery engendered many forms of illegal and legal enslavement and coercive labor that would cast a shadow on the lives of women and men in Brazil and around the Atlantic World leading up to, and after, 1888. The politics of black liberation must be examined in relation to indigenous lives. Enslaved people's flight and geographic claims in the Atlantic frontier at times engendered solidarities with Indians but also threatened the latter's precarious territorial control. Abolitionist laws and black people's engagement with the legal system may be evidence of an expanding popular legal and political culture and a growing national concern with black citizenship. Our conclusions are tempered, however, by the absence of such laws and legal recourse for Indians, who were effectively placed outside of the nation's body of laws. Indigenous experiences thus demand that we reconsider the temporal, geographic, and racial contours of the Age of Emancipation.

Citizenship remains vital to Brazilian political culture today. As legal citizenship in the aftermath of the military dictatorship (1964–85) continues to legitimate inequalities, Brazilians of all walks of life have asserted their own definitions.[4] Here again, examining the contours of black and indigenous people's experiences together sheds light on the complexities of Brazilian citizenship and the different iterations of national belonging. Citizenship and land remain closely intertwined. Their relationship has assumed center stage in the political claims-making of African-descended communities, galvanized by the Unified Black Movement (MNU, founded

---

[4] Holston, James. *Insurgent Citizenship: Disjunctions of Democracy and Modernity in Brazil* (Princeton, NJ: Princeton University Press, 2008).

1978) and gaining momentum through the 1988 Constitution. Article 68 of the Constitution stated that "definitive ownership will be recognized, and the respective title will be issued by the State, to those descendants [*remanescentes*] of the quilombos occupying their lands." The federal government's Palmares Cultural Foundation subsequently expanded the definition of a quilombo in 1994 to mean "any black rural community composed of descendants from slaves, who survive through subsistence agriculture, with cultural manifestations strongly linked to the past." This was later expanded again to include urban communities and other reinterpretations of African cultural legacies.[5]

Propelling the transformation of what constituted a quilombo from a historical community of fugitive slaves was the concerted action of rural Afro-descendants, urban black activists, nongovernmental organizations, scholars, and progressive legislators. Together they "transformed the legal figure of the *quilombo*-descendants into a form of compensation for slavery, a settlement for Brazil's debt with Afro-descendants since slavery's abolition in 1888." The right to land ownership thus became a means to claim a fuller citizenship, dovetailing with Afro-Brazilians' claims to the land forged during slavery and after emancipation.[6] In the process, the quilombo has become a state-guaranteed right. Ilka Boaventura Leite has shown how "from being a form of opposition to the regime of slavery, the quilombo thus came to signify the enjoyment of full citizenship through its inclusion in land tenure regularization, housing, health, and educational and cultural policies." The quilombo's historical practice of resistance now "represents part of the grounds for state recognition," and in the process, resistance becomes integrated into the "body of the nation."[7]

These familiar words of nineteenth-century liberal statesman José Bonifácio, whose vision it was to bring Indians into a homogeneous national body through assimilation and miscegenation, are now evoked to understand quilombo recognition. With land rights bringing to the fore more expansive rights, quilombo recognition is a form of reparations that promises the greater inclusion of Afro-descendants into Brazilian

---

[5] Ilka Boaventura Leite, "The Transhistorical, Juridical-Formal, and Post-Utopian Quilombo," in *New Approaches to Resistance in Brazil and Mexico*, ed. John Gledhill and Patience A. Schell (Durham, NC: Duke University Press, 2012), 251.

[6] de la Torre, *People of the River: Nature, Community, and Identity in Black Amazonia, 1835–1945* (Chapel Hill: University of North Carolina Press, forthcoming), 3–4; Chapter 5.

[7] Leite, "Transhistorical Quilombo," 262–63.

citizenship. However, understanding quilombos as an exercise and claim of citizenship is not a post-1988 phenomenon. We hear echoes of the quilombolas of São Mateus of the 1880s, whose "insurgent geographies" were a political practice of citizenship that expressed their own terms of national inclusion, rather than signaling their isolation. In that sense, quilombos were not redefined beginning in 1988, but have been constantly reinventing their relationship to the dominant society and express the broader aspirations of black communities during and after slavery.

What then of Indians? The 1824 Constitution left citizenship open to Brazilian-born slaves, once freed, but maintained a silence on indigenous citizenship. Their ambiguous citizenship, whose violent and exclusionary consequences we have witnessed in this book, has continued to cast its shadow on the present. The orphan status conferred on Indians freed from slavery on the conclusion of the Botocudo Wars in 1831 was reaffirmed in the 1916 Civil Code of the First Republic, which maintained Indians' legal incapacity until they became "adapted to the civilization of the country." In 1928 Indians were transformed into wards (*tutela*) of the state, a condition reaffirmed by the 1973 Indian Statute.[8] The coerced assimilation and territorial loss that served as preconditions for Indians' citizenship in the nineteenth century was also echoed in the idea of "emancipation" – of releasing all Indians from *tutela* and integrating them into national society as full citizens – that was floated by the military dictatorship in 1978. As Alcida Ramos has shown, while the government claimed that emancipation would pave the way for "Indians to become politicians, generals, and even presidents of the Republic," its real intention was to remove state protection of Indian lands, making them available for privatization. Vehement opposition from the public and many indigenous groups led to the proposal's abandonment.[9] A dramatic change seemed to arrive with the 1988 Constitution which, for the first time in Brazilian

---

[8] Tracy Devine Guzmán, *Native and National in Brazil: Indigeneity after Independence* (Chapel Hill: University of North Carolina Press, 2013), 42–43; Alcida Rita Ramos, *Indigenism: Ethnic Politics in Brazil* (Madison: The University of Wisconsin Press, 1998), 18–19, 98.

[9] Article 9 of the 1973 Indian Statute, echoing older assimilationist views, states that individual Indians who are integrated into the "national communion" may request legal emancipation from *tutela* status. On 1978, see Alcida Rita Ramos, "A Hall of Mirrors: The Rhetoric of Indigenism in Brazil," *Critique of Anthropology* 11, no. 2 (1991): 164. Significantly, the Brazilian state denies Indians full land ownership. They are only allowed to possess the land – i.e., have the exclusive usufruct of all resources that exist on their land – but not the subsoil. The Union is the proprietor; the Indians are the possessors. Ramos, *Indigenism*, 96–97, 244–45.

history, recognized indigenous identities as a legitimate permanent state and no longer a temporary condition on the way to full assimilation. The 1988 Constitution also *implied* the end of Indians' state wardship by recognizing their capacity to represent themselves in court. However, because the 1973 Indian Statute was never repealed and thus remains in effect, and the government agency FUNAI (National Indian Foundation) continues to offer special protections to Indians, it is at best unclear whether Brazilian Indians today remain wards.[10]

Ironically, it was also the military dictatorship that created an opening for indigenous land rights. The 1973 Indian Statute stated in Article 3 that "Indian or forest dweller is every individual of pre-Columbian origin and ancestry who identifies himself and is identified as belonging to an ethnic group whose cultural characteristics distinguish him from the national society." Jan French has shown how this law, whose original intention was to facilitate the military government's colonization of the Amazon region by demarcating indigenous territories and relocating indigenous populations, became reinterpreted in the Northeast. Article 3 presented an opportunity that allowed assimilated people to self-identify as Indian and gain state recognition and land usufruct rights, since as long as Indians are legally recognized as such, the law protects the inalienability of their lands.[11] And if being "outside of society" was precisely what had led members of the Constituent Assembly in the 1820s to exclude "wild," autonomous Indians such as the Botocudo from Brazilian citizenship, in this new statutory definition, self-ascription and official recognition as Indians distinct "from the national society" was precisely what garnered them state-sponsored land rights – in exchange for relinquishing full citizenship.[12] Perhaps the most intriguing consequence of these new "legalized identities" has been that whereas nineteenth-century indigenous policy, science, and violence had collectively made Indians "disappear" from much of the national territory, today the process of reverse assimilation opened up by these legislations is leading Indians to "reappear," since "if some people can cease being Indians, there is no impediment for others to become Indians."[13]

To explore the meanings and forms of black and indigenous citizenship today thus challenges us once again to resist the homogenizing

---

[10] Ramos, *Indigenism*, 259–60; Jan French, personal communication.
[11] Jan French, *Legalizing Identities: Becoming Black or Indian in Brazil's Northeast* (Chapel Hill: University of North Carolina Press, 2009), 69; Ramos, *Indigenism*, 244.
[12] French, *Legalizing Identities*, 63–64; Guzmán, *Native and National in Brazil*, 42.
[13] French, *Legalizing Identities*, 68–69 and personal communication.

temptations of citizenship and liberal nationhood. Official recognition as *remanescentes de quilombos* is an avenue to a fuller citizenship for Afro-Brazilian people that centers on land recognition but extends to much more expansive rights, from housing to education. Recognition as Indians, by contrast, rests on the renunciation of full citizenship rights but provides rights over the land and other benefits in exchange. All this must occur within the purview of the state.[14] If these are imperfect solutions of a nation reluctant to fully embrace difference among its residents and accept alternative modes of citizenship, the histories of black and indigenous people of the nineteenth-century Atlantic frontier and today speak to other modalities that continue to challenge these terms of national belonging. They show us new ways of thinking about our present, past, and possible futures, and the stories we tell about them.

[14] Leite, "Transhistorical Quilombo," 262; Guzmán, *Native and National in Brazil*, 48.

Bibliography

Archives

Rio de Janeiro, Brazil
  Arquivo Nacional
  Biblioteca Nacional
  Instituto Histórico e Geográfico Brasileiro
  Museu do Índio
  Arquivo dos Capuchinhos (courtesy of José Bessa, UERJ)
Bahia, Brazil
  Arquivo Público do Estado da Bahia, Salvador
  Co-Catedral do Santo Antônio de Caravelas
Espírito Santo, Brazil
  Arquivo Público do Estado do Espírito Santo, Vitória
  Cartório do Primeiro Ofício, São Mateus
Lisbon, Portugal
  Arquivo Histórico Ultramarino

Newspapers and Serials

Almanak Administrativo, Mercantil e Industrial da Bahia (BA)
Almanak (ES)
Correio Mercantil (RJ)
Correio Paulistano (SP)
Diario do Rio de Janeiro (RJ)
Espírito Santense (ES)
Estandarte (ES)
Folha da Victoria (ES)
Gazeta da Bahia (BA)
Liberal Mineiro (MG)
Norte do Espírito Santo (ES)
Philantropo (RJ)

Província do Espírito Santo (ES)
Revista Ilustrada (RJ)

Brazilian Provincial Presidential Speeches and Reports (*Fallas* and *Relatórios*) from Bahia, Espírito Santo, and Minas Gerais, 1823–1889. Available at the Center for Research Libraries Brazilian Government Documents Collection (www-apps.crl.edu/brazil).

Brazilian Ministerial Reports (Empire; Justice; Agriculture, including Indians). Available at the Center for Research Libraries Brazilian Government Documents Collection (www-apps.crl.edu/brazil).

Printed Primary Sources

Agassiz, Louis, and Elizabeth Cabot Cary Agassiz. *A Journey in Brazil*. Boston: Ticknor and Fields, 1868.

Aguiar, Durval Vieira de. *Descripções praticas da provincia da Bahia com declaração de todas a distancias intermediarias das cidades, villas e povoações*. Bahia: Typographia do "Diario da Bahia," 1888.

Alencar, José Martiniano de. *Iracema: A Novel*. Translated by Clifford E. Landers. New York: Oxford University Press, 2000.

Almeida, Hermenegildo Antonio Barbosa d'. "Viagem ás vilas de Caravelas, Viçosa, Porto Alegre, de Mucury, e aos rios Mucury, e Peruípe." *RIHGB* 8, no. 4 (1846): 425–52.

Almeida, Miguel Calmon du Pin e. *Ensaio sobre of fabrico do açucar*. Edited by José de F. Mascarenhas, Waldir Freitas Oliveira, and José Honório Rodrigues. Salvador: FIEB, 2002.

Memoria sobre o estabelecimento d'uma companhia de colonisação nesta provincia. Salvador: Typographia do Diario de G. J. Bezerra e cia, 1835.

Anais do Senado do Império do Brasil. 2a sessão da 18a legislatura. Vol. IV. Rio de Janeiro: Typographia Nacional, 1882.

Annaes do Parlamento brazileiro, Assembléa constituinte, 1823, Vol. 5. Rio de Janeiro: H. J. Pinto, 1880.

Argollo, M. de Teive e. *Memoria descriptiva sobre a Estrada de Ferro Bahia e Minas*. Rio de Janeiro: H. Laemmert, 1883.

Avé-Lallemant, Robert. *Viagem pelo norte do Brasil no ano de 1859*. Rio de Janeiro: Instituto Nacional do Livro, Ministério da Educação e Cultura, 1961.

Azambuja, Bernardo Augusto Nascentes de. *Relatório sobre as colônias ao sul da província da Bahia, apresentado ao Ministério da Agricultura, Commércio, e Obras Públicas*. Rio de Janeiro: Typographia Nacional, 1874.

Barbosa, Januário da Cunha. "Se a introdução dos escravos africanos no Brasil embaraça a civilização dos nossos indígenas, dispensando-se-lhes o trabalho, que todo foi confiado a escravos negros. Neste caso qual é o prejuizo que sofre a lavoura Brasileira." *RIHGB* 1, no. 3 (1839): 123–33.

Bonifácio, José. *Projetos para o Brasil*. Edited by Miriam Dolhnikoff. São Paulo: Companhia das Letras, 1998.

Brazil. *Código criminal do imperio do Brazil annotado com as leis, decretos, avisos e portarias publicados desde a sua data até o presente, e que explicão, revogão ou alterão algumas das suas disposições, ou com ellas tem immediata connexão.* Rio de Janeiro: A. Goncalves Guimarães, 1860.

Brazil, and Directoria Geral de Estatística. *Recenseamento da população do Imperio do Brazil a que se procedeu no dia 1°. de agosto de 1872.* Rio de Janeiro: A Directoria, 1873.

Cardim, Fernão. *Tratados da terra e gente do Brasil.* Edited by Ana Maria de Azevedo. Lisboa: Comissão Nacional para as Comemorações dos Descobrimentos Portugueses, 1997.

Companhia do Mucury. História da empresa. Importância dos seus privilégios. Alcance de seus projetos. Rio de Janeiro: Typographia Imperial e Constitucional de J. Villeneuve e comp., 1856.

Costa, João Severiano Maciel da. *Memória sobre a necessidade de abolir a introdução dos escravos africanos no Brasil: sobre o modo e condições com que esta abolição se deve fazer; e sobre os meios de remediar a falta de braços que ela pode ocasionar.* Coimbra: Imprensa da Universidade, 1821.

Costa, José Candido da. *Comarca de Caravellas. Creacão de uma nova província, sendo capital a cidade de Caravellas.* Bahia: Typographia de Camillo de Lellis Masson & C., 1857.

Couty, Louis. *L'esclavage au Brésil.* Paris: Librairie de Guillaumin, 1881.

O Brasil em 1884: esboços sociológicos. Brasília and Rio de Janeiro: Senado Federal, Casa Rui Barbosa, 1984.

Cunha, Manuela Carneiro da, ed. *Legislação indigenista no século XIX: uma compilação (1808–1889).* São Paulo: EDUSP, 1992.

Debret, Jean-Baptiste. *Viagem pitoresca e histórica ao Brasil, T.1.* São Paulo: Livraria Martins, 1954.

Ewbank, Thomas. *Life in Brazil, Or, A Journal of a Visit to the Land of the Cocoa and the Palm with an Appendix, Containing Illustrations of Ancient South American Arts.* New York: Harper & Brothers, 1856.

Fonseca, Luís Anselmo da. *A escravidão, o clero e o abolicionismo.* Bahia: Imprensa Economica, 1887.

Freyreiss, Georg W. "Viagem ao interior do Brasil nos annos de 1814–1815." *Revista do Instituto Historico e Geographico de São Paulo* XI (1906): 158–228.

Hartt, Charles Frederick. *Thayer Expedition: Scientific Results of a Journey in Brazil, by Louis Agassiz and His Travelling Companions: Geology and Physical Geography.* Boston: Fields, Osgood & Co., 1870.

Lacerda, João Batista. "A força muscular e a delicadeza dos sentidos dos nossos indigenas." In Melo Morais Filho (ed.), *Revista da Exposição Antropologica Brasileira,* 6–7. Rio de Janeiro: Typographia de Pinheiro & C., 1882.

Lacerda, João Batista, and José Rodrigues Peixoto. "Contribução para o estudo anthropologico das raças indígenas do Brasil." *Arquivos do Museu Nacional* 1 (1876): 47–75.

Magalhães, José Vieira Couto de. *Anchieta, as raças e linguas indigenas.* São Paulo: C. Gerke & Cia., 1897.

Malheiro, Agostinho Marques Perdigão. *A escravidão no Brasil, ensaio histórico-jurídico-social.* Vols. 1 and 2. Rio de Janeiro: Typographia Nacional, 1866.

Martius, Karl Friedrich von. "Como se deve escrever a História do Brasil." *Revista de Historia de América* 42 (1956): 433–58.

Naud, Leda Maria Cardoso. "Documentos sôbre o índio brasileiro, 2a parte." *Revista de informação legislativa* 8, no. 29 (1971): 227–336.

Ottoni, Teófilo Benedito. *Breve resposta que ao relatório da liquidaçõ da companhia do Mucury por parte do governo.* Rio de Janeiro: Typographia de M. Barreto, 1862.

Condições para a encorporação de uma companhia de commercio e navegação do rio Mucury, precedidas de uma exposição das vantagens da empreza. Rio de Janeiro: Typographia de J. Villeneuve, 1847.

Notícia sobre os selvagens do Mucuri. Belo Horizonte: Editora UFMG, 2002.

Pacó, Domingos Ramos. "Hámbric anhamprán ti mattâ nhiñchopón? 1918." In *Lembranças da terra: histórias do Mucuri e Jequitinhonha,* ed. Eduardo Magalhães Ribeiro, 198–211. Belo Horizonte: CEDEFES, 1996.

Patrocínio, José do. "O grande projeto (May 5, 1887)." In *Oito anos de parlamento,* by Afonso Celso. Biblioteca básica brasileira. Brasília: Senado Federal, 1998.

Pederneiras, Innocencio Velloso. *Commissão de exploração do Mucury e Gequitinhonha. Interesses materiaes das comarcas do sul da Bahia. Comarcas de Caravellas e Porto Seguro. Relatório do capitão do imperial corpo d'engenheiros, I.V. Pederneiras, chefe da mesma commisão.* Bahia: Typographia de João Alves Portella, 1851.

Reinault, Pedro Victor. "Relatorio da exposição dos rios Mucury e Todos os Santos, feita por ordem do Exm. governo de Minas Geraes pelo engenheiro Pedro Victor Reinault, tendentes a procurar um ponto para degredo." *RIHGB* 8 (1846): 356–75.

Saint-Hilaire, Auguste de. *Segunda viagem ao interior do Brasil, Espírito Santo.* Translated by Carlos Madeira. São Paulo: Companhia Editora Nacional, 1936.

Viagem pelas províncias de Rio de Janeiro e Minas Geraes, Vol. 2. São Paulo: Companhia Editora Nacional, 1938.

Schwartz, Stuart B., ed. *Early Brazil: A Documentary Collection to 1700.* New York: Cambridge University Press, 2010.

Sluiter, Engel. "Report on the State of Brazil, 1612." *HAHR* 29, no. 4 (November 1, 1949): 518–62.

Sousa, Gabriel Soares de. *Tratado Descritivo do Brasil em 1587.* Edited by Francisco Adolpho de Varnhagen. Recife: Fundação Joaquim Nabuco Massangana, 2000.

Steains, Wm. John. "An Exploration of the Rio Doce and Its Northern Tributaries (Brazil)." *Proceedings of the Royal Geographical Society and Monthly Record of Geography* 10, no. 2 (February 1, 1888): 61–84.

Taunay, Carlos Augusto. *Manual do agricultor brasileiro.* Edited by Rafael de Bivar Marquese. São Paulo: Companhia das Letras, 2001.

Tölsner, Karl August. *Die colonie Leopoldina in Brasilien. Schilderung des anbaus und der gewinnung der wichtigsten, dort erzeugten culturproducte, namentlich des kaffees, sowie einiger anderen.* Göttingen: Gebrüder Hofer, 1860.

Tovar, Manoel Vieira de Albuquerque. "Informação de Manoel Vieira de Albuquerque Tovar sobre a navegação importantissima do Rio Doce, copiada de un manuscrito oferecido ao Instituto pelo socio correspondente o Sr. José Domingues de Athaide de Moncorvo." *RIHGB* 1 (1839): 134–38.

Tschudi, Johann Jakob von. *Reisen durch Südamerika.* Leipzig: F. A. Brockhaus, 1866.

Varnhagen, Francisco Adolfo de. "Memorial orgânico – Offerecido á nação." Guanabara: *Revista mensal, artística, scientifica e litteraria Tomo I* (1851): 356-402.

Os Indios bravos e o sr. Lisboa, Timon 3: Pelo autor da "Historia geral do Brazil." Apostilla e nota G aos nos. 11 e 12 do "Jornal de Timon"; contendo 26 cartas ineditas do jornalista, e um extracto do folheto "Diatribe contra a Timonice," etc. Lima: Imprensa Liberal, 1867.

Vasconcellos, Ignacio Accioly de. *Memoria Statistica da Provincia do Espírito Santo no Anno de 1828.* Vitória: Arquivo Público Estadual, 1978.

Vianna, Francisco Vicente, and José Carlos Ferreira. *Memória sobre o estado da Bahia.* Bahia: Typographia e encadernação do "Diario da Bahia," 1893.

Wied-Neuwied, Maximilian. *Viagem ao Brasil nos anos de 1815 a 1817.* São Paulo: Companhia Editora Nacional, 1958.

Secondary Sources

Abreu, João Capistrano de. *Chapters of Brazil's Colonial History, 1500–1800.* Translated by Arthur Brakel. New York: Oxford University Press, 1998.

Abreu, Martha. "Slave Mothers and Freed Children: Emancipation and Female Space in Debates on the 'Free Womb' Law, Rio de Janeiro, 1871." *JLAS* 28, no. 3 (1996): 567–80.

Meninas perdidas: os populares e o cotidiano do amor no Rio de Janeiro da belle époque. Rio de Janeiro: Paz e Terra, 1989.

Agamben, Giorgio. *Homo Sacer: Sovereign Power and Bare Life.* Stanford, CA: Stanford University Press, 1998.

Aguiar, Maciel de. *Os últimos zumbis: a saga dos negros do Vale do Cricaré durante a escravidão.* Porto Seguro: Brasil-Cultura Editora, 2001.

Brincantes & quilombolas. São Mateus: Memorial, 2005.

Alberto, Paulina L. *Terms of Inclusion: Black Intellectuals in Twentieth-Century Brazil.* Chapel Hill: University of North Carolina Press, 2011.

Albuquerque, Wlamyra Ribeiro de. *O jogo da dissimulação: abolição e cidadania negra no Brasil.* São Paulo: Companhia das Letras, 2009.

Algranti, Leila Mezan. *O feitor ausente: estudo sobre a escravidão urbana no Rio de Janeiro.* Petrópolis: Vozes, 1988.

Almada, Vilma Paraíso Ferreira de. *Escravismo e transição: o Espírito Santo (1850–1888).* Rio de Janeiro: Graal, 1984.

Almeida, Maria Regina Celestino de. "Reflexões sobre política indigenista e cultura política indígena no Rio de Janeiro oitocentista." *Revista USP* 79 (2008): 94–105.

"Índios mestiços e selvagens civilizados de Debret." *Varia Historia* 25, no. 41 (June 2009): 85–106.

Anderson, Benedict R. O'G. *Imagined Communities: Reflections on the Origin and Spread of Nationalism*. London; New York: Verso, 1991.

Andrews, George Reid. *Blacks & Whites in São Paulo, Brazil, 1888–1988*. Madison: University of Wisconsin Press, 1991.

Afro-Latin America, 1800–2000. Oxford: Oxford University Press, 2004.

Appelbaum, Nancy P., Anne S. Macpherson, and Karin Alejandra Rosemblatt, eds. *Race and Nation in Modern Latin America*. Chapel Hill: University of North Carolina Press, 2003.

Araujo, Ana Lucia. *Brazil through French Eyes: A Nineteenth-Century Artist in the Tropics*. Albuquerque: University of New Mexico Press, 2015.

Azevedo, Celia Maria Marinho de. *Onda negra, medo branco: o negro no imaginário das elites – século XIX*. Rio de Janeiro: Paz e Terra, 1987.

Maçonaria, anti-racismo e cidadania: uma história de lutas e debates transnacionais. São Paulo: Annablume, 2010.

Azevedo, Elciene. *Orfeu de carapinha: a trajetória de Luiz Gama na imperial cidade de São Paulo*. Campinas, SP: Editora UNICAMP, 1999.

"Para além dos tribunais: advogados e escravos no movimento abolicionista em São Paulo." In *Direitos e justiças no Brasil: ensaios de história social*, ed. Silvia Hunold Lara and Joseli Maria Nunes Mendonça, 199–238. Campinas, SP: Editora UNICAMP, 2006.

Barickman, B. J. "'A Bit of Land, Which They Call Roça': Slave Provision Grounds in the Bahian Recôncavo, 1780–1860." *HAHR* 74, no. 4 (1994): 649–87.

"'Tame Indians,' 'Wild Heathens,' and Settlers in Southern Bahia in the Late Eighteenth and Early Nineteenth Centuries." *The Americas* 51, no. 3 (January 1, 1995): 325–68.

"Persistence and Decline: Slave Labour and Sugar Production in the Bahian Recôncavo, 1850–1888." *JLAS* 28, no. 03 (October 1996): 581–633.

A Bahian Counterpoint: Sugar, Tobacco, Cassava, and Slavery in the Recôncavo, 1780–1860. Stanford, CA: Stanford University Press, 1998.

Barman, Roderick J. *Brazil: The Forging of a Nation, 1798–1852*. Stanford, CA: Stanford University Press, 1988.

Barr, Juliana. *Peace Came in the Form of a Woman: Indians and Spaniards in the Texas Borderlands*. Chapel Hill: University of North Carolina Press, 2007.

Beattie, Peter M. "'Born Under the Cruel Rigor of Captivity, the Supplicant Left It Unexpectedly by Committing a Crime': Categorizing and Punishing Slave Convicts in Brazil, 1830–1897." *The Americas* 66, no. 1 (2009): 11–55.

"Slaves, Crime, and Punishment in Imperial Brazil." *Luso-Brazilian Review* 45, no. 2 (2009): 191–93.

Punishment in Paradise: Race, Slavery, Human Rights, and a Nineteenth-Century Brazilian Penal Colony. Durham, NC: Duke University Press, 2015.

Beckles, Hilary. *Centering Woman: Gender Relations in Caribbean Slave Society*. Kingston: Ian Randle and Oxford: James Currey, 1999.

Natural Rebels: A Social History of Enslaved Black Women in Barbados. New Brunswick, NJ: Rutgers University Press, 2000.

Berlin, Ira, and Philip D. Morgan, eds. *The Slaves' Economy: Independent Production by Slaves in the Americas*. London: Frank Cass, 1995.

Bieber, Judy. "Of Cannibals and Frenchmen: The Production of Ethnographic Knowledge in Early Nineteenth-Century Brazil." *Interletras: Revista Transdisciplinar de Letras, Educação e Cultura* 1, no. 5 (December 2006). www.interletras.com.br/ed_anteriores/n5/arquivos/v5/artigointerestudosSneadWertheimEliane.pdf.

"Catechism and Capitalism: Imperial Indigenous Policy on a Brazilian Frontier, 1808–1845." In *Native Brazil: Beyond the Convert and the Cannibal, 1500–1900*, ed. Hal Langfur, 166–97. Albuquerque: University of New Mexico Press, 2014.

"Mediation through Militarization: Indigenous Soldiers and Transcultural Middlemen of the Rio Doce Divisions, Minas Gerais, Brazil, 1808–1850." *The Americas* 71, no. 2 (2014): 227–54.

"'Philadelphia' in Minas Gerais: Teófilo Otoni's North American Vision for Indigenous Brazil," paper presented at Linguistic and Other Cultural Exchanges across Brazilian History: The Indigenous Role, University of Chicago, Chicago, IL, October 2016.

Bittencourt, Gabriel Augusto de Mello. *Café e modernização: O Espírito Santo no século 19*. Rio de Janeiro: Ed. Cátedra, 1987.

Brantlinger, Patrick. *Dark Vanishings: Discourse on the Extinction of Primitive Races, 1800–1930*. Ithaca, NY: Cornell University Press, 2003.

Brito, Jailton Lima. *A abolição na Bahia, 1870–1888*. Salvador: EDUFBA, 2003.

Brown, Alexandra K. "'A Black Mark on Our Legislation': Slavery, Punishment, and the Politics of Death in Nineteenth-Century Brazil." *Luso-Brazilian Review* 37, no. 2 (December 1, 2000): 95–121.

Brown, Kathleen M. *Good Wives, Nasty Wenches, and Anxious Patriarchs: Gender, Race, and Power in Colonial Virginia*. Chapel Hill: University of North Carolina Press, 1996.

Brown, Vincent. *The Reaper's Garden: Death and Power in the World of Atlantic Slavery*. Cambridge, MA: Harvard University Press, 2008.

Bush, Barbara. *Slave Women in Caribbean Society: 1650–1838*. Kingston: Heinemann, 1990.

Cadena, Marisol de la. *Indigenous Mestizos: The Politics of Race and Culture in Cuzco, Peru, 1919–1991*. Durham, NC: Duke University Press, 2000.

Camp, Stephanie M. H. *Closer to Freedom: Enslaved Women and Everyday Resistance in the Plantation South*. Chapel Hill: University of North Carolina Press, 2004.

Campbell, Gwyn, Suzanne Miers, and Joseph Calder Miller, eds. *Women and Slavery*. 2 vols. Athens: Ohio University Press, 2008.

Carmo, Alane Fraga do. *Colonização e escravidão na Bahia: a Colônia Leopoldina (1850–1888)*. M. A. thesis, Universidade Federal da Bahia, 2010.

Carroll, Patrick J. "Black-Native Relations and the Historical Record." In *Beyond Black and Red: African-Native Relations in Colonial Latin America*, ed. Matthew Restall, 245–67. Albuquerque: University of New Mexico Press, 2005.

Carvalho, José Murilo de. *Cidadania no Brasil: o longo caminho*. Rio de Janeiro: Civilização Brasileira, 2001.

Carvalho, Marcus J. M. de. *Liberdade: rotinas e rupturas do escravismo no Recife, 1822–1850*. Recife: Editora Universitária UFPE, 1998.

Castilho, Celso Thomas. *Slave Emancipation and Transformations in Brazilian Political Citizenship*. Pittsburgh: University of Pittsburgh Press, 2016.

Castro, Hebe Maria Mattos de. *Das cores do silêncio: os significados da liberdade no sudeste escravista, Brasil século XIX*. Rio de Janeiro: Arquivo Nacional, 1995.

Escravidão e cidadania no Brasil monárquico. Rio de Janeiro: Jorge Zahar, 2000.

Caulfield, Sueann. *In Defense of Honor: Sexual Morality, Modernity, and Nation in Early-Twentieth Century Brazil*. Durham, NC: Duke University Press, 2000.

Chalhoub, Sidney. *Visões da liberdade: uma história das últimas décadas da escravidão na corte*. São Paulo: Companhia das Letras, 1990.

"The Politics of Silence: Race and Citizenship in Nineteenth-Century Brazil." *Slavery & Abolition* 27, no. 1 (April 2006): 73–87.

"The Precariousness of Freedom in a Slave Society (Brazil in the Nineteenth Century)." *International Review of Social History* 56, no. 03 (2011): 405–39.

A força da escravidão: ilegalidade e costume no Brasil oitocentista. São Paulo: Companhia das Letras, 2012.

Childs, Matt D. *The 1812 Aponte Rebellion in Cuba and the Struggle against Atlantic Slavery*. Chapel Hill: University of North Carolina Press, 2009.

Claudio, Affonso. *Insurreição do Queimado: episódio da história da Província do Espírito Santo*. Vitória, E.S.: Editora da Fundação Ceciliano Abel de Almeida, 1979.

Côgo, Anna Lucia. *História do Espírito Santo no século XIX: a região de São Mateus*. Doctoral dissertation, Universidade de São Paulo, 2007.

Conrad, Robert. *The Destruction of Brazilian Slavery, 1850–1888*. Berkeley: University of California Press, 1972.

"Neither Slave nor Free: The *Emancipados* of Brazil, 1818–1868." *HAHR* 53, no. 1 (1973): 50–70.

Corzo, Gabino La Rosa. "Subsistence of Cimarrones: An Archaeological Study." In *Dialogues in Cuban Archaeology*, ed. L. Antonio Curet, Shannon Lee Dawdy, and Gabino La Rosa Corzo, 163–80. Tuscaloosa: University of Alabama Press, 2005.

Costa, Emília Viotti da. *Da senzala à colônia*. São Paulo: Editora da UNESP, 1997.

The Brazilian Empire: Myths & Histories. Chapel Hill: University of North Carolina Press, 2000.

Cowling, Camillia. "Debating Womanhood, Defining Freedom: The Abolition of Slavery in 1880s Rio de Janeiro." *Gender & History* 22, no. 2 (2010): 284–301.

Cunha, Euclides da. *Rebellion in the Backlands (Os Sertões)*. Chicago: University of Chicago Press, 1944.
Cunha, Manuela Carneiro da. *Negros, estrangeiros: os escravos libertos e sua volta à África*. São Paulo: Ed. Brasiliense, 1985.
Antropologia do Brasil: mito, história, etnicidade. São Paulo: Editora Brasiliense, 1986.
História dos índios no Brasil. Rio de Janeiro: Editora Schwarcz, 1992.
Cunha, Olivia Maria Gomes da, and Flávio dos Santos Gomes, eds. *Quase-cidadão: histórias e antropologias da pós-emancipação no Brasil*. Rio de Janeiro: Editora FGV, 2007.
Danner, Mark. *The Massacre at El Mozote: A Parable of the Cold War*. New York: Vintage Books, 1994.
Das, Veena, and Deborah Poole, eds. *Anthropology in the Margins of the State*. Santa Fe: School of American Research Press and Oxford: James Curry, 2004.
Dean, Warren. *Rio Claro: A Brazilian Plantation System, 1820–1920*. Stanford, CA: Stanford University Press, 1976.
"The Frontier in Brazil." In *Frontier in Comparative Perspectives: The United States and Brazil*, 15–27. Washington, DC: Latin American Program, Wilson Center, 1990.
With Broadax and Firebrand: The Destruction of the Brazilian Atlantic Coastal Forest. Berkeley: University of California Press, 1995.
de la Torre, Oscar. *The People of the River: Nature, Community, and Identity in Black Amazonia, 1835–1945*. Chapel Hill: University of North Carolina Press, In press.
Delrio, Walter, and Claudia N. Briones. "The 'Conquest of the Desert' as a Trope and Enactment of Argentina's Manifest Destiny." In *Manifest Destinies and Indigenous Peoples*, ed. David Maybury-Lewis, Theodore Macdonald, and Biorn Maybury-Lewis, 51–83. Cambridge, MA: Harvard University Press, 2009.
Delrio, Walter. *Memorias de expropiación: sometimiento e incorporación indígena en la Patagonia, 1872–1943*. Bernal, Buenos Aires: Universidad Nacional de Quilmes, 2005.
Díaz, María Elena. *The Virgin, the King, and the Royal Slaves of El Cobre: Negotiating Freedom in Colonial Cuba, 1670–1780*. Stanford, CA: Stanford University Press, 2000.
Dubois, Laurent. *A Colony of Citizens: Revolution & Slave Emancipation in the French Caribbean, 1787–1804*. Chapel Hill: University of North Carolina Press; Omohundro Institute, 2004.
"An Enslaved Enlightenment: Rethinking the Intellectual History of the French Atlantic." *Social History* 31, no. 1 (February 1, 2006): 1–14.
"Avenging America: The Politics of Violence in the Haitian Revolution." In *The World of the Haitian Revolution*, ed. David Patrick Geggus and Norman Fiering, 111–24. Bloomington: Indiana University Press, 2009.
Earle, Rebecca. *The Return of the Native: Indians and Myth-Making in Spanish America, 1810–1930*. Durham, NC: Duke University Press, 2007.

Echeverri, Marcela. *Indian and Slave Royalists in the Age of Revolution: Reform, Revolution, and Royalism in the Northern Andes, 1780–1825.* New York: Cambridge University Press, 2016.

Eisenberg, Peter L. *The Sugar Industry in Pernambuco; Modernization without Change, 1840–1910.* Berkeley: University of California Press, 1974.

Ellis, Stephen. "Interpreting Violence: Reflection on the West African Wars." In *Violence,* ed. Neil L. Whitehead, 107–24. Santa Fe: School of American Research, 2004.

Espindola, Haruf Salmen. *Sertão do Rio Doce.* Governador Valadares, MG: Editora Univale, 2005.

Euraque, Darío. *Conversaciones históricas con el mestizaje y su identidad nacional en Honduras.* San Pedro Sula, Honduras: Centro Editorial, 2004.

Farias, Juliana Barreto, Flávio dos Santos Gomes, and Carlos Eugenio Libano Soares. *No labirinto das naçoes: africanos e identidades no Rio de Janeiro, século XIX.* Rio de Janeiro: Arquivo Nacional, 2005.

Fausto, Boris. *A Concise History of Brazil.* Cambridge: Cambridge University Press, 1998.

Ferreira, Ricardo Alexandre. *Senhores de poucos escravos: cativeiro e criminalidade num ambiente rural, 1830–1888.* São Paulo: Ed. UNESP, 2005.

Ferrer, Ada. *Insurgent Cuba: Race, Nation, and Revolution, 1868–1898.* Chapel Hill: University of North Carolina Press, 1999.

Fields, Barbara. *Slavery and Freedom on the Middle Ground: Maryland during the Nineteenth Century.* New Haven, CT: Yale University Press, 1987.

Fonseca, Hermógenes Lima da, and Rogério Medeiros. *Tradições populares no Espírito Santo.* Vitória: Departamento Estadual de Cultura, Divisão de Memória, 1991.

Fraga Filho, Walter. *Mendigos, moleques e vadios na Bahia do século XIX.* São Paulo: Editora Hucitec, 1996.

Encruzilhadas da liberdade: histórias de escravos e libertos na Bahia, 1870–1910. Campinas, SP: Editora UNICAMP, 2006.

French, Jan Hoffman. *Legalizing Identities: Becoming Black or Indian in Brazil's Northeast.* Chapel Hill: University of North Carolina Press, 2009.

Furtado, Júnia Ferreira. *Chica da Silva: A Brazilian Slave of the Eighteenth Century.* Cambridge: Cambridge University Press, 2009.

Gileno, Carlos Henrique. "A legislação indígena: ambigüidades na formação do Estado-nação no Brasil." *Caderno CRH* 20, no. 49 (April 2007): 123–33.

Godlewska, Anne, Neil Smith, and Jonathan Crush, eds. "Post-Colonialism, De-Colonization, and Geography." In *Geography and Empire.* Oxford and Cambridge, MA: Blackwell, 1994.

Gomes, Flávio dos Santos. "Quilombos do Rio de Janeiro no século XIX." In *Liberdade por um fio: história dos quilombos no Brasil,* ed. Flávio dos Santos Gomes and João José Reis, 263–90. São Paulo: Companhia das Letras, 1996.

A hidra e os pântanos: mocambos, quilombos e comunidades de fugitivos no Brasil (séculos XVII-XIX). São Paulo: Editora UNESP, 2005.

Palmares: escravidão e liberdade no Atlantico Sul. São Paulo: Ed. Contexto, 2005.

Histórias de quilombolas: mocambos e comunidades de senzalas no Rio de Janeiro, século XIX. São Paulo: Companhia das Letras, 2006.

"Roceiros, mocambeiros e as fronteiras da emancipação no Maranhão." In *Quase-cidadão: histórias e antropologias da pós-emancipação no Brasil,* ed. Olivia Maria Gomes da Cunha and Flávio dos Santos Gomes, 147–69. Rio de Janeiro: Editora FGV, 2007.

Gomes, Flávio dos Santos, and Carlos Eugênio Líbano Soares. "Sedições, haitianismo e conexões no Brasil: outras margens do atlântico negro." *Novos Estudos* 63 (2002): 131–44.

Gomes, Mércio Pereira. *The Indians and Brazil.* Gainesville: University Press of Florida, 2000.

Gomez, Michael A. *Exchanging Our Country Marks: The Transformation of African Identities in the Colonial and Antebellum South,* 1st ed. Chapel Hill: University of North Carolina Press, 1998.

Gotkowitz, Laura. *Histories of Race and Racism: The Andes and Mesoamerica from Colonial Times to the Present.* Durham, NC: Duke University Press, 2012.

Goulart, José Alipio. *Da fuga ao suicídio: aspectos da rebeldia do escravo no Brasil.* Rio de Janeiro: Conquista, 1972.

Graden, Dale Torston. *From Slavery to Freedom in Brazil: Bahia, 1835–1900.* Albuquerque: University of New Mexico Press, 2006.

Grinberg, Keila. "Freedom Suits and Civil Law in Brazil and the United States." *Slavery & Abolition* 22, no. 3 (2001): 66–82.

Código civil e cidadania. Rio de Janeiro: Jorge Zahar, 2008.

Guardino, Peter F. *Peasants, Politics, and the Formation of Mexico's National State: Guerrero, 1800–1857.* Stanford, CA: Stanford University Press, 1996.

Guy, Donna, and Thomas Sheridan, eds.*Contested Ground: Comparative Frontiers on the Northern and Southern Edges of the Spanish Empire.* Tucson: University of Arizona Press, 1998.

Guzmán, Tracy Devine. *Native and National in Brazil: Indigeneity after Independence.* Chapel Hill: University of North Carolina Press, 2013.

Haberly, David T. *Three Sad Races: Racial Identity and National Consciousness in Brazilian Literature.* Cambridge and New York: Cambridge University Press, 1983.

Hahn, Steven. "'Extravagant Expectations' of Freedom: Rumour, Political Struggle, and the Christmas Insurrection Scare of 1865 in the American South." *Past & Present* no. 157 (1997): 122–58.

Hall, Gwendolyn Midlo. *Slavery and African Ethnicities in the Americas: Restoring the Links.* Chapel Hill: University of North Carolina Press, 2005.

Hartman, Saidiya V. *Scenes of Subjection: Terror, Slavery, and Self-Making in Nineteenth-Century America.* New York: Oxford University Press, 1997.

Hemming, John. *Amazon Frontier: The Defeat of the Brazilian Indians.* Cambridge, MA: Harvard University Press, 1987.

Herzog, Tamar. *Frontiers of Possession: Spain and Portugal in Europe and the Americas.* Cambridge, MA: Harvard University Press, 2015.

Higgins, Kathleen J. *"Licentious Liberty" in a Brazilian Gold-Mining Region: Slavery, Gender, and Social Control in Eighteenth-Century Sabará, Minas Gerais*. University Park: Penn State University Press, 1999.

Holanda, Sérgio Buarque de. *Caminhos e fronteiras*. São Paulo: Companhia das Letras, 1995.

Holloway, Thomas H. *Policing Rio de Janeiro: Repression and Resistance in a 19th-Century City*. Stanford, CA: Stanford University Press, 1993.

Holston, James. *Insurgent Citizenship: Disjunctions of Democracy and Modernity in Brazil*. Princeton, NJ: Princeton University Press, 2008.

Holt, Thomas C. *The Problem of Freedom: Race, Labor, and Politics in Jamaica and Britain, 1832–1938*. Baltimore: Johns Hopkins University Press, 1992.

Howell, David L. *Geographies of Identity in Nineteenth-Century Japan*. Berkeley: University of California Press, 2005.

Hu-DeHart, Evelyn. *Yaqui Resistance and Survival: The Struggle for Land and Autonomy, 1821–1910*. Madison: University of Wisconsin Press, 2016.

Johnson, Walter. *Soul by Soul: Life Inside the Antebellum Slave Market*. Cambridge, MA: Harvard University Press, 2009.

Karasch, Mary. "Slave Women on the Brazilian Frontier in the Nineteenth Century." In *More than Chattel: Black Women and Slavery in the Americas*, ed. David Barry Gaspar and Darlene Clark Hine, 79–96. Bloomington: Indiana University Press, 1996.

"Catechism and Captivity: Indian Policy in Goiás, 1780–1889." In *Native Brazil: Beyond the Convert and the Cannibal, 1500–1900*, ed. Hal Langfur, 198–224. Albuquerque: University of New Mexico Press, 2014.

Kelley, Robin D. G. *Race Rebels: Culture, Politics, and the Black Working Class*. New York: The Free Press, 1996.

Kiddy, Elizabeth W. "Who Is the King of Congo? A New Look at African and Afro-Brazilian Kings in Brazil." In *Central Africans and Cultural Transformations in the American Diaspora*, ed. Linda M. Heywood, 153–82. Cambridge and New York: Cambridge University Press, 2001.

Kodama, Kaori. "Os debates pelo fim do tráfico no periódico 'O Philantropo' (1849–1852) e a formação do povo: doenças, raça e escravidão." *Revista Brasileira de História* 28, no. 56 (2008): 407–30.

Os índios no Império do Brasil: a etnografia do IHGB entre as décadas de 1840 e 1860. Rio de Janeiro: Editora Fiocruz and São Paulo: EDUSP, 2009.

Kraay, Hendrik. *Race, State, and Armed Forces in Independence-Era Brazil: Bahia, 1790s-1840s*. Stanford, CA: Stanford University Press, 2004.

"Arming Slaves in Brazil from the Seventeenth Century to the Nineteenth Century." In *Arming Slaves: From Classical Times to the Modern Age*, ed. Christopher Leslie Brown and Philip D. Morgan, 146–79. New Haven, CT: Yale University Press, 2006.

Krauthamer, Barbara. "A Particular Kind of Freedom: Black Women, Slavery, Kinship, and Freedom in the American Southeast." In *Women and Slavery*, Vol. 2, ed. Gwyn Campbell, Suzanne Miers, and Joseph Calder Miller, 100–27. Athens: Ohio University Press, 2008.

Landers, Jane G. *Black Society in Spanish Florida*. Urbana: University of Illinois Press, 1999.

Langer, Erick D. "The Eastern Andean Frontier (Bolivia and Argentina) and Latin American Frontiers: Comparative Contexts (19th and 20th Centuries)." *The Americas* 59, no. 1 (2002): 33–63.

Expecting Pears from an Elm Tree: Franciscan Missions on the Chiriguano Frontier in the Heart of South America, 1830–1949. Durham, NC: Duke University Press, 2009.

Langfur, Hal. *The Forbidden Lands: Colonial Identity, Frontier Violence, and the Persistence of Brazil's Eastern Indians, 1750–1830*. Stanford, CA: Stanford University Press, 2006.

"Frontier/Fronteira: A Transnational Reframing of Brazil's Inland Colonization." *History Compass* 12, no. 11 (November 1, 2014): 843–52.

"Introduction: Recovering Brazil's Indigenous Pasts." In *Native Brazil: Beyond the Convert and the Cannibal, 1500–1900*, ed. Hal Langfur, 1–28. Albuquerque: University of New Mexico Press, 2014.

Langfur, Hal, and Maria Leônia Chaves de Resende. "Indian Autonomy and Slavery in Colonial Minas Gerais." In *Native Brazil: Beyond the Convert and the Cannibal, 1500–1900*, ed. Hal Langfur, 132–65. Albuquerque: University of New Mexico Press, 2014.

Larson, Brooke. *Trials of Nation Making: Liberalism, Race, and Ethnicity in the Andes, 1810–1910*. Cambridge and New York: Cambridge University Press, 2008.

Lasso, Marixa. *Myths of Harmony: Race and Republicanism during the Age of Revolution, Colombia 1795–1831*. Pittsburgh: University of Pittsburgh Press, 2007.

Lauderdale Graham, Sandra. *House and Street: The Domestic World of Servants and Masters in Nineteenth-Century Rio de Janeiro*. Cambridge and New York: Cambridge University Press, 1988.

Leite, Ilka Boaventura. "The Transhistorical, Juridical-Formal, and Post-Utopian Quilombo." In *New Approaches to Resistance in Brazil and Mexico*, ed. John Gledhill and Patience A Schell, 250–68. Durham, NC: Duke University Press, 2012.

Lemos, Marcelo Sant'Ana. "*O índio virou pó de café? a resistência dos índios Coroados de Valença frente à expansão cafeeira no Vale do Paraíba (1788–1836)*." M. A. thesis, Universidade do Estado do Rio de Janeiro (UERJ), 2004.

Lightfoot, Natasha. *Troubling Freedom: Antigua and the Aftermath of British Emancipation*. Durham, NC: Duke University Press, 2015.

Lima, Henrique Espada. "Wages of Intimacy: Domestic Workers Disputing Wages in the Higher Courts of Nineteenth-Century Brazil." *International Labor & Working-Class History* 88 (2015): 11–29.

Lima, Ivana Stolze. *Cores, marcas e falas: sentidos da mestiçagem no Império do Brasil*. Rio de Janeiro: Arquivo Nacional, 2003.

Lima, Valéria. J.-B. *Debret, historiador e pintor: a viagem pitoresca e histórica ao Brasil (1816–1839)*. São Paulo: Editora UNICAMP, 2007.

Lockhart, James, and Stuart B. Schwartz. *Early Latin America: A History of Colonial Spanish America and Brazil*. Cambridge and New York: Cambridge University Press, 1983.

Lucchesi, Dante, and Alan N. Baxter. "Un paso más hacia la definición del pasado criollo del dialecto afro-brasileño de Helvécia (Bahia)." In *Lenguas criollas de base lexical espanola y portuguesa*, ed. Klaus Zimmermann, 119–41. Madrid: Iberoamericana and Frankfurt: Vervuert, 1999.

Lucchesi, Dante, Alan N. Baxter, and Ilza Ribeiro. *O português afro-brasileiro*. Salvador: UFBA, 2009.

Mahony, Mary Ann. "Creativity under Constraint: Enslaved Afro-Brazilian Families in Brazil's Cacao Area, 1870–1890." *Journal of Social History* 41, no. 3 (2008): 633–66.

Maio, Iacy Mata. *Os treze de maio: ex-senhores, polícia e libertos na Bahia no pós- Abolição (1888–1889)*. M. A. thesis, Universidade Federal da Bahia, 2002.

"'Libertos de treze de maio' e ex-senhores na Bahia: conflitos no pós-abolição." *Afro-Ásia* 35 (2007): 163–98.

Mallon, Florencia E. *Peasant and Nation: The Making of Postcolonial Mexico and Peru*. Berkeley: University of California Press, 1995.

Mamigonian, Beatriz Gallotti. "O direito de ser Africano livre: os escravos e as interpretações da Lei de 1831." In *Direitos e justiças no Brasil: ensaios de história social*, ed. Silvia Hunold Lara and Joseli Maria Nunes Mendonça, 129–60. Campinas, SP: Editora UNICAMP, 2006.

Mamigonian, Beatriz Gallotti, and Keila Grinberg, eds. "Dossiê: "Para inglês ver? Revisitando a lei de 1831"." *Estudos Afro-Asiáticos* 1–3 (2007).

Marquese, Rafael de Bivar. *Feitores do corpo, missionários da mente: senhores, letrados e o controle dos escravos nas Américas, 1660–1860*. São Paulo: Companhia das Letras, 2004.

Marquese, Rafael de Bivar, and Márcia Regina Berbel. "A ausência da raça: escravidão, cidadania e ideologia pró-escravista nas Cortes de Lisboa e na Assembléia Constituinte do Rio." In *Território, conflito e identidade*, ed. Cláudia Maria das Graças Chaves and Marco Antonio Silveira, 63–88. Belo Horizonte: Argumentum, 2007.

Martins, José de Souza. *Fronteira: a degradação do outro nos confins do humano*. São Paulo: Editora Hucitec, 1997.

Martins, Robson L. M. "Em louvor a 'Sant'Anna': notas sobre um plano de revolta escrava em São Matheus, norte do Espírito Santo, Brasil, em 1884." *Estudos Afro-Asiáticos* no. 38 (2000): 67–83.

Matory, James Lorand. *Black Atlantic Religion: Tradition, Transnationalism, and Matriarchy in the Afro-Brazilian Candomblé*. Princeton, NJ: Princeton University Press, 2005.

Mattos, Izabel Missagia de. *Civilização e revolta: os Botocudos e a catequese na província de Minas*. São Paulo: EDUSC ANPOCS, 2004.

"Educar para dominar." *RAPM* 1, no. 100 (2011): 98–109.

Meinig, D. W. *The Shaping of America: A Geographical Perspective on 500 Years of History*. New Haven, CT: Yale University Press, 1986.

Mello, Evaldo Cabral de. *A outra independência: o federalismo pernambucano de 1817 a 1824*. São Paulo: Editora 34, 2004.

Mendonça, Joseli Maria Nunes. "Sob cadeiras e coerção: experiências de trabalho no Centro-Sul do Brasil do século XIX." *Revista Brasileira de História* 32, no. 64 (2012): 45–60.

Metcalf, Alida C. *Family and Frontier in Colonial Brazil: Santana de Parnaíba, 1580–1822*. Austin: University of Texas Press, 2005.

Mintz, Sidney W. *Caribbean Transformations*. New York: Columbia University Press, 1989.

Monteiro, John M. *Negros da terra: índios e bandeirantes nas origens de São Paulo*. São Paulo: Companhia das Letras, 1994.

"As 'raças' indígenas no pensamento brasileiro do império." In *Raça, ciência e sociedade*, ed. Marcos Chor Maio and Ricardo Ventura Santos, 15–22. Rio de Janeiro: Editora FIOCRUZ, 1996.

"The Heathen Castes of Sixteenth-Century Portuguese America: Unity, Diversity, and the Invention of the Brazilian Indians." *HAHR* 80, no. 4 (2000): 697–719.

Tupis, Tapuias e Historiadores: Estudos de História Indígena e do Indigenismo. Tese de Livre Docência, UNICAMP, 2001.

Moreira, Vânia. "Índios no Brasil: marginalização social e exclusão historiográfica." *Diálogos Latinoamericanos* 3 (2001): 87–113.

"Terras Indígenas do Espírito Santo sob o Regime Territorial de 1850." *Revista Brasileira de História* 22, no. 43 (2002): 153–69.

"História, etnia e nação: o índio e a formação nacional sob a ótica de Caio Prado Júnior." *Memoria Americana* no. 16–1 (June 2008): 63–84.

"A guerra contra os índios botocudos e a formação de quilombos no Espírito Santo." *Afro-Ásia* 41 (2010): 57–83.

"De índio a guarda nacional: cidadania e direitos indígenas no Império (Vila de Itaguaí, 1822–1836)." *Topoi* 11, no. 21 (2010): 127–42.

Morel, Marco. "Cinco imagens e múltiplos olhares: 'descobertas' sobre os índios do Brasil e a fotografia do século XIX." *História, Ciências, Saúde* 8 (2001): 1039–58.

"Independência, vida e morte: os contatos com os Botocudos durante o primeiro reinado." *Dimensões* no. 14 (2002): 91–113.

Morgan, Jennifer L. *Laboring Women: Reproduction and Gender in New World Slavery*. Philadelphia: University of Pennsylvania Press, 2004.

Mott, Maria Lúcia de Barros. *Submissao e Resistência: a mulher na luta contra a escravidão*. São Paulo: Editora Contexto, 1991.

Moura, Clóvis. *Rebeliões da senzala: quilombos, insurreições, guerrilhas*. Rio de Janeiro: Conquista, 1972.

Nardoto, Eliezer, and Herinéa Lima. *História de São Mateus*. São Mateus, ES: Editorial Atlântica, 2001.

Needell, Jeffrey D. "Brazilian Abolitionism, Its Historiography, and the Uses of Political History." *JLAS* 42, no. 02 (2010): 231–61.

Nimuendajú, Curt. "Social Organization and Beliefs of the Botocudo of Eastern Brazil." *Southwestern Journal of Anthropology* 2, no. 1 (1946): 93–115.

Nishida, Mieko. *Slavery and Identity: Ethnicity, Gender, and Race in Salvador, Brazil, 1808–1888*. Bloomington: Indiana University Press, 2003.

Novaes, Maria Stella de. *A Escravidão e a abolição no Espírito Santo: história e folclore*. Vitória, ES: Instituto Histórico e Geográfico, 1963.

Oberacker Jr., Carlos H. "A Colonia Leopoldina-Frankental na Bahia meridional." *RIHGB* 142, no. 354 (1987): 116–40.

Oliveira, João Pacheco de. "'Wild Indians,' Tutelary Roles, and Moving Frontier in Amazonia: Images of Indians in the Birth of Brazil." In *Manifest Destinies and Indigenous Peoples*, ed. David Maybury-Lewis, Theodore Macdonald, and Biorn Maybury-Lewis, 85–117. Cambridge, MA: Harvard University Press, 2009.

O'Toole, Rachel Sarah. *Bound Lives: Africans, Indians and the Making of Race in Colonial Peru*. Pittsburgh: University of Pittsburgh Press, 2012.

Palazzolo, Jacinto de. *Nas selvas dos vales do Mucuri e do Rio Doce, como surgiu a cidade de Itambacuri, fundada por Frei Serafim de Gorizia, missionario capuchino, 1873–1952*. São Paulo: Companhia Editora Nacional, 1954.

Pang, Eul-Soo. *O Engenho Central do Bom Jardim na economia baiana: alguns aspectos de sua história, 1875–1891*. Rio de Janeiro: AN/IHGB, 1979.

Paraiso, Maria Hilda Baqueiro. "Guido Pokrane, o imperador do Rio Doce," n.d.

"Os Botocudos e sua trajetória histórica." In *História dos índios no Brasil*, ed. by Manuela Carneiro da Cunha, 413–30. Rio de Janeiro: Editora Schwarcz, 1992.

O tempo da dor e do trabalho: a Conquista dos Territórios Indígenas nos Sertões do Leste. Doctoral dissertation, Universidade de São Paulo, 1998.

"Guerra do Mucuri: conquista e dominação dos povos indígenas em nome do progresso e da civilização." In *Indios do Nordeste: temas e problemas: 500 anos*, ed. Marcos Galindo, Luiz Sávio de Almeida, and Juliana Lopes Elias, 129–66. Maceió: EDUFAL, 2000.

"As crianças indígenas e a formação de agentes transculturais: o comércio de kurukas na Bahia, Espírito Santo e Minas Gerais." In *Resistência, Memória, Etnografia*, ed. Luiz Savio de Almeida, Christiano Barros Marinho da Silva, Amaero Hélio Leite da Silva, et al., 51–96. Maceió: EDUFAL, 2007.

Parron, Tâmis. *A política da escravidão no Império do Brasil, 1826–1865*. Rio de Janeiro: Civilização Brasileira, 2011.

Paton, Diana. "Punishment, Crime, and the Bodies of Slaves in Eighteenth-Century Jamaica." *Journal of Social History* 34, no. 4 (2001): 923–54.

Penningroth, Dylan C. *The Claims of Kinfolk: African American Property and Community in the Nineteenth-Century South*. Chapel Hill: University of North Carolina Press, 2003.

Perrone-Moisés, Beatriz. "Índios livres e índios escravos: os princípios da legislação indigenista do periodo colonial (séculos XVI a XVIII)." In *História dos índios no Brasil*, ed. Manuela Carneiro da Cunha, 115–30. Rio de Janeiro: Editora Schwarcz, 1992.

Petrone, M. Thereza Schorer. *O imigrante e a pequena propriedade, 1824–1930*. São Paulo: Brasiliense, 1982.

Pirola, Ricardo Figueiredo. *A lei de 10 de junho de 1835: justiça, escravidão e pena de morte.* Doctoral dissertation, UNICAMP, 2012.

Poole, Deborah. "Between Threat and Guarantee: Justice and Community in the Margins of the Peruvian State." In *Anthropology in the Margins of the State,* ed. Deborah Poole and Veena Das, 35–65. Santa Fe: School of American Research Press and Oxford: James Curry, 2004.

Prado, Fabricio. "The Fringes of Empires: Recent Scholarship on Colonial Frontiers and Borderlands in Latin America." *History Compass* 10, no. 4 (April 1, 2012): 318–33.

Price, Richard. *Maroon Societies: Rebel Slave Communities in the Americas.* Baltimore: The Johns Hopkins University Press, 1996.

Price, Sally. *Co-Wives and Calabashes.* Ann Arbor: University of Michigan Press, 1993.

Radding, Cynthia. *Landscapes of Power and Identity: Comparative Histories in the Sonoran Desert and the Forests of Amazonia from Colony to Republic.* Durham, NC: Duke University Press, 2005.

Ramos, Alcida Rita. "A Hall of Mirrors: The Rhetoric of Indigenism in Brazil." *Critique of Anthropology* 11, no. 2 (1991): 155–69.

Indigenism: Ethnic Politics in Brazil. Madison: University of Wisconsin Press, 1998.

Reis, João José. *Slave Rebellion in Brazil: The Muslim Uprising of 1835 in Bahia.* Baltimore: Johns Hopkins University Press, 1993.

"Escravos e coiteiros no quilombo do Oitizeiro, Bahia 1806." In *Liberdade por um fio: história dos quilombos no Brasil,* ed. Flávio dos Santos Gomes and João José Reis, 332–72. São Paulo: Companhia das Letras, 1996.

"'The Revolution of the Ganhadores': Urban Labour, Ethnicity and the African Strike of 1857 in Bahia, Brazil." *JLAS* 29, no. 2 (May 1997): 355–93.

Rebelião escrava no Brasil: a história do levante dos malês em 1835. São Paulo: Companhia das Letras, 2003.

Reis, João José, and Flávio dos Santos Gomes, eds. *Liberdade por um fio: história dos quilombos no Brasil.* São Paulo: Companhia das Letras, 1996.

Reis, João José, and Eduardo Silva. *Negociação e conflito: a resistência negra no Brasil escravista.* São Paulo: Companhia das Letras, 1999.

Restall, Matthew. *Black Middle: Africans, Mayas, and Spaniards in Colonial Yucatan.* Place of publication not identified: Stanford University Press, 2013.

ed. *Beyond Black and Red: African-Native Relations in Colonial Latin America.* University of New Mexico Press, 2005.

Rios, Ana Lugão, and Hebe Maria Mattos de Castro. *Memórias do cativeiro: família, trabalho e cidadania no pós-abolição.* Rio de Janeiro: Civilização Brasileira, 2005.

Rocha, Levy. *Viagem de Pedro II ao Espírito Santo.* 2a. ed. Rio de Janeiro: Revista Continente Editorial, 1980.

Rodrigues, Jaime. *O infame comércio: propostas e experiências no final do tráfico de africanos para o Brasil, 1800–1850.* Campinas, SP: Editora UNICAMP, 2000.

Rosen, Hannah. *Terror in the Heart of Freedom: Citizenship, Sexual Violence, and the Meaning of Race in the Postemancipation South*. Chapel Hill: University of North Carolina Press, 2009.

Ruiz, Jason. *Americans in the Treasure House: Travel to Porfirian Mexico and the Cultural Politics of Empire*. Austin: University of Texas Press, 2014.

Rushforth, Brett. *Bonds of Alliance: Indigenous and Atlantic Slaveries in New France*. Chapel Hill: University of North Carolina Press; Omohundro Institute, 2012.

Russell-Wood, A. J. R. "Acts of Grace: Portuguese Monarchs and Their Subjects of African Descent in Eighteenth-Century Brazil." *JLAS* 32, no. 02 (May 2000): 307–32.

Russo, Maria do Carmo de Oliveira. *A escravidão em São Mateus, ES: economia e demografia (1848–1888)*. Doctoral dissertation, Universidade de São Paulo, 2011.

Sadlier, Darlene J. *Brazil Imagined: 1500 to the Present*. Austin: University of Texas Press, 2008.

Saïd, Edward W. *Culture and Imperialism*. New York: Knopf, 1993.

Salvatore, Ricardo Donato. *Wandering Paysanos: State Order and Subaltern Experience in Buenos Aires during the Rosas Era*. Durham, NC: Duke University Press, 2003.

Sampaio, Patrícia Melo. "Política indigenista no Brasil imperial." In *O Brasil imperial*, Vol. 1, 1808–1831, ed. Keila Grinberg and Ricardo Salles, 175–206. Rio de Janeiro: Civilização Brasileira, 2009.

Sanders, James E. *Contentious Republicans: Popular Politics, Race, and Class in Nineteenth-Century Colombia*. Durham, NC: Duke University Press, 2004.

Santos, Claudia. "French Travelers and Journalists Debate the Lei do Ventre Livre of 1871." In *New Frontiers of Slavery*, ed. Dale W. Tomich, 225–47. Albany: SUNY Press, 2016.

Sartorius, David A. *Ever Faithful: Race, Loyalty, and the Ends of Empire in Spanish Cuba*. Durham, NC: Duke University Press, 2014.

Schultz, Kirsten. *Tropical Versailles: Empire, Monarchy, and the Portuguese Royal Court in Rio de Janeiro, 1808–1821*. London: Routledge, 2001.

Schwarcz, Lilia Moritz. *The Spectacle of the Races: Scientists, Institutions, and the Race Question in Brazil, 1870–1930*. New York: Farrar, Straus and Giroux, 1999.

The Emperor's Beard: Dom Pedro II and His Tropical Monarchy in Brazil, 1st ed. Translated by John Gledson. New York: Hill & Wang, 2003.

Schwartz, Stuart B. "Resistance and Accommodation in Eighteenth-Century Brazil: The Slaves' View of Slavery." *HAHR* 57, no. 1 (February 1977): 69–81.

Sugar Plantations in the Formation of Brazilian Society: Bahia, 1550–1835. Cambridge and New York: Cambridge University Press, 1985.

Slaves, Peasants, and Rebels: Reconsidering Brazilian Slavery. Chicago: University of Illinois Press, 1996.

Schwartz, Stuart B. and Hal Langfur. "*Tapanhuns, Negros da Terra*, and *Curibocas*: Common Cause and Confrontation between Blacks and Natives in Colonial Brazil," in *Beyond Black and Red: African-Native Relations in*

Colonial Latin America, ed. Matthew Restall (Albuquerque: University of New Mexico Press, 2005), 85–96.

Scott, Rebecca J. *Degrees of Freedom: Louisiana and Cuba after Slavery*. Cambridge, MA: Belknap Press of Harvard University Press, 2008.

"Paper Thin: Freedom and Re-Enslavement in the Diaspora of the Haitian Revolution." *Law and History Review* no. 4 (2011): 1061–88.

Serulnikov, Sergio. *Subverting Colonial Authority: Challenges to Spanish Rule in Eighteenth-Century Southern Andes*. Durham, NC: Duke University Press, 2003.

Seyferth, Giralda. "Construindo a nação: hierarquias raciais e o papel do racismo na política de imigração e colonização." In *Raça, ciência e sociedade*, ed. Marcos Chor Maio and Ricardo Ventura Santos, 41–58. Rio de Janeiro: Editora FIOCRUZ, 1996.

Sheller, Mimi. *Democracy after Slavery: Black Publics and Peasant Radicalism in Haiti and Jamaica*. Gainesville: University Press of Florida, 2000.

Sidbury, James, and Jorge Cañizares-Esguerra. "Mapping Ethnogenesis in the Early Modern Atlantic." *The William and Mary Quarterly* 68, no. 2 (April 1, 2011): 181–208.

Silva, Ligia Osorio. *Terras devolutas e latifúndio: efeitos da lei de 1850*. Campinas, SP: Editora UNICAMP, 1996.

"Fronteira e identidade nacional." In *Anais do V Congresso Brasileiro de História Econômica*, 2003.

Silva, Ligia Osorio, and María Verónica Secreto. "Terras públicas, ocupação privada: elementos para a história comparada da apropriação territorial na Argentina e no Brasil." *Economia e Sociedade* 8, no. 1 (1999): 109–41.

Silva, Ricardo Tadeu Caires. *Os caminhos da abolição: escravos, senhores, e direitos nos últimas décadas da escravidão (Bahia, 1850–1888)*. Doctoral dissertation, Universidade Federal do Paraná, 2007.

Siriani, Sílvia Cristina Lambert. "Os descaminhos da Imigração alemã para São Paulo no século XIX – aspectos políticos." *Almanack* 2 (2005): 91–100.

Skidmore, Thomas E. *Black Into White: Race and Nationality in Brazilian Thought*. Durham, NC: Duke University Press, 1993.

Slatta, Richard W. *Gauchos and the Vanishing Frontier*. Lincoln: University of Nebraska Press, 1992.

"Comparing and Exploring Frontier Myth and Reality in Latin America." *History Compass* 10, no. 5 (May 1, 2012): 375–85.

Slemian, Andréa. "Seriam todos cidadãos? Os impasses na construção da cidadania nos primórdios do constitucionalismo no Brasil (1823–1824)." In *Independência: história e historiografia*, ed. István Jancsó, 829–47. São Paulo: Editora Hucitec, 2005.

Slenes, Robert W. *Na senzala, uma flor: esperanças e recordações na formação da família escrava: Brasil Sudeste, século XIX*. Rio de Janeiro: Editora Nova Fronteira, 1999.

"The Brazilian Internal Slave Trade, 1850–1888: Regional Economics, Slave Experience, and the Politics of a Peculiar Market." In *The Chattel Principle: Internal Slave Trades in the Americas*, ed. Walter Johnson, 325–70. New Haven, CT: Yale University Press, 2004.

Soares, Mariza de Carvalho. "Descobrindo a Guiné no Brasil Colonial." *RIHGB* 161, no. 407 (2000): 71–94.

People of Faith: Slavery and African Catholics in Eighteenth-century Rio de Janeiro. Durham, NC: Duke University Press, 2011.

Sommer, Barbara A. "Colony of the Sertão: Amazonian Expeditions and the Indian Slave Trade." *The Americas* 61, no. 3 (2005): 401–28.

"Why Joanna Baptista Sold Herself into Slavery: Indian Women in Portuguese Amazonia, 1755–1798." *Slavery & Abolition* 34, no. 1 (March 1, 2013): 77–97.

Sommer, Doris. *Foundational Fictions: The National Romances of Latin America*. Berkeley: University of California Press, 1993.

Sposito, Fernanda. "Liberdade para os índios no Império do Brasil. A revogação da guerra justa em 1831." *Almanack* 1 (2011): 52–65.

Nem cidadãos, nem brasileiros: Indígenas na formação do Estado nacional brasileiro e conflitos na província de São Paulo (1822–1845). São Paulo: Alameda, 2012.

Stein, Stanley J. *Vassouras, a Brazilian Coffee County, 1850–1900: The Roles of Planter and Slave in a Plantation Society*. Princeton, NJ: Princeton University Press, 1985.

Stepan, Nancy. *The Hour of Eugenics: Race, Gender, and Nation in Latin America*. Ithaca, NY: Cornell University Press, 1991.

Stolcke, Verena. *Coffee Planters, Workers, and Wives: Class Conflict and Gender Relations on São Paulo Plantations, 1850–1980*. New York: St. Martin's Press, 1988.

Sweet, James H. *Domingos Álvares, African Healing, and the Intellectual History of the Atlantic World*. Chapel Hill: University of North Carolina Press, 2011.

Taussig, Michael. "Culture of Terror – Space of Death. Roger Casement's Putumayo Report and the Explanation of Torture." *Comparative Studies in Society and History* 26, no. 3 (July 1, 1984): 467–97.

Thornton, John K. "'I Am the Subject of the King of Congo': African Political Ideology and the Haitian Revolution." *Journal of World History*, 4, no. 2 (1993): 181–214.

Africa and Africans in the Making of the Atlantic World, 1400–1800. Cambridge; New York: Cambridge University Press, 1998.

Thurner, Mark. "Peruvian Genealogies of History and Nation." In *After Spanish Rule: Postcolonial Predicaments of the Americas*, ed. Andrés Guerrero and Mark Thurner, 141–75. Durham, NC: Duke University Press, 2003.

Tomich, Dale W. *Through the Prism of Slavery: Labor, Capital, and World Economy*. Rowman & Littlefield, 2004.

Toplin, Robert Brent. *The Abolition of Slavery in Brazil*. New York: Atheneum, 1975.

Treece, Dave. *Exiles, Allies, Rebels: Brazil's Indianist Movement, Indigenist Politics, and the Imperial Nation-State*. Westport, CT: Greenwood Publishing Group, 2000.

Trouillot, Michel-Rolph. *Silencing the Past: Power and the Production of History*. Boston: Beacon Press, 2015.

Troutman, Philip. "Grapevine in the Slave Market: African American Geopolitical Literacy and the 1841 Creole Revolt." In *The Chattel Principle: Internal Slave Trades in the Americas*, ed. Walter Johnson, 203–33. New Haven, CT: Yale University Press, 2004.

Turner, Frederick Jackson. *The Frontier in American History*. New York: Henry Holt and Co., 1921.

Vainfas, Ronaldo. "Colonização, miscigenação e questão racial: notas sobre equívocos e tabus da historiografia brasileira." *Tempo. Revista do Departamento de História da UFF* 8 (1999): 7–22.

Wade, Peter. *Blackness and Race Mixture: The Dynamics of Racial Identity in Colombia*. Baltimore: Johns Hopkins University Press, 1993.

Race and Ethnicity in Latin America. London and New York: Pluto Press, 2010.

Walker, Charles. *Smoldering Ashes: Cuzco and the Creation of Republican Peru, 1780–1840*. Durham, NC: Duke University Press, 1999.

Weinstein, Barbara. "Slavery, Citizenship, and National Identity in Brazil and the U.S. South." In *Nationalism in the New World*, ed. Don Harrison Doyle and Marco Antonio Villela Pamplona, 248–71. Athens: University of Georgia Press, 2006.

"Erecting and Erasing Boundaries: Can We Combine The 'Indo' And The 'Afro' In Latin American Studies?" *Estudios Interdisciplinarios de América Latina y el Caribe* 19, no. 1 (2007).

The Color of Modernity: São Paulo and the Making of Race and Nation in Brazil. Durham, NC: Duke University Press, 2015.

Weyrauch, Cléia Schiavo. *Pioneiros Alemães de Nova Filadélfia*. Caxias do Sul: Editora da Universidade, 1997.

White, Deborah G. *Ar'n't I a Woman?: Female Slaves in the Plantation South*. New York: W. W. Norton, 1999.

Whitehead, Neil L. "Introduction." In *Violence*, ed. Neil L. Whitehead, 3–24. Santa Fe: School of American Research, 2004.

Womack, John. *Zapata and the Mexican Revolution*. New York: Vintage Books, 1970.

Index